Disease and the Modern World

1500 to the Present Day

Mark Harrison

polity

First published in 2004 by Polity Press Ltd.

Reprinted 2005, 2006

Polity Press
65 Bridge Street
Cambridge CB2 1UR, UK

Polity Press
350 Main Street
Malden, MA 02148, USA

A catalogue record for this book is available from the British Library.

Library of Congress Cataloging-in-Publication Data

Harrison, Mark, 1964
    Disease and the modern world: 1500 to the present day / Mark
Harrison.
        p. cm. – (Themes in history)
Includes bibliographical references and index.
    ISBN 0-7456-2809-5 – ISBN 0-7456-2810-9 (pbk.)
    1. Medicine – History. 2. Diseases – History. I. Title. II. Series:
Themes in history (Polity Press)
    R131.H247 2004
    610′.9′03 – dc22

                                                          2003017371

Typeset in 10.5 on 12 pt Times
by SNP Best-set Typesetter Ltd., Hong Kong
Printed and bound in Great Britain by
Marston Book Services Limited, Oxford

For further information on Polity, visit our website: www.polity.co.uk

Disease and the Modern World

THEMES IN HISTORY SERIES

Published

M. L. Bush, *Servitude in Modern Times*

Peter Coates, *Nature: Western Attitudes since Ancient Times*

Mark Harrison, *Disease and the Modern World: 1500 to the Present Day*

Colin Heywood, *A History of Childhood: Children and Childhood in the West from Medieval to Modern Times*

J. K. J. Thomson, *Decline in History: The European Experience*

David Vincent, *The Rise of Mass Literacy: Reading and Writing in Modern Europe*

Contents

Acknowledgements

Like any other synthetic work intended as a textbook or for the general reader, this book depends heavily on the scholarship of others, and I would like to acknowledge my great debt to them. One book that I would have liked to have made more use of was Howard Phillips and David Killingray's volume on *The Spanish Influenza Pandemic*, which I did not receive until my manuscript had reached the copy-editing stage. Although I have referred to this book in chapter 7, I was unable to incorporate its many insights. Readers with a particular interest in the influenza pandemic would do well to consult this book, which contains some of the best work yet produced on the subject.

I am lucky enough to know or to have known many of the scholars who produced the original scholarship upon which this book is based, among whom I would like to mention the late Roy Porter, who provided me with invaluable advice when I began writing this book. I owe an even greater debt to my friend and former colleague Michael Worboys, who has probably done more than anyone else to influence my thinking about disease. I would also like to thank Loreen Salleh and the referees for their helpful suggestions, and the people at Polity for their assistance, especially Jean van Altena for her excellent copy-editing. Finally, I would like to thank my family, friends and colleagues for their forbearance and support.

Introduction

Today, every country may be regarded as modern in its most fundamental respects. The very fact that we can compare a country's economic performance, its population and its mortality figures is evidence of this. Virtually every nation on earth is organized in a way that enables its resources to be measured, monitored and evaluated – in other words, a form of organization that is typically modern. Countries that have undergone modernization may continue to contain pre-modern social arrangements or ideas, but only if they are compatible with the key elements of modernity.[1] The intrinsic features of modernity according its most famous analyst, Max Weber, were the rise of capitalism, the dominance of reason over faith, and the organization of society along bureaucratic lines. All were aspects of a process that Weber referred to as rationalization: a form of reasoning in which every aspect of human life became subject to calculation, measurement and control. By the nineteenth century, according to Weber, rationalization had stripped away community feeling, religious belief and moral value, and had replaced them with legal, political and economic regulation.[2]

Some may object that modernity is now a thing of the past, and that we are living in a postmodern world in which reason is no longer the guiding light and in which technology has lost its redemptive power. But while there are some reasons to see the recent past as distinctive, a historian of the long term may be more cautious. From the Renaissance onwards, successive generations of intellectuals have found the need to label their own times as different or special. Like Agnes Heller, I think it makes more sense to see postmodernism not as something that comes after modernism but as a critical, reflective tendency within it; a tendency that comes to the fore from time to time, questioning our ability to understand the world and our capacity to make it after our own image.[3] In any case, it would be a mistake to exaggerate the changes that have occurred over the last two decades or so, as there is little sign of any fundamental shift in patterns of social organization. For good or ill, we are still very much part of the modern world.

Modernity is clearly a problematic concept, and there may be drawbacks to using it as a central theme for a book on the history of disease; nevertheless I believe, like Fernand Braudel, that a general history requires 'an overall model, good or bad, against which events can be interpreted'.[4] I aim to show that disease was central to the development of modern states and their machinery of government. From the Renaissance onwards, the control of disease became one of the most important functions of the state, along with the protection of its people from external aggression. Thus the threat of plague and other diseases met with co-ordinated state action in the form of quarantine, medical relief, isolation of victims, and measures to cleanse the environment. One cannot entirely discount humanitarian motives for these measures, but the growth of state activity had much to do with a new perception of the economic and military value of the population. This perception may, itself, have owed much to the depredations of plague, which increased the scarcity and price of labour. Public health measures also developed as means of controlling potentially dangerous or unruly elements within society, such as soldiers, beggars and prostitutes, all of whom were stigmatized as bearers of disease. The scale and scope of these measures widened considerably in the coming years, with the state aiming to maximize the potential of its population.

At numerous points, the history of disease also illuminates the growth of capitalism and its corollary, the formation of a new kind of class society. For one thing, disease rapidly became a marker of class: mortality differed greatly among social groups, as did the kinds of disease they tended to suffer from. In the Renaissance and for much of the seventeenth century, plague appeared to show a 'preference' for the poor, rather like cholera in the nineteenth century. Gout, by contrast, was a disease of luxury and a marker of wealth and status; and disease is still one of the most poignant indications of a world divided by inequalities of wealth and opportunity. In rich, 'Western' countries, most people live well beyond seventy years of age and die from heart disease, cancer or degenerative diseases. In the poor countries of Asia, Africa and Latin America, life expectancy is far lower, with many dying in infancy from infectious diseases and, increasingly, from AIDS and AIDS-related illnesses. There, the vast majority of people are denied the basic sanitary and medical provisions of those who inhabit the developed world.

Another aspect of economic development that looms large in this book is the global expansion of the market economy and of capitalist systems of production. This process began in the sixteenth century with the colonization of parts of Asia and most of central and southern America by the Spanish and the Portuguese, and was boosted during the seventeenth century with the arrival of commercial fleets from Holland, England and France. During the eighteenth century, these trading concerns began to transform themselves into territorial powers and to establish dominions in parts of South and South-East Asia. The trading companies were gradually brought under stricter control, and their territories came to be administered directly by European states. In the nineteenth century, there was a fresh wave of colonial expansion, most notably in Africa, from the 1880s. Alongside these 'formal' colonies, European countries enjoyed unequal terms of trade with poorer, independent nations that formed part of an 'informal', commercial empire.[5] With the demise of formal colonial rule in the second half of the twentieth century, the informal empire of old set the pattern for new relationships between rich and poor countries. Transnational companies also came to exert a tremendous influence over the economic policies of independent nations, which feared the withdrawal of capital investment.

The emergence of a global economy since the sixteenth century has been one of the most striking and definitive features of the modern world. The economic fortunes of the imperial 'core' (which lay in Europe for most of this period) were in large measure dependent upon the exploitation of colonized ('peripheral') nations, and for some time on a system of formal slavery.[6] Whether or not similar patterns of exploitation have persisted beyond the end of colonial rule is a moot point. Some economists and historians maintain that the life-style enjoyed by rich nations like the USA continues to depend upon the poverty of other countries, while others claim that poor countries have only themselves to blame.[7] Either way, these global connections are integral to many chapters in this book. European expansion was in large part facilitated by the spread of Old World pathogens to the New World, while the presence in many tropical countries of diseases deadly to Europeans encouraged the use of African slave labour. But few diseases spread from the New World to the Old, the only important exception being syphilis, which had a profound effect upon European medicine and culture.

By the nineteenth century, the emergence of new technologies such as the steamship and the railway had revolutionized travel and made possible more frequent connections between different parts of the world. In the 1840s, for example, it was possible for a steamship to reach Britain from its Caribbean colonies in about a week, whereas the journey would formerly have taken several weeks under sail. The increasing speed and frequency of contact between different parts of the world served as a further stimulus to the movement of pathogens. In the early nineteenth century, cholera spread from India across much of the world, and at the close of the century, bubonic plague travelled rapidly from southern China to Hong Kong, India and many other parts of the globe. At the end of the First World War, massive and rapid population movements helped to transmit the deadly virus causing the influenza pandemic of 1918–19, which claimed the lives of at least 25 million people. In our more recent past, the advent of air travel has opened up the frightening possibility of virulent strains of influenza or 'new' infections like Ebola and Severe Acute Respiratory Syndrome (SARS) spreading beyond their places of origin in a matter of hours.

Globalization has affected the history of disease in other ways, too. During the twentieth century, the rise of international health organizations such as the League of Nations Health Organization and the World Health Organization (WHO) have led to universal expectations of health standards acceptable in a civilized society. Infant mortality rates and what has become known as the 'human development index' have become key measures of progress and national pride. Organizations such as the WHO have also led global efforts to tackle disease, most notably the successful campaign to eradicate smallpox. The idealistic rhetoric of the immediate post-war period has moderated, but global targets are still a feature of disease prevention today.

As well as the material fabric of the modern world, we must also consider the intellectual changes that, for many historians and sociologists, are characteristic of modernity. During the Renaissance, more value began to be placed on direct observation and experience. Although stimulated by the rediscovery of ancient texts, this desire to see the world anew culminated in the modification or rejection of old authorities – a process that led to the Scientific Revolution of the seventeenth century and, later, to the Enlightenment. New ways of knowing came into being, such as those based on experimentation and quantification; tools like the microscope opened up new vistas in the natural world; and new idioms were developed to describe and classify natural phenomena.[8] As a result, the natural world was shorn of much of its magical and religious symbolism – a process that Weber described as 'disenchantment'. Disease came increasingly to be seen as a natural entity that could be understood and cured in wholly natural ways. By the end of the seventeenth century, it was unusual for a physician or anyone educated in natural philosophy to ascribe an outbreak of disease to divine retribution.

In the course of the eighteenth century, diseases came to be classified much as any other natural phenomena. As well as closely observing the symptoms of various diseases, medical practitioners began to look inside the body and to locate disease in particular organs, then in tissues, and, by the nineteenth century, in individual cells. Disease changed from being a generalized disorder of the body to a thing possessing a characteristic pathology. During the second half of the nineteenth century, the discovery of the causal organisms of many bacterial and parasitic diseases established a new paradigm for medicine and for thinking about disease. The laboratory became the arbiter of whether a disease existed and, increasingly, the source of new medicines and vaccines that could cure or prevent specific infections. Germ theories of disease continue to influence the way people think about all kinds of illness, including what are generally known as mental diseases, although some critics regard these germ-based models as inappropriate and simplistic.[9] The identification of genes related to specific diseases has also led many people to think about disease in narrow, reductionist ways, although geneticists themselves frequently stress that environmental factors are often crucial in determining if or when a trait is developed.

As a way of thinking and a mode of social organization, modernity has tended to sweep all before it, but it would be wrong to give the impression that its march entailed a simple diffusion of Western ideas and technologies. The reality as it pertains to disease and medicine, as in so many other areas, is far more complex. Modern ideas of disease emerged in some regions of the world as the result of a dialogue – albeit usually an unequal one – between Western medical practitioners and those of indigenous systems of medicine, such as Chinese medicine, Ayurveda (the Hindu medical tradition) and Unani-tibb (Islamic medicine). All parties have been changed to some extent by this encounter.[10] Western practitioners were changed less, but they acquired a vastly larger repertoire of therapeutic practices and medicines as a result. Indigenous or 'traditional' medical systems were also changed, and most came to incorporate some aspects of Western medicine, such as physiology and anatomy, which subtly altered conceptions of disease and its treatment. While Western medicine has become the dominant system in most parts of the world, these other systems have continued to flourish, sometimes with state support. Thus, in many parts of the world – including now in the West – it is possible to consult a range of practitioners for the same ailment and to be invited to consider disease in radically different ways. This heterogeneity is, perhaps, a facet not so much of postmodernity but of a global world fashioned by the process of modernization.

The relationship between disease and the rise of the modern world is probably most obvious if we examine the history of infectious diseases, particularly epidemic diseases, which have been among the principal threats to the order and prosperity of modern states. But both these terms – 'infectious diseases' and 'epidemic diseases' – are highly problematic, and some definition of what I understand by them is necessary. By 'infectious diseases', I mean those diseases that are thought to arise outside the body, whether in a corrupted atmosphere, or as a result of contamination from an 'infected' article or person. This broad definition encompasses the varied and changing meanings of the term 'infection', which have ranged from person-to-person transmission to the idea that disease was generated by rotting matter. The term 'infection' is practically synonymous today with the term 'contagion', and it is sometimes difficult to distinguish between them historically, too. But 'contagion' has generally had a more specific meaning, referring to the transmission of disease from person to person, and so is less serviceable as a focus for a general work of this kind. The term 'epidemic', which is also sometimes used in this book, is another elastic category and defies precise definition. Like the terms 'infection' and 'contagion', it has a long history stretching back to the ancient Greeks, and has been used loosely to refer to serious outbreaks of disease that are localized in time and space. Writers in the Hippocratic tradition used to use the term 'epidemic' to refer to peculiar 'constitutions' of the atmosphere that produced distinctive sets of maladies, but now the term is generally used to denote an incidence of disease that is above the statistical norm.

As if these problems were not enough, there is little agreement about the concept of disease itself. Historians, philosophers, doctors, sociologists and anthropologists have all grappled with the problem of disease, but no one has been able to produce a definition that has satisfied all. They even disagree about whether disease is a real entity that can be verified scientifically.[11] Some, like Christopher Boorse, believe it is possible to distinguish between 'disease' (which can be objectively verified) and 'illness', which cannot.[12] 'Disease' in this sense is sometimes defined as a deviation from the biological norm, and sometimes as an impediment to survival and reproduction. As a tool of analysis, this distinction has its uses: it acknowledges that illness has a biological and a social component, and it allows us to acknowledge the reality of suffering among non-human animals. But it does not resolve the problem of the specificity and existence of particular diseases – what is sometimes known as their *ontological* status. There are many conditions such as myalgic encephalomyelitis (ME) and various 'mental diseases' that might be said to impair survival but which cannot be easily verified. The same is true of Alzheimer's disease and other degenerative disorders, which manifestly impair bodily function. Are these distinct diseases or parts of the natural ageing process? In other words, while impairment of function can easily be identified, the existence of conditions such as ME cannot. Definitions of disease that are derived from statistical norms can also lead to anything unusual being described as a disease, even when it might not be unhealthy; some abnormalities may even enhance an organism's chances of survival or reproduction.

This 'realist' approach to the problem of disease differs markedly from that of those who contend that all diseases – physical and 'mental' – are culturally specific and value-laden, an approach more common among anthropologists and sociologists than among physicians. The disease/illness distinction makes little sense to those who believe that all disease is subjective, for they believe that disease cannot be isolated from its social and cultural context. The distinction rests, they argue, on an ideal of scientific purity that has never been attained.[13] Some sociologists go even further and argue that just as diseases are 'constructs' of medicine, so 'objectivity' itself is a construct of sociology. Objectivity in other words has no objective existence![14] If so, one wonders why we should take any arguments seriously, including those that deny the objectivity of disease.

However, there have been some attempts to reconcile these conflicting traditions. One such is the work of Charles Culver (a psychiatrist) and Bernard Gert (a philosopher), who see both 'biological' and 'cultural' elements of disease as fundamentally linked. Gert and Culver envisage disease as part of a more general category that they term 'maladies', including injuries, disabilities and death. Each society, they argue, has a rather different interpretation of these maladies, and it is only if a particular person or society perceives them as 'evil' that they can be classed as a disease. For example, what might be regarded as a dangerous mental state in one culture might be welcomed in another as a sign of divine inspiration. Such sensitivity to cultural contexts is very appealing, especially to many historians and anthropologists, yet it presents certain difficulties. What happens, for example, when society does not recognize a dysfunction that impairs someone's health? There are many examples throughout history that testify to this problem, where sick individuals have been neglected or even stigmatized because their illness has not been socially legitimated.

These are weighty and perhaps intractable problems, but they have to be confronted at some level by historians of disease. Whether or not we think that disease has an objective existence affects what we are prepared to say about it and what kind of histories we aim to write. Is it valid, for instance, to write the history of a particular disease – such as plague or malaria – when what has been understood by these terms has changed markedly over time? Can historians ever be sure that they are writing about the same disease as people in the past? Does it matter what a disease really was, or are society's responses to it all that should concern us?

Historians of medicine have been aware of these problems for many years. As early as the 1930s, the German historian Ludwik Fleck drew attention to the dangers of assuming a constant identity to disease when discussing the case of syphilis in his path-breaking book, *The Genesis and Development of a Scientific Fact*. The term 'syphilis' was rarely used before the nineteenth century, so this makes it problematic to write histories of 'syphilis' that stretch back to its apparent origins in Europe in the 1490s.[15] But with a few notable exceptions,[16] the vast majority of historians have been less cautious. Some have thought nothing of writing histories of disease that span many centuries,[17] and many have set out with the express aim of identifying the 'true' causes of mortality in the past, retrospectively diagnosing disease on the basis of contemporary descriptions of symptoms and patterns of mortality. But this way of writing the history of disease was challenged in the late 1970s by historians influenced by the sociology of knowledge, and particularly the work of sociologists based at the University of Edinburgh.[18] From the 'Edinburgh School' came the notion that scientific and medical knowledge was 'socially constructed', and not a simple reflection of 'reality'. Knowledge, in other words, was produced rather than discovered.

Historians indebted to the Edinburgh School have argued that medical knowledge has typically served professional and political interests. This comes through strongly in Karl Figlio's influential study of chlorosis, or the 'green sickness', so-called because of the severe anaemia that gave those afflicted a greenish pallor. The condition was frequently diagnosed in nineteenth-century Britain, but had largely disappeared by the 1920s. Figlio argued that the reason lay in fashions of diagnosis that reflected the relationship between classes in Victorian Britain. Capitalist development, he argued, was facilitated by the exploitation of youthful female labour, which led to great social value being attached to work, and stigma being attached to idleness. Chlorosis, which was typified by debility, was idleness in pathological form, a disease that amplified all the characteristics of the 'delicate', idle adolescent.[19]

Figlio's article was followed by many other explorations of the relationship between disease and professional or political power,[20] perhaps the most notorious of which is François Delaporte's history of the Paris cholera epidemic of 1832. Delaporte boldly asserts that ' "disease" does not exist', and that it is 'illusory to think that one can "develop beliefs" about it or "respond" to it'. 'What does exist is not disease but practices,' he claims.[21] However, Delaporte is not actually denying the existence of the causal organism of cholera, but is emphasizing – in a rather sensational way – that human beings can know the world only through concepts, and that it is impossible to draw a distinction between disease and cultural practices. Our culture, in other words, actively forms our idea of what a disease is. In the case of cholera in 1832, Delaporte argued that disease practices were structured by prevailing power relationships, traditional humoral thinking about disease giving way to new theories which stressed the role of the lower classes in the generation and spread of cholera.

Delaporte's work owes a great deal to that of Michel Foucault, which, in recent years, has provided the basis for many 'social-constructionist' studies in the history of medicine. He takes from some of Foucault's earlier works the insight that knowledge is inextricably bound up with power, and employs a methodology similar to that of Foucault in *The Archaeology of Knowledge*. Foucault's *Discipline and Punish* has also proved influential, especially upon historians who have examined disease concepts and hygienic practices in modernizing countries. For example, the growing emphasis upon indiscipline and sloth as causes of disease has been seen as characteristic of the transition from paternalistic to capitalistic societies, just as attempts to control disease have increasingly entailed impersonal forms of discipline and surveillance.[22] Foucault's work has also provided the inspiration for some recent work on disease and identity. His later work on sexuality and 'the care of the self', for example, has suggested new ways in which to explore the subjective experience of disease, and historians are beginning to examine how notions of individuality are bound up with ideas of disease and its transmission.[23]

These approaches meld easily with those of historians who have employed anthropological insights into pollution and contagion. Historians have shown particular fondness for Mary Douglas's work, most notably her book *Purity and Danger*, which was first published in 1966. Strictly speaking, the book is more concerned with concepts of pollution than with disease, although they are fundamentally linked. She argues that Nature (in the form of disease) is often invoked to sanction or prohibit violations of a society's moral order. Thus, particular types of disease are interpreted as punishments for the transgression of what a society regards as its moral boundaries; these transgressions have included adultery, incest, disloyalty to the tribe or ruler, and blasphemy. Douglas's work shows that certain moral and social rules are upheld and defined by the belief in contagion. It also tells us a good deal about hygienic practices and other measures taken to prevent or dispel disease. Rather than interpreting these in a strictly materialistic way, as was the fashion among anthropologists in the early twentieth century, Douglas argued that hygienic practices had a ritualistic element. Thus 'dirt', in her opinion, is basically 'matter out of place', and modern notions of dirt, which are closely associated with disease, have something in common with older ideas of ritual pollution.[24] In both modern and pre-modern societies, she argues, hygienic practices have symbolic meanings: they are ways of ordering and classifying our world, even if the forms of these rituals bear little resemblance to one another. Douglas's insights continue to inspire a great deal of historical work on disease, and have been fruitfully combined with concepts fashionable in the new discipline of Cultural Studies.[25]

Another strand of writing on disease stems from the Actor Network Theory of Bruno Latour. Latour's approach is in some ways reminiscent of the sociology of knowledge, because it sees knowledge formation as a social process.[26] However, it differs radically, in that it abandons 'interest-based' accounts of scientific knowledge in favour of a more complex model that allows for simultaneous points of interaction and influence, and the formation of alliances. Latour also stresses the importance of non-human elements in this process, and employs the term 'actants' to describe them. Actants can include all autonomous figures that comprise the material world, including microbes, technologies and ideas. According to Latour, 'No actant is so weak that it cannot enlist another. Then the two join together and become one for a third actant. . . . An eddy is formed, and it grows by becoming many others.'[27] As a result, networks of actants emerge, each connected with many others, simultaneously depending on and influencing one another. Through these networks, ideas, observations, skills and interests are transformed into statements in line with a particular argument: a process of *translation* in which allies are identified, shaped and enrolled. According to Latour, it is in this way, and not through the force of logic or powerful interests, that scientific ideas are formed and come to dominate, including ideas about disease. Indeed, the case study used by Latour was the rise of Pasteurian germ theories of disease in France. According to Latour, Pasteur's ideas gained acceptance because he was able to form alliances with various groups, ranging from farmers to military doctors, who came to see Pasteurian ideas as compatible with their own interests and outlook.

One thing that Latour emphasizes strongly is that even material objects must be regarded as actants, as players in their own right. Thus even microbes have the capacity to shape knowledge about disease and to redirect it. It is a view that goes somewhat against the grain of social-constructionist approaches, because it reasserts the primacy and irreducibility of the material world; but it also comes close to attributing agency to non-human subjects, something that many historians find difficult to accept.[28] Latour has also been criticized for misrepresenting what sociologists of knowledge understand by 'interests', by equating them with the self-proclaimed goals of scientists. However, most sociologists and historians do not take such statements at face value, and see interests as the socio-political factors that have a bearing on an individual's thoughts and actions.[29] Thus, while Latour avoids the pitfalls of crude determinism, he closes off a potentially fruitful line of inquiry.

Many historians share Latour's view that knowledge cannot be reduced to social relations alone, and few now call themselves 'social constructionists'. Some refer to themselves simply as 'constructionists', a term which suggests that scientific knowledge has to be actively manufactured but which lacks the political connotations of much earlier work in the sociology of knowledge. Many also regard the term 'social' as redundant, because all knowledge is in some sense social.[30] Others, like the historian Charles Rosenberg, have dispensed with the term 'construction' altogether. Rosenberg argues that the 'social-constructionist' approach has simplified medical knowledge, making it seem like a mere rationalization of the prevailing order. He further points out that constructionists have focused on a handful of spurious diagnoses such as hysteria and chlorosis, for which a pathological mechanism has not been or cannot be proved. The social constructionists, in other words, have chosen easy targets.

Rosenberg insists that disease and disease practices are shaped to a significant extent by biological reality: different pathogens and different symptoms, he argues, tend to elicit different responses.[31] As an alternative to 'construction', he has proposed the metaphor of 'framing', which recognizes the biological reality of disease while acknowledging that disease does not exist as a social entity until it has been named and explained. This is quite different from saying that the meaning of a disease is determined entirely by social factors: 'Biology', Rosenberg insists, 'shapes the . . . choices available to societies in framing conceptual and institutional responses to diseases: tuberculosis and cholera, for example, offer different pictures to frame for society's would-be framers.'[32]

The metaphor of 'framing' has proved popular with those historians who find the notion of 'construction' too contrived, and among those who see the 'biological' aspects of disease as to some extent shaping 'social' responses. But historians like Adrian Wilson insist that there is no real distinction between the 'biological' and the 'social', since both are human constructs.[33] It is unlikely that Rosenberg intended to invest these labels with any essential meaning, however. Rosenberg is also right to suggest that certain types of disease – in so far as they can be identified retrospectively – have produced characteristic social 'responses', as the following chapters attest. Where the metaphor of 'framing' fails somewhat is in capturing the dynamic nature of knowledge; it suggests that nature is simply viewed, rather than actively shaped, by scientific investigators, as Latour reminds us in his study of Pasteur's laboratory.

Wilson's target is not only Rosenberg's notion of 'framing', but the 'naturalist-realist' approach more generally – an approach that seeks to establish the 'true' identity of diseases in the past. Among the 'neo-realists' considered by Wilson are many distinguished historians, such as Alfred W. Crosby and William H. McNeill, whose work will be considered at more length in the following chapters.[34] But Wilson alerts us to a problem that deserves attention at the outset: the problem of retrospective diagnosis. The extent to which retrospective diagnosis is valid is hotly debated among historians. There are those (we might call them 'historicists') who see little point in attempting to identify and classify the afflictions of the past, but many still feel that the enterprise is justified if pursued with caution. In reality, both historicism and qualified realism can be fruitful methodologies, depending on which questions the historian chooses to ask. Wilson's invitation to study *ideas about disease* rather than diseases, alerts us to the different ways in which disease was conceived over time and across cultures, and it avoids the common assumption that a modern disease category such as 'plague' or 'cholera' necessarily referred to the same thing in the past. The *history of diseases*, on the other hand, can help us to reconstruct life in past times, to explain the rise and fall of civilizations, to identify social differences in the incidence of ill health, and to assess the consequences of economic and environmental change.

Disease can only be fully understood as a historical phenomenon if we attempt both forms of inquiry. It is important to see the past as far as possible in its own terms, while realizing that we can never entirely divest ourselves of the present. Nor is there any reason why we should do so. Providing we do not distort the views of historical actors, there is much to be gained from using modern knowledge about disease in order to elucidate the past. After all, if we are to understand the ways in which people made sense of disease, it is useful to know what they were confronted with. The evidence available to us necessarily imposes limitations on our ability to re-create the past and to identify any disease with certainty; but it may be possible within certain bounds of probability. Reading textual sources to identify diseases is fraught with problems, but this is no reason to give up altogether: some diseases, such as plague and yellow fever, have symptoms that are distinctive, and may also display epidemiological characteristics that enable them to be distinguished from one another. In some cases, it is also possible to correlate textual evidence with that from paleopathology, which has the capacity to demonstrate the existence of diseases such as leprosy and syphilis by examining human remains.[35] Our motto might therefore be, 'Let a thousand flowers bloom'.

This book began life as a history of disease from ancient times, rather than a history of disease in what I have perhaps foolishly called the 'modern world'. It soon became apparent that my original plan was impossible within the word limit and that it had to be scaled down in some way. I felt uncomfortable with a project restricted to 'the West', as the European colonies have always been one of my main interests, so limiting the time-scale was the only realistic option. Though problematic, the concept of modernity offered a way of imposing some kind of unity on an otherwise diverse range of sources, while enabling me to cover a broad geographical range. The scope of this book widens gradually, as modern forms of society emerged or were imposed around the globe. I have decided to opt for a more or less chronological structure, using case studies to explore broader issues, while at the same time providing enough detail to demonstrate their complexity, together with the richness of the subject-matter.

One obvious difficulty in such an approach, and in writing any synthetic work of history, is deciding what to include and what to exclude. Although I thought I had a fairly good command of the literature before I began, I was surprised by just how much had been written on disease and by the extent of my ignorance. Writing *Disease and the Modern World* has therefore been a great learning experience, but, unfortunately, there was not sufficient space to discuss much of what I read. The original manuscript was considerably longer than the final version, and that, too, omitted a good deal. Readers with some knowledge of the field may be surprised or disappointed to find that some subject dear to them has not been covered. I can only say that I am aware of these limitations, and offer my apologies in advance. I have chosen to concentrate on the social, economic, demographic and intellectual aspects of the history of disease, and specifically on infectious diseases, chiefly because the literature in these areas allowed me to explore more easily the theme of modernity, and particularly the rise of the modern state, which is closely related to the threat of disease. In so doing, I have highlighted some areas that have not been given sufficient attention in the existing literature – such as the relationship between war and disease – while saying rather less about others, like cultural representations.

As many of the terms used in the book are rather technical, I have provided an extensive glossary. For ease of reference, I have also provided full publication details for each of the works referred to on the first occasion they are cited in each chapter. It was not possible to provide a full bibliography, but a select bibliography of key works is located at the end of the book.

1

Disease and Medicine before 1500

In order to understand the significance of the changes wrought by the advent of modernity during the sixteenth and seventeenth centuries, we must look briefly at the world they transformed. This period is generally known as the Middle Ages, or the medieval period, and spans the centuries between the demise of the Roman Empire in the fifth century AD and the new world created by the Renaissance and the Reformation. Until the year 1000 or thereabouts, Europe was a poor, agricultural society with few large towns or cities. Epidemics and famines occurred with dreadful regularity, including the plague, which periodically ravaged Europe and the Near East between 541 and 767.[1] The intellectual glories of Greece and Rome were known only to a few, in monastic orders on Europe's western fringe, and it was only beyond Europe's boundaries – in the Byzantine Empire and the Islamic Near East – that classical learning truly flourished. In the West, the intellectual vacuum was filled almost entirely by the Catholic Church and its interpretations of Holy Scripture. But in the three centuries after 1000, Europe became more prosperous and cosmopolitan. Agriculture thrived in warm, stable climatic conditions, and produced enough of a surplus to enable the population to double. The surplus also permitted a flourishing trade in commodities such as wool and wine. Merchants, landlords and artisans prospered, towns grew, and cathedrals and churches were built to the glory of God and their benefactors. Monarchs established their authority over barons and knights, and left many parts of Europe more settled and at peace than before. In Paris and other medieval cities, universities emerged from monastic schools and began to resurrect the ancient scholarship that had been lost in much of Europe since the fall of Rome. In the thirteenth century, Europe was probably better off, better fed, better educated and in better health than at any time since the fall of the Roman Empire.

Disease in the Western medical tradition

Between 1000 and 1300, most European countries were periodically beset by dynastic conflicts, but the relative stability of the 'High Middle Ages' permitted intellectual life to flourish in a way that it had not for centuries. This was as true of medicine as of other branches of learning. Until the eleventh century, medicine had seldom been taught in monastic schools, and in the few instances where it was part of the curriculum, it was taught alongside other areas of natural knowledge. The object was not to produce a class of healers, but to enable monks to better understand the works of God. All this began to change at Salerno towards the end of the eleventh century. Salerno was a Norman dukedom in what is now southern Italy. Lying at the intersection of several important trade routes between Europe, Byzantium and the Arab world, it developed as a cosmopolitan centre of learning, and it was through Salerno that classical Greco-Roman medicine began to re-enter mainland Europe. For many years after the fall of the Roman Empire, little was known of the medical writings of antiquity, such as the Hippocratic corpus (fifth–fourth centuries BC) and the many works of Galen of Pergamum (AD 129–216). But in the Arab world, these works were still widely used and had been translated into Arabic. Several scholars had added to them, most notably Rhazes or Razi (d. 925) and Ibn Sina, known to the West as Avicenna (d. 1037). These writers were interested in the philosophical as well as the practical dimensions of medicine, and Avicenna systematized Galenic medicine by placing it within an Aristotelian philosophical framework.[2]

The Arabic literature that entered Europe through Salerno soon began to attract the attention of scholars throughout the Italian peninsula. Constantine the African (c.1020–87) is perhaps the best known of these, and translated many Arabic medical works into Latin, the lingua franca of Catholic Europe. In the first half of the twelfth century, Greek and Roman works (which had been rendered into Arabic), together with some Arabic originals, became widely known in the monasteries of Italy, and a new canon of medical authority emerged in the form of the *Articella*, or 'Little Art of Medicine'. Simultaneously, in Spain, which had experienced several centuries of Moorish rule, there was a great deal of additional trans-lation of medical and philosophical works from Arabic into Latin. The texts translated included the *Canon* of Avicenna and the works of Rhazes. Translators in Spain imparted an even greater Aristotelian slant to medicine than those in Italy. Following the synthesis between classical philosophy and Christian doctrine by Thomas Aquinas (1225–74), Aristotelianism was to become the main philosophical system underpinning Christian teaching in the West. Aristotle's 'Prime Mover' was equated with the Christian God, while, in medical texts, the purpose of organs and other bodily structures was said to be God-given. This new way of thinking aroused curiosity about the body, because it seemed that its design could reveal the mind of the Creator.

The learned medicine that had been recovered for the West was taught in a systematic way in the monasteries of the Catholic Church, and later in the universities that emerged from monastic schools. The first of these was the University of Bologna, founded around 1180, which was quickly followed by universities in Paris (*c*.1200), Oxford (*c*.1200), Salamanca (*c*.1218), Montpellier (*c*.1220) and Padua (*c*.1220). In all, fifty universities were founded between 1180 and 1479. Although its temporal power was increasing at this time, the Church did not interfere too much with the teaching of medicine. For example, it permitted the dissection of human bodies when this was introduced into the curricula of some universities during the four-teenth century. As medical knowledge became more systematized, it was offered as a separate degree. The MB, or bachelor of medicine degree, was taken after a preliminary period of training in philoso-phy and the arts (the MA degree), and took around seven years in total. The MD, or doctor of medicine degree, was a more advanced qualification taken after at least ten years of study. In view of the long period necessary to qualify, few students opted to read for either degree. At Oxford in the fifteenth century the average was one student every two years! The exception was the University of Padua, where medical students comprised around 10 per cent of the student body (around nine per year). By the mid-fifteenth century Padua had acquired an excellent reputation for practical learning, whereas northern European universities tended to be more clerical and the-ological in outlook.[3]

The system of medicine taught at these universities through to the end of the fifteenth century was essentially Galenic and Hippocratic, as understood from recent translations of Arabic texts. At the core of this system was the humoral theory of disease, which originated in the writings of Hippocrates and his followers on the Greek island of Cos. Rather than attributing disease to the action of gods and spirits, the Hippocratics sought natural explanations, grounded in the relationship between human beings and their environment. The central Hippocratic idea was that the body was composed of fluids known as humours. Initially, there were thought to be three humours – blood, bile and phlegm – but over time practitioners began to differentiate between two types of bile, yellow and black (also known as melancholy). When the four humours were in balance, the body was deemed to be healthy; when out of kilter, it became diseased. Each humour was closely associated with a particular season of the year: blood with spring, summer with yellow bile, autumn with black bile, and winter with phlegm. Further associations were made with the four ages of man (childhood, adolescence, maturity, old age), with the four elements (earth, fire, air and water), and, in medieval times, with the four Evangelists (Matthew, Mark, Luke and John).[4] This complex network of associations helps to explain why the humoral system endured for so long. In a predominantly agricultural society, the link between the body and the seasons made sense, while the accretion of other meanings made it compatible with Christian theology.

Medical practice and medical institutions

For university-trained physicians, the treatment of disease consisted in correcting or preventing an imbalance between the humors. Such an imbalance could occur for any number of reasons. Certain seasons of the year tended to produce an excess of one humour, giving rise to characteristic symptoms; for example, spring was said to bring about an increase in blood, sometimes culminating in fever. Certain forms of behaviour could have the same effect: an inactive life-style could produce an excess of the heavy, watery humour, phlegm; too much activity, on the other hand, stirred the blood, inducing fever – hence the expression 'feverish activity'. Each individual was also born with a propensity to produce too much of one humour, making them liable to certain diseases. Someone with too much black bile, for example, was said to have a 'melancholic' disposition, with a tendency to sadness and depression. To counteract their tendency to disease, an individual might be prescribed a regimen of diet and exercise of a contrary kind. A phlegmatic person, for example, might be asked to avoid cold and heavy food and to eat light meats and vegetables. Physicians also prescribed depletive treatments such as bleeding, vomiting and purging to take off 'corrupt' or 'excessive' humours, or tonics to stimulate the production of deficient humours.

In the later Middle Ages, the system of humoral medicine was taught using such influential authorities as Galen and Avicenna. It was chiefly through their eyes that the writings of the Hippocratics and other Greek physicians were seen. As well as offering their own interpretations and opinions, these writers added a good deal that was new. Galen, who is credited with at least 350 works, wrote extensively on the philosophy of medicine, on anatomy and physiology (based mostly on animal dissections), and on the diagnosis of disease. Only a small number of Galen's works were known to scholars and physicians in the Middle Ages, but his example inspired some to innovate and make independent observations in areas like anatomy.[5]

The physicians comprised a tiny minority of those who made a living from healing in medieval Europe. They often worked in conjunction with apothecaries, who supplied them with drugs, but apothecaries also practised independently, and some made a very good living indeed. The number of apothecaries appears to have increased enormously in the fifteenth century, because the use of medicaments (as opposed to dietetic medicine) became more fashionable, and because of the importation of exotic new drugs from the Orient. Barber-surgeons were equally numerous, their red and white poles denoting one important part of their trade – the therapeutic letting of blood. They also performed small operations such as the removal of bladder and kidney stones. Most barber-surgeons learned their trade as apprentices for five or six years, before going on to practise in their own right. Only in a few places, such as the Italian university of Padua, was surgery offered as an academic subject. Below the barber-surgeons and apothecaries were a multitude of healers, most of whom practised their trade alongside another occupation. These included bone-setters, experts in stone cutting and eye diseases, midwives, astrologers, priests and sorcerers. But the most common resort for the majority of those who fell sick was someone in their family or village who was skilled in making remedies from local plants. Only in a handful of cities such as Freiburg was there any attempt to restrict or regulate medical practice as such, although some cities passed laws regulating the conduct of apothecaries, who were often suspected of fraudulently selling medications.[6]

From the eleventh century, provision was also made for the care of the sick within institutions. The trend began with the charitable actions of members of lay religious brotherhoods and Augustinian canons, who unlike members of monastic orders, were not required to withdraw from society. The infirmaries and charitable houses they established were a response to the growth of cities at this time, and to growing numbers of destitute sick. These institutions were soon joined by a variety of hospitals founded by kings, bishops, lords, merchants, guilds and municipalities. They were endowed as charitable institutions and staffed by members of various religious orders, including the Knights Hospitallers of St John of Jerusalem. In most cases, nursing and medical treatment was performed by members skilled in physic who did not, however, possess any qualification. But by the thirteenth century, many hospitals had one or more trained physicians, and in some Italian cities they were funded by the state.[7]

The term 'hospital' (*hospitale* in Latin) embraced four main types of institution: almshouses, hospices for poor wayfarers and pilgrims, infirmaries for the sick poor, and leper houses. The latter were among the earliest hospitals founded in many countries, despite the fact that leprosy was widely regarded as incurable. It was a disease rich in biblical symbolism and one to which the Christian West gave a disproportionate amount of attention. The appearance of its victims marked them out clearly from the rest of the population. The symptoms included scaly skin, a gruff rasping voice, collapsed tissues, loss of extremities such as fingers, and degeneration of bones. In the absence of any reliable form of diagnosis, it is impossible to say whether those termed 'lepers' in the Middle Ages had actually contracted Hansen's disease, as it is now termed. It is quite likely that many were suffering from chronic skin complaints. We have no way of knowing for certain, but this does not prevent us from trying to understand how contemporaries viewed leprosy and how those designated as lepers were treated. Almost invariably, this entailed isolation from the rest of society, whether they were confined in special communities or left to wander in search of alms. Either way, lepers were required to wear special clothing and to warn others of their approach with a bell or rattle. From 1100 the preferred solution was to isolate lepers in special houses (leprosaria) outside towns, normally without any assistance except food and shelter. Although each house was small in size, the number of leprosaria was large: by 1226, France had around 2,000 such institutions, and by 1250, England had 130.[8] The rapid growth in leper houses has led some historians to the conclusion that Christian society had a mania for persecution – a desire to segregate and punish that was later vented on the poor and the mad.[9]

The segregation of lepers was justified on the grounds of the biblical injunction in Leviticus 13.46 that the 'unclean' should dwell outside the camp, and in 1179 the Third Lateran Council ordered that all lepers be cast out of society. What, then, was so 'unclean' about the leper? One common misconception is that leprosy has always been regarded as a 'contagious' disease, in the sense that it could be passed easily from person to person. This was far from the case. To the extent that leprosy was seen as contagious, it was in the sense that lepers corrupted the air around them, exposing others to similar corruption. But such explanations do not appear to have existed until the thirteenth century, several decades after the order from the Third Lateran Council. Far more common was the view that lepers were unclean because of some form of moral contamination. More than most diseases, leprosy was associated with sin, at least in the Jewish and Christian traditions. In the Middle Ages it was closely linked with the sin of lust, which led some churchmen to claim that the disease was spread sexually. Leprosy served alongside other diseases as a way of condemning forms of behaviour proscribed by the Church, which was attempting to exert more control over the lives of ordinary people, most of whom probably had few sexual inhibitions. Prostitution, for example, was an openly accepted feature of medieval life. But along with other 'evils' like sodomy and masturbation, it was an aspect of life which offended the pious, and which the Church sought to stigmatize using every means at its disposal.[10] This is not to say that leprosy was entirely a 'construction' of the medieval Church, although its incidence may have been exaggerated. Rather, the disease came to be understood in a new way, with leprosy being more closely associated with sin and contamination than in the great medical works of the Western and Islamic traditions.

By the mid-fourteenth century, however, the number of leprosy hospitals went into steep decline, and by the fifteenth century most were redundant. There is little agreement about why this decline occurred. Some have claimed that there were never many cases of leprosy, and that the growth of these institutions during the twelfth and thirteenth centuries owed more to fear of the disease than to actual need. Others have attributed the decline to the onset in the 1340s of the Black Death: with the collapse in agricultural revenues, the charitable imperative began to dry up, and turned in some cases to open hostility. Alternative explanations include diminishing virulence, more accurate methods of diagnosis, and climatic changes that made it more difficult for the bacillus to spread.[11] None of these explanations is entirely convincing in itself, but the fact that 1350 seems to have been an important turning point suggests that the Black Death was in some way involved.

The world the plague made

One of the great ironies of medieval Europe is that the prosperity that had created the High Middle Ages was to bring about its demise. A burgeoning population and the growth of cities and trade laid the foundations for a new and more deadly disease environment. Marginal land brought into cultivation during the thirteenth century was unable to keep pace with demand. Food had to be brought in from further afield, and supplies became expensive and uncertain. It was a society balanced on the edge of disaster, and in the fourteenth century it teetered over. A series of famines between 1315 and 1317 was followed by outbreaks of disease among cattle and sheep. In the coming years, productivity continued to fall, with land and food becoming more expensive, and labour – which was still plentiful – even cheaper. Medieval society was thus already in crisis before the arrival of what we call the 'Black Death' (a term not used until the nineteenth century). But it was the arrival of plague that really sounded the death knell for the old order, and which provided the conditions in which the modern world would emerge.

The plague first appeared in Europe in 1347, on the Mediterranean island of Sicily. In all likelihood the disease had travelled there from Central Asia via the Middle East. Before the end of the year, it had appeared in many of the Italian ports, and had spread by sea to Marseilles and by land to Pisa by early 1348. Within the year it had spread over most of central and western Europe, and had crossed the Channel to the south coast of England. During 1349 plague spread over the rest of the British Isles and over the sea to Norway. The following year, the Black Death laid waste to Scandinavia and eastern Europe. Most of Europe was gravely affected, although a few enclaves, such as Bohemia and parts of Poland, remained relatively free from it, possibly because it arrived during the winter, when the cold inhibited its spread.

The Black Death was one of the greatest biomedical catastrophes in human history, and certainly in the history of Europe. It is estimated that the disease killed around 20 million people – not so many as the influenza pandemic of 1918–19 but far more in proportion to the populations that it affected. The Black Death probably killed between 30 and 50 per cent of Europe's inhabitants: devastation on a scale that is scarcely imaginable today, even in the poorest countries.[12] Indeed, many aspects of the Black Death remain shrouded in mystery. We cannot even be certain what caused this terrible mortality. For a long time, it was taken for granted that the Black Death was a form of plague, caused by the bacterium *Yersinia pestis*, which lives as a parasite in burrowing rodents. The plague germ is normally carried from rodent to rodent by the bite of fleas. Many rodents can carry plague, but the biggest threat to human beings is the black rat (*Rattus rattus*), which finds it easy to enter human dwellings. The disease spreads to humans through the bite of the rat flea (*Xenopsylla cheopis*), and possibly also of the human flea. The disease can also be spread easily from one human being to another in its pneumonic form, by coughing and sneezing.

What we know about plague today seems to tally with the spread of the Black Death, though by no means exactly. The steppes of Central Asia, where plague was first recorded in the 1330s, are known to be the home of rodents that carry the bacillus. Although some scholars have doubted that true plague could spread as rapidly as the Black Death, the symptoms described in fourteenth-century texts resemble fairly closely the classical symptoms of plague in its various forms: headaches, black-outs, digestive problems and, of course, the characteristic 'buboes' – hard swellings of the lymph nodes in the armpits, the groin or on the neck. Some descriptions also appear to refer to plague in its pneumonic and septicaemic forms – that is, when the plague organism infects the blood.

It is likely that the vast majority of deaths attributed to the Black Death were caused by plague as we understand it today; but some anomalies remain. In 1984 the British zoologist Graham Twigg noted that the Black Death affected thinly populated areas as badly as urban areas. Some of the outbreaks also occurred in winter, whereas bubonic plague normally occurs in summer. Moreover, Twigg noted that contemporary accounts often described death as occurring within a few days, rather than a week or two, as is normally the case with plague. Some of the afflicted also appeared to die without fever or any sign of buboes. Twigg therefore conjectured that at least some of the mortality attributed to the Black Death was caused by anthrax, which begins with similar symptoms to plague. Twigg's thesis met with scepticism initially, but recent evidence has shown that anthrax did exist in Europe at that time.[13] In all probability, what we call the Black Death was probably a composite crisis, predominantly caused by plague but accompanied by other diseases, including anthrax.[14]

This argument will probably rumble on and on, but some historians feel that the true nature of the Black Death is less important than its social, economic and demographic consequences. The medieval world was very different from our own, and the coming of plague was interpreted very largely in the light of Catholic theology. As far as the Church was concerned, there was one obvious conclusion to be drawn from the plague: that God was punishing humanity for some form of wickedness. That wickedness and those responsible for it had to be identified and rooted out. As plague afflicted one in every two or three people, it was clear that the community as a whole was culpable to some extent, and its religious observances had to be examined. People were exhorted to acts of penance, pilgrimage and propitiation, which included processions of flagellants which moved from town to town scourging their flesh with whips to remove the sins of humanity. There was also the possibility that the community was being punished for harbouring ungodly beliefs. The most visible 'heresy' was Judaism, as Jews were normally required to wear special clothing, which immediately marked them out. As the Jews had rejected Christian teaching, they had often been accused of being in league with the devil, and had been regularly subjected to persecution. In England, for example, mass killings of Jews were followed by their expulsion by Edward I in the 1290s. Plague roused the latent anti-Semitism that pervaded most of Europe, and it was rumoured that Jews were spreading plague deliberately by poisoning wells and other nefarious activities. In France, Germany, Italy and Switzerland there were numerous attacks on Jews and their property, and in some cities they were systematically slaughtered or expelled.

Most of these attacks were spontaneous rather than the result of specific commands, and many clerics, including the popes, condemned attacks on Jews, pointing out that they, as well as Christians, had died from plague. But in a catastrophe as terrible as the Black Death, all minority groups and strangers were suspect, as people desperately tried to make sense of what was happening to them. The Jews were only the most numerous of several groups singled out as scapegoats for the disease, including lepers, Muslims (in Spain and Portugal), foreigners and even those who practised 'foul trades', including prostitutes, butchers, tanners and fishmongers. What all these scapegoats had in common was some association with dirt, pollution and illness. Individuals who engaged in 'filthy' or 'unnatural' acts were targeted for the same reason. Fornication, adultery, sodomy and masturbation were all said to be predisposing causes of plague, and attitudes towards them began to harden as a result of the epidemic and the shortage of labour that occurred thereafter. In such a climate it became easier to stigmatize non-reproductive sexual activities as unnatural.[15]

It is interesting to compare these responses with those in Islamic countries affected by the Black Death. Here, there were no messianic movements resembling the flagellants, and no persecution of minorities: the Christian belief in plague as a divine punishment had no parallel in Islamic society; nor was there any notion of original sin or guilt arising from man's essential depravity. Rather, Islamic religious leaders viewed plague as a permanent aspect of the human condition, rather like war. As Michael Dols concludes in his book on the Black Death in the Middle East, a 'sense of reverent resignation pervades the accounts of the popular Muslim reaction to plague epidemics through to the nineteenth century'.[16]

In the West there is no doubt that many people took comfort from watching the persecution and expulsion of Jews and other stigmatized peoples, in the belief that such actions expunged the evil that had invited divine retribution. But such confidence was merely skin-deep. The Black Death and subsequent visitations of plague provided a regular reminder that death could strike anyone at any time and, in the wake of the plague, new rituals and art forms began to reflect the transience of human life. One such was the *danse macabre*, which in many contemporary paintings was depicted as an eternal procession in which the dead alternate with the living. People from all walks of life joined in the dance in a manner that reflected the social hierarchy of the time. In most depictions, the figure of death holds out a hand to the living, who are invited to follow him. The moral purpose of these images was to remind the living that mortality could strike at any time, and that the trappings of rank counted for nothing in the end.[17]

But not all responses to plague were fatalistic, and by the fifteenth century, some cities in northern Italy had begun to place their trust in reason as well as faith. The Renaissance had given birth to a culture of civic humanism, in which rulers were deemed to have a moral obligation to look after their people. People were also seen as an important resource of the state – a realization that probably owed a great deal to the devastation caused by the Black Death. Having lost between two-thirds and one-half of its population, Europe after the Black Death experienced a severe shortage of labour. This rapid decline in population accelerated the demise of serfdom, and higher wages resulted in a new class of prosperous 'yeoman' peasants.[18] Rulers were aware that a similar decline in population would place them at a further disadvantage *vis-à-vis* their subjects. With this in mind, the rulers of some Italian cities began to consult physicians, seeking their advice on how best to prevent plague.

In the fourteenth and fifteenth centuries, the vast majority of physicians saw plague as a form of pestilential fever, rather than a new disease, and it was understood as a humoral imbalance rather than a specific entity.[19] Physicians normally recommended dealing with plague as they would any other pestilential fever, by taking measures to counteract putrefaction. Plague was attributed variously to 'corruptions' of the air caused by rotting matter, malignant conjunctions of the planets, an excess of humidity, and the foul breath of the sick.[20] There was no real departure from the classical tradition in Western medicine, which had no clear idea of contagion distinct from those of miasma and noxious vapours.[21]

Physicians may have been reluctant to depart from medical orthodoxy, but those responsible for implementing measures against plague were not. These powers lay with magistrates, who were far more inclined than either physicians or churchmen to think of the plague as contagious, in the sense of its being transmitted from person to person. Magistrates were open to the idea that filth and bad air might aggravate the disease, but most saw plague as something that was imported – an observation that seemed to accord with its sequential progression.[22] Magistrates therefore took measures to check contagion and clean their cities. In Venice, for example, a permanent committee of nobles was formed in 1446 to tackle plague by reducing overcrowding in prisons, establishing rules for burial, and forbidding entrance into the city to anyone who seemed to be sick. This followed a number of temporary committees, the first of which was established in 1348.[23] Similar measures were taken in Florence and other Italian cities. Many cities also began to confine the sick in special hospitals, which were often former leper houses; indeed, the confinement of plague victims was modelled on the confinement of lepers. By the end of the fourteenth century, even the smallest Italian cities possessed their own pest houses. Some also began to institute quarantines, prohibiting the entrance of all peoples and certain materials from outside. In 1377, for example, the republic of Ragussa (now Dubrovnik in Croatia) instituted a thirty-day quarantine against persons from plague-stricken areas, which was increased to forty days in 1397. Marseilles followed suit in 1383, and was joined by Venice (1423), Pisa (1464) and Genoa (1467).[24] These quarantines and other measures against plague provided the model and the inspiration for many later initiatives in public health. As will become clear in the following chapter, plague – and the threat of plague – was an important stimulus to the emergence of the modern state.

2

Early Modern Europe

In early modern Europe epidemics provided a regular reminder of
the frailty of human life. The vast majority of people died from acute
infectious diseases, but the nature of these infections is usually hard
to determine. We will probably never know the identity of the mysterious 'sweating sickness' that ravaged northern Europe during the
sixteenth century, to say nothing of less well-documented outbreaks.[1]
It is also difficult to disentangle the mortality caused by disease from
that attributable to other crises, such as war and famine. Many of the
worst incidents of mortality in early modern Europe – as in all pre-
industrial societies – were due to 'mixed crises' during which epidemic disease arose from dearth or conflict. Indeed, the Wars of
Religion that afflicted much of Europe in the sixteenth and early seventeenth centuries were responsible for the spread of many diseases
– notably plague and typhus – and for the economic devastation that
caused severe famine and malnutrition.[2]

As in many poor countries today, death rates were highest among
the young, although they varied greatly from region to region. Infant
mortality rates (mortality among children under one year of age) in
Tudor and Stuart England were generally lower than in continental
Europe. Britain's geographical isolation may well have played a part
in this, as did the fact that it was spared the perpetual religious
warfare of the early seventeenth century. Britain had its own bloody
wars, and these contributed to mortality from disease; but mortality
during the English Civil War paled in comparison with the Thirty
Years War (1618–48), during which much of central Europe experienced severe outbreaks of plague, typhus, scurvy and dysentery. The
greater frequency of atrocities in the religious wars of continental

Europe produced more population movement, which may in turn have contributed to the spread of disease.[3]

As a general rule, rural parishes tended to fare much better than urban ones. Throughout the whole of the period 1558 to 1837, the parish of Hartland in Devon, England, had an infant mortality rate below 100 per thousand and a life expectancy at birth of fifty-five – a level not obtained nationally until 1920.[4] Some rural parishes were so isolated that they were able to escape epidemics altogether, and country people may also have been better equipped to deal with periods of dearth than their urban counterparts, who often lacked the means to grow their own food. But some parts of the countryside were as, or more, unhealthy than the cities. This was especially true of malarious areas like the Mediterranean basin and low-lying parts of England and the Netherlands. In mosquito-infested, marshy areas, infant mortality sometimes approached 300 per thousand, while many among the adult population were periodically debilitated by malaria.[5]

This death rate was at the upper range of infant mortality in early modern Europe, which was normally between 150 and 300 per thousand. The fact that between one and three children died within a year of their birth has led some historians, most notably Philippe Ariès and Lawrence Stone, to conclude that parents were relatively indifferent to the death of their young offspring and did not form any attachment to them until later in life.[6] But most recent work has shown that parental grief was just as evident then as it is today.[7]

If a person survived the trials of childhood to reach the age of thirty, he or she could expect to live for another thirty years, depending on geographical location and social status.[8] Geographically, the crucial factors determining mortality were the relative isolation of many country parishes, the space between individual dwellings, and the availability of clean food and drinking water. The most dreaded of diseases – plague – was mainly an urban phenomenon, as its relatively inefficient bacillus could thrive only in filthy and overcrowded conditions where rats abounded. Plague's 'preference' for the least salubrious areas of town led many to believe that it was divinely ordained as a scourge of urban vice: not only sexual immorality – which we shall consider in a moment – but also avarice and deception. The writers of some Renaissance tragedies referred to the stacked corpses of plague victims as 'merchandise' or 'flitches of bacon', suggesting a relationship between the predations of commerce and those of disease.[9]

Social status probably had a greater impact upon life expectancy than geography, although the two were inextricably linked. The poor inhabited the most overcrowded and filthy areas and the most dilapidated dwellings, ridden with vermin of every kind, and, despite well-organized networks of charity, they were often unable to purchase adequate amounts of food. Thus, most diseases, with the notable exception of the 'sweating sickness', affected the poor far more than the rich. Bills of mortality in London, for example, show higher infant mortality in the poorest parishes and life expectancy from birth of up to a third lower than in more prosperous areas.[10] Counter-intuitively, there was no great difference in the life expectancy of men and women, despite the fact that women faced the additional danger of childbirth. Maternal mortality accounted for up to 20 per cent of female deaths between the ages of twenty-five and thirty-four, and the risk of dying in childbirth was between 6 and 7 per cent if a woman experienced six full-term pregnancies.[11] But the hazardous nature of some male employments and incessant warfare meant that death rates remained roughly the same.

The ever-present danger of an epidemic meant that there was constant anxiety about health, and a great demand for medical care. Although most illness was treated within the family, the demand for medical attention was such that it supported a wide variety of medical practitioners. The social structure of healing was much the same as in the Middle Ages. At the apex of the medical hierarchy were the university-trained physicians. They were few in number, and they practised largely among the rich; their outlook was generally elitist and conservative. However, in the Italian states, whose universities led the medical Renaissance, there were a larger number of physicians than in most other countries, and the boundaries between them and other practitioners, like surgeons, were less apparent. Unlike their English counterparts, the surgeon-physicians of Italy catered to all but the poorest patients, and were prepared to treat even the most loathsome diseases. In most countries there were also practitioners of physic (internal medicine), who lacked university training, but who regarded themselves as qualified by virtue of their knowledge or experience. Here, the Reformation had some effect on medical practice. Just as some Protestants rejected priestly intercession, some healers rejected classical authorities, or believed they could make sense of them without a formal education. Some of these men gained considerable reputations, much to the chagrin of physicians, who for the most part retained the restrictive mentality of the medieval guilds.[12] There were a few notable exceptions, however. Some physicians brimming with the egalitarian spirit of the Reformation wrote texts for the guidance of unlicensed practitioners, though partly in order to restrict them to the treatment of common diseases.

Specialist practitioners of physic were massively outnumbered by those who plied their trade as surgeons. Most were still barbers or barber-surgeons, offering services like hair cutting along with minor operations such as cutting for bladder stones (lithotomy) and the removal of teeth. However, some specialized solely in the treatment of wounds and disease, especially in Italy and Spain, where surgery was taught in the universities as well as by apprenticeship.[13] The sick also had recourse to apothecaries, who treated patients, in addition to dispensing medicines. Some apothecaries practised surgery, and provided a range of medical services not unlike the modern general practitioner. These services were often within the means of the poor, but those of bone-setters, teeth-pullers, stone-cutters, herbalists and dispensers of *specifics* (remedies for particular diseases) were probably cheaper. Many areas had resident specialists, but there were a growing number of itinerant healers – more, at least, than in the Middle Ages, when populations were more firmly rooted to their place of origin.[14]

The practice of physic and some other branches of healing underwent a great change during the sixteenth and seventeenth centuries. The chief reason was the rebirth, or Renaissance, of European culture in the fifteenth and sixteenth centuries, during which there was a desire to emulate and ultimately to surpass the learning of classical Greece and Rome. This movement began in the rich city-states of northern Italy and gradually spread throughout Europe. The process was fuelled by the rediscovery of many original Greek texts after the fall of Constantinople to the Ottoman Turks in 1453 and the flight of learned men to Italy. The desire to return to pristine original sources, and to reject their corrupt medieval versions, was also stimulated by the Reformation and the insistence of Protestants that the Bible was the sole fount of spiritual authority. Even in countries that remained Catholic, reform-minded clerics believed that a return to Greek sources would lead to a better understanding of the Bible than the old Latin or medieval commentaries.[15]

In medicine, the immediate effect of the Renaissance was to strengthen the authority of classical authors such as Galen. No fewer than 590 editions of Galen's works appeared between 1500 and 1600, including the first complete edition of Galen's corpus, which was published in Greek in 1525. These editions brought to attention aspects of Galen's work that were unknown during the Middle Ages, including his method of diagnosis, which progressed from the general to the particular. Under the influence of medical Hellenists, this method was soon taught in universities such as Padua, and came to be seen by many physicians as the key to medical knowledge. Some were prepared to go beyond the ancient masters. For example, Sanctorius Sanctorius (1561–1636), a friend of Galileo, questioned the certainty of touch in diagnosis, and devised the first thermometer and hydrometer as more certain measures of humoral imbalance. These instruments were supposed to help Galenic medicine, but they served gradually to undermine it. For Galen, hot and cold existed as distinct qualities, and not as a continuum, as Sanctorius implied.[16] This was part of a more general shift in learned medicine from the theoretical to the practical aspects of the art, from received opinion to empirical observation of the signs and symptoms of illness. Renaissance medicine thus prefigured some of the changes normally associated with the Scientific Revolution of the seventeenth century.[17]

The new approach to natural knowledge was also evident in the field of anatomy, which became an increasingly important foundation of medical knowledge. Stimulated by the rediscovery of Galen's anatomical works, and a naturalistic approach derived from Renaissance art, physicians began to open up and examine the body themselves, rather than relying on ancient texts. The endeavours of successive Paduan anatomists, including Andreas Vesalius (1514–64) and Hieronymus Fabricius (1533–1619), revealed that much of Galen's anatomy was inaccurate, because it had been based on dissections of animals rather than human beings.[18] Anatomy also received a boost from the Reformation. Public anatomical demonstrations had been very rare in medieval Europe, but became common in the wake of Vesalius's demonstrations at Padua. Anatomy had a special appeal to Protestants because, as well as providing practical tuition, it revealed to all the design and workmanship of the Creator. Protestant universities like the one at Wittenberg, in Saxony, were quick to emulate Vesalius. Many Protestants believed that body and soul were fundamentally interlinked, so that a better knowledge of anatomy would ultimately shed light on the workings of the soul.[19]

By the time William Harvey began to study medicine at Padua in 1600, many aspects of Galenic anatomy and physiology had already been called into question. Scholars had become increasingly interested in the functions as well the structure of the body, and began to experiment with individual organs to determine their purpose. This research was fuelled by a new emphasis in learned circles on the experimental natural philosophy of Aristotle.[20] It was this impetus that drove Harvey to experiment with the heart and the blood vessels, and ultimately, in 1628, to publish his theory of the circulation of blood in animals. Harvey was criticized by some of the more conservative Galenic physicians, but his theory of circulation soon commanded assent among the majority. The great achievements of the Paduan anatomists and Harvey began to undermine the traditional Galenic view of the body, but they did not immediately sound the death knell for humoral medicine. Although the movement of the humours now appeared to be very different from that stated by

Galen, disease was still seen as the result of an imbalance between them. Therapeutics also changed very little. Although the old debate over where to bleed the patient (for example, the arms, the torso or the head) was rendered meaningless by the theory of circulation, bleeding could still be rationalized in terms of the removal of 'bad' blood from the system as a whole.[21]

The great strides made in the Renaissance encouraged physicians to believe that many diseases could be fully understood and treated. Like other humanists, they had great confidence in what could be achieved using human intelligence independently of faith. Many now regarded it as their religious duty to reveal the work of God in Nature and to use the gifts that he had given humanity to rid the world of suffering. But the most radical challenge to traditional attitudes towards disease came from outside the realm of learned medicine, in the person of the Swiss medical practitioner Paracelsus (1493–1541). Paracelsus had nothing but contempt for learned medicine and for classical learning in general, and wrote mostly in German rather than Latin. He created a new system of natural philosophy based on three chemical principles (salt, sulphur and mercury), which he believed were more fundamental than the Aristotelian elements of earth, air, fire and water. He likewise rejected the notion of the four humours and the system of medicine based upon it. Paracelsus believed that disease often came from outside the body and that each organ acted as an 'alchemist' that separated the pure from the impure. Illness occurred when the directive force in an organ failed, allowing poisons to accumulate. This was a localized theory of disease quite unlike the fluid system of the Galenists. Whereas Galenic physicians always cured by giving medicines that produced a contrary effect to the disease, Paracelsus believed that like could cure like: that poisons within the body could be removed by giving small quantities of a similar poison. He attributed the supposed healing powers of many popular shrines to such phenomena occurring naturally, thereby challenging widely held views about miraculous cures and the power of the saints. By demystifying 'miracles', Paracelsus may have played an important part in what Max Weber termed the 'disenchantment of the world view', yet he believed that the cosmos was pervaded by magical harmonies.[22]

Paracelsus appears to have had no formal university education and to have learned medicine largely from experience. Growing up in a mining village, he was able to see how locals made use of minerals as well as plants to treat disease. His rejection of classical authorities in medicine was also consistent with the Reformation and the desire to purify Christianity; indeed, he was closely associated with the militantly anticlerical peasants' movement in southern Germany. Paracelsus's early tracts dealt with matters of the spirit, and were critical of the rituals of the Roman Church and the corruption of Christianity by religious orders. His later works dealt more specifically with medicine and natural philosophy: medicine, like religion, ought to be stripped to its bare essentials, he insisted. According to Paracelsus, one needed only two books: the Book of Nature and the Book of God (the Bible). His ideas were not widely known during his lifetime, because few of his works were published until after his death. Few universities taught his doctrines for obvious reasons; but by 1575, Paracelsus had many followers among medical practitioners, especially in Protestant countries. Those at the forefront of medical reform tended to accept the cosmological basis of Paracelsus's ideas as well as his chemical remedies; but most practitioners, including many physicians, rejected the more radical elements while incorporating chemical remedies into their Galenic practices. As we shall see, doctors could not afford to ignore the growing popularity of chemical remedies for diseases such as syphilis.

The 'Great Pox': syphilis

Syphilis was one of two diseases (the other being plague) that had a profound effect upon Western medicine during the early modern period. Western medicine had traditionally focused on *diseased people* rather than on diseases as separate entities; disease was seen as the outcome of congenital weakness or behaviour that disrupted the humoral balance, and treatment consisted in restoring the body to equilibrium. But from their first appearance, plague and syphilis were seen as specific entities, afflicting multitudes simultaneously and in similar ways. This led many to look for causes of these diseases outside the body, seeking explanations in everything from rotting refuse to malign conjunctions of the planets. It was also noticed that plague and syphilis tended to appear in individuals who had been in contact with those suffering from these diseases, and this gave rise to theories of contagion and infection, in which disease was attributed to the transmission of some infectious matter or 'influence'. These theories had important implications for both the treatment of disease – which became increasingly specific – and its prevention, which increasingly took the form of collective or state action on behalf of the population as a whole.

The disease we now call syphilis is a bacterial disease caused by a spirochete organism – *Treponema pallidum* – that was discovered in 1905. It is one of four infections caused by the bacterial genus *Treponema*, the others being yaws, endemic syphilis (*bejel*) and pinta.

Although epidemiologically and symptomatically distinct, these conditions are practically identical, which has led some scientists to claim that they are merely variants of the same disease. Unlike the other infections, syphilis usually enters the body through sexual intercourse, and can also be transmitted to unborn babies through the bloodstream of an infected mother. The disease has three stages. The primary stage of syphilis is characterized by painful pimples on the genitalia; these usually heal within a few weeks, forming hard-edged ulcers known as venereal chancres. The secondary stage comes two or three months after the chancres have healed, and its symptoms include sore throat, fever, joint pains and debility. At this stage, a rash covers the entire body with the exception of the face, and ulcers appear on the genital organs, the mouth and other moist parts of the body. The signs of the secondary stage usually disappear after a few months, and it can be some time until the development of the tertiary stage. At this point, the skin and bones develop non-malignant tumours called gummas, which can also appear on the liver and the testicles. At the same time, the central nervous system and brain can be affected, leading to a condition called paresis or 'general paralysis of the insane'. This condition is marked by progressive dementia and muscular weakness. In the fifteenth and early sixteenth centuries, syphilis was particularly virulent, and parts of the body were eaten away by the disease, so that the victim resembled a person in an advanced stage of leprosy. For some unknown reason, the virulence of the disease declined around the middle of the sixteenth century, and afterwards there were fewer fatal cases.

The origins of syphilis in Europe are obscured by five centuries of bitter controversy. One theory – the 'Columbian' – is that syphilis originated in the Americas and was brought to Europe by Columbus's men in March 1493. According to this theory, the disease spread to Naples in 1494, when Spanish soldiers were sent to defend the city against the invading armies of Charles VIII of France. Although the Spaniards withdrew before the arrival of the French armies, they had been in the city long enough to infect many of the women. During the siege, the disease spread from the Neapolitans to the attacking army through the exchange of female camp followers, which was then a common practice. The disease wreaked havoc amongst those besieging the city, and the survivors – mercenaries from all over Europe – returned to spread the disease across the continent.[23] Reports of a new disease resembling syphilis as understood today appeared in quick succession: in France and Germany in 1495; in Holland and Greece in 1496; in England and Scotland in 1497; and in Hungary, Russia and Poland in 1499. Each country blamed its neighbour: the Germans referred to the disease as the 'French

Disease', as did the English; the French called it the 'Italian Disease'. The disease then spread quickly beyond Europe, and within a few years the Portuguese had carried it to Africa, India and Japan, where it was known as 'mankabassam' (the 'Portuguese sickness').[24] The name 'syphilis' – which came from the title of a poem by the physician Girolamo Frascatoro (*c.*1478–1553) – was not widely used at this time, and terms such as the 'French Disease' or 'pox' remained in common usage until the late eighteenth century. This means that it is difficult for us to be certain whether the 'pox' was syphilis as understood today, although there are many indications that it was.

Most observers agreed from the very beginning that the pox was a new disease, although its origins remained shrouded in mystery. It was not for several decades that people speculated the disease had come from America. The first person to claim so was G. Fernandez de Orviedo, who in 1525 alleged that Columbus's men had contracted the disease on the Caribbean island of Hispaniola (now shared by Haiti and the Dominican Republic). Another early exponent of the Columbian hypothesis was the Spanish surgeon R. Diaz de Isla, who published an account of his work in his *Treatise Against the Serpentine Malady* (1539). De Isla was the first person to treat the disease, having attended the crew of Columbus when they disembarked at Barcelona. But the Columbian theory did not receive universal assent. Some physicians denied that the disease was new to Europe, pointing to similarities between the 'French Disease' and descriptions of elephantiasis and leprosy in the texts of ancient authors such as Galen and Hippocrates.[25] The professional authority of these physicians rested on their claim that the Greeks and Romans had described all the diseases known to man. But their opinions remained those of an eminent minority, and the idea that the pox was a new disease, imported from the Americas, survived the sixteenth century as the dominant one. The Columbian theory appealed to those who saw syphilis as evidence of the decay or weakness of nature in the New World, legitimating European dominance over the peoples of the Americas.[26]

Today, the dispute over the origin of syphilis is most closely associated with the historian Alfred W. Crosby and his notion of the 'Columbian Exchange'. Crosby contended that syphilis was the only serious disease to be transmitted from the New World to the Old, whereas Europeans had brought with them a host of pathogens to which native peoples had no immunity. This very unequal exchange worked to the advantage of Europeans, enabling relatively few invaders to quickly gain the upper hand (see chapter 4). Crosby was convinced that syphilis had been imported into Europe because of the coincidence between the date of Columbus's return and the sub-

sequent epidemic of syphilis in southern Europe. Unlike earlier advocates of the Columbian hypothesis, he was also able to draw upon the
work of paleopathologists, whose analysis of skeletons appeared to
show no evidence of venereal syphilis in Europe before Columbus's
voyage, but plenty of evidence in the Americas. But some have
claimed that European skeletons dating from before 1493 show characteristic signs of syphilitic infection, such as star-shaped scars on the
skull and the vestiges of inflammation in the bones. These 'pre-
Columbian' theorists usually explain the sudden appearance of the
disease in epidemic form in the 1490s in terms of a sudden increase
in virulence. Another possibility is that treponemal infections indigenous to Europe combined with those imported from overseas, such
as yaws, which may have been brought from Africa to Europe by the
Portuguese.[27]

On balance, though, it seems that the Columbian theory is still the
strongest. The evidence for syphilis in pre-Columbian Europe is controversial, because some of the signs of syphilis are difficult to distinguish from the damage caused by other diseases, such as leprosy.
In any case, the numbers of skeletons that arguably show signs of
syphilis before 1492 are tiny. In what used to be Czechoslovakia, for
example, tens of thousands of skeletons were analysed for evidence
of syphilis before 1492, but none was found, whereas there was a great
deal of evidence from skeletons dated after 1492; the same is true for
all other European and Asian countries where investigations of a
similar scale have been conducted.[28] At the same time, there are many
indications of syphilis in skeletons dating from before 1492 in the
Americas. The textual evidence is less conclusive, because descriptions of the 'pox' or 'French Disease' vary considerably, and contain
diagnostic categories quite different from those used today. Nevertheless, the sudden appearance, in epidemic form, of a disease that
most contemporaries believed to be new provides further evidence
to support the Columbian hypothesis.

The long-running debate over the origins of syphilis serves to illustrate one of the greatest difficulties in writing the history of disease:
the problem of retrospective diagnosis. Most historians of 'syphilis'
have written with disarming certainty about a disease with a European history stretching over five centuries; they have simply assumed
that modern syphilis and the 'Great Pox' are one and the same.[29] An
alternative approach is suggested in *The Great Pox: The French
Disease in Renaissance Europe* (1997), which presents the history of
a disease as contemporaries would have understood it, leaving aside
the question of whether the disease they wrote about was really
syphilis as understood today. This approach provides valuable
insights into the world of Renaissance physicians and other com-

mentators. It also reveals the diversity of medical opinion, and provides an antidote to simplistic assumptions about contemporary theories of contagion and treatment. But the authors of *The Great Pox* are perhaps unduly prescriptive in insisting that 'the historian is wrong to identify a modern category, such as a named disease, in the past'.[30] It is true that it is difficult to translate the names of old diseases into modern terms, and that descriptions of the 'French Disease' were sometimes brief and obscure. Yet some form of retrospective diagnosis must be attempted if we are to explain why so many people were afflicted by this hideous disease, why it suddenly appeared in the mid-1490s, why it spread in the way it did, and why it had a very different impact than other diseases.

If we set out strictly to write the history of the 'French Disease', then we must also confine ourselves *solely* to historical accounts that refer to that particular malady; even a comparison with the 'Italian Disease' would be out of the question, because one cannot assume that it refers to the same thing. Nor would it be possible to chart shifts in the perception of disease over time. Such restrictions are neither necessary nor desirable: although we can never be sure of the identity of a disease, we can make an educated guess. The majority of contemporaries agreed that the 'French Disease', or 'pox', was new to Europe, and that it was widely (though not exclusively) associated with sexual transmission. Many of the symptoms of this disease also resemble those of modern syphilis, and this textual evidence is supported by evidence from bones. Although some diseases leave marks on bone similar to those of syphilis, from the balance of evidence we can be reasonably sure that the 'French' and 'Italian' diseases were the same as the syphilis we know today.

What, then, can we say about the social impact of the 'pox', or if we feel bold enough, of syphilis? The fact that it was closely associated with war led some to apocalyptic interpretations: the pox seemed to be one of many punishments sent by God to purge humanity of its wickedness, and its associations with vice and immorality underscored this connection. But different parts of Europe drew rather different conclusions from its appearance. In Reformation Germany, for example, it was seen as a punishment more for blasphemy than licentiousness, becoming a potent symbol of the corruption of the Roman Church.[31] However, the pox did not elicit much in the way of an official response. Unlike plague, it killed slowly, and did not cause massive social dislocation; there was also uncertainty over how best to prevent the disease. While there seemed to be a link between the pox and sexual intercourse, physicians also believed that it could be spread by other means. How else was one to explain the fact that several churchmen had contracted the disease? But there were a few occasions on which the state did intervene. In northern France persons suffering from pox were sometimes driven from the cities, and in 1497 the Scottish city of Aberdeen expelled its prostitutes in the belief that they were responsible for the disease. The pox also contributed to a decline in communal bathing, and in some parts of Europe innkeepers were forbidden to accept persons suffering from it.[32]

The coming of the pox was also the main stimulus for the establishment of hospitals for chronic illness, which in the Italian states were known as *incurabili*. Most of these institutions were built to house the incurable poor, and were quite distinct from infirmaries dealing with acute cases of disease and the pest houses used in times of plague. The hospitals, which were established by religious fraternities from the 1490s, were not solely for persons suffering from pox, although many were dedicated to St Job, the patron saint of its victims. The construction of the *incurabili* can be seen, in part, as a means of preserving social order. The pox contributed to a more intolerant attitude towards the poor: its victims did not die rapidly, and, unable to work, they roamed the streets in search of alms. Syphilitic beggars were regarded as an eyesore and a nuisance. In some places, like the papal state of Rome, they were rounded up and hospitalized, on the grounds that they polluted the atmosphere.[33]

The name *incurabili* expressed the common opinion that the pox was incurable: physicians initially had no effective remedy, or even a plausible account of how it spread. It had often been noticed that the pox passed from person to person, which suggested that the disease was not simply an imbalance of the humours. Although the touch of an infected person (or sexual intercourse) could conceivably cause such an imbalance, the relationship between the cause and its violent effects seemed disproportionate. Learned medicine, though not necessarily wrong, seemed to be incomplete. The most famous theory developed to account for the spread of the pox was that of the physician Frascatoro, who believed that the disease was carried in a 'seed' that germinated in a person if conditions were right. This theory has sometimes been seen as a precursor of modern germ theories, but it was quite different. For one thing, the seeds were merely one element of Frascatoro's theory of contagion, which also included the distinctly unscientific idea that contagion could occur at a distance through a kind of magical 'sympathy'. The idea that the cosmos was fundamentally interlinked was common among physicians at this time, and many believed that disease was spread through sympathetic attraction.[34]

The pox also stimulated important new developments in the treatment of disease. When the pox first appeared in Europe, physicians resorted to the traditional remedy of bleeding, in order to draw off corrupted humours. Their lack of success led them to try a host of new remedies, including guaiacum, a decoction made from the guaiac tree native to Hispaniola. This treatment became popular, because it originated in the same place as the disease itself, conforming to the popular view that God had provided remedies for all the ills that affected mankind. Physicians reasoned that if such a remedy were to exist, God would surely have placed it close to the source of the disease. The exotic origins of the guaiac tree also appealed to those bent on reforming learned medicine: it was free from any associations with Galen and other classical authors. The remedy proved especially popular in the Germanic states, where there was a close association between religious and medical reform. The most famous treatise extolling its virtues – *On the Guaiac Medicine and the French Disease* by Ulrich von Hutten – was published in Mainz in 1519. Hutten, who contracted and later died from the pox, was condemned along with Luther in the first papal bull against those attempting to reform the Church; he also wished to reform the medical establishment.[35] Although he was not a physician, Hutten had allies among fellow reformers who were qualified in medicine. One such, Heinrich Stromer, who was the dean of the medical faculty of Leipzig, helped Hutten to write his treatise, and many others began to use decoctions of guaiac.

The connection between medical and religious reform was also evident in the more radical guise of Paracelsus – known by some as the 'Luther of medicine' – who was opposed to both bleeding and the use of guaiacum. Just as Protestants wanted every man to be able to read the Bible for himself, in his own language, so Paracelsus wanted every man to be his own physician. He believed that it was the duty of those with knowledge of medicine to lead people to the remedies that God had created, both plants and chemicals. He felt that guaiacum was inappropriate, because it had to be imported from overseas, local plants being best suited to the treatment of the local manifestations of disease. However, the treatment favoured by Paracelsus was not a plant but a chemical – mercury – which he saw as an antidote to the specific poison causing pox. He may have chosen mercury because it was already a common folk remedy for skin diseases.

The initial reaction of physicians to Paracelsus's specific treatment for the pox was hostile. They had been taught to avoid universal remedies, and to stress the individuality of their patients. Nevertheless, mercury became a popular remedy among unqualified practitioners called empirics, and eventually among physicians, who were conscious of losing business. It was used both as an internal medicine and as an ointment applied to the infected parts. Paracelsus's influence was greatest in Protestant countries, where chemical medicine was in harmony with vigorous traditions of alchemy and the pious rejection of pagan and Romish culture.[36] From a modern perspective, the increasing use of mercury can also be explained by the fact that it was the only treatment that had any perceptible effect upon syphilis. It remained in common use until the development of more effective medicines in the twentieth century, hence the saying: 'A night with Venus, a lifetime with Mercury.' But mercury had its drawbacks: it caused patients to sweat profusely, corroded the membranes of their mouths, loosened their teeth, and even ate away their bones. Paracelsus himself was well aware of its toxicity, and always gave mercury in dilution.[37]

As well as introducing the most beneficial treatment for pox, the writings of Paracelsus contributed to the belief that it was a distinct disease, taking a similar course in nearly all its victims. Like other natural entities, it seemed to possess a past and a future, becoming weaker towards the middle of the sixteenth century, once the vigour of its 'youth' had subsided. Together with plague, to which we shall now turn our attention, pox contributed to an entirely new conception of disease as a 'thing' that could be understood and controlled using knowledge of its history.

Plague

After the catastrophe of the Black Death in the mid-fourteenth century, epidemics of a disease resembling plague continued to occur sporadically in Europe throughout the next three centuries. It is impossible to be certain that an epidemic was truly plague as understood today, but historical epidemiologists have pointed to certain features that are characteristic of the disease. Parish records kept in England from 1528, for instance, show a high number of deaths occurring during the summer and autumn, which is typical of bubonic plague, as rat fleas, which transmit the disease to humans, are active only in warm weather. Although other epidemic diseases occurred in summertime, the localized nature of the outbreaks makes it probable that they were plague, as most other infectious diseases affect a wider area simultaneously.[38] This pattern also suggests that the plagues of early modern Europe were primarily bubonic rather than pneumonic or septicaemic.[39] Pneumonic plague, which is communicated by coughing and sneezing, is primarily a winter disease, but most outbreaks of the plague during the fifteenth and sixteenth century occurred during the summer, a notable exception being the severe epidemic at Basel in 1610–11.[40] Compared to the Black Death, plague was less widespread, being largely confined to cities, and it caused fewer deaths than during its first appearance, possibly because the population may have acquired some immunity after repeated visitations. In the sixteenth century, plague usually killed around 10 per cent of the affected population, although in a few cases it killed far more: in Lübeck (1548), Rostock (1564) and Norwich (1579), for example, mortality was as high as one-third or even one-half of the population.[41] For those afflicted with plague, death came quickly. At Rennes, in 1605, 20 per cent of those infected died within twenty-four hours, 43 per cent within forty-eight hours, and 80 per cent within five days. All were at risk, the young and healthy, as well as the old and frail, although the poor seem to have been at greater risk than the rich. It is no wonder that plague was still by far the most dreaded of all epidemics.

Since the first outbreaks of plague during the fourteenth century, it had become clear that the disease accompanied the movement of peoples and merchandise. For instance, it was widely thought that plague was carried to the English village of Eyam, in 1665, in boxes of cloth.[42] Plague also appeared to spread from port to port, and the Edinburgh plague of 1568 was probably imported by a merchant from Copenhagen.[43] Another important factor in the spread of plague was the endemic warfare that followed the Reformation and the growth of independent nation-states. For example, the plague in Portsmouth, England, in 1563, may have been caused by the return of English soldiers from a military expedition to France;[44] and the introduction of the plague into northern Italy in 1629 was attributed to a Milanese mercenary who had been trading garments with German soldiers.[45]

It therefore seemed that plague could be carried by persons or in merchandise, often over long distances. However, there was no fundamental difference between explanations that stressed the transmissibility of plague and those that attributed it to noxious miasma. Both explanations were compatible and existed within a complex hierarchy of causes derived from Aristotelian philosophy. At its apex were primary or 'remote' causes, which were usually divine in nature: visitations of plague and other natural disasters as divine punishments for worldly sins. But God exercised his punishment by manipulating the natural world, working through 'secondary causes' such as contamination and putrefaction. One common theory was that plague was caused by an unfavourable conjunction of stars and planets, causing an atmospheric disturbance that putrefied the air.[46]

Such beliefs were widespread among medical practitioners and laymen, and led them to predict the course of epidemics through astrology. However, both astrological and supernatural explanations of plague became less common during the seventeenth century. In Protestant countries, the Reformation led many to doubt miraculous explanations of the appearance and disappearance of disease, and this new scepticism received an added impetus from the Scientific Revolution. Yet, as we shall see in the following chapter, astrological explanations of disease did not disappear altogether, and were reformulated in ways that made them more seem more scientific.

The gradual decline in astrological and supernatural explanations of epidemics – at least among the educated – meant that officials often looked no further than the local or 'exciting' causes of an outbreak. Disease-inducing miasmas were attributed variously to unburied corpses, stagnant pools of water, and accumulations of filth, not to mention the unhygienic habits of the poor. It was thought that unclean persons, or those suffering from plague, could communicate the disease to other people by corrupting the air around them. These miasmas could also be transported in clothes and bedding, or even by domestic animals.[47] Other so-called exciting causes included poor diet, exhaustion and exposure to inclement weather, which explained why some persons were affected by disease and not others. The tendency of plague to 'select' its victims carefully was also explained by reference to 'predisposing causes', including intemperance, immorality and constitutional disposition.[48] Those who possessed hot or humid constitutions were thought susceptible to plague because their open pores enabled the miasma to enter more easily; frenzied or licentious activities could have a similar effect.[49]

Since moral corruption was commonly blamed for visitations of plague, its arrival was usually greeted with penance and prayer. But penitential acts were rarely as extreme as those in the Middle Ages, and amounted to little more than public displays of fasting and prayer. In Catholic Europe special masses were offered to particular saints, but Protestants preferred sermons, fasts and prayer meetings, combined with more worldly action.[50] This is not to say that Catholic countries were content only with displays of piety and contrition, for it was Catholic Europe that took the lead in the civic response to plague. Deference to saints, for example, could provide a powerful incentive to practical action. In Venice beggars were removed from sacred parts of the city such as St Mark's, not simply to remove potential sources of pollution but also to end the defilement of holy places.[51]

Displays of piety did not always translate into greater attendance at church, however. Church-going brought with it an increased risk of infection, and was often avoided for this reason – not least by the clergy themselves. In the London plague of 1625, for example, there was widespread anger at 'runaways' who had abandoned their parishioners.[52] Some priests even justified their flight as a moral duty, equating unnecessary exposure to infection with suicide – a mortal sin. Martin Luther, however, famously admonished his fellow priests for fleeing from plague, declaring it a dereliction of Christian duty.[53] When the faculty of Wittenberg University withdrew to Jena in 1527, Luther was one of the very few to remain and even took plague victims into his home. The same could not be said for the dons of Oxford and Cambridge, who decamped to houses in the country whenever an epidemic struck. Benefactors had given the colleges property especially for this purpose.[54] Other measures of personal protection included the use of incense and posies to counteract the effects of miasma, the wearing of talismens and magical amulets, and the avoidance of potentially infected bedding and linen.

But the most significant thing about the response to plague in the early modern period is the growth of state provisions to control epidemic disease. As we saw in the previous chapter, official attempts to control plague began during the fourteenth century, when the first commissions of health were established in Milan, followed by the creation of permanent boards of health in Florence and Venice. These bodies controlled the movement of persons and merchandise between infected towns by imposing *cordons sanitaires*. Within cities, infected persons and their contacts were confined in pest houses (*lazaretti*); infected areas of the city were fumigated by fire and incense; and measures were taken to ensure the rapid burial of the dead, usually in large anonymous graves, or 'plague pits'. A growing number of Mediterranean states also began to insist that ships entering their ports carried clean bills of health, and that infected vessels were placed in quarantine.[55]

The Italian city-states had extensive trading links with the East, and were directly at risk from the spread of plague from its reservoirs in Central Asia.[56] But mere proximity to the source of plague is not a sufficient explanation of why the Italian states were the first to take measures against it. After all, we might have expected the cities of the Middle East to have introduced plague regulations even sooner than the Italians. The fact that such measures appeared in Italy rather than the Ottoman Empire can be explained to some extent by religious differences. Notions of original sin and divine chastisement propelled Christians to action, whereas death from plague, in Islamic cultures, was often equated with martyrdom.[57] Within Christendom itself, the development of plague regulations probably owed more to political conditions than geographical location. Regulations were most evident in states where political power was concentrated in the hands of a few. Thus Florence, for example, did not attack plague with the same vigour as more autocratic states such as Milan and Mantua. Being autocracies, the latter were able to override vested interests opposed to taxation or quarantine, and to act upon the humanistic maxim that a healthy population was a state's most precious asset.[58] By the later fifteenth century, civic competition had prompted most Italian states to introduce plague regulations, and, in time, they were emulated throughout Europe.[59] After the dark years of the Black Death, and the *danses macabres* of the following century, life had recovered its value and importance.

The measures introduced in some of the Italian city-states were rarely sufficient to hold plague at bay, although in a few cases – such as Barcelona and northern Italy in the later sixteenth century – quarantine may have protected cities against plague.[60] The eventual disappearance of plague from Europe during the early eighteenth century (the last major outbreak being at Marseilles in 1720–2) has also been attributed to the imposition of quarantine. But fighting plague was an expensive business: in addition to the disruption of commerce, there was the cost of maintaining the inhabitants of pest houses, their guards and all the other people employed in anti-plague work. In Milan in 1576, the disinfection of 1,563 homes cost the community 122,000 livres – equivalent to 50 kilos of gold. The expense of feeding those in quarantine exhausted the city's coffers within days, and the town's administration was forced to raise extraordinary taxes and loans. Heavy additional taxation was the norm in most Italian cities during and after an epidemic.[61]

Until recently the establishment of boards of health and quarantines were seen as natural, almost inevitable, responses to invasions of plague.[62] But plague legislation may have had more to do with long-term shifts in attitudes towards the poor than the threat of plague itself. It was over a century before the sanitary commissions formed during the Black Death were accompanied by additional measures to control plague. When some of the Italian states did begin to make new provisions, in the late fifteenth century, they focused almost exclusively on the poor. The poor were thought to suffer most because they lived in the least healthy parts of town and because of their 'repulsive' habits. Their rootless existence also made them a threat to more respectable folk. As Ann Carmichael has argued, the removal of the poor into pest houses, and restrictions on their movement, served not only to prevent the spread of infection but also to deal with the growing problem of social unrest. As well as containing the sick, pest houses provided a means of tackling urban poverty, and were often used between epidemics to house the indigent. This explains why such measures were implemented despite the absence of a clearly defined theory of contagion.[63]

In the north of Europe, the official response to plague was initially more muted, as the case of England shows. Prior to 1518, when Cardinal Wolsey first suggested that infected persons and places should be clearly identified, England had no public precautions against plague. Wolsey's initiative was not so much a response to the immediate threat of plague, but an expression of his desire to place England on a similar footing to the Italian states, which he esteemed as the source of the Renaissance. His scheme to identify infected people and places was first introduced in London, but was later copied in Oxford by Thomas More, the author of *Utopia* (1516). More embraced the humanistic notion that the health of the population was an asset to the state, and in *Utopia* he imagined large, well-run suburban hospitals which provided humane treatment for the sick while at the same time preventing the spread of infection.[64]

In the course of the sixteenth century, localized attempts to prevent plague gathered ground in England. By the 1550s, the principle of segregation was widely proclaimed, and many towns had constructed pest houses to confine the infected. In the coming decades, towns such as York also employed watchmen to prevent the movement of plague victims and their contacts. But segregation was not the only method employed. There was no hard and fast division between contagious and miasmatic notions of disease, and all sources of infection had to be countered. The isolation of the sick removed one source of foul air, but more general cleansing was also deemed necessary, such as the lighting of fires to purify the atmosphere. These scenes were familiar during epidemic visitations well into the nineteenth century, but some anti-plague measures are truly extraordinary to modern eyes. In London, in 1563, there was a massacre of dogs in the belief that they spread the disease, and in Edinburgh, two years later, there was a curious prohibition on the sale of leeks, chives and onions.[65]

All such measures were taken under the auspices of permanent town councils. During the seventeenth century, these municipal bodies began to increase their sanitary functions, with towns such as Gloucester acquiring municipal privies. Even rural communities became subject to sanitary regulation. From 1590, the inhabitants of the Wiltshire village of Castle Combe, for instance, were forbidden to deposit dung or to carry out noxious trades in certain parts of the village.[66] However, as in the Italian city-states, it would be a mistake to see such measures simply as a response to plague, or the threat of plague: they reflected broader concerns about public order and a new cultural sensibility which was part of what the German sociologist Norbert Elias has termed the 'civilizing process'. Elias described a shift from the communal eating and bathing of the Middle Ages to sharply defined distinctions between public and private spheres – a shift that was closely bound up with responses to plague and pox.[67]

After centuries of plague, the poor had become objects of both pity and fear. In 1578 the Privy Council made a Plague Order that provided for the certification of deaths, the appointment of searchers to discover the whereabouts of plague victims, the regulation of burials, and segregation of the sick in their houses. The measures were unprecedented, in the sense that they were funded by taxation, in much the same manner as provisions for the poor under the new Poor Law of 1572. Both the Poor Law and the Plague Order were responses to the growing problem of the rootless poor.[68] Just as the Poor Law aimed to keep the poor within their parish, the Plague Order placed restrictions on their movement. The Plague Act (1604), which encompassed the earlier Plague Order, allowed penal sanctions to be used to contain infected persons, and permitted watchmen to use violence to enforce segregation. Anyone found wandering with a plague sore could be hanged. These measures were potentially very oppressive, and weighed most heavily on the poor, though epidemics did occasionally improve their lot, since local authorities were forced to recruit scavengers, watchmen and grave-diggers from among the lowest orders of society, allowing them to wield power temporarily over their 'betters'.[69]

Popular, as opposed to official, reactions to plague are difficult to ascertain, because they were recorded only, if at all, in court proceedings arising from crime, or in other official sources. As they dealt with the preoccupations of the governing classes, these records may place too much emphasis on disorder, and may exaggerate the threat posed by the lower orders. However, epidemics of plague were often accompanied by attacks on foreigners and minority groups. The Irish in England, Slavs and Albanians in Venice, and migrant workers in Savoy were all blamed for introducing or propagating the disease.[70] Women were prominent among the victims of persecution, being accused of licentiousness and vanity or of poisoning their menfolk.[71] For the same reason, sick servants often found themselves thrown out on to the street, while better-off householders enlisted the help of officials to segregate their poorer neighbours. But the coming of plague seldom provoked generalized disorder or persecution on the scale of the Black Death. This can be explained by the fact that many European cities were visited by plague every few decades, breeding a certain familiarity with the disease.

If popular disturbances occurred, they were normally due to the measures imposed to combat plague rather than to fear of the disease itself. There was strong resistance, for example, to attempts to close down alehouses and places where people gathered for sport and entertainment. Interference was even more strongly resented when officials disturbed long-established customs such as those surrounding the burial of the dead. There were numerous protests against the burial of plague victims in unconsecrated ground, the burial of the dead in shrouds rather than wooden coffins, and the prohibition of large public funerals.[72] But the most unpopular measure by far was the segregation of infected individuals. In 1635, for example, Dutch sailors rioted in Plymouth and Yarmouth when attempts were made to quarantine their ships, and there were numerous attempts to break out of isolation or bribe watchmen.[73] Segregation was also denounced by some of the clergy, who regarded it as 'abhorrent to religion and humanity'. But there seemed to be no practicable alternative. The evacuation of infected cities like London was thought to be prohibitively expensive, although it was attempted in some Italian cities during the 1570s.[74] Quarantine was also relatively popular in the Italian states, and there was little protest against it by comparison with other parts of Europe.[75]

Like pox, plague brought with it a desperate search for remedies, which ranged from prayers and magical amulets to the patent medicines peddled by quacks and empirics. Physicians often continued to treat plague according to Galenic principles, bleeding their patients and lancing their buboes in order to restore the balance of the humours, or employing Galenic antidotes such as theriac, or 'treacle' – a medicine containing opium. There were also numerous remedies based on the doctrine of sympathy, including the application of a live hen or cock to the bubo in order to 'draw out' the poison. It was believed that chickens possessed this property because they were accustomed to eating toads and other supposedly poisonous creatures. Chemical remedies, such as oil of vitriol and gold, also began to gain popularity – among physicians as well as the empirics.[76]

Each visitation of plague prompted a certain amount of medical innovation, but perhaps the most significant outbreak from a medical point of view was the Great Plague of London in 1665–6. This was the first major epidemic in the English capital for over thirty years, and it coincided with – and contributed to – a major revolution in medicine. A crucial difference from previous epidemics was that more medical practitioners remained in the city than before, and some made a serious study of the disease. As many as forty-six treatises on plague appeared during or immediately after the epidemic, dealing with its causes, incidence and treatment. These treatises are notable for being concerned almost entirely with the natural, as opposed to the supernatural, causes of the disease.

But here agreement ended: plague treatises were a battleground for conservative Galenists and followers of the neo-Paracelsian physician J. B. van Helmont (1579–1644). The former continued to see the cause of disease as an imbalance of the humours, whereas the latter believed that disease was due to a disorder of the body's vital spirits. According to the Helmontians, such a disorder could be caused by some disruptive force outside the body (poisoned gas arising from 'fermentation' of the earth) or simply by fear of the plague. Unlike the Galenists, the Helmontians believed that plague was a specific disease, like syphilis, an idea that some reform-minded physicians were beginning to share.[77] There were also some new conceptions of plague, which derived from recent developments in natural philosophy. These included the corpuscular theory of infection and the idea of the *contagium animatum*, which were propounded by the mechanistic natural philosopher Pierre Gassendi (1592–1655) and the Jesuit polymath Athanasius Kircher (1602–80). But whether plague was attributed to 'atoms', worms or gases, these hypotheses served to explain rather than to challenge traditional theories of plague transmission; they should not be regarded as a step towards the germ theory and modern theories of contagion.[78]

The new emphasis upon the specificity of disease was closely associated at the time, and subsequently, with the reforming physician Thomas Sydenham (1624–89). Sydenham had little time for Galenic dogma. Like the Hippocratics, he believed that the only way to learn about disease was by direct observation of the patient at the bedside. This enabled him to monitor the progress of disease and the success of various remedies. His observations led him to believe that plague was a disease with a distinctive natural history and an identity separate from that of the patient, manifesting itself in much the same way no matter whom it attacked. As one popular saying had it, plague was the same whether it afflicted Socrates or a simpleton. This was in marked contrast to Galenic theories of disease, which were essentially individualistic. Sydenham's bedside medicine, by contrast, was a conscious revival of the Hippocratic tradition, as was his interest in the relationship between disease and meteorological conditions. The Hippocratic writings contained books on epidemics and on 'Airs, Waters and Places', in which the atmosphere was closely linked to outbreaks of disease. These works had been widely known to medical practitioners since the Renaissance, but Sydenham regarded them as fundamental to his practice.[79]

Medicine and the 'new science'

The changes taking place in medicine during the plague epidemics of the 1660s were part of the movement conventionally known as the

Scientific Revolution.[80] Some scholars doubt whether there was such a thing, but the idea is worth holding on to, if only because it demonstrates the ways in which medicine was being affected simultaneously by developments in chemistry, mechanics and experimental philosophy. Not all physicians welcomed the new philosophy, because it seemed to place more emphasis on observation and experimentation than on classical authorities, and because it left little room for the individuality of the patient. But others, inspired by the likes of Sir Francis Bacon (1561–1626), author of several influential treatises on the reform of learning, began to pursue investigations in natural history in the hope of finding new cures for disease. The search was stimulated by voyages of discovery and colonial expansion (see chapter 4) and by Puritan visionaries who aimed to make cures available to all. Nicholas Culpeper's *Herbal* (1653) is the most famous of many such examples.[81]

The Baconian quest for useful knowledge also inspired the reform of other branches of medicine. Bacon wrote that medicine ought to be divided into three parts: the preservation of health, the curing of disease, and the prolongation of life. He advocated systematic fact gathering and experimentation to further all these objectives. One of those who took Bacon seriously was the English natural philosopher Robert Boyle (1627–91), who is best known for his work on chemistry and air pressure. In his book *The Usefulnesse of Experimental Naturall Philosophy* (1663), Boyle also wrote on the application of experimental philosophy to physic. He believed that natural philosophy could help the physician better to understand physiology, by observing the effects of temperature upon the body, and pathology, by examining the processes of putrefaction, coagulation and dissolution. What Boyle termed the 'hygienical' part of physic (the preservation of health) could also be improved by a better understanding of cookery and food preservation, he claimed. And, of course, he stressed that chemists and natural philosophers could assist in finding more effective cures for disease.[82]

There were many others besides Boyle who were engaged in pathological and physiological inquiries. Thomas Bartholin (1616–80), for instance, explored the lymphatic system; Franciscus Sylvius (1614–72) proposed a new theory of digestion, the active agent of which was acid, rather than heat as in the Galenic system; Thomas Willis (1621–75) and Robert Hooke (1635–1702) explained why arterial (bright) and venous (dark) blood were different colours, elucidating the link between the heart and the lungs; Francis Glisson (1597–1677) pioneered the study of morbid anatomy with a treatise on what appeared to be a new disease, rickets, in 1654.[83]

These and other developments attest to a radical rethinking of the body and its functions – thinking that sometimes went in controversial directions. This was true, especially, of those investigations inspired by the mechanical philosophy of René Descartes (1596–1650). Descartes was the first open supporter of Harvey's discovery of the circulation of the blood, but he went further than Harvey in likening the heart to an automatic pump powered by its own heat. According to Descartes, the human body was maintained not by one or more 'life-forces', as Harvey had imagined, but solely by the interrelations of its mechanical parts. There were several attempts subsequently to apply Cartesian principles to physiology, such as that by Giovanni Alfonso Borelli (1608–79). A reputed mathematician and astronomer, Borelli was inspired by Descartes to turn his attention to animate forms, publishing his influential book *On the Motion of Animals* in 1680–1. He attempted to compute the mechanical pull exerted by the muscles, and began to look at the heart and vasculature as a single hydraulic system.[84]

Investigations of the human body and other objects were now aided by a new tool in the form of the microscope, which had been constructed around 1600 in Holland. In the 1650s and 1660s, Marcello Malphigi (1628–94) a professor of medicine at Pisa, used the microscope to discover the minute capillaries that connected the arteries and the veins, providing conclusive evidence for the circulation of the blood. The Dutchman Antoni van Leeuwenhoek (1632–1723) described for the first time what were later termed bacteria and protozoa, as well as human spermatozoa. His discoveries sparked heated debates over the spontaneous generation of the lower orders of animals, some of which were to have direct implications for theories of disease. Robert Hooke, Boyle's assistant, also described numerous phenomena, including blood vessels, in a compendium entitled *Micrographia* (1665). As we shall see in the following chapter, these new ways of seeing and understanding the body had a profound effect upon the ways in which disease was understood, treated and prevented.

3

Disease and Social Order: The Enlightenment and its Legacy

What we know today as the Enlightenment spanned the period between the Scientific Revolution of the seventeenth century and the French Revolution of the eighteenth, although its legacy has proved enduring. It was a period of great optimism about the perfectibility of humankind: ideas of political liberty and toleration flourished, and there was growing confidence that society could be improved by enlightened and rational govenment. The decline of certain epidemic diseases – most notably the plague – contributed to this feeling of optimism; it seemed that even the most dreaded of pestilences could be banished if people put their minds to it. Attention began to turn to those diseases that remained: to chronic complaints such as gout and to common, though often lethal, maladies such as smallpox and fevers. There was particular concern about new 'crowd diseases' which ravaged armies and other confined populations, while intermittent and remittent fevers (most likely malaria) continued to cause death and debility in many lowland areas of Europe.

But all these maladies now seemed amenable to control, provided that order and discipline could be imposed. Inspired by the achievements of Isaac Newton (1642–1727) and others working in the physical sciences, medical practitioners attempted to discover the laws that governed the operation of disease and to classify diseases according to scientific principles. From the late seventeenth century a growing number of physicians inspired by Descartes, and later by Newton, began to think of the body as if it were a machine, composed of pipes, pulleys and levers.[1] Modish practitioners induced their patients to 'purge and vomit mathematically', as one critic put it.[2] For these mechanistic physicians, there was no place for the notions of soul and spirit that had permeated Galenic medicine, and even the theories of Harvey.

At the forefront of the new medicine was Herman Boerhaave (1668–1738), a professor at Leiden University in the Netherlands. Boerhaave was the leading medical figure of his day, and had many disciples throughout Europe. He believed that the solid parts of the body were composed of fibres, and that its fluid components flowed through these fibrous vessels in accordance with the laws of hydrodynamics. Disease occurred when the vessels became blocked or constricted, and could be relieved by bleeding and purging. It was a theory that retained certain aspects of the old humoral system, but within a new, mechanical framework.[3] Boerhaave's German contemporary Friedrich Hoffman (1660–1742) interpreted Descartes' mechanical philosophy rather differently. He placed much greater emphasis than Boerhaave on the nervous system, which he envisaged as a network of fine canals carrying minute particles that linked different parts of the body in a kind of 'sympathy'. Hoffman saw health as a state of optimal nervous tension, with disease occurring when the tension was either too great or too little. But the mechanical approach to medicine had its critics. Hoffman's colleague at Halle, Georg Stahl (1660–1734), believed that the body's 'mechanical' actions were subordinate to those of a soul, or 'anima'. According to Stahl, the soul enlivened the body and prevented disease, but adverse environmental conditions or emotional turmoil could unsettle it, affecting the tone of bodily fibres. The result was impairment of circulation and putrefaction of the humours.[4]

Many physicians found Stahl's ideas appealing because they allowed for interaction between body and soul, thus avoiding the materialism (and implicitly the atheism) of mechanical philosophy. A pious Lutheran, Stahl believed that the anima was immortal, and that disease occurred when it was misdirected. One of those inspired by Stahl was the Swiss physician Albrecht von Haller (1708–77), who believed that the body possessed two vital qualities: its nervous *sensibility* to pain and the *irritability* of its muscles. In his eight-volume work *The Elements of Physiology* (1757–76), he distinguished organs by their different levels of irritability, and explained their actions accordingly. The most 'irritable' organ was the heart, and it was its state of constant excitement that enabled it to pump blood rapidly around the body. Haller's view of the human body was therefore quite different from both the dualism of Boerhaave and Hoffman and the vitalism of Stahl, because the qualities of sensibility and irritability existed independently of the soul.[5]

Haller had a profound influence on the ways in which eighteenth-century physicians came to view disease, and induced many practitioners to see the nervous system as the seat of all illness. One of those indebted to Haller was the Scottish physician William Cullen (1710–90), professor of medicine at Edinburgh University and one of the most influential writers and teachers of the eighteenth century. Cullen was attracted by the mechanical systems of Boerhaave and Hoffman (Boerhaave had taught many of the first members of the Edinburgh medical faculty),[6] but Cullen borrowed from Haller the idea that the motion of fluids and solids was governed by the nervous system. Like Haller, he rejected the idea that bodily functions were co-ordinated by the soul, although he believed in the existence of an immortal faculty within the body. The body was sustained, rather, by nervous excitement, at a sufficient level to maintain chemical balance, correct posture and locomotion, as well as the circulation of the blood. Nervous excitement was generated by environmental stimuli such as heat and cold, together with internal stimulation from the mind. These theories were advanced in Cullen's *Institutions of Medicine* (1772) and *First Lines of the Practice of Physic* (1776–8). Here and in his lectures, he argued that disease resulted from either too much or too little stimulation. Too much excitement produced muscular spasms, which resulted in disturbances of the circulation or the body's chemical balance; too little produced debility and paralysis of bodily functions.[7]

Cullen was also famous for his attempt to classify diseases according to distinctive types. Like others who admired Sydenham's natural-historical approach to disease, Cullen set out to classify ailments in terms of their symptoms – an enterprise which came to be known as nosology. In addition to observing the symptoms of patients, Cullen used evidence from post-mortem dissections – something that Sydenham did not do. Cullen's attempt to classify disease followed in the footsteps of the Italian physician Giorgio Baglivi (1668–1707), the French physician F. B. de Sauvages (1706–67) and Carl von Linné (1707–78), the Swedish naturalist who had famously classified living organisms into species and genera.[8] But Cullen's scheme of classification was less elaborate than that of de Sauvages, and he made more use of post-mortem evidence than any of his fellow nosologists.[9]

Cullen published his nosology in 1769 as a guide for medical students. He divided diseases into four classes: pyrexiae (which included fevers and fluxes), neuroses, cachexia (swellings and skin diseases) and locales (a miscellany). These systems of classification were quite unlike the natural histories of the Renaissance, which were full of mythical allusions. Natural historians now aimed to lift the veil of superstition and reveal the natural world in its barest form.[10] Moreover, diseases were treated as if they were distinct entities existing independently of an individual's experience of suffering. Yet Cullen insisted that his classification of diseases was merely a guide, and that others might see things differently.[11] Each physician, he insisted, ought to be guided by the evidence of his senses.

Tempered by the scepticism of his friend, the philosopher David Hume (1711–76), Cullen was seldom dogmatic. He attracted many pupils but few disciples, quite unlike his most famous antagonist John Brown (1735–88). A former pupil of Cullen, Brown reduced all bodily processes to one simple principle – nervous excitability. Some admirers likened Brown's theory to the achievements of Newton, but others could see little difference between Brown's system and that of his teacher. After all, both Cullen and Brown stressed the primacy of the nervous system as the seat of disease. The real difference lay in Brown's insistence that all diseases were essentially one: the result of either too much or too little nervous stimulation. This also led Brown radically to simplify the treatment of disease. Cullen preferred gently to assist the body's natural processes, whereas Brown advocated the use of wine and opium, then regarded as stimulants, to revitalize its energies. Many physicians regarded Brown's system as too simplistic, but it appealed to those who challenged the authority of learned medicine, whether in Edinburgh, London or on the Continent.[12] Even those who rejected Brown's theories were increasingly inclined to use stimulants in the treatment of diseases like fever. This owed something to Cullen's insight that the onset of fever was marked by 'debility', a reduction in nervous energy, and to accumulating evidence that bleeding and other depletive treatments were sometimes fatal, especially when patients were already weakened by fatigue or exposure to climatic extremes.[13]

Cullen believed that debility was often caused by exposure to bad weather and putrid air. He taught that 'The remote cause of fever is a poison that weakens the nervous power and energy of the brain'. This poison could be produced either by 'contagion', which Cullen defined as the contamination of a healthy body by foreign matter from a diseased person, or by miasmas, which arose from rotting matter, especially in conditions of great humidity. As contagion was usually spread through the atmosphere – when sick and healthy shared confined and ill-ventilated spaces – there was no rigid distinction between contagious and miasmatic diseases: both were due to matter suspended in the air, and were affected by the atmosphere. Marshes, for example, were considered unhealthy in all climates, because stagnant water and rotting vegetation gave rise to noxious miasma. But the power of marsh effluvia to cause disease was intensified by heat and moisture. Marsh fevers like 'intermittent fever' thus appeared to be more deadly in the tropics than in the fens of England, an observation that Cullen had made personally while working for a short time in the West Indies.[14]

The increasing frequency of travel to different climates, together with the nervous theory of disease, provided an additional stimulus to those investigating the link between disease and meteorological conditions. Since the Renaissance there had been growing interest in Hippocratic medicine, including those parts of the Hippocratic corpus that dealt with epidemics and the relationship between disease and the environment. Thomas Sydenham, for example, had shown a keen interest in the relationship between the atmosphere and epidemic diseases, as did the Italian physician Bernadino Ramazzini (1633–1714), who undertook a series of investigations culminating in his *History of the Constitution of the Years 1690 . . . and 1694*.[15] Others followed suit, notably the English physician John Arbuthnot, whose *Essay Concerning the Effects of Air on Human Bodies* (1733) was later used by Montesquieu to provide support for the theory of climatic influence expounded in *The Spirit of the Laws* (1749).[16] Many medical practitioners continued to trace the influence of climate upon disease, most sharing Cullen's view of the primacy of the nervous system. Some, like John Clark (1744–1805), a surgeon with the East India Company, wrote specifically on the effects of tropical climates; others, like Robert Robertson (1742–1829), wrote on fevers in all climates.[17] On the Continent, too, there was growing interest in the relationship between climate and disease. The French hygienist J. N. Hallé (1754–1822), the physician A. Fourcroy (1755–1809), as well as many non-medical writers, made important observations on the relationship between meteorology and disease. By the 1790s there were even calls for the unification of medicine with the earth sciences.[18]

One curious aspect of these developments was a renewed interest in the influence of planetary bodies. Physicians had grown increasingly sceptical about the claims of medical astrologers, but new explanations were offered for old beliefs. Robert Boyle, for instance, wrote 'An Apology for Astrology', in which he speculated that 'celestial particles' interacted with the minute building blocks of terrestrial matter. Newton's work on gravity also inspired some practitioners to rationalize astrology in mechanical terms, including the London physician Richard Mead (1673–1754) and the poet, doctor and evolutionary theorist Erasmus Darwin (1731–1802). Notions of planetary influence were also popular amongst medical practitioners in the tropical colonies, where the moon was thought to exercise a particularly strong influence on fevers.[19]

Views of disease were also transformed by morbid anatomy, which came increasingly to the fore during the eighteenth century. Although some physicians had already investigated signs of disease in dead bodies,[20] post-mortem dissections were still relatively uncommon, and had little bearing on medical practice. But during the eighteenth century morbid anatomy began to receive more attention, a development that is generally attributed to the influence of the venerable Paduan professor Giovanni Battista Morgagni (1682–1771).[21] In 1761, at the age of nearly eighty, Morgagni published a monumental work entitled *On the Sites and Causes of Disease.* The work was based on around 700 autopsies, in which Morgagni claimed to find tell-tale signs of particular diseases; these were analysed closely alongside the case histories of individual patients. His book was well received, and was translated into English in 1769 and German in 1774. Its importance lay in the fact that it correlated symptoms with anatomical lesions, enabling physicians to locate particular diseases in specific organs.

One of those inspired by Morgagni was Matthew Baillie (1761–1823), a nephew of the surgeon-anatomists William Hunter (1718–83) and John Hunter (1728–93). Baillie trained at William's Great Windmill Street Anatomy School in London and at St George's Hospital, where John was head surgeon. In 1793 Baillie published his *Morbid Anatomy of Some of the Most Important Parts of the Human Body*, which matched symptoms to morbid changes in particular organs. John Hunter also conducted many pathological investigations himself, most notably in his work on gunshot wounds, in which he paid special attention to tissue inflammation.[22] The fact that Baillie's book went through many editions in England and overseas attests to a growing interest in morbid anatomy, but the conventional picture of the eighteenth century is that only a handful of practitioners pursued similar lines of inquiry. It is true that opportunities for dissection were restricted by statute, but illicit supplies of cadavers allowed surgeons at some charitable infirmaries to conduct pathological investigations,[23] while military and naval surgeons enjoyed the best opportunities of all. When a soldier or sailor died overseas, there was nothing to prevent a surgeon from opening up his body. Global conflicts like the Seven Years War (1756–63) provided ample opportunities to investigate the morbid effects of fevers, scurvy and dysentery, for example. Such investigations were common even before the publication of the influential works of Morgani and Baillie, and they informed numerous treatises on fever.[24]

At the close of the eighteenth century, pathological anatomy took a new turn with the work of the Frenchman Marie François Xavier Bichat (1771–1802). During the Revolutionary period, Bichat joined the army as a surgeon, which provided him with ample opportunity to dissect those who had died from disease. In 1794 he settled in Paris, where the city's hospitals, formerly under religious orders, had been taken over by the Revolutionary state. Under the new dispensation, the sick poor, who were treated in the infirmaries, became the subjects of detailed clinical and post-mortem investigations. Bichat conducted hundreds of autopsies, which formed the basis of two important works, his *Treatise on Membranes* (1799) and *General Anatomy* (1801). Bichat refined pathology by paying more attention to morbid changes in tissues and membranes, rather than organs as a whole. He described twenty-one different tissues, including muscular and nervous tissue, and insisted that these should become the basis of medical instruction.[25]

With Bichat's tissue pathology, medicine acquired 'an objective, real, and at last unquestionable foundation for the description of diseases'.[26] Combined with detailed scrutiny of the patient's symptoms in hospital, pathological anatomy was an essential feature of what Michel Foucault called the 'anatomico-clinical gaze'. This was the defining feature of a new form of medicine, often referred to as 'hospital' or 'clinical' medicine, which gradually displaced the more individualistic, patient-centred medicine of the eighteenth century.[27] But the distinctiveness of Parisian medicine has been questioned by several historians, who point out that clinical medicine had many different origins, some of which pre-date the hospitals of Revolutionary Paris. Othmar Keel has argued that tissue pathology was already evident in the work of John Hunter, for example, while many features of clinical medicine were present at universities like Vienna.[28] Laurence Brockliss has also shown that French students sought clinical training in medicine, as well as surgery, well before the Revolution.[29] But if any institutions can claim to be the true originators of clinical medicine, it is the hospitals of the army and the navy. As we have seen, military and naval hospitals, especially those in the colonies, were at the forefront in morbid anatomy. The regulated environment of these hospitals also permitted the mass observation of patients, together with standardized treatment and therapeutic experimentation on a scale way beyond that allowed in civilian institutions. The collection and collation of medical statistics – which was another key element of the anatomico-clinical method – also developed predominantly in military and naval hospitals.[30]

One key innovation that *did* originate in civilian medicine was the development of a new diagnostic technique closely related to pathological anatomy. In 1816 Théophile Hyacinthe Laënnec (1781–1826), a physician at the Salpêtrière Hospital in Paris, devised the first stethoscope, which allowed doctors to listen for pathological changes within the body. In his *Treatise on Auscultation* (1819), Laënnec showed that it was possible to detect diseases like pneumonia and phthisis (later termed tuberculosis), a disease to which he was himself to succumb. The stethoscope enabled physicians to claim objective knowledge of their patients' bodies, quite independently of the reporting of symptoms or other conventional forms of diagnosis. It was a major boost to the authority and status of the medical practitioner. Laënnec was subsequently elevated to the status of a national hero, but there were many contemporaries of similar distinction. One such was Laënnec's colleague Gaspard Laurent Bayle (1774–1816), who was the first person to show that phthisis was a separate disease. On the basis of port-mortem examinations, Bayle differentiated between different types of phthisis, observing tubercular nodes in different parts of the body. He later made similar observations on cancer.[31]

After the final defeat of Napoleon in 1815, students from all over Europe and North America flocked to Paris to imbibe the new spirit of medicine, and on returning to their native lands, imparted it to new generations of students.[32] But the pathologists had their critics. Another Parisian doctor, F. J. V. Broussais (1772–1838), railed against pathological anatomy and the tendency of his colleagues to localize disease. His *Examination of the Medical Doctrines and of the Systems of Nosology* (1821) treated diseases not as separate entities but as derangements of the body's normal functions.[33] In other words, disease was systemic rather than specific. Broussais believed that most diseases resulted from gastro-intestinal irritation, a condition that he believed was best treated by blood-letting. Largely as a result of Broussais' influence, bleeding became fashionable once more, before falling out of favour towards the middle of the century. But Broussais' influence lived on in the physiological theories of Claude Bernard and Rudolf Virchow, who will be examined in the following chapter.

Disease prevention: public and private spheres

New theories of disease raised the prospect of a more rational approach to prevention – a subject that began to receive far more attention from medical practitioners than before. A growing number were employed in hospitals – which proliferated rapidly during the eighteenth century – and in the new standing armies and navies formed in most European countries. As a result, medical practitioners were increasingly inclined to think of health collectively. Rather than ministering simply to the needs of individual patients, some began to think of themselves as guardians of society, diagnosing the social causes of disease and prescribing social as well as medical remedies. It was an aspiration that chimed with the general mood of the Enlightenment and new theories about the role of the state. Although the prevention of disease had been an object of statecraft since the Renaissance, the enlightened regimes of eighteenth-century Europe took a much broader interest in matters of health. Health was now seen as the natural state of the human body, contrasting sharply with the medieval view that it tended inevitably to putrefaction and decay. It was widely believed that the body natural and the body politic could be perfected by the application of reason. Like many other social ills, disease appeared to be a consequence of unruliness and irrationality that could be conquered by reason and good government.

The new role envisaged for medicine was encapsulated in the idea of 'medical police'. The term referred not to a 'police force' in the modern sense, but to a range of mechanisms that aimed to ensure the health and wealth of the nation. The main aim of medical police was the 'preservation, upkeep and conservation of the labour force', but it was also concerned with broader problems of social order.[34] The concept of medical police was most clearly articulated in the context of cameralism, a paternalistic, German variant of the mercantilist theory of statecraft that dominated Europe during the Enlightenment.[35] Mercantilism often entailed commercial protectionism, as well as military and naval action to sever the economic arteries of opposing nations. Within this context, it was seen as desirable to maintain the health of workers and military recruits.

The main exponent of medical police was the German municipal physician Wilhelm Rau (1721–72), who urged that medical care should be available to the population as a whole, and not just to the rich. The principle was further extended by Johann P. Frank (1745–1821) who envisioned state-supervised regulations governing everything from personal hygiene to water supplies, and from marriage to transportation. An important element in Frank's scheme was a team of health inspectors invested with powers to quarantine, disinfect and cleanse. Having been educated in France, and having served various administrations in the German states and Austria, Frank's views were widely known throughout Europe. However, his proposals were too authoritarian and too expensive to gain much support.[36] Even in autocratic nations like Prussia and Austria, regulations were confined largely to medical practice and the sale of drugs.[37]

But though the idea of medical police had little appeal, most European states began to accept that they should take a more active role in disease prevention, particularly in respect of epidemic disease. The clearest illustration of this is the growth of quarantines to check the passage of disease by land and by sea. By the mid-eighteenth century, the Habsburg Empire maintained a cordon sanitaire along its 1,500 km border with Turkey, in order to keep plague at bay in Eastern Europe.[38] However, maritime quarantine was probably a more effective barrier against plague, and it may have helped to confine it to the eastern Mediterranean. The sole exception was the terrible epidemic that occurred in Marseilles in 1720–2.[39] Cordons sanitaires around Marseilles were unable to prevent the plague from spreading to neighbouring provinces, but strict quarantines against French shipping did prevent it from reaching other countries like England.[40]

States also began to improve their intelligence about epidemics. During the reign of Louis XIV, for example, the French state began to wrest control of public health from the localities in order to make information available at the centre. Later, the Royal Academy of Medicine was established in 1772, partly in order to maintain a network for reporting epidemics and to provide medical assistance to rural areas facing outbreaks of disease. Following a severe epidemic of cattle disease (probably rinderpest), a central Commission on Epidemics was established in 1776 to gather information about its causes. It spent most of its time investigating the link between epidemics and environmental factors such as weather, soil and seasonality.[41] These investigations were similar to those of Sydenham and Ramazzini; indeed, rinderpest was first described by Ramazzini in 1712. He had suggested that the disease was similar to smallpox: an observation that led some to experiment with inoculation. As we shall see in a moment, the practice of inoculation – of artificially inducing a mild case of smallpox with smallpox crusts – had just been introduced into Europe from the Middle East. In the case of rinderpest, similar practices conferred immunity, but at the cost of keeping the disease circulating amongst cattle. For this reason, most people tended to prefer the drastic but effective expedient of slaughter.[42]

Infant mortality was another growing concern in many countries.[43] By the eighteenth century, children were increasingly seen as the foundation of national prosperity, and this led to new codes of behaviour concerning relationships between children and adults. These codes lacked legal force, but there was a growing expectation that parents should pay attention to the cleanliness and hygiene of their offspring. According to Michel Foucault, 'the healthy, clean, fit body' and a 'purified, cleansed aerated domestic space' became two of the family's main concerns.[44] But despite the flood of publications on child rearing, there is little evidence of any widespread change in behaviour, except among the more prosperous sections of society. The vast majority of people were unaware of these new fashions for child rearing, or paid little attention to them. The only time at which child health may have been materially affected by the state itself was immediately after delivery, because of new regulations governing the practice of midwifery. After 1730, French midwives were compelled to undergo a two-year apprenticeship at a provincial hospital, for example. Yet, even this requirement was often dispensed with in practice.[45]

Although the state began to intervene in a modest way in many European countries, it did not do so in the complete and systematic manner envisaged by the advocates of medical police. This situation did not alter significantly until the nineteenth century. Some countries, like Great Britain, were resistant to any form of state regulation, even of the sale of drugs. There was much greater emphasis in Britain on medicine as a free trade, and no special measures were introduced to curtail the sale of drugs or to license medical practice. But there were many people in Britain who did think of the population as a national resource, just like the advocates of medical police. John Graunt's *Natural and Political Observations upon the Bills of Mortality* (1662) and William Petty's *Essays on Political Arithmetic* (1687) stressed the importance of gathering data on the population in order to improve its health, largely for economic reasons.[46]

Nevertheless, the initiative in matters of health remained very much with private individuals, as the proliferation of charitable hospitals and dispensaries attests. Between 1720 and 1745, no fewer than five large general hospitals were established in London alone.[47] These initiatives set off a chain reaction, which saw the foundation of numerous provincial hospitals and dispensaries. Most of these institutions were intended for the 'deserving poor', who received medical care free of charge, the aim being to heal social divisions and encourage a sense of loyalty and gratitude towards their patrons.[48] As in France, many of these initiatives were aimed at children, such as the London Foundling Hospital established in 1741 and the London Lying-in Charity Hospital founded in 1757, partly with the aim of teaching better midwifery.[49]

Private philanthropists also took the lead in promoting inoculation against smallpox, a disease that was responsible for 10 per cent of all deaths in Europe at this time. Inoculators used the dried scabs of smallpox pustules to induce a mild form of the disease that conferred lifelong protection; the matter was usually rubbed on to abrasions on the skin or on the membranes of the nose. The practice was well established in many areas of Asia, Africa and the Balkans, but in

Western Europe it was not generally known until the eighteenth century.[50] In England, the Royal Society began to investigate small-pox in earnest after the deaths of Queen Mary in 1694 and the Duke of Gloucester in 1700, and in the coming years it received a series of reports describing the practice of inoculation overseas. Dr Edward Tarry claimed to have seen 4,000 people inoculated in Turkey, for example, and it was reported that the children of the French consul at Aleppo, Syria, had successfully undergone the operation. The first two Britons to be inoculated – in 1716 – were the sons of Mr Heffernan, the Secretary to the British ambassador in Turkey. This was soon overshadowed by the publicity given by Lady Mary Wortley Montagu, whose uncommon beauty had been destroyed by an attack of smallpox. She witnessed the inoculation in Constantinople after travelling there with her husband, who had been appointed British ambassador. Wortley Montagu decided immediately to inoculate her son, and after her return to England, her daughter was also inoculated.[51] This was the first inoculation to be performed in Britain, and it was witnessed by several eminent physicians. Their favourable reports induced other aristocrats to follow suit, though the death of some children showed that the procedure was far from totally safe.[52]

Variolation, as inoculation came to be known, was seldom practised without some form of embellishment. Physicians subjected their patients to a strict regimen for three to six weeks before the operation, which normally entailed the exclusion of alcohol and meat from their diet, the aim being to eliminate harmful substances so as to strengthen the body before it was given the smallpox 'poison'; the process was normally assisted by purging and bleeding. When the patient was deemed ready, an incision was made deep into the skin, and the smallpox lymph rubbed into it. The wound was normally dressed for several weeks to reduce the threat of contagion, and in some cases patients were shut up in special houses until their fever had passed. There then followed a lengthy period of convalescence, during which the patient underwent detoxification.[53]

These procedures transformed inoculation from a simple folk practice into a lengthy and expensive procedure, and it is hardly surprising that its popularity was confined to the upper classes, at least until the middle of the century. Other obstacles included the severe fevers (and sometimes fatalities) that followed, not to mention the fatalism of the lower classes, some of whom believed that inoculation flouted the will of God. But after 1750, the practice of variolation began to spread more quickly. The immediate reason was the great smallpox epidemic of 1751–3, which claimed thousands of lives in large cities like London. The procedure itself was also simpler, safer and cheaper than before, thanks to a new arm-to-arm method of inoculation developed in South Carolina by the Charleston physician James Kirk-patrick. His report, which was well supported by statistical evidence, was translated into several European languages, and did much to broaden the interest in variolation. In 1747 Kirkpatrick's report induced the London Foundling Hospital to inoculate all children admitted to it, and in many English country towns, charities took responsibility for inoculating the poor, enlisting the expertise of local surgeons and apothecaries, many of whom saw in inoculation a prof-itable sideline.[54]

Inoculation was also gradually introduced into other European countries. In France, it was supported strongly by the Royal Academy of Sciences, despite some resistance from the Catholic Church and conservative elements within the medical profession. Doubts about the efficacy and safety of variolation did not, however, deter the aris-tocracy from inoculating themselves and their children. Inoculators such as the charismatic Genevan physician Dr Théodore Tronchin (1709–81) enjoyed a high reputation among the French elite, and inoculated several children of the royal family. Tronchin's success may have owed something to the fact that he selected his patients carefully, refusing to inoculate any who might be unable to bear the procedure.[55] Like other prominent inoculators, he made a good living from touring the courts of Europe: the death of Louis XV from small-pox had provided a salutary lesson.[56] Yet it was only in Britain that inoculation became widespread among the poorer sections of society, partly because British surgeons and apothecaries had a more experi-mental outlook than many practitioners on the Continent. Many British landowners, too, had imbibed the spirit of improvement, and induced their tenants and retainers to undergo the procedure. But even in Britain there were large gaps in coverage, and smallpox remained one of the principal endemic diseases. Despite some claims to the contrary, it is unlikely that inoculation made any major impact upon mortality.[57]

It was not long before a more effective solution to the problem of smallpox arrived in the form of vaccination – the practice pioneered by Edward Jenner (1749–1832). Jenner was a clergyman's son from the rural county of Gloucestershire, in England, who had established a medical and surgical practice in his home town of Berkeley. He was a typical figure of the Enlightenment, with interests in many areas. A keen naturalist, he made important discoveries about the nesting behaviour of the cuckoo, and it may have been this bent for natural history that led Jenner to take an interest in local stories about the immunity of milkmaids to smallpox. Jenner found that those who had contracted cowpox from their animals did not suffer from the similar but far more serious disease, smallpox. In 1796 he put these observations to practical use, experimentally injecting a local boy, James Phipps, with cowpox. He then attempted to infect the child with smallpox using the technique of variolation, but found that no symptoms appeared. Subsequent tests provided further confirmation of Jenner's hypothesis, and he published his results in *An Inquiry into the Causes and Effects of the Variolae Vaccinae* (1798).[58]

Jenner's theory was far from watertight, as he still had to explain why some people who contracted cowpox also contracted smallpox. He suggested that this anomaly might be due to there being two types of cowpox, 'true' and 'spurious', and warned that vaccine lymph would have to be of the right kind to be effective. Many of his critics found this explanation implausible, if not ridiculous.[59] Some even imagined that vaccination would 'animalize' them, a fear famously satirized by the cartoonist James Gilray, who depicted those who had undergone the operation with cows' heads. However, vaccination quickly attracted some influential supporters. Eminent physicians in London and on the Continent lauded Jenner, and the emperor Napoleon was a great admirer, as was Thomas Jefferson, who vaccinated his own children. In 1802, only four years after the publication of his *Inquiry*, Jenner received the enormous sum of £10,000 from the British government, and a further £20,000 in 1807. As we shall see in the next chapter, vaccination against smallpox encountered stubborn resistance on many counts throughout the nineteenth century; yet it saved innumerable lives, and was undoubtedly the most tangible example of medical progress during the eighteenth century.

War, disease and medicine

Quarantine and vaccination apart, the Enlightenment was more notable for its ideas than its actions in the field of public health. Ambitious plans and fine sentiments were rarely backed up with concerted action by the state. The only real exceptions were the armies and navies of the major European powers, all of which saw major developments in hygiene and sanitation – developments that would later provide precedents for reforms in the civilian sphere. These initiatives stemmed from a combination of practical and humanitarian concerns: there was widespread revulsion at the barbarism of religious wars like the Thirty Years War (1618–48), and this was expressed in a more humane attitude towards the sick and the wounded. This new sensibility led many to question the necessity of death from disease: a consideration that was all the more important in view of the rising cost of manpower. A series of interconnected developments in technology and tactics – which has been described as the 'Military Revolution' – meant that men needed to be trained for longer than before, making it more difficult and expensive to replace them.[60] For this reason, the state began to take a keen interest in the prevention of disease in the armed forces, and it was in the armies and navies of Europe that the idea of medical police was most fully realized.

Though the eighteenth century is often said to have been an age of 'limited warfare', its battles were hugely wasteful of human life, and many thousands died from disease in the protracted sieges that typified many campaigns in Europe and its colonies. In summer, the concentration of men and animals around fortifications provided fertile breeding grounds for water- and fly-borne diseases such as dysentery. In winter, when men and animals were huddled together in tents and huts, the conditions were ripe for louse-borne infections such as typhus. Thus the siege of Lille by the British coalition, which ended in 1708, cost the investing armies 14,000 casualties, nearly all to disease. The following year the Allies lost a further 15,000 men, in addition to thousands of sick, during the sieges of Douai, Béthune, Aixe and St Venant.[61] The situation was no better at sea. The confined and usually filthy conditions below decks resulted in regular outbreaks of fluxes (dysentery) and 'ship fevers' like typhus. At the beginning of the Seven Years War, levels of sickness in the Royal Navy were so high that many of its ships were unserviceable.[62]

Military and naval surgeons were acutely aware of the costs to the state of near continual warfare. In his *Œconomical and Medical Observations* (1764), the British military surgeon Richard Brocklesby wrote of the loss to disease of 'so many useful members of the Body Politick' when urging sanitary reforms in the Army.[63] The military surgeon Donald Monro, a scion of the famous Edinburgh medical dynasty, spelled out the connection between disease and the national interest at greater length: 'In a commercial Country like our own,' he argued, 'where Numbers of Hands are constantly wanted for carrying on our Manufactories, we have a strong political Argument to add to that drawn from the Dictates of Humanity, why the Life of every individual should be most carefully attended to.' 'The Preservation of the Lives of Soldiers', he continued, 'is then with us a Matter of the highest Importance, in order to make as low as possible the Number of Recruits who must be perpetually drawn off for Service to War.'[64] By the end of the century, it had become common to refer to servicemen as 'commodities', whose lives were worth preserving for economic reasons alone.[65]

Indeed, most European countries now thought it worthwhile investing in a permanent medical service for their armies and navies, and some, like Russia, even provided special tuition for military and naval surgeons.[66] For the same reasons, a number of impressive hospitals were established for the exclusive use of the armed forces. Hitherto, what little care had been available was provided by religious orders or charities. In 1629 it was stipulated that every French military fortress should be equipped with an infirmary and a surgeon, and this had been achieved by 1708.[67] In 1670 the grand Hôtel des Invalides was also established to provide medical care and indoor relief for retired soldiers. It was an institution that symbolized the benevolence of the Sun King, Louis XIV, but may also have been intended as a means to control a potentially volatile and dangerous section of French society.[68] Similar objectives may have been behind the establishment of the Chelsea (military) and Greenwich (naval) hospitals in England, in 1691 and 1705 respectively.[69]

Institutions like the Hôtel des Invalides were established for the general care of ex-servicemen and were not simply infirmaries, though specialist military and naval infirmaries became more common in the course of the eighteenth century. In the early 1700s, the majority of sick and wounded sailors were placed in taverns and other private quarters, which naval doctors regarded as dens of disease and iniquity. But by the 1750s the Royal Navy was sending its casualties to purpose-built institutions like the hospital at Haslar, near Plymouth. Here, patients could be kept under naval discipline, and their environment could be closely regulated to prevent disease.[70] The achievements of these hospitals in treating disease were impressive. At Haslar, 9,862 out of 14,418 patients admitted between 1753 and 1757 were discharged as cured, no less than 68 per cent.[71] Similar hospitals were established in other European countries,[72] in addition to the improvement of mobile hospitals that accompanied troops into battle.[73] But though it was possible to keep order in the larger military and naval hospitals, conditions in most of the field hospitals left much to be desired. The French seem to have had the best hospital organization, because hospitals were under the control of medical officers. Although hygiene was beginning to figure in manuals on military discipline, most combatant officers had little knowledge or interest in such matters. And even the best intentions counted for little if men were determined to flout sanitary orders *en masse*.[74]

For these reasons it was easier to maintain sanitary discipline within the confines of naval vessels than it was in armies, and especially armies on the march. When it came to naval hygiene, it was the British who led the way. From the 1750s, naval surgeons began to investigate many of the common diseases afflicting seamen, one of which was scurvy, a disease that had begun to figure as a major problem during the seventeenth century. Recent discoveries such as the chronometer enabled ships to stay at sea for longer periods, without losing time or incurring danger by having to land to correct longitude. This conferred an important tactical advantage, but it also meant that crews were denied fresh produce for longer periods, and that they suffered increasingly from deficiency diseases like scurvy (which is now known to be caused by a lack of vitamin C). Scurvy was a problem on most long voyages and, most notoriously, on Lord Anson's circumnavigation of the globe in 1740–1, which resulted in the deaths of 1,051 seamen out of 1,955 engaged for the voyage, mostly from scurvy.[75]

Various investigations were conducted to help prevent and treat scurvy, including James Lind's famous trial, which took place on *HMS Salisbury* in 1754. Lind chose twelve patients suffering from scurvy, and gave two of them a quart of cider every day; two, oil of vitriol; two, vinegar; two, sea water; two, a combination of garlic, radish, balsam and myrrh; and two, oranges and lemons. At one time or another, all of these substances had been touted as 'antiseptics' that preserved the body against putrefaction. The two sailors who ate the citrus fruits were fit for duty within six days, the others remained sick. With hindsight it is easy to recognize that Lind had identified the best means of preventing scurvy, but, at the time, citrus fruits did not seem like the most obvious solution to the problem. There were many other competing theories and remedies that seemed equally plausible, and even for Lind, citrus fruits were merely one measure among many. He thought scurvy was due just as much to poor discipline, filth and laziness as to poor diet.[76]

Lind's treatise had no immediate impact on victualling, but it did draw attention to the more general problem of poor sanitary discipline and disease on naval vessels, leading some enlightened individuals to improve conditions on and below decks. This was most evident during the voyages of Captain Cook (1728–79) in the 1770s, which were notable for their very low incidence of disease, including scurvy. Cook insisted on good hygiene and on measures to keep up morale, along with a diet of fruit and vegetables that included preserved cabbage and citrus fruits. In the coming years, the paternalistic regime of Captain Cook became the model for like-minded naval officers, and many other captains took similar measures to secure the health of their men. But for every commander like Cook, there were dozens who neglected the health of their crews or who lacked knowledge of how to preserve it; too much still depended on the whim of individual officers.[77]

Conscious of the waste of skilled manpower, the British Admiralty began to codify the measures that had been introduced on naval vessels in the preceding decades. These included the introduction of uniforms and the divisional system, which ensured that a junior officer was responsible for the cleanliness of each part of a ship. One particularly important regulation (passed in 1795) was that all naval vessels should make provision for the distribution of citrus juices in order to prevent scurvy. Experiments with citrus juices on naval vessels during the American War of Independence showed that they were successful in preventing the disease, confirming Lind's earlier observations. The combined effect of these measures was evident in the rapid fall in the death rate on board British naval vessels towards the end of the eighteenth century. Whereas the average sick rate during the American War of Independence had been 29.7 per cent of official strength, the rate for the period 1796–1806, at the height of the French Wars, was only 11.8 per cent. Scurvy was practically non-existent on British naval vessels; whereas it was still a problem on French ships; the incidence of other diseases like typhus and dysentery was also much lower.[78] Perhaps for the first time in history, medical knowledge had conferred a significant advantage in battle.

The retreat of plague

These measures coincided with the beginnings of a great transformation in Europe's epidemiological profile. Plague, which had formerly accounted for a good deal of epidemic mortality, disappeared from Western Europe after making a final appearance in Marseilles.[79] Epidemics of typhus, however, continued to occur frequently and, like smallpox, became more visible as plague withdrew, arousing the interest of governments and medical men.[80] But what impact did attempts to prevent these and other diseases have upon mortality in Europe? Before we can answer this question, we need to look more closely at the changes that did occur, the most important being what has been termed the 'stabilization of European mortality'. Until the late seventeenth century, most European countries experienced high general death rates punctuated by numerous crises caused by dearth, war and epidemics. During the eighteenth century, these fluctuations began to level out, and in a few countries, there was probably an overall decline in mortality. However, the pattern of mortality varied enormously from place to place. In England, the decline in mortality crises began after the retreat of plague in 1666, and accelerated during the second half of the eighteenth century.[81] But in most other European countries, the decline began later, and was less dramatic than in England.[82] In France the plague of Marseilles, which killed in the region of 80,000 people,[83] was followed by severe epidemics of dysentery in 1738–42 and 1779, of influenza in 1740, and what were probably typhus and typhoid in 1740–2. There was some improvement later in the century, notwithstanding a severe crisis in the 1770s.[84] In most countries infant mortality remained high until the 1790s, with rates reaching 300 deaths per thousand births in epidemic years in Western Europe, and it was even higher in the poorer countries to the East.[85]

These epidemics were still often only elements in mixed crises consisting of war, famine and disease, so it is often hard to isolate mortality from disease alone. In France and Spain, for example, there were close links between epidemics and crises of subsistence;[86] but documentary evidence is limited, and accurate assessments of mortality patterns over time and between countries are difficult to make.[87] Nevertheless, there seems to be enough reliable evidence for us to accept Michael Flinn's conclusion that European mortality began to stabilize during the eighteenth century. It is also likely, as Flinn claims, that this owed something to human intervention. In England, rising agricultural productivity provided the basis for improved health and lower mortality from disease.[88] Urbanization and better connections between markets also led to formerly localized diseases becoming endemic on a national or regional scale. This had the effect of levelling out mortality, if not actually decreasing it. Another likely cause of stabilization was the end of the bitter civil wars that had marred the previous century. These had produced epidemics of plague, typhus and dysentery, as well as widespread famine.[89]

For the same reasons, it is difficult to make any categorical statements about underlying trends in European mortality, trends that demographic historians refer to as 'non-crisis mortality'. In so far as generalizations are possible, it seems that any downward trend was modest, and that there was no substantial decline anywhere until after 1750.[90] Yet there does seem to be a real difference between mortality in England and that in many parts of mainland Europe. In England, there was probably a modest decrease in mortality during the eighteenth century, possibly due to the protection afforded by its island location, together with advances in agriculture and the drainage of malarious marshes. But in most other European countries, there is no evidence of an overall decline in mortality until after 1800.[91]

In all countries, differences between town and country were still a significant feature of mortality, with rural areas continuing to enjoy higher life expectancy than towns and cities. In England and Wales, for example, infant mortality rates could vary from 45 per cent below the national average in rural parishes to 75 per cent or above in county towns. Mortality was highest of all in the capital, London, although it began to decline towards the end of the century.[92] But there were important exceptions to this 'urban penalty'. In Spain, life expectancy varied from twenty-five years of age in some rural areas (probably due to poor drainage and malaria) to over forty in the most salubrious.[93] In France, too, the countryside suffered most from the epidemics of dysentery that occurred in 1738–42. The epidemics were most severe in the economically depressed areas of the north-west. Here, many families were crowded into single rooms; sanitation and personal cleanliness were practically non-existent and food, which was scarce, was often of poor quality. Peasants lived in close proximity to their animals, and their dwellings were plagued with flies, which were the main carriers of diseases like dysentery.[94] However, poverty was a crucial determinant of mortality in all areas, with the most socially marginal groups suffering higher mortality regardless of location.[95]

There is little agreement among historians about the causes of Europe's changing epidemiological profile. Some historians ascribe mortality decline largely to changes in the virulence of certain diseases and other natural shifts in the balance between pathogens and their human hosts. Wrigley and Schofield, for example, argue that medical, social and economic factors were far less important than environmental factors such as climatic change. There was indeed a close correlation between temperature and death rates: in the winter, cold weather killed many older people through pneumonia, bronchitis and influenza; in the summer, hot weather killed many infants and young children through diseases of the digestive tract.[96] Sequential seasonal extremes – hard winters and dry summers – were the worst combination, sometimes leading to a complete cessation of economic activity, and hence to malnutrition and disease.[97] Viewed over the long term, mortality decline tended to occur when the climate became cooler, as in the 1690s, when there were several hard winters. The eighteenth century was also cooler on average than the preceding century, although there were two brief periods of warming, one of which, in 1773–83, coincided with episodes of famine and disease in several parts of the world.[98] This relationship is in some respects counter-intuitive, as we might expect cooler weather to have a deleterious effect on agriculture. Yet cold weather also tends to check the growth of certain pathogens and their vectors, and this may go some way to explaining the diminished incidence of diseases like plague.[99]

While accepting the role of immunity and natural factors in disease, other historians place greater emphasis on human agency, witting or not. Stephen Kunitz, for example, ascribes mortality decline in

Europe chiefly to state intervention, economic integration and the decline of military activity.[100] But most of the factors that Kunitz mentions were not much in evidence before 1800. One measure that may have had some effect in preventing epidemics is quarantine, but the efficacy of land quarantines, in particular, is questionable. Other 'public health' measures like inoculation undoubtedly had some impact, but the lack of state support for inoculation meant that protection tended to be ephemeral and localized. Despite the claims of historians like Razzell, there seems to be little evidence that inoculation had much impact on mortality rates. However, at the local level, measures to improve the more prosperous towns and cities probably did have an effect upon mortality. Cities like Edinburgh and London experienced intermittent, though significant, bouts of building: neat rows of stone-built houses and warehouses began to replace narrow shambles of timber and thatch; sewers and water mains were laid or redesigned.[101] In the latter part of the eighteenth century, these localized improvements may have affected the transmission of diseases like typhus, because they lowered the population of disease-bearing arthropods.[102] The increased availability of cotton cloth at this time, and a fall in the price of garments, also enabled more clothes to be boiled and divested of lice.[103] In general, though, the most important human determinants of mortality were probably economic change and the cessation of internecine warfare. It was only in the relatively privileged enclaves of the army and the navy that the Enlightenment's medical advances had any appreciable impact.

4

The World beyond Europe

New World peoples, Old World diseases

The world that emerged from the Renaissance and the Reformation was a world that looked increasingly to the future. Though scholars and statesmen still revered Classical civilization, they looked forwarded in confident anticipation of progress. They looked increasingly beyond Europe, too. The rise of the West depended very largely on its willingness to seek out, and ultimately to control, new lands, commodities and peoples.[1] In the process, Western medicine was confronted with new challenges and opportunities, in the forms of disease and medicinal plants. And with the movement of peoples came the passage of microbes, hastening what Emmanuel Le Roy Ladurie has described as the 'unification of the globe by disease'.[2] But while germs were distributed far more widely than before, the burden of disease was far from equal. Long exposure to infections like smallpox and measles gave Europeans an immunity that the peoples of America and the Pacific lacked. In the Old World there were more domesticated animals, which acted as reservoirs of infection, and all the key centres of population had long been joined by trade, which ensured regular mixing of germs.[3] Once Europeans landed in the New World, Old World infections spread rapidly and fatally among the local inhabitants, leaving Europeans relatively unscathed. Spanish censuses and tax surveys suggest that the indigenous population halved within two decades after the first reported epidemics.[4]

The best-known account of these epidemics is Alfred W. Crosby's book, *The Columbian Exchange* (1972).[5] Crosby argues that the importation of lethal pathogens was one aspect of a process of 'ecological imperialism' that allowed white settlers rapidly to attain dominance over Native Americans.[6] Without the advantage conferred by disease, he insists, the Spanish would never have been able to overcome the militaristic civilizations of Mexico and the Andes. He therefore dismissed the 'Black Legend' that attributed the collapse of Amerindian societies predominantly to Spanish brutality. While there were numerous instances of murder and exploitation, none seemed sufficient to explain the massive demographic collapse that occurred in the Americas soon after contact with Europeans. But there was plenty of documentary evidence from the sixteenth and seventeenth centuries that pointed to terrible epidemics among Native Americans in the years following the Spanish invasion. It thus seemed more plausible that the fall of the Aztec and Incan empires had been caused by disease rather than military power alone. Violent epidemics of measles, smallpox and typhus had allowed a numerically weak invading force to gain the advantage.

Epidemics erupted sporadically throughout the first three centuries of European rule, but the most serious mortality among Native Americans occurred in the first century after the Spanish invasion. The first smallpox epidemic seems to have begun in 1519, shortly after the arrival of a Spanish slaving vessel. The disease was sustained in its passage across the Atlantic by the cargo of young, non-immune slaves carried from Africa to American plantations.[7] But the rapid collapse of the indigenous population was due to a mixture of new pathogens, rather than to a single disease. Spanish and Aztec records show wave after wave of epidemics with distinctive characteristics, their symptoms and patterns of transmission resembling smallpox, measles, typhus, plague and influenza.[8] The same pattern was evident in North America, where English settlers established colonies along the eastern seaboard. From the formation of an abortive settlement at Sagadahoc in Maine, in 1607, to the founding of Plymouth in 1620, possibly as many as 90 per cent of New England's natives perished from smallpox and other infectious diseases.[9]

For those who survived, the implications were catastrophic. Epidemic disease gravely weakened military resistance to European invaders, and when Cortés laid siege to the Aztec capital of Tenochtitlán in 1521, the city had already lost around 100,000 of its inhabitants to smallpox and other diseases. Many more died from disease during the siege, which lasted for seventy-five days. Had there been no epidemic, the Aztecs would almost certainly have been able to repel the Spaniards.[10] Resistance was also weakened by the bitter dynastic struggles that followed the death of some Amerindian leaders, such as those that led to the collapse of the Incan Empire in

1525. As smallpox spread south from the Aztec lands of Mexico, it claimed the lives of many Incas, including their ruler, Huayna Capac, and his designated heir. Pizzaro and his men took advantage of the succession crisis to plunder the imperial capital of Cuzco.[11]

The hierarchical nature of Aztec and Incan societies made them particularly vulnerable to the effects of disease. Having a less hierarchical structure, the Native American tribes of the North may have been less affected by the death of prominent figures than the royal dynasties of the South. This may account for the endurance of some tribal societies in North America despite their decimation by disease. A society accustomed to dynastic leadership could fragment more easily. For the same reason, the subjects of the South and Central American empires may have been more fatalistic in their attitudes towards infection. Many believed that the ravages of disease were a form of divine intervention, while European invaders viewed them as providential – a sign that they were destined to exercise dominion over their new lands. As William McNeill has put it, 'stunned acquiescence in Spanish authority was the only possible response. ... The extraordinary ease of Spanish conquests and the success a few hundred men had in securing control of vast areas and millions of people is unintelligible on any other basis.'[12]

But the depiction of a demographic catastrophe brought about by smallpox and other Old World diseases has not gone unchallenged. The controversy surrounding the 500th anniversary of Columbus's voyage to the Americas gave a new lease of life to the old 'Black Legend'. Some scholars dismissed documentary evidence for the terrible epidemics as Spanish fabrications, while the methods used by historians to compute the decline of the Amerindian population were questioned.[13] Francis Brooks, for example, argued that the 1520 epidemic in Mexico was no more serious than epidemics of smallpox back in Europe. Reports of terrible mortality among the Aztecs (the loss of one-third to one-half of their population) were nothing more than a myth, he claimed.[14]

By calling into question the best-documented of what were later called 'virgin soil' epidemics, Brooks was mounting a challenge to what had become the orthodoxy among historians of the Columbian contact. This challenge prompted the historian Robert McCaa to re-examine the evidence for the Mexican epidemic of the 1520s.[15] After reading the sources used by Brooks, and other extant sources in Spanish and Nahuatl (the Aztec language), he 'moved from a guarded sympathy' with Brooks's argument to 'the discovery of overlooked sources, misread texts, flawed reasoning, and false analogies and, finally, to disagreement with fundamental points'. After sifting the evidence, he became confident that the mortality from smallpox in

Mexico was several times greater than in Europe, even though it was probably less than the Spanish believed. Indeed, the majority of historians who have studied the epidemics in Columbian America still agree that Native American populations were devastated by a series of epidemics soon after contact with Europeans, and that this fatally weakened resistance to European invasion.[16] As one historian has recently remarked, 'The century and a half after 1492 witnessed, in terms of the number of people who died, the greatest human catastrophe in history, far exceeding even the disaster of the Black Death of Medieval Europe.'[17]

But can we be sure about the true extent of population decline in Columbian America? Can we really identify the diseases that devastated its native population? Quite apart from the absence of population statistics, contemporary descriptions of diseases varied widely, and there was no consistency in the names attached to them. A case in point is the epidemic that ravaged the peoples of what is now central Mexico in the mid-1540s. The disease appeared to coincide with the arrival of a group of Spanish friars, and was referred to by the local people simply as *cocoliztli* or *hueycocoliztli*, meaning 'sickness' or 'great sickness'.[18] Native sources described its symptoms as fever, spots and bleeding from the nose, mouth and anus. In his book *Rats, Lice and History*, Hans Zinnser concluded that the disease was probably typhus,[19] but others are less certain.[20] The most recent studies conclude that typhus remains the most likely explanation,[21] but some speculate that the disease might even have been anthrax or plague.[22] Whatever the true nature of the disease, contemporary accounts suggest strongly that it was imported into central Mexico, and that it took a terrible toll upon the local population. In individual towns the number of dead often exceeded 10,000, while Torquemada estimated the total number of deaths as high as 800,000.[23]

Much of the scholarship on disease and conquest in the New World has been rather too confident about diagnosing the diseases of the past; but in the case of smallpox, for instance, it is possible to be more certain because of its peculiarly distinctive symptoms. Both Spanish and Amerindian sources mention a pustular disease which, though often fatal, left survivors permanently disfigured or blind. The pustules were sometimes depicted graphically, and the Spaniards had no hesitation in designating the disease 'smallpox' – a malady with which they were familiar in Europe.[24] One must always exercise caution when dealing with such accounts, but the fact that the sources distinguish clearly between different afflictions, some of which closely resemble smallpox, indicates that it was one of the chief diseases ravaging the Americas in the sixteenth and seventeenth centuries.

Even if the presence of smallpox in Columbian America is acknowledged, is the 'true' identity of a disease really that significant?[25] Some historians, particularly those of a constructionist inclination, argue that it is not, and that what really counts is how disease was understood at a particular time in history.[26] According to this view, the projection of a modern disease category on to the sixteenth century would be, at best, irrelevant and, at worst, a misleading distortion. But the case of smallpox in the New World shows that the true identity of a disease is important. The fact that it can be shown beyond reasonable doubt that the epidemics were imported diseases such as smallpox, rather than diseases indigenous to the Americas, provides compelling evidence to support the hypothesis of the Columbian exchange, and that the demise of Amerindian societies was due as much to imported infections as to any military advantage that Europeans may have possessed.

America was not the only continent to suffer the ravages of 'virgin soil' epidemics. The same fate awaited the Pacific islands and Australia, which did not receive regular visits from Europeans until the last third of the eighteenth century. In a popular work on the European discovery and colonization of the Pacific, Alan Moorhead described the arrival of Europeans as having a 'fatal impact' upon indigenous civilizations, partly on account of the traffic of new germs, partly on the brutality of settlers.[27] The diseases that characterized the first phase of the encounter between Europeans and Pacific islanders were sexually transmitted. At first the women of the islands offered themselves freely to Europeans, who eagerly took advantage of their sexual hospitality. But after a while, their menfolk began to exploit the situation. As Captain Cook put it on leaving New Zealand during his second voyage, in 1773, the local men had 'obliged their wives or daughters to prostitute themselves whether they will or no', for nothing more than a 'spike nail or any other thing they value'. He lamented that 'we debauch their Morals already too prone to vice and we interduce [sic] among them wants and perhaps diseases which they never before knew and which serve only to disturb that happy tranquility they and their fore Fathers had injoy'd'.[28] On reaching Tonga in 1774, Cook noted in his journal that his crew were suffering from venereal disease, and that he 'took all imaginable care to prevent its being communicated to these people', and he asserted that his 'endeavours succeeded'.[29]

Venereal diseases nevertheless became rife throughout the Pacific islands. For many observers, their prevalence came to symbolize the lost innocence of noble savages, corrupted by a supposedly superior civilization. But gonorrhoea and syphilis were far from being the most deadly infections introduced into the Pacific: measles, smallpox and a host of other Old World infections proved lethal in a population that had not previously encountered them. The impact of these diseases is most dramatically illustrated by the case of Hawaii, which had enjoyed a long period of isolation, broken only by the arrival of Captain Cook in 1778. The population of the Hawaiian archipelago plummeted from an estimated 400,000 in 1778 (some modern demographers have put the figure as high as 800,000) to fewer than 40,000 by 1893. Crosby has therefore considered Hawaii a test case for his hypothesis that rapid population decline in areas previously isolated from the Old World was due primarily to the importation of new pathogens.[30] Considering alternative explanations for the sharp fall in population on the islands, Crosby discounted deliberate genocide by settlers and the exploitation of aboriginal labour. The main reason for such a catastrophic population decline, he argued, had to be the introduction of new diseases. Evidence from human skeletons shows that Hawaiians suffered from very few infectious diseases before contact with Europeans, whereas the new arrivals suffered from many, including the most deadly and infectious diseases known to humanity. 'We can usefully picture the Hawaiian disease environment as a briar patch', he suggested, 'and the continental equivalent as a jungle.'[31]

The epidemiologist Stephen Kunitz, however, has argued that Polynesian depopulation was caused not simply by the introduction of new pathogens.[32] Whereas Crosby attributed the decline of the indigenous population to their lack of immunity, Kunitz places far more emphasis on the expropriation of land and the exploitation of labour. As Hawaiians left their isolated houses and communities and ventured to the ports in search of work, they experienced overcrowding and malnutrition, which increased their susceptibility to disease. And, as many were drawn into prostitution, which thrived in new port settlements such as Honolulu, they also contracted chronic infections such as syphilis and gonorrhoea.[33] In order to illustrate his point that disease alone cannot account for depopulation, Kunitz contrasts the experience of Hawaii with that of other South Pacific islands, showing that different populations responded differently to the introduction of new diseases. He shows that most islands experienced a mortality decline in the hundred years following European contact, but that it was steeper on some islands (such as Hawaii and New Zealand) than others (such as Samoa and Tonga). The population also recovered at different rates and at different times, beginning much earlier in Tahiti than Hawaii, for instance.[34] Population collapse and slow recovery were most evident on islands that experienced the predations and territorial dispossession associated with large-scale European settlement, while lower decline and early recovery occurred on islands with fewer European whites and a more formal colonial structure. Kunitz therefore concluded that the type of colonial rule was of paramount importance, and that social forces mediated between newly introduced pathogens and their human hosts.

The importance of social and economic factors in long-term population decline is still a matter of debate.[35] Those, like Kunitz, who criticize the 'biological determinism' of Crosby and McNeill point out that the mode of European colonization was crucial in determining the demographic history of each colony. While acknowledging that population decline was also due to illness caused by 'extreme overwork' and 'a general lack of will to live after their whole culture had been destroyed by alien invasion', Crosby may have underestimated the significance of economic and social factors in mediating the impact of disease. However, he is surely correct to argue that the rapid fall in population that occurred in most Pacific and Amerindian societies soon after the first contact can have no other plausible explanation. This immediately becomes clear if we contrast the demographic experiences of Asian and African colonies with those of the New World. Nowhere in the Asian and African colonies was there such a severe collapse of population, and, for the first century or so of colonial contact, it was Europeans, rather than the indigenous inhabitants, that were at a biological disadvantage. The reason was that many European diseases – with the notable exception of tuberculosis – were also widely distributed in Africa and Asia. But the different positions typified by Crosby and Kunitz are best seen as complementary. While it seems likely that short-term population decline was due to the importation of new diseases, long-term trends can be explained only by socio-economic factors such as the nature and extent of European settlement.

The slave trade and the Atlantic exchange

The Atlantic slave trade was one of the largest maritime commercial ventures in history. Between 1492 and 1870, at least 10 million slaves – mostly from western and central Africa – were transported to the Americas and the Caribbean. There, they were compelled to work in mines and on plantations, and to become the servants and concubines of Europeans. The shippers, in order of scale, were the Portuguese, the English, the French, the Dutch, the Spaniards and the North Americans. At the height of the slave trade, in the 1780s, the English and French were each transporting approximately 40,000 slaves a year. The slaves were usually procured by barter with African chiefs or merchants who had established themselves along the African coast.[36] Most of the slaves were obtained from inland areas that had hitherto been isolated from one another: the mixing together of different pathogens and the removal of Africans from the disease environment to which they were accustomed resulted in tremendous mortality from diseases like malaria.[37] In the overcrowded 'barracoons' used to imprison slaves prior to transportation, and in the cramped conditions of slaving vessels, African diseases mixed freely with those of Europeans, producing a deadly cocktail of dysentery, malaria, smallpox and yellow fever. This lethal mixture of diseases was transported with the slaves to the New World, which had previously been free from malaria and yellow fever.[38] The first documented appearance of yellow fever was in Barbados, in 1647, where 5,000 persons died of a 'new distemper' characterized by black vomit. The disease was probably imported on Dutch vessels carrying slaves for the island's sugar plantations, as its mosquito vector (_Aedes aegypti_) could have survived the crossing in water barrels carried as supplies.

It was not simply the climate that allowed diseases such as yellow fever to become established. James Goodyear has argued persuasively that there was a connection between epidemic yellow fever and sugar cultivation and related industries such as milling and refining. Using examples from the Caribbean and mainland North America, he points to a close correlation between the advent of sugar plantations or sugar manufacture and epidemics of yellow fever. In all cases, the presence of sugar antedated outbreaks of yellow fever. Goodyear points out that female _Aedes aegypti_ prefer to feed on sweet substances such as cane syrup, and sugar production ensured that sucrose was available all year round.[39] Sugar plantations had the highest mortality and morbidity rates in the Caribbean islands. Their proximity to ports meant that they received new waves of infection easily and quickly. Further, plantations were generally established in moist, lowland areas, where there were ample breeding grounds for mosquitoes. Poor diet, poor housing and brutality no doubt reduced resistance to disease.[40]

Malaria probably established itself in much the same way, there being no evidence that either disease was present in the Americas before the Columbian contact. Conditions in the plantations were particularly favourable to the spread of both diseases, as people, plants and animals were concentrated in poorly drained lowland areas which provided the perfect breeding ground for disease-bearing mosquitoes.[41] By the 1650s, malaria was recorded along the eastern coasts of Southern and Central America, and by the 1680s, it was found among English settlers in North America; it appears to have been present in both its *vivax* and *falciparum* forms.[42] It is important to stress that only some Africans possessed the sickle cell traits that conferred a degree of protection against permanent liver damage or death from malaria. Even fewer would have carried the Duffy negative factor – which gives immunity to vivax malaria – in their blood.

Many of the smallpox epidemics that ravaged the Americas were also due to the importation of slaves. The first smallpox epidemic on the South American mainland was attributed to an African slave who landed at Yucatan in 1519.[43] The slave trade has also been identified as the source of most of the smallpox epidemics in colonial Brazil. Dauril Auden and Joseph Miller have shown a strong correlation between epidemics in parts of Africa from which the Portuguese drew their slaves and epidemics in Brazil. They also stress the importance of drought and famine as sources of these epidemics. Droughts led to the concentration of people in relatively moist areas, and to wars between rival tribes: conditions that were conducive to the transmission of smallpox and, presumably, other diseases. Captives from these wars were also sold on as slaves to the Portuguese. Further concentration prior to embarkation and in overcrowded slaving vessels continued to foster the spread of disease.[44]

Although some slaves would have enjoyed immunity to smallpox, and in some cases to malaria and yellow fever, their ability to withstand such infections would almost certainly have been compromised by poor nutrition. Even before leaving Africa, it is likely that many slaves would have been malnourished, not only because of periodic famines, but also because their diet was typically lacking in vitamins A and B1 due to a deficiency of animal proteins and fats. For cultural reasons, and because of poverty, similar diets were common among slaves in the West Indies. This may explain the apparently high incidence of diseases such as beriberi – due to lack of vitamin B1 – and of complaints such as night-blindness, due to lack of vitamin A. Beriberi appears to have taken a heavy toll in human life, and may help to account for the difference between the population growth rates of slave populations in Caribbean and North American plantations. The latter experienced a tenfold growth rate, but the slave populations of the Caribbean decreased in the order of 5:2, and had constantly to be replenished.[45] The diet of slaves on North American plantations seems to have been more nutritious, and there is no evidence of beriberi, which was capable of killing the very young. Some deficiency diseases such as pellagra were common on American plantations, but pellagra was a chronic disease that rarely resulted in death.[46]

The magnitude and the causes of African mortality in the Atlantic slave trade are difficult to determine. Although loss of life on slaving vessels was usually recorded, many of the so-called death books have been lost. Those that survive from Spanish and Portuguese vessels show that mortality on voyages from the notoriously unhealthy Bight of Benin to South America could be as high as 40 per cent. Brazilian historians have suggested that the average mortality on voyages in the sixteenth century was 15–20 per cent, falling to 10 per cent by the 1800s. Mortality on English vessels also seems to have declined over this period. Between 1680 and 1688 the Royal African Company lost 24 per cent, or 14,388, of its total cargo of around 60,000 slaves. But by the early eighteenth century the average mortality had apparently diminished to around 10 per cent and, by the 1780s, to just below 6 per cent.[47] Records for the nineteenth century are more complete, and show somewhat higher mortality rates, averaging 9 per cent for the crossing to the Americas.[48] Nevertheless, it is clear that a substantial decline in mortality did occur, the most likely causes of which are better provisions of food and water, more attention to hygiene, the statutory limitation of carrying limits from the 1780s, and changes in ship design, which enabled faster passage.

Surprisingly the mortality on voyages along the African coast was higher than that recorded for the mid-Atlantic passage. Records from British naval squadrons which intercepted slaving vessels at the bights of Biafra and Benin – the principal slaving centres during the nineteenth century – show that the death rate on voyages to Sierra Leone, where the slaves were released, averaged almost 18 per cent between 1821 and 1839. The main reason for this high mortality appears to have been the length of time it took to make the voyage. The average time of thirty-four days was actually longer than many transatlantic crossings, owing to the difficulties of sailing against prevailing winds and dangerous currents along the West African coast.[49] In fact, the length of voyages appears to have been the most important factor affecting mortality on slave vessels. Using the records of French slaving vessels, Klein and Engermann found little evidence that the crowding of vessels had any appreciable effect on mortality. But they did find a positive correlation between mortality and the length of voyage: the longer the voyage, the greater the risk of the spoilage or depletion of provisions. In some cases, poor weather may have forced longer voyages, which led to provisions becoming exhausted before the end of the journey.[50]

These are not the only reasons for variations in mortality on slaving vessels. Much depended on when and where the slaves were obtained. Philip Curtin has suggested that the higher mortality among slaves shipped from the Congo, as opposed to the bights of Biafra and Benin, may have been due to the fact that slaves from the Congo were drawn from further inland, and thus reached the vessels in a weaker state.[51] Famine and epidemics in some regions might also explain variations in mortality. Another important variable affecting mortality was the number of children on board. Ships carrying a high proportion of children tended to have higher mortality rates, probably because of children's poorly developed immune systems.[52] The variability of conditions on board ships was another crucial factor. One particularly important provision was an adequate supply of water, because the climate, the overcrowded conditions, and the effects of dysentery meant that slaves suffered severely from dehydration. During the eighteenth century, many captains also began to insist on the maintenance of hygiene, ranging from regular cleaning of decks to the shaving and washing of slaves.[53]

Such measures may have contributed to the control of water-, fly- and food-borne diseases like dysentery, which was probably the biggest single cause of mortality on slaving vessels. Yet they would have done little to prevent the second biggest killer, smallpox. During the eighteenth century, losses from smallpox were a major concern for those involved in the slave trade. The disease was highly contagious, as well as highly fatal, and could reduce the worth of a human cargo by as much as one-half; it also posed a deadly threat to the European crews. One means of reducing the disease was simply to kill its victims and throw them overboard, before they had chance to spread the contagion. This practice was still evident in the nineteenth century, although it declined after the widespread introduction of vaccination during the 1820s.[54] Even in the eighteenth century there were effective alternatives to these brutal means of disease control. Inoculation was one obvious alternative. As we saw in the previous chapter, inoculation was widely practised in India, North Africa, parts of West Africa,[55] and the Middle East, from where it was introduced into Europe in the early eighteenth century.[56] By the 1720s, inoculation was being performed on British slaving vessels, and by 1770 it was fairly common on French ships making the mid-Atlantic passage.[57] Inoculation was also used extensively on British and French plantations,[58] but less widely on Brazilian plantations, though missionaries in Portuguese America occasionally experimented with it. It was only at the very end of the eighteenth century that the Portuguese Crown and its colonial agents became truly interested in inoculation.[59]

Disease among Europeans

The exchange of diseases between the Old World and the New was, as Alfred Crosby states, 'wondrously one-sided'.[60] There were only two exceptions to what was generally a one-way traffic across the Atlantic. One is the tropical American chigger, which reached Africa in 1872, and spread across the continent. This was rarely fatal, the most serious complication being tetanus in the affected limbs. The other, as we saw in chapter 2, was syphilis, although the American origins of the disease are still a matter of dispute. Tertiary syphilis was often fatal, but as a cause of mortality it ranked well below other diseases that afflicted Europeans in their colonial possessions. By the late seventeenth century, malaria and yellow fever were rife along the West African coast and in tropical parts of the Americas. Europeans were already familiar with malaria ('ague', 'intermittent' or 'remittent' fever, as it was generally known), but in Africa and the Caribbean they encountered it in a more deadly form. The type of malaria then common in Europe was *vivax* malaria, which is caused by a different species of parasite than the one which causes the more deadly *falciparum* malaria. This new form of fever, along with yellow fever, claimed the lives of countless Europeans, and led to the west coast of Africa being dubbed 'The White Man's Grave'.[61]

As the accompanying table shows, these diseases caused a considerable drain on manpower among troops stationed in the Caribbean as well as in West Africa. In wartime, when large numbers of fresh troops poured into the Caribbean, the numbers dying from disease beggared belief. Seventy per cent of the British and American force besieging Cartagena in 1741 died from disease, as did 40 per cent of the British force at Havana in 1762. Around half the French troops sent to St Dominique in 1792 perished within the year, and around 10,000 British soldiers and seamen died on the island between 1793 and 1796, mostly from yellow fever.[62] Most of the losses on these occasions occurred among troops who had been brought to the tropics during the hot or rainy seasons, giving them little time to acclimatize. Although some medical practitioners believed that yellow fever was contagious, most believed that it was due simply to a failure to adapt to a new climate. In the Caribbean, for example, it was widely recognized that the incidence of yellow fever was much higher among new arrivals than among those long resident on the islands. This conviction had certain military consequences: the comparatively high wastage rate of new arrivals served to increase the military value of colonial militia and black troops, who were apparently acclimatized to the tropics. In reality, most had survived a mild bout of yellow fever in childhood: a disease that either killed or conferred lifelong immunity. Greater value was also attached to fortifications, because it was thought that besieging armies would be more exposed to the causes of disease.[63]

Death rates of British troops stationed in Britain in the early nineteenth century, compared with those stationed in the colonies

Location	Average death rate per 1,000 troops per annum
Great Britain	15
India	30–75
West Indies	85–138
West Africa	483–668

Source: R. B. Sheridan, *Doctors and Slaves: A Medical and Demographic History of Slavery in the British West Indies, 1680–1834* (Cambridge University Press, New York and Cambridge, 1985), p. 12.

For much of the eighteenth century, it seems that these heavy losses were viewed fatalistically as the inevitable cost of war in hot climates. Some rulers even saw military expeditions as a way of ridding their kingdoms of dangerous and disruptive elements.[64] But it would be a mistake to take this argument too far, for, as we saw in the previous chapter, the cost of manpower was increasing due to the extra time and money that had to be invested in training soldiers and sailors. Small wonder that the medical literature of the period drew attention to the human and financial costs of service overseas. In his *Essay on Diseases Incidental to Europeans in Hot Climates* (1768), the naval surgeon James Lind wrote: 'The recent examples of the great mortality in hot climates, ought to draw the attention of all the commercial nations of Europe, towards the important object of preserving the health of their countrymen.' 'Unhealthy settlements', he warned, 'require a constant supply of people, and of course drain their mother country of an incredible number, and some of its most useful inhabitants.'[65] Such statements illustrate the growing tendency to see manpower as a 'commodity', possessing a precise monetary value. A new, humanitarian sensibility was also beginning to emerge, and this made casualties from disease harder to justify. The huge losses of the French Wars captured the imagination of poets and other Romantic writers, who drew attention to the plight of servicemen and their destitute families.[66]

Growing unease with tropical service was apparent within the armed forces themselves. The British physician Thomas Trotter, who had served with the Navy in the West Indies, as well as on slaving vessels, ended his professional life as a trenchant critic of colonialism and slavery, and of the impressment of seamen. The conditions endured by sailors, he believed, were little better than those of slaves.[67] Long periods of service in the colonies, he felt, would cause Europeans to degenerate, as their bodies were ill adapted to life in a hot climate – a belief shared by other army and naval surgeons such as James Johnson and Benjamin Moseley.[68] By the same token, colonial riches threatened to undermine the nation's manly qualities by producing an addiction to luxury.[69] The poor performance of the British Navy against the American fleet in the war of 1812 seemed to confirm this pessimistic appraisal.[70]

Trotter was writing at the turn of the nineteenth century, by which time European views of the tropics were becoming more negative.[71] But only a few years earlier there had been considerable optimism about adaptation to life in tropical climates. Writers such as Richard Towne and John Hunter in Jamaica believed that Europeans would undergo a period of 'seasoning' in which their bodies would become attuned to the climate, rendering them more resistant to disease. Hunter even maintained that Europeans would become blacker over generations, indicating a very flexible conception of physical difference or 'race'.[72] Practitioners working in the colonies also began to develop distinctive forms of medical practice, which made extensive use of locally available drugs to treat fevers and other common ailments. Many of these remedies were discovered as a result of dialogue with practitioners of indigenous medicine, some of whom were employed by Europeans. The British and Dutch East India Companies, for example, employed large numbers of indigenous peoples as assistants to work in their armies and hospitals in Asia. Some of the local remedies became so popular that they were traded as commodities and used back in Europe too. The best-known example is the bark of the cinchona tree of South America. Usually called 'Peruvian' or 'Jesuits' bark', it was used with some success in decoctions to treat malarial fevers.[73] Rhubarb from China was another popular imported drug, being used as a purgative to treat bowel disorders. At the height of its popularity in the late eighteenth century, between 20,000 and 30,000 pounds of rhubarb were being imported annually into Britain alone.[74]

Despite the availability of local remedies, the colonies remained a hazardous place for Europeans, and after the ravages of yellow fever in the 1790s, the prospect of Europeans enjoying good health in the

Caribbean, especially, appeared remote. Africans, by contrast, seemed to enjoy a degree of immunity from these fevers. Some doctors began to speculate that this was due to an innate characteristic that white settlers could never obtain: an observation that contributed to the development of 'scientific racism' in the early nineteenth century.[75] Doctors even began to open up the bodies of African slaves to find what they believed to be evidence of distinctive racial pathologies.[76] By the 1790s, the dominant view was that Europeans could not settle in the tropics except as a managerial class, directing the labour of races more suited to such conditions.[77] However, the extent to which the 'Africanization' of the Caribbean was determined by differential immunity is a moot point. Sheldon Watts, for example, has argued that the declining proportion of white labourers in the West Indies was due more to the growth of economic opportunities in Europe than the perceived risk from disease.[78] The likelihood is that it was a combination of both; nevertheless, Watts alerts us to the possibility that disease may have served an ideological function in justifying the system of slave production that developed on the islands. However, some contemporaries drew the conclusion that different races should remain in those regions to which their bodies were best adapted.[79]

Whatever the reasons for the changing racial profile of the Caribbean, there can be no doubt that fear of disease led to distinctive patterns of European settlement. Medical opinion during the seventeenth and eighteenth centuries was unanimous in attributing most tropical fevers to noxious vapours, or 'miasma', arising from putrefying matter. Low-lying, marshy areas and the banks of rivers and lagoons were seen as particularly unhealthy places: as the water subsided, they became littered with vegetation that rotted quickly beneath the tropical sun. Marshes were thought to be unhealthy in any climate, but in the tropics the abundance of vegetation and the rate of decay were quicker. This, together with the debilitating effects of heat and humidity upon the human body, appeared to explain the lethality of many tropical environments.[80]

These theories gave rise to the belief that it was better for Europeans to settle in high, dry areas, and to clear the undergrowth from around their habitations. This followed the experience of settlers in North America, which seemed to suggest that the clearance and cultivation of land had led to a decline in fever. The salubrity of Barbados, for example, was attributed to the fact that it had more land under cultivation than other Caribbean islands.[81] These ideas served to justify the introduction of European methods of land cultivation into other regions of the world, and contributed to a providential view of white settlement or colonial rule.[82] But it soon became clear that the removal of tropical vegetation could be taken too far.

During the eighteenth century, a number of island colonies started to suffer from the effects of drought and soil erosion, which some botanists and medical writers began to attribute to the disruption of a delicate environmental balance. Some even made links between deforestation and climatic change. On tropical islands such as Mauritius, St Helena and St Vincent, the British, French and Dutch colonial authorities began to take remedial action by planting trees and establishing forest reserves.[83]

Careful stewardship of the environment also provided a justification for colonial rule in India, where the East India Company had acquired large tracts of land.[84] But there were important differences between India and other tropical regions. The climate of India seemed far less deadly than that of the Caribbean or tropical Africa, and until the early 1800s, many European visitors thought it no less salubrious than Europe itself. India was free from many epidemic diseases common in Europe, such as plague and typhus, and many travellers commented that chronic diseases such as rheumatism were less severe. Some even chose to remain in India because they thought it better for their health. While the risk of disease in India was freely acknowledged, the stifling heat of the hot season and the fevers of the rainy season were balanced by healthy weather in the cooler months. For this reason, belief in the possibility of acclimatization and of large-scale European settlement persisted longer in India than it did in the Caribbean. It was not until the 1830s that the possibility of settling white farmers in substantial numbers was discounted, and even then, belief in some degree of climatic adaptation was not unusual.[85]

It is hard to determine why a more pessimistic view came to prevail during the nineteenth century, but one factor was undoubtedly the high mortality suffered by European troops in the First Burma War of 1824–6. The high death rate of British and Indian troops in the jungles of Burma, by contrast with the local inhabitants, suggested that each race had its 'proper place', to which it had become uniquely adapted over many generations.[86] The cholera epidemics of 1817 onwards were another important factor. Hitherto, cholera had been endemic to deltaic Bengal, with only occasional outbreaks outside the region, in some port cities and forts, to which it may have spread as a result of coastal trade. But when the disease became epidemic in 1817, it spread right across India, and ultimately to many other parts of the world. The spread of 'Asiatic cholera' to Europe in the 1830s gave the impression that India was a deadly continent, and great effort had to be expended in order to convince the population of Britain that service in India need not result in death or invalidity.[87]

One consequence of this more pessimistic outlook was the frantic search for areas of India that were relatively healthy. In the years after the First Burma War, British medical officers wrote dozens of 'medical topographies' that detailed the chief diseases of different localities and their apparent causes.[88] Diseases like fever were still understood in environmentalist terms, as the product of marshes and uncultivated land, but there was now also a sense that Indian habits were to blame. Increasingly, the British saw it as their role to cleanse the Indian people, just as it was to manage the Indian environment.[89] The growing alienation of the British from the Indian climate was one reason for the establishment of hill stations where Europeans could recover their health (and also their racial identity). The most famous of these was Simla, where the British Government of India moved each year during the hot season. The hill stations resembled a cross between an alpine village and rural England; they were a reassuring refuge from the heat and diseases of the plains and, increasingly, from political turmoil.[90]

In colonial North America, the experience of disease was different again. Mortality among the English colonists was high. Many died from malaria and yellow fever – diseases that had been introduced into North America from Africa as a result of the slave trade. It is also possible that the less serious *vivax* strain of malaria was imported from the fens of England.[91] When settlers cleared the forests in order to farm or establish plantations, they created ideal breeding conditions for disease-bearing mosquitoes, which had hitherto been rare or absent. In the early seventeenth century, up to 40 per cent of new arrivals died in the first couple of years. Even if the outcome was not fatal, most new settlers experienced an attack of malaria or yellow fever, which came to be known as 'seasoning' fever, after which they were thought to be better adapted to life in the New World.[92] Mortality was far higher in the malarious southern colonies than in the North. [93] Virginia, Maryland and South Carolina were notoriously unhealthy, and Charleston in South Carolina was described as the 'great charnel house of the country'.[94] The difference between the northern and southern colonies can be illustrated by a comparison of life expectancy between the two. Adult males who survived to maturity in the towns of Plymouth and Andover, Massachusetts, had the prospect of living an additional forty-four to forty-eight years – more than twice as long as adult males in Chesapeake Bay, Virginia. This gave a distinctive shape to the population structure of the southern colonies. Because of the death of so many men before they reached the end of their normal procreative years, the size of most families remained small.[95] North Carolina was somewhere between these two extremes, experiencing higher death rates than New England but lower death rates than its southern neighbours, perhaps because it was more isolated from the main trade routes. Life expectancy at age twenty for adult white males was around thirty years.[96]

In most parts of America, colonists became accustomed to the burden of diseases like malaria.[97] Disease was not necessarily a barrier to settlement, especially during the seventeenth and eighteenth centuries, when conditions were little better in Europe itself. Mortality rates in New England were only slightly higher than in relatively healthy parts of Europe, such as south-east England, although the pattern of mortality was different. During the seventeenth century, New England suffered periodic epidemics with long periods of good health in between. This pattern had been characteristic of England in the fifteenth and sixteenth centuries, but was less marked in the seventeenth. It was only at the end of the eighteenth century that the mortality patterns of new and old England began to converge, as mortality rates in New England fell to similar levels.[98] In the South, this convergence did not occur for at least another half-century: southern states were afflicted by the deadly *falciparum* form of malaria, as well as the more benign *vivax*. They were also plagued by yellow fever to a greater extent than the North. Despite this, death rates in the South were probably not much higher than those in the most unhealthy parts of Europe.[99] At any rate, it is unlikely that perceived differences in mortality between America and the Old World made much difference to potential settlers.[100] The main determinant of migration to North America was not so much its salubrity, as the better economic opportunities available in the New World.

During the nineteenth century, death rates also began to decline in European settlements in other parts of the world. In India, the Caribbean and Africa, average death rates dropped by between 85 and 95 per cent, with the sharpest decline occurring after 1850. The decline was probably due to improvements in sanitation and water supplies, and the relocation of troops to highland areas to escape malaria. Other measures, such as vaccination against smallpox and the therapeutic and prophylactic use of quinine (extracted from cinchona bark in the 1820s), also played their part, but were probably less significant than the environmental measures just described. But despite the fall in mortality, the difference between the mortality rates of soldiers at home and overseas remained fairly stable until the First World War, showing that there was still a much greater risk from disease in the colonies than at home.[101] Sanitation and hygiene usually proved difficult to enforce on military campaigns, especially as many officers regarded the subjects as beneath their dignity. Consequently, mortality in colonial warfare remained high throughout the nineteenth century.[102] And, whereas mortality decreased as a whole, rates of sickness among European troops did not fall significantly in some colonies until after 1900.[103] Sickness therefore remained a barrier to large-scale settlement in many colonies, if not to formal imperial rule.

5

Disease in an Age of Commerce and Industry

The growth of commerce and empire described in the last chapter contributed to a process that has become known as the Industrial Revolution: a rapid growth in factory-based production that transformed the economies of Europe and, later, the rest of the world. But historians are deeply divided over the nature of this 'revolution'. Many claim that it was not a revolution at all, and that industrialization occurred gradually as one of several interconnected processes that brought into being the modern world. Industrialization, perhaps, occurred more slowly, and began much earlier than is sometimes thought. As if problems of definition were not enough, historians also differ greatly about the causes and consequences of industrialization.[1] As far as health and disease are concerned, there is little doubt that industrialization led in the long term to a rise in real incomes and to falling death rates. But the fall came after a period when mortality either increased or remained much the same as it had been before industrialization.[2] In most cases, the immediate effect of industrialization was to concentrate people in conditions of non-existent or inadequate sanitation, in which many of the basic necessities of life, like water and staple foodstuffs, deteriorated appallingly. Diseases like typhoid and dysentery thrived as a result of water contaminated by sewage; tuberculosis and smallpox were widespread; and typhus was a regular winter visitor to the dwellings of the poor. A new disease – cholera – also spread along the trade routes opened up by commercial and imperial expansion, and found a congenial home in the slums and tenements of industrial cities.

Cholera remained a significant threat to Western countries until the 1890s, but many nations became increasingly confident that they could prevent its incursions through quarantine and sanitary reform. States also began to intervene directly in other areas too, passing legislation that made vaccination against smallpox compulsory. By the end of the century, death rates from many of the major infectious diseases were falling, marking the transition to the mortality profile that characterizes most developed countries today. But while there were many common features in the ways that nations responded to the sanitary problems of industrialization, there were also significant differences. Each country took a slightly different path to modernization, striking a balance between conflicting priorities such as commerce and disease prevention, and between the rights of the individual and those of the state.

Smallpox and the vaccination controversies

At the beginning of the nineteenth century, vaccination against smallpox was unique in being the only truly effective measure against infectious disease. Some years before governments threw their weight behind sanitary reform, a number of countries began to make vaccination compulsory. At first, compulsion was confined only to certain sections of the population, normally those over which the state had direct control or for whom it had direct responsibility. In Britain – the birthplace of vaccination – all soldiers not protected by inoculation were required to undergo vaccination from 1799, and some local authorities began to deny poor relief to those who had not been vaccinated. From 1807, vaccination was also required of new recruits to the Bavarian army, and in Baden and Westphalia the same was demanded of all who became apprentices or entered trades. In some states, these selective measures were later accompanied by compulsory vaccination of all infants. Bavaria led the way in 1807, with other, mostly Germanic, states following in quick succession. But despite its reputation for state intervention, Prussia decided against compulsion initially, and made vaccination compulsory only when a locality was threatened by an epidemic. Under normal circumstances, vaccination was enforced only in state institutions such as workhouses and in the army. Nevertheless, in Prussia the mechanisms for mass vaccination were in place very early, and it was difficult for parents to resist the pressure of influential figures such as parsons and schoolmasters. With such an efficient system of medical policing, compulsion seemed unnecessary.[3]

In England, which is normally noted for its liberal political traditions, compulsory vaccination was introduced earlier than in more autocratic countries like Prussia. In 1840 local Poor Law institutions were required to appoint qualified medical practitioners and to provide free vaccination; in the same year, inoculation was made illegal. Following a campaign by the Epidemiological Society – a medical pressure group – another Act was passed in 1853, requiring that all infants be vaccinated within three months of birth. However, the Act suffered from the absence of any effective means to enforce it, and it took the next twenty years or so to establish an administrative infrastructure to support it. A severe epidemic of smallpox in 1871–2 provided the final boost, and led to the passage of the Vaccination Acts of 1871 and 1874. The Acts enabled the appointment of vaccination officers to enforce compulsion throughout the country, and introduced harsh penalties for parents who defaulted. The epidemic of 1871–2, which seems to have been a pan-European phenomenon linked to the Franco–Prussian War, also led to vaccination being made compulsory in Prussia (now part of a unified Germany) in 1874. Germany too instituted a system of revaccination, which required children to be vaccinated at the age of twelve. This followed the realization that vaccination did not confer protection for life. But England, formerly in advance of Prussia in legislative terms, did not follow its lead, and consequently suffered higher levels of disease.[4]

There was now a general convergence in vaccination policy across Europe, and even the French, who had hitherto pursued the most liberal policies towards vaccination, began to rethink their position. The Franco–Prussian War sparked off the worst smallpox epidemic of the century, with clusters of troops and prisoners of war acting as foci for the spread of disease.[5] The French army, which was poorly vaccinated by comparison with the Prussians, suffered far higher rates of smallpox. The French lost more than 23,000 soldiers to smallpox, while the Prussians lost only 500. By the 1880s, the medical profession and many deputies to the assembly of the Third Republic were backing compulsion, but the vagaries of the French parliamentary system stymied attempts to introduce legislation. It was not until 1902 that legislation making vaccination compulsory was finally passed.[6]

All countries which introduced compulsory vaccination experienced opposition from those who objected to compulsion or to vaccination in its own right. In most countries, doubt was cast on the effectiveness of vaccination, often accompanied by claims that it actually caused disease. The dangers may have been exaggerated, but they

were real enough. Vaccination was not the relatively painless procedure we know today. There were no fine needles, with multiple inci-
sions being made on the skin with lancets; lymph from an infant
vaccinated eight days earlier was taken from a blister on its arm and
smeared on to the cuts. The procedure was not only painful and dis-
figuring; it was conducive to infection. For most of the nineteenth
century, vaccination was carried out from arm to arm, which meant
that diseases like erysipelas and syphilis might be spread; some even
feared that mental illness could be spread in this way. Above all, vaccination seemed to violate the integrity of the body. Some attributed
smallpox to a poison produced by the body itself, which could be
corrected only by a restoration of equilibrium.

These fears existed in most countries, but there were some significant national differences. The anti-vaccination movement in England
was generally less inclined than its continental equivalents to reject
vaccination out of hand; its chief complaint was about compulsion
rather than vaccination itself. In Britain, anti-vaccination campaigners found a good deal of support among the working class, who could
ill afford the fines levied on recalcitrant parents. Those who could not
afford to pay the fines faced the sale of their possessions. More generally, people felt oppressed by what they saw as interference by the
state. Campaigners complained that vaccination was analogous to the
branding of cattle and slaves, and its opponents engaged in noisy –
though often good-humoured – demonstrations, which paraded vaccination 'martyrs' (those who had been imprisoned for violation of
the law) through the streets. Sales of goods seized in distraint were
also disrupted and attacked.[7]

These demonstrations were at their most dramatic in the wake of
the 1871 Vaccination Act, but were largely ineffective. By the 1880s,
the anti-vaccination movement had become more moderate, with the
establishment of organizations like the National Anti-Compulsory
Vaccination League, which had a largely middle-class membership.
The politics of persuasion had replaced the politics of demonstration.
The members of these new organizations began to claim that vaccination was unnecessary, because smallpox, like cholera and fever, was
essentially a 'filth' disease that could be controlled by environmental
improvements. Deaths from smallpox among the unvaccinated were
explained by the fact that these tended to be the poorest members
of society, and hence those who inhabited the most insalubrious areas.
Several prominent sanitarians – including Florence Nightingale –
were among those opposed to vaccination.[8]

In the 1880s, the anti-vaccination movement began to find a voice
in Parliament, where it demanded an end to compulsion. The result
was the appointment in 1889 of a Royal Commission. The Commis-

sion reaffirmed the value of vaccination, but was critical of the heavy-handed prosecution of those who avoided it, concluding that this had done more harm than good. In 1898 a new Vaccination Act was passed, which permitted the exemption of those who declared a conscientious objection to the procedure. A landslide victory by the Liberal Party resulted in a further gain for the anti-vaccinators in 1907, when the certificate of objection required by the 1898 Act was replaced with a simple declaration.[9]

The anti-vaccination movement was powerful on the Continent too, though ultimately less successful than in England. Some historians have claimed that this was because the English movement had a broader social base, whereas in Germany, the passage of the 1874 Act resulted in a petition with more than 30,000 signatures being placed before the Reichstag. By the end of the century, three times as many were petitioning for an end to compulsion. Perhaps the most crucial difference between the British and continental movements was that the latter were more inclined to reject vaccination out of hand, whereas the British movement was geared more specifically to ending compulsion. In the long run, this may account for the success of the British movement and the failure of its more radical continental counterparts. On the Continent, the indignation of the campaigners was directed more at the medical profession – and its unshakeable conviction that it was in the right – than it was against the government.[10] In countries like Germany there seems to have been more of a commitment to 'holistic' and 'natural' means of preventing and treating smallpox than in Britain, though it was by no means absent there either.[11]

Although resistance did not – except in the case of Britain – modify compulsion, it did provide an incentive to introduce technical improvements, so as to reduce the risks associated with vaccination and increase its effectiveness. The most important innovation was the use of lymph obtained from calves – a technique pioneered in Naples in 1848. The lymph was usually preserved using glycerin, though some other preservatives were tried. The technique was adopted most enthusiastically in countries like Germany, in an attempt to assuage opposition to vaccination – apparently with some success. By the late 1890s, calf lymph had almost entirely replaced lymph obtained from humans. Perhaps because there was less opposition to vaccination (as opposed to compulsion) in Britain, the authorities there were slower to introduce lymph obtained from calves.[12]

The most striking result of smallpox vaccination was the decline in mortality that occurred in all countries that introduced it. As such, vaccination made a major contribution to the mortality decline that took place in most European countries towards the end of the nineteenth century. But there were significant variations. In Germany, where there were no exceptions to compulsion, and – more importantly – where there was compulsory revaccination, the death rate fell from the mid-1880s, and remained negligible thereafter. From twenty-five deaths per million people living in 1882, the number had fallen to one-tenth by 1897. In Britain, where there was no compulsory revaccination, and where legislation was not always effectively enforced, the number of deaths declined, but far more unevenly, and smallpox mortality continued to be characterized by peaks and troughs. During the epidemic of 1902, for example, smallpox deaths shot up to seventy-eight per million living, whereas no similar mortality had been observed in Germany since 1874.[13]

Outside of advanced industrial nations, the impact of smallpox vaccination was far less obvious. In British India, where vaccination was introduced at the very beginning of the nineteenth century, the procedure was touted as a cure to India's 'great scourge'. Many thousands died of smallpox annually, and the disease occupied a special place in Hindu rituals, with annual devotions being made to the smallpox deity Sitala. But vaccination faced a major obstacle in the form of inoculation, which was firmly entrenched in Bengal and the north of India, as well as in some localities in the west and south. Where inoculation was well established, it was often accompanied by religious rites, and was not easily dislodged by the more secular process of vaccination. Vaccination encountered other difficulties too. High-caste Hindus objected to the use of low-caste children as vaccinifers, because they feared ritual pollution. At times of political tension, it was also rumoured that vaccination was a British plot to poison the Indian people.[14]

However, historians may have placed too much emphasis upon cultural reasons for resistance to vaccination. Many Indians feared the procedure for the same reasons as people in Europe: namely, that it was painful and sometimes gave rise to secondary infections. As the hot climate diminished the potency of lymph, multiple scarring of the body was deemed necessary in order to get the vaccine to 'take'. This only heightened fears of infection and disfigurement. Attempts to substitute calf for human lymph also met with difficulties because many Hindus believed that their sacred animal was being mistreated. In view of this suspicion, vaccination was made compulsory only in certain large towns and cities, and was seldom strictly enforced. For these reasons, it had no appreciable effect upon smallpox during the nineteenth century, but as vaccine technology improved, and as the procedure became more efficacious and less painful, demand for vaccination began to increase, and this served to reduce the frequency and severity of epidemics.[15]

Quarantine, commerce and political economy

At the beginning of the nineteenth century, the fortunes of developed nations were tied more closely than ever to those of distant parts of the globe: a new reality that came to be experienced biologically as well as economically. The increased frequency of maritime trade and the movement of armies around the globe produced a new distribution of diseases. Cholera and yellow fever moved from their tropical domains to affect many temperate parts of Europe and North America; plague, which had been confined for some years to West Asia, threatened once again to invade more developed nations to the north and west.

The chief bulwark against these diseases was quarantine, which, in the course of the eighteenth century, had become a familiar, though unwelcome, fact of life. Ships leaving the Middle East often found themselves impounded at European ports when plague was reported in the Levant; their cargo was sometimes destroyed, and their crews and passengers subjected to vexatious and lengthy quarantines. Some of the Mediterranean states made a good deal of money from charges on impounded vessels, so they had little incentive to change. In any case, quarantine still had a good deal of popular support in Mediterranean countries where the prospect of infection from plague and yellow fever was most immediate.[16] Northern European states also imposed quarantine against vessels from suspect regions, but after more than a century of freedom from plague, the prospect of infection seemed remote. For some, the absence of plague provided evidence that quarantine worked, but a growing number regarded quarantine as anachronistic and unnecessarily restrictive. Some even began to question whether quarantinable diseases like plague and yellow fever were contagious.

Quarantine had always had its critics,[17] but as the eighteenth century drew to a close, the clamour against it grew, especially in those countries and among those communities that had the greatest interest in freedom of commerce. Quarantine seemed like a vestige of a less enlightened era: it encouraged corruption, despotism and economic stagnation at a time when the wealth of nations depended on liberty and free trade.[18] In the late eighteenth century, disaffection with quarantine was most evident in the maritime cities of America. From the middle of the century, quarantine had been imposed against some of the West Indian islands in the belief that epidemics of yellow fever along America's eastern seaboard had been imported from the Caribbean. Cities like Philadelphia were often free from infection for many years, but every so often a major epidemic broke out, as in 1762, when several hundred people died. This led some to argue that quarantine was no protection against yellow fever, and that the disease was the product of local conditions. Prominent among the opponents of quarantine was the eminent physician Dr Benjamin Rush. Rush had both medical and political reasons for opposing quarantine. He was adamant that yellow fever was not contagious and that it was caused by miasmas arising from rotting matter, and, as a staunch republican and an exponent of liberty, he also opposed quarantine on the grounds that it was an unnatural constraint upon human freedom. For Rush, freedom was an essential pre-condition for human health, while health was the foundation of liberty.[19]

The connection between medicine and politics became particularly evident during the serious outbreak of yellow fever that occurred in Philadelphia in 1793. A few cases of what were thought to be a bilious remittent fever occurred at the beginning of August but, by the nineteenth, Rush declared that yellow fever had returned to the city for the first time since 1762. By the end of the month, around 300 people had died from the disease, and panic had set in. Between 10 and 15 per cent of the city's estimated 55,000 inhabitants fled. By the time the epidemic had subsided, in excess of 4,000, and possibly as many as 5,000 people had died.[20] The epidemic was 'the most appalling collective disaster that had ever overtaken an American city',[21] and had a profound effect on those who survived. One correspondent told Rush: 'It is not possible for me to pass the streets without walking in a line with the dead. Passing infected houses, and looking into open graves. . . . [M]y head is gone, and my heart is torn to pieces.'[22]

The epidemic was a devastating blow to a city that was the medical and political capital of a new republic; Rush himself had been a signatory of the Declaration of Independence. The disease arrived at a time when the young republic was beginning to divide between Jeffersonian Republicans and Hamiltonian Federalists, and yellow fever was one of the issues around which this new party system began to crystallize. Federalists blamed the epidemic on the arrival of refugees from the French island of St Domingue, following the slave revolt of 1793. Everyone was aware that many of the refugees were sick, and it seemed likely that they had imported the disease, especially as Philadelphia had been free from yellow fever for thirty years. Nearly all physicians who had Federalist sympathies supported the importation theory, as did many who were non-aligned. Republican physicians, however, were mostly united in their opposition to the importation theory. With Rush, they insisted that the disease was the product of local miasmas arising from insanitary areas around the docks.

Party leaders adroitly exploited the medical controversy over yellow fever. Federalists used importation theory to back demands for quarantine and exclusion of the radical French, whereas Republican merchants saw 'importationism' as a pretext to wreck their lucrative trade with the Caribbean. However, this was not the main aim of the Federalists. Although they talked of ending all trade with the French islands, their intention was to arouse public suspicion of the French and of radical Republicans in America. Merchants also supported the Federalist Party, so it had little reason to end all commerce with the West Indies. For the Federalists, quarantine was a weapon that could be used to discredit their opponents and to forge a strong sense of national identity. Indeed, it was later used, during the 'quasi-war' with France, in 1798, to block the immigration of suspected subversives from St Domingue. The Federalists' endorsement of quarantine and importation theory proved to be very popular, as the Republican alternative – the idea of a home-grown plague – offended patriotic sensibilities. Some local merchants also feared that miasmatic theory could be used to discredit Philadelphia, providing a pretext for moving the capital elsewhere. Yet quarantine was not pursued to the exclusion of the sanitary measures advocated by Rush and fellow Republicans.[23] Both received popular support, and a combination of quarantine and sanitary improvement became the normal course of action in most American cities afflicted by yellow fever.[24]

Yellow fever also divided the medical profession in France. A number of French physicians had witnessed the devastating epidemic on the island of St Domingue in 1793, and had been among the refugees to Philadelphia. One of these, Jean Devèze, adopted the anti-contagionist stance of Republican physicians like Rush. Another witness to the St Domingue and American epidemics was the army doctor Louis Valentin. Along with fellow military practitioners, Valentin believed that contagionist arguments had become too extreme and exclusive. While he was prepared to allow 'contagion' from the breath of the sick (as, incidentally, did Rush), he believed that yellow fever was predominantly a disease of rotting matter. Sanitation, not quarantine, was therefore the best means of preventing epidemics. However, the issue of whether or not yellow fever was contagious did not become a truly pressing one until the disease appeared in Spain in 1800. The Montpellier Faculty of Medicine declared the disease contagious and advocated quarantine, but this was immediately challenged by a number of physicians.[25]

The controversy erupted again nearly two decades later, after yellow fever appeared in Cadiz in 1819, and Barcelona in 1822. A commission sent to Spain under the direction of Étienne Pariset (1770–1847) concluded that yellow fever was contagious. The government accepted this conclusion, and in 1822 established a High Council of Health under the Ministry of the Interior which oversaw the operation of quarantine and lazarettos along France's borders. But these measures did not meet with universal approval. Local authorities resented the intrusion of the government in Paris, and merchants warned of losing commercial traffic; liberals also feared that the government would use quarantine to exclude its political enemies. The opposition to quarantine was voiced in the main by members of the medical profession. The older generation of anti-contagionists that included men like Devèze was joined by the likes of Nicolas Chervin (1783–1843), another radical physician who had witnessed yellow fever in the Americas as well as in Spain. Chervin's views were in line with those of the French Academy of Medicine, which was becoming increasingly critical of the restored Bourbon monarchy.[26]

Attacking the official line on quarantine became a way of attacking the dynasty and its corrupt ways. Indeed, some of the fears expressed by opponents of quarantine were realized in 1823, when the government turned the cordon sanitaire into an army to quash a revolution in Spain. After the July Revolution of 1831, the tide began to turn against contagionism and quarantine. Chervin was elected a fellow of the Academy of Medicine the following year, and became its main spokesman on yellow fever. However, there was some unease over his radical anti-contagionism, as the majority of those who took up this position were prepared to allow some measure of 'contagion' from the exhalations of the sick. But although the two sides called each other 'anti-contagionists' and 'contagionists', contagion was a protean concept, and it is difficult to draw a clear line between the two positions.[27] To all intents and purposes, the debate was about quarantine and under what conditions, if at all, it should be imposed. The anti-contagionists were never able to prove to most people's satisfaction that yellow fever was not transmissible, but they did cast doubt on the government's reasons for erecting a cordon sanitaire. After the July Revolution, however, official attitudes towards quarantine in France began to change. The 'bourgeois monarchy' of Louis-Philippe was more inclined to listen to liberal and commercial interests, and in 1845 all quarantine for yellow fever was abolished.[28]

A new scourge – cholera – reopened the question of quarantine during the 1830s. Until 1817 the disease had been largely confined to the Ganges delta in Bengal, though there had been sporadic outbreaks along the Indian coast. But in that year, as war raged between the British and the Marathas of western and central India, cholera spread from its 'home' in deltaic Bengal to afflict much of the subcontinent. From there, it spread by sea and by land to many parts of Asia and Europe.[29] When cholera spread across Asiatic Russia in the 1820s, the Russian authorities took little interest and did not impose quarantine. But when the disease spread from Bokhara to Orenburg, where it caused severe losses, local officials began to suspect that the disease was infectious and called for quarantine. But still St Petersburg did not act. It was only when the disease reached central Russia, in 1830, that the government changed its mind about quarantine, but by then it was too late. Although quarantines were brutally enforced in other parts of Russia, all the major cities became infected.[30] Some medical men in other countries agreed that quarantine was the right course of action, and declared confidently that the disease was contagious. But the failure of quarantine to check cholera in Russia convinced many that the disease was not contagious, and that it must be produced by atmospheric and insanitary conditions. By the time cholera had spread to Western Europe, there was little agreement on why the disease occurred.[31]

Most governments did not have the luxury of debating the causes of cholera, and thought it wise to err on the side of caution. In Britain the competent authority was the Privy Council, which decided to proceed as if it were dealing with an outbreak of plague. When it learned that cholera had reached the Baltic port of Riga, the Council imposed a quarantine against all ships from Russia and the Baltic. The effects on the Baltic trade were serious: whereas the quarantine station at Stangate normally handled only 200 to 300 ships per year, in 1831 it handled more than 3,000. Merchants protested that the quarantines were causing unemployment and poverty, even though these measures seemed to have little effect in preventing the spread of cholera.[32]

In France, the majority of physicians were not strongly contagionist, but they did support quarantine at ports and along national borders. The Royal Academy of Medicine objected to the use of quarantines internally, however. The Academy was confident that the external cordon would keep cholera at bay, and declared that if it were to break out in France, it would be due to some factor other than importation. The French government acted in accordance with medical opinion and established quarantines along its borders, but it was impossible to seal a nation as large as France. Concentrations of troops along the borders served only to favour the spread of cholera; regulations also varied from place to place, and were not systematically enforced. By May 1832, the cholera had reached Paris.[33]

What, then, can we conclude from the responses to the first cholera epidemic, and from earlier debates about yellow fever? In a seminal essay of 1948, Erwin Ackerknecht argued that the public health measures adopted by different states varied in accordance with their political orientation: a claim that has often been repeated. Liberal states like Britain, it is argued, tended to adopt liberal measures; autocracies like Russia and Prussia tended to adopt coercive ones.[34] However, there seems to be little evidence of any clear association between politics and quarantine in the cases we have examined so far. Most countries responded in much the same way to the threat of epidemic disease, by imposing maritime quarantine. In the absence of medical consensus, quarantine was a wise precaution, whereas miasmatic theories offered no basis for an immediate response. Contagionism was a doctrine that could be understood by laymen, whereas anti-contagionism, with its talk of mysterious atmospherical causes, was the province of medical experts, in whom most people still had little confidence.[35] Yet, regardless of political orientation, all countries progressively relaxed their quarantines, a fact which tends to support the argument recently advanced by Peter Baldwin, that there was no close relationship between the political complexion of states and their sanitary policies.[36]

In the two or three decades after the end of the first cholera epidemic, most countries made their quarantine restrictions less onerous. Nevertheless, there were some important differences, which tended to become more evident over time. By mid-century, Britain and France had moved away from quarantine, and the outlook of the medical profession was increasingly opposed to contagionism in the case of diseases like cholera and yellow fever. However, states like Austria–Hungary and Sweden moved more hesitantly when it came to relaxing quarantine.[37] These differences became evident during attempts to reach an international agreement on quarantine in the Mediterranean from the late 1830s. France and Britain were eager to see a uniform system of regulations created, to put an end to the capricious and often damaging quarantines imposed by some of the Italian states. The main obstacle to an agreement was Austria–Hungary, which, while acknowledging the desirability of reform, did all it could to delay an international summit.[38]

Baldwin argues that these growing differences owed less to political or economic factors than to 'geo-epidemiology' – that is, to each state's historical experience of disease. He concludes that countries close to historic foci of epidemics tended to behave differently from those for which the threat was more remote. In the case of plague, it is true that parts of the Hapsburg Empire were closer to the traditional sources of plague than were Britain or France; but southern France was arguably just as much at risk as the Italian states for which quarantine had become an institution and an easy source of revenue. Moreover, if proximity to infection was the chief factor in quarantine policy, then it could work both ways. Quarantine restrictions against yellow fever were abandoned in some British Atlantic colonies like Barbados during the 1850s, even though vessels suspected of carrying the disease were still subjected to quarantine in Britain itself. In this case, proximity to the source of infection served as an incentive to relax restrictions, because the frequency of outbreaks in the Caribbean made commerce and movement between the islands difficult unless quarantine was discontinued.[39]

In the 1860s, however, international opinion began to swing back in favour of restricting importation. This shift occurred in response to an outbreak of cholera among Muslim pilgrims to Mecca in 1865, which culminated in epidemics across Europe and North America. The pandemic focused attention on the new dangers posed to the world by a revolution in communications. The recent introduction of steamships on Mediterranean routes and to and from India, together with the massive expansion of railways, meant that cholera could be transmitted rapidly from endemic zones like India and Java to all parts of the world. The advent of telegraph communication – which provided warnings of impending epidemics – served only to heighten the sense of panic. Most nations that sent delegates to the International Sanitary Conference held in Constantinople in 1866 therefore favoured some kind of quarantine.[40] All delegates agreed that the quarantines of old had been too restrictive, and a new approach to quarantine was advocated, which entailed the inspection of persons suspected of suffering from cholera, the notification of disease, and the disinfection of persons, ships and merchandise.[41]

But the advent of medical inspection was more evident in some countries than others. France swung sharply from its old anti-contagionist position whole-heartedly to embrace the new approach. Prussia (and later the united Germany), on the other hand, did not. Under the influence of the prominent hygienist Max Pettenkofer, Germany advocated a more liberal line, based on the theory that the cholera 'seed' could thrive only in favourable 'soil'. According to Pettenkofer's theory, quarantine could theoretically prevent the importation of cholera, but in practice this was unlikely. The emphasis ought to be placed, he argued, on sanitary measures.[42] Britain stood somewhere between France and Germany. In a pioneering work of epidemiology, Dr John Snow (1813–58) had traced an outbreak of cholera in London to a particular source of drinking water

– the Broad Street Pump. He concluded that the agent causing the disease must be transmitted in water.[43] Snow's theory was initially regarded as too exclusive, but by the 1860s there was more evidence to support his claims, including statistics compiled by the Registrar-General, William Farr (1807–83).[44] Thereafter, most government medical officers struck a balance between the probable transmissibility of cholera and the local conditions that fostered it. A two-pronged attack was made on the disease: sanitary reform, on the one hand, and a modified system of 'quarantine' – based on medical inspection – on the other.[45]

The mixed reception given to medical inspection appears to support Baldwin's contention that there was no clear relationship between politics and sanitary policy. Germany's softer line on quarantine ran counter to the increasingly conservative tenor of German politics. Similarly, France persisted with its relatively hard line on quarantine, even after the fall of Napoleon III and the proclamation of the Third Republic. Other factors must therefore be implicated in the direction taken by these states. The reason, according to Baldwin, was that countries bordering the Mediterranean, like France, were more directly at risk from the threat of cholera than either Britain or Germany.[46]

Yet there is more to politics than ideology, and changing international alignments had a profound effect upon sanitary policy. The protracted debates over the quarantines imposed at the Suez Canal, which opened in 1869, are a case in point. In 1882 the British unilaterally ended their 'dual control' of Egypt with France, and subsequently occupied the country. Thereafter, French delegates to the Egyptian Board of Health, established after the 1866 sanitary conference, opposed all British attempts to liberalize quarantine. Britain was anxious to do this, as the quarantines imposed at Suez were an impediment to trade and the free movement of troops and mail between Britain and India. Disputes between Britain and France were played out at subsequent conferences, where Britain began to align itself with the nations of the Triple Alliance: Germany, Austria–Hungary and Italy. Although Bismarck had initially pursued a policy antagonistic to that of Britain, after 1885 he developed an interest in closer co-operation, seeking Britain's support in the event of hostilities with Russia. Germany's recent colonial acquisitions in East Africa also meant that Bismarck had an interest in relaxing restrictions on ships passing through the Canal. Italy's support for its Alliance partners is also interesting in view of Baldwin's claims about geo-epidemiology. If proximity to sources of infection was the main factor determining policy, then Italy should have opposed the liberalization of quarantine at Suez, but its political alliance with Germany dictated otherwise.[47]

Cholera and the tensions of modernization: the epidemics of 1830–1832

The arrival of cholera in Europe during the 1830s created panic on a scale not seen since the great plague epidemics of the seventeenth century. The numbers killed by cholera were far lower than in some of the great plagues of yesteryear, but its mysterious 'Asiatic' origins and the way in which it seized its victims made it terrifying. Cholera arrived with little warning: the unfortunate individual was gripped by a sudden bout of vomiting and severe diarrhoea, and within only a few hours severe dehydration caused the body's tissues to collapse, the blood to coagulate, the skin to turn blue, and the internal organs to fail. The disease was not always fatal, but it was profoundly humiliating, especially if suffered in public. In one fell swoop, the disease stripped away all the trappings of polite society.

Cholera also highlighted social tensions. The privileged classes of Europe charted its approach with growing unease, watching anxiously as it made its way from Asia to Europe. Many wondered whether they ought to leave the cities for the relative safety of the countryside, removing themselves from the most likely seats of disease and also of political rebellion. In many European countries, there was evident dissatisfaction with the prevailing order, and the imminent arrival of cholera threatened to turn simmering discontent into full-blown revolution. Fear of cholera and fear of insurrection became inextricably linked in many parts of Europe. Some reactionary groups like the Carlists in France claimed that cholera travelled along the same routes as subversive political ideas. They believed the disease had spread from Poland, following the rebellion of November 1830, to Germany and then to England; Polish refugees were also blamed for bringing the disease to Paris at the time of the July Revolution. The Catholic Church, for its part, saw in cholera an opportunity to restore its ties with a population that had turned its back on God. The cholera, it claimed, had been sent to punish countries like France for rejecting monarchical and religious authority.[48]

The political situation in Great Britain was rather different from that on the Continent. It had not experienced a revolution, nor did it possess an autocratic monarchy; but it was a country in the midst of social and political upheaval. Class divisions in the new industrial towns were stark, and many workers resented the conditions in which they had to labour. Nor was the countryside immune from the effects of industrialization. In 1831 there were riots in the agricultural south of England following the introduction of mechanized threshing machines. The same year also saw the first disturbances connected with the movement for parliamentary reform. The propertied classes feared that Britain was on the brink of revolution, and that the arrival of cholera would be all that was required to trigger it. When cholera did arrive in the summer of 1831, some of the well-to-do followed their continental cousins and took flight to the country, but many stayed put, some taking an active part in organizing measures against cholera, others denying that the disease had even arrived. For members of the commercial middle class, it was important to convey a sense of 'business as usual'. But for others, the arrival of cholera heralded a major catastrophe. Some saw the disease as divine punishment for wickedness and moral corruption, especially among the lower classes. Others, who lamented the passing of the old, paternalistic order, saw the disease as a symptom of the social dissolution that had followed industrialization.[49]

On the other side of the Atlantic, the educated elite in American cities drew rather different conclusions. Though many were fearful of the disease spreading to America, the cities of the eastern seaboard seemed cleaner, and their inhabitants more pious, than those in Europe; it was assumed that the moral and physical purity of a free people would ensure that cholera would never take root in America. But though favoured by the Lord, most acknowledged that America was far from perfect. The streets of cities like New York were littered with filth and rubbish and contained many dens of iniquity, and the sense of unease mounted after cholera crossed the Atlantic to Canada.[50] By the end of June 1832, several cases of cholera had been reported in New York City, and from there the disease spread quickly along the network of railways and canals which was a source of pride to so many Americans, and a symbol of their modernity.

Despite all their rhetoric about Old World corruption, the response of the elite was much the same as in continental Europe. Those who could afford to do so left New York City, and visitors were struck by the deathly silence of its streets. Business stagnated, and those who depended on a weekly wage were driven to destitution. There were collections to relieve the plight of the poor, and the city's authorities and church groups arranged alternative work, for a few at least. But for the victims of cholera, pity was mixed with contempt. Cholera was seen as a disease that afflicted the lewd and the lazy. Most Americans regarded it as a form of divine punishment: a belief that appeared to be supported by medical opinion. It was widely believed that sexual promiscuity and indulgence in alcohol left people 'over stimulated' and defenceless against disease. But a few regarded the epidemic as evidence not of divine justice but of human *in*justice. Radicals like George Henry Evans argued that poverty was caused by low wages rather than fecklessness; it seemed to be no accident that those who suffered most from cholera – blacks and recent immigrants – were among the most oppressed and most exploited people in America.[51]

In all industrialized countries, cholera was regarded as a disease of the lower classes, of prostitutes and of the dissolute, so it is hardly surprising that the poor were suspicious of the intentions of ruling classes. In countries where there was great hatred of the ruling elite, there were rumours that the deaths attributed to cholera were really the result of poisoning. In Russia, Hungary and France, it was believed that doctors had spread poison in wells at the behest of their rulers, the aim being to reduce a population that had become too large to be governed effectively. The rumours may have been sparked by the decision to pour chlorate of lime into water supplies in order to purify them.[52] Cholera was also a factor in the political riots that occurred in Paris in April and June 1832, and barricades were erected in all streets severely affected by the disease. Although cholera was not actually the cause of the insurrections, it highlighted pre-existing social tensions, and increased fear and loathing of those in authority.[53]

Suspicion of the ruling classes was heightened by their tendency to dismiss the epidemic as nothing more than 'summer diarrhoea'. Such denials often came as the authorities prepared for the worst, establishing facilities for isolation and temporary hospitals. The ambiguity of these responses led the poor to think that there were ulterior motives behind the desire to separate the sick from their families. In parts of Britain, for example, the poor refused to believe in the existence of cholera, and saw hospitalization as a medical plot to remove them for dissection. Cholera arrived in the wake of a scandal over the murders perpetrated by Burke and Hare in Edinburgh, who sold fresh cadavers to the medical school for dissection.[54] The Edinburgh scandal heightened long-standing fears about dissection among the poor, whose graves had been robbed regularly to provide bodies for anatomy theatres, and who feared dissection as an additional punishment, sometimes carried out after judicial execution.[55] Doctors were attacked by crowds who claimed that they 'merely wanted to get the poor into their clutches to Burke them'.[56] All thirty riots and major disturbances connected with cholera in Britain in 1832 were aimed at the medical profession in some way.[57]

Enforced hospitalization was unpopular in other countries too. In Hamburg, one official lamented the belief that cholera had been deliberately encouraged by the well-off. 'This delusion', he reported, 'has become so deeply rooted that despite the most careful preparations in the cholera hospital . . . it has been possible to admit the victims to it only against great resistance on the part of their relatives and friends.' Mobs gathered outside the hospital, and tried to prevent cholera victims from being removed from their homes.[58] In Moscow, unrest was far more serious: hospitals were sacked, patients released, and several doctors were killed.[59] In some cases it was believed that medical practitioners would subject those admitted to hospital to experiments. This was one of the reasons why some cholera hospitals were attacked in the USA and, in some cases, with good reason. In the slave-owning South, blacks were subjected to some horrific experiments; in one instance, a southern physician poured boiling water on the leg of a black patient to test the theory that cholera caused nervous impairment.[60]

It was difficult for anyone to have much confidence in medical practitioners when they were so spectacularly unsuccessful in their attempts to treat cholera. Practitioners tried a wide range of medicines, none of which seemed to work. In Britain, calomel (mercurous chloride) was a popular medicine, having been used extensively in India in the treatment of stomach complaints. Calomel was normally given in the form of 'blue pills', which were renowned for their purgative action. The aim was to beat the disease at its own game, by expelling the harmful matter more quickly. Another popular remedy was opium, which was given as a sedative to reduce purging, vomiting and cramping. Hot baths were used to treat the stomach cramps caused by cholera, but some practitioners went to the opposite extreme. Doctors in Germany declared, 'Cold water has conquered cholera!',[61] and cold-water treatment was popular with groups like the Mormons in the USA, who claimed that it helped to prevent vomiting and purging. Other home-grown treatments, like Thomsonian botanical remedies, flourished as the American public's already fragile confidence in medicine was shaken further.[62]

Suspicion of medical practitioners was due partly to their being seen as representatives of the ruling elite. In truth, most were marginal men, struggling to gain acceptance in genteel society;[63] but there is no doubt that many of the measures taken to combat cholera weighed heavily on the poor. In Britain, the government ordered that all rags and hangings in infected dwellings should be destroyed, and that the victim's clothes and furniture should be doused with disinfectant water. There was no mention of compensation for survivors or the victim's families.[64] Lack of respect for the property of the poor was one thing, but an even more sensitive matter was the disrespect shown to traditional burial practices. To prevent infection, most countries ordered bodies to be interred within a few hours of death. This ran contrary to practices like laying out the body and left little time for ceremonials. Rapid burial also led many to fear premature interment – a common concern in many previous epidemics.[65] Consequently, there was great distress and widespread defiance of regulations. In Britain, many of the large disturbances were fomented by Irish Catholics, whose burial customs typically involved a wake around the body.[66]

Behind the cholera protests in most countries were demands for social justice. Cholera and the measures taken to control it were among many perceived threats to the traditional values of a culture that existed beyond the bounds of respectable society. But while there was a good deal of similarity in responses to government intervention, there were important differences too. In Russia and other autocratic countries, and in France, which was gripped by Revolutionary fervour, cholera was widely seen as a conspiracy by one class against another. Cholera protests were therefore closely bound up with political disturbances such as the July Revolution.[67] But Britain and America were rather different. Britain was also riven by class divisions, but both the government and the propertied classes did their best to keep tensions to a minimum. Only a small number of the wealthy fled the cities, and the government took steps to redress the grievances of the poor. Doctors were told to stop the dissection of cholera victims, and coercion was rarely used to enforce hospitalization or isolation.[68] In the USA religion and ethnicity played a more important part than they did in Europe. The main objects of preventive measures were poor immigrants and blacks, and it is not surprising that Irish immigrants were at the fore of the comparatively few protests that were made. The medical profession was regarded with some suspicion in the USA, but attacks on medical practitioners were less violent and less widespread than they were in Europe, perhaps because the profession was less monopolistic and more loosely connected with the state.[69]

Urban disease and sanitary reform

As the most dramatic of the epidemic diseases that afflicted industrialized countries, cholera has long been seen as the chief stimulus to the great sanitary reforms of the nineteenth century. Certainly, few diseases produced as much fear as cholera, and few illustrated so clearly the interdependence of rich and poor. But cholera may have been more of a distraction than an impetus to sanitary reform. Sanitarians had to work hard on public opinion in order to use it for their own ends, and their main concern was not so much cholera but the epidemics of fever that appeared regularly in industrial cities. As a cause of death and debility, cholera was surpassed by 'continued fever' (a term which then embraced typhus, relapsing fever and typhoid), scarlet fever, smallpox and measles. These epidemic diseases killed fewer people than chronic maladies such as tuberculosis. Reformers thus sought to treat cholera as merely one among many fevers that thrived in the squalour of their towns and cities. The fact that an Asiatic fever could flourish in Europe was a sign that it was not yet fully civilized or, indeed, that it may have degenerated.[70]

But the unhealthiness of large conurbations was hardly a revelation. Throughout the eighteenth century, medical men pointed to the close relationship that existed between poverty, filth and disease, but governments had shown little inclination to intervene in matters of public health, and the urban environment remained the responsibility of local authorities. A few authorities managed to achieve a good deal, but mostly in older, richer towns. The industrial towns that developed rapidly from the late eighteenth century generally lacked strong local government, and were unable to cope with the filth generated by large numbers of humans and animals newly brought together. Partly in response to these conditions, the state began to take a more active role. Britain – the first nation to industrialize and hence to experience these problems – led the way, but other industrializing nations like France, Germany and the United States soon followed suit. By the end of the nineteenth century, sanitation had become an index of civilization across the Western world.

Today, most people have a very specific conception of what sanitation entails. It has become synonymous with sewers and other great feats of Victorian engineering, with pure water and the removal of slums. But at the beginning of the nineteenth century, the word 'sanitary' had no fixed meaning. It was used loosely, if at all, to describe anything pertaining to health.[71] It was by no means inevitable that sanitary reform would become synonymous with sanitary engineering, or even that the state would intervene in any way to counteract the problems of urban squalor. Lest we regard sanitary reform as inevitable, we should remember that, even today, different peoples are prepared to tolerate different degrees of 'filth'. Moreover, what people understand by 'filth' is not the same the world over, but is a reflection of what is deemed unacceptable within their particular system of values.[72] So, what was 'sanitary reform' and why did it happen? Why did disease come to warrant greater attention from the state?

Apart from the fact that Britain was the first nation to experience industrialization, it seems an unpromising arena for state intervention. Compared with more authoritarian countries like Prussia and Austria–Hungary, Britain's state apparatus was poorly developed. The prevailing ideology was also far from interventionist, being a mixture of liberal political economy and Malthusianism. Each individual was expected to take care of his or her own health, and high mortality was tolerated as part of the natural order. As we saw in the last chapter, it was only in the armed forces that the state took anything like an active role, and even among its soldiers and sailors, it was tolerant of thousands of deaths from disease.

Around the turn of the century, things began to change. New currents of thought became more prominent, and began to have an influence on public life. The most important of these was the utilitarian philosophy of Jeremy Bentham and his followers. Utilitarians believed that all human beings had a natural capacity for happiness – by which they meant the power to earn a living and to learn – and that they ought not to be prevented from doing so by illness or untimely death. Bentham's ideas had a profound influence on the key figure in the first phase of English sanitary reform, Edwin Chadwick (1800–90) who headed the Board of Commissioners of the New Poor Law. Chadwick's solution to the problems of urbanization was simple: to remove filth. Most fevers, he believed, were the product of noxious miasmas arising from rotting matter; they could be prevented by legislation that compelled individuals to keep their environment clean and by efficient systems for the disposal of waste. Sanitary reform would enable the poor to make full use of their natural capacities, thereby reducing their reliance on public funds. It would work hand in hand with the New Poor Law, with its workhouses and principle of 'less eligibility', which would serve as disincentives to indigence.[73]

Secular Benthamites like Chadwick found unlikely bedfellows in the form of evangelical Christians. The Evangelicals were a diverse group: they were primarily concerned with saving souls, though some favoured action by the state to lift mankind from its presently degraded condition. In the course of the nineteenth century, the emphasis within Evangelicalism shifted from the individual's relationship with God to a gospel of social action, exemplified by the mid-century writings of Charles Kingsley and Charles Dickens. Their Christian idealism drew on the spirit of the medieval guilds and the Renaissance city-states, and provided the inspiration for a great deal of civic improvement.[74]

As a layman and civil servant, Chadwick had little patience with medical controversies over the causation of disease. In the Poor Law Commissioners' report on the *Sanitary Condition of the Labouring Population of Great Britain*, Chadwick quoted selectively from a wide range of medical writers, choosing to stress those aspects that supported his claims about filth. He also made use of statistics to bypass medical debate, such as tables showing the comparative life chances of different classes and different areas.[75] But he did rely heavily on one medical authority: the Benthamite physician Thomas Southwood Smith (1788–1861). Smith had rather dogmatic views on the causes of fever, and was firmly opposed to the idea of contagion. He attributed most outbreaks of fever – including cholera – to a 'poison' produced by putrefying matter.[76]

Many medical practitioners thought these views too simplistic. Although most agreed that miasma was a cause of fevers, they usually saw it as one cause among many.[77] Poor diet, fatigue, squalid surroundings, military defeat, separation from loved ones, and harsh conditions of employment were all said to be possible causes of disease.[78] Indeed, some medical practitioners claimed that poverty and the anxiety engendered by life in a commercial and industrial society had created a host of new diseases, ranging from 'hypochondriacal despondency' to fevers and digestive problems.[79] The medical critique of industrial society was most famously expressed in William Pultenay Alison's *Observations of the Management of the Poor in Scotland, and its Effects on the Health of Towns* (1840). Alison identified poverty, rather than filth, as *the* sanitary problem of the day. The commonest cause of disease, he insisted, was destitution. What was needed was more generous provision for paupers, not just the removal of filth. Alison favoured a system of outdoor relief, rather than the gloomy workhouses advocated by Chadwick and his commissioners; he also recommended that fever hospitals be made more humane, so that the poor would no longer be afraid of them. None of these men was a political radical, however. Many were Tories who looked back fondly to a pre-industrial order that seemed more generous and humane in its social dimensions. For men such as Alison, industrialization and degeneration seemed to go hand in hand.[80]

Some doctors clearly had a wider vision of public health than that advocated by Chadwick, but it was his vision which came to dominate the public agenda, and which provided the model for public health in other countries. The environmental improvements advocated by Chadwick fitted the political needs of the Poor Law Commissioners and of successive governments seeking an antidote to radical or revolutionary reform. Chadwick's programme of reform transformed social problems into environmental problems; it did not entail any interference in the market, it promised to lessen the burden of poor relief, and continued to assume that individuals were masters of their own destiny. Sanitarianism of the Chadwickian variety was congruent not only with the doctrines of political economy, but also with some of the new currents in medicine, particularly pathological anatomy. Pathological anatomy sometimes led its practitioners to make reductive statements about the nature of disease, which was increasingly perceived as behaving in a law-like manner, akin to the principles of political economy. Another correlate can be found in epidemiology. William Farr, the Registrar-General, whose statistics Chadwick utilized in his reports, believed that it was possible to predict the course of epidemics. The connections between Chadwickian sanitarianism and the Industrial Revolution thus lay, as John Pickstone has observed, 'as much in the structures of knowledge as in the structures of cities'.[81]

By the time the Health of Towns Commission reported in 1844–5, the transition to a wholly environmental approach to public health was complete. The report concerned itself entirely with technical details concerning sewerage, water supply and drainage: the holy trinity of Chadwick's 'Sanitary Idea'. It emphasized the need for high-pressure, constant water supplies, water-carriage waste removal and the recycling of sewage, which would be used as a fertilizer. Recycling had an almost religious significance for sanitarians: transforming waste into fertilizer was not only 'useful' in the Benthamite sense, but symbolized the restoration of divine harmony.[82] The Commission also established the framework for sanitary legislation over the next half century. Sanitation was to involve central government, but the execution and management of sanitary services were to rest with local authorities. These principles were enshrined in what became the Public Health Act of 1848. The Act created a General Board of Health that was empowered to create local boards of health, either when petitioned by at least one-tenth of the ratepayers, or by compulsion when mortality in a district exceeded twenty-three per thousand for a period of seven years. The General Board was modelled on the Poor Law Commission and suffered from the latter's unpopularity, and its demise came quickly. In 1854 Chadwick and his colleagues were purged from the Board, and in 1858 its functions were assumed by the new medical department of the Privy Council. The local boards survived, however, and, in the course of the century acquired further powers of municipal administration.[83]

Spurred by the British public health movement, most cities in northern Europe began to build new systems to distribute water and evacuate liquid waste. In 1852, one Belgian observer commented that a 'water mania' was spreading across Europe, not unlike the 'railway mania' of the preceding decade.[84] But each country had its own traditions of public administration, which, on the Continent, tended to be more centralist than in Britain, where local government was the main engine of sanitary reform. Continental countries had also taken their own hesitant steps towards a system of public health, and had somewhat different medical traditions. Chadwick's influence was great, but the sanitary idea was subtly modified in the different contexts in which it was adopted.

In early nineteenth-century France, for example, the hygienist movement was comprised of a small group of activists within the medical elite. Inspired by the Enlightenment and progressive thinkers during the Revolutionary and Napoleonic eras, these reformers linked medicine to politics, and envisaged doctors taking an active role in social reform. Two of the main exponents of hygienic reform were the public health investigators Louis Villermé (1782–1863) and A.-J.-B. Parent-Duchâtelet (1790–1836), who in 1829 launched the first public health journal to appear in any language, the *Annals of Public Health and Legal Medicine*. The hygienists conducted important research on many subjects, reporting on the health problems created by urbanization and drawing up plans for sanitary reform. In the capital, Paris, there were substantial improvements in drainage, water supplies and steps to control dangerous trades. But the hygienists were constrained by the bodies through which they had to work. Responsibility for matters relating to health was dispersed throughout several ministries, and there was no real infrastructure save the Health Council established in Paris during the Napoleonic period. The first national public health institutions were created after the Restoration, like the quarantine authorities already described. But in most cases sanitary regulations continued to be local in scope, and the health councils established in 1848 had a purely advisory role.[85]

In the 1850s sanitary conditions in Paris were already far better than those in most European cities, but they were not good enough for France's new ruler, the emperor Napoleon III. Napoleon was attracted to Chadwick's vision of public health, and he regarded British sanitary engineering as the epitome of progress. Chadwick was invited to meet Napoleon on several occasions. When asked what he thought of Paris, Chadwick is said to have replied: 'Fair above, Sire, foul below.'[86] Napoleon was determined that nothing should detract from the glory of his empire, and aimed to transform the capital below ground as well as above. Like Chadwick, he also saw a link between sanitary reform and social order. The city's ancient sewers had long been associated with revolution. Revolutionaries had hid in the sewers, and the Restoration monarchy had hesitated to have the sewers to its palace cleaned for fear that gunpowder would be placed beneath. For Victor Hugo, author of *Les Misérables*, the putrid sewers of mid-century Paris came to symbolize moral disintegration and political disorder.[87]

A new sewerage system promised to cleanse much of the filth and corruption remaining from the old regime. The task fell not to local authorities, as in Britain, but to Baron Georges Haussmann, prefect of the Seine. From 1854 he presided over a five-fold increase in the area covered by the sewerage system, which grew from 143 kms to 773 kms at the end of the Second Empire. Practically every street in Paris was now equipped with its own sewer. The engineer who designed the new system was Eugène Belgrand, who took advantage of the natural incline of the River Seine to flush water from one side of the city to the other. Water from the river was trapped in small reservoirs, from which it was released periodically to cleanse the system. Above ground, Haussmann made use of his powers to expand the system of street cleaning and refuse collection. The supply of piped drinking water also increased. Paris soon became the envy of the civilized world, and its streets were said to be cleaner than those of London or Berlin. The death rate from water-borne diseases also fell sharply after 1854, a fact which most observers attributed to the sewerage system and accompanying measures.[88]

In France, as in Britain, what started off as a broad vision of public health reform had been transformed into a more limited programme of sanitary engineering. The same was true in Prussia, which experienced industrialization and its consequences somewhat later. There, a group of physicians influenced by developments in Britain and France joined forces in the revolutionary year of 1848 to campaign for health reforms. The most prominent figures in this group were Rudolf Virchow, Solomon Neumann and Rudolf Leubuscher, all of whom believed that the state had an obligation to ensure the health of its population. They insisted that governments should be responsible for regulating environmental conditions, housing and food, and that they had the right to interfere with personal liberty for the public good. Virchow also proposed that the poor should be provided with the services of physicians paid for by the state, and proclaimed the right of every citizen to work. But with the defeat of the revolution, most of the programme outlined by Virchow and his colleagues was sidelined. Under the more authoritarian leadership of Bismarck, Prussia, and later the united Germany, concentrated on the more attainable goal of sanitary reform. Some action was taken to improve working conditions but, otherwise, the ideas of the liberal reformers did not mature until the end of century.[89]

With Europe in the grip of 'water mania', a few ambitious souls attempted to export Chadwick's model to the colonies. British India was the first colony in which such an experiment was attempted. In 1855 the municipal engineer of Calcutta – the capital of British India – proposed a combined underground system of drainage and sewerage, in which five deep receiving sewers would run across Calcutta with their outflow in the Salt Lake to the east. The scheme was accepted, and was financed by a loan from government and local taxes. But the funds generated were insufficient, and the scheme proceeded slowly. As in most other countries, not least in Britain, sanitary reform was opposed by a coalition of vested interests in the form of slum landlords, ratepayers and the like. In India the imperial government lacked the will to overcome these interests, perhaps because it feared a political backlash: a terrible prospect in view of the Mutiny and Rebellion of 1857–8. Moreover, for sanitary reform to be successful, it required at least the compliance, if not the active cooperation, of the people, and the colonial situation was not conducive to forming such alliances. Even then, the sanitary problem was far too large to be dealt with simply by engineering: Calcutta contained many thousands of people who were either homeless or lived in properties that could not be connected to a sewer, and to whom Western notions of hygiene meant nothing.[90]

The public health reforms of the mid-nineteenth century were a response to the twin problems of industrialization and urbanization, which brought unprecedented numbers of people together in relatively confined spaces. The epidemic diseases that thrived in these conditions hit the poor hardest, but they also threatened the privileged classes and, on some occasions, paralysed social and economic life. While cholera was not the immediate impetus for sanitary reform, it served as a paradigm for urban interdependence, and highlighted the threat posed to all persons by the presence of disease within the environment of the city.[91] While the affluent could move away from the worst urban squalor and the locus of disease, they could never be sure that they were wholly beyond its reach. Moreover, they were concerned that epidemics would ignite smouldering discontent among those marginalized by the social and political order. The response to these problems varied from one country to another, depending on the country's historical experience of disease and its economic and political orientation. But all countries experienced a narrowing of the scope of public health around the middle of the century, with broad, almost utopian visions losing ground to the technocratic solution proposed by Chadwick. Although Chadwick met with opposition from some exponents of *laissez-faire*, his approach harmonized with the prevailing order, and his proposals were designed to reinforce it. But sanitary reform, like vaccination, was also an art of the possible. In prosperous countries it could be achieved relatively quickly, and its results were soon evident in lower death rates; it was only in the colonies that it failed to deliver.

6

The Individual and the State

Between 1870 and 1914 there was a fundamental change in the way in which diseases were understood. By the outbreak of the First World War, the causal organisms of malaria, anthrax, tuberculosis, cholera, plague, typhoid and many other major diseases had all been identified. In some cases – such as malaria – their vectors had been identified too, opening up new vistas for the prevention of disease. A new era in medicine had arrived, in which the laboratory was king.[1] Yet there were important continuities, too. The search for bacteria and parasites can be seen as merely one aspect of a pre-existing programme of research that aimed to find the causes of disease.[2] More importantly, perhaps, there was no single germ theory, but a range of germ theories and practices that flourished independently in various branches of medicine, nursing and public health.

Germ theories may have been less revolutionary than previously thought, but they did contribute to a reorientation of public health away from the environment and towards the individual. More than ever before, individuals were seen as carriers of disease, and new methods were designed to prevent them from spreading infections. In the decades following the first bacteriological discoveries, the balance between the rights of the individual and the powers of the state shifted further in favour of government. Human activities regarded as pathogenic were regulated more closely than before, and individuals were compelled to undergo vaccination in the name of public health. This regulatory environment began to alter public consciousness, and encouraged people to think differently about disease. Disease was now defined by the presence or absence of micro-organisms rather than by its symptoms. As the only people trained to detect and control these organisms, medical experts came to acquire a status and authority they had not enjoyed previously. They also became the main custodians of public health, an undertaking that was increasingly professionalized and bureaucratic. All these developments were closely related, though not in any simple or deterministic way, and were characteristic features of the 'modern' societies analysed by Weber and his contemporaries at the turn of the twentieth century.

Disease and scientific medicine

The laboratory revolution in medicine depended upon one relatively simple piece of technology – the microscope. Improved magnification enabled doctors to observe the processes of disease at a cellular level, the most important development being the emergence of what became known as cellular pathology. Cellular therapy was pioneered by Rudolf Virchow (1821–1902), professor of medicine at the University of Berlin, who came to see the cell as the primary locus of life and hence, also, of disease. He concluded that disease could be spread from diseased cells to the rest of the body by the process known as mitosis, or cell division. All diseases could therefore be traced as chemical and physical changes within cells, an insight that led Virchow to make several observations of lasting importance on such diseases such as thrombosis and leukaemia.[3] Virchow was convinced that cellular pathology would revolutionize medicine, and urged physicians to accustom themselves to 'thinking microscopically', to conceive of minute structures within the body that were invisible to the naked eye.[4]

Many doctors were already doing just that, though not necessarily in the sense meant by Virchow. Some were using the microscope to search for the causal agents of disease, and in the first half of the nineteenth century numerous poisons, viruses, germs, fungi and other putative agents became the subject of medical controversy. Much of the reasoning behind these investigations was analogical: doctors saw similarities between disease and processes like fermentation and putrefaction, which were then being elucidated by chemists such as Justus von Liebig (1803–72). Liebig showed how sugar could be broken down into various components to form alcohol, and was beginning to understand the process of putrefaction. He also turned his attention to pathology, suggesting that some diseases were caused by specific poisons which acted in a similar way to yeast and which produced molecular changes in the blood. Liebig referred to this process as 'zymosis', and the zymotic theory of disease gained many adherents, particularly in Britain, where it was endorsed by William Farr, the country's first state epidemiologist.[5]

Liebig thought that these poisons acted as catalysts, accelerating the body's natural tendency to decay, just as he believed that yeast assisted the process of fermentation. In the late 1850s Louis Pasteur (1822–95) challenged Liebig's theory. He saw fermentation as a biological rather than a chemical process, and concluded that it could not occur without the presence of yeast. Extending his researches to putrefaction, he argued that decomposition was also the work of living organisms. After studying two distinct diseases in silkworms, he concluded in the 1860s that each was caused by infection with different species of bacteria. Pasteur's theory was still controversial, but he was not the only one who identified micro-organisms as the cause of disease. One such was the Italian Agostino Brassi (1773–1856), who had shown that another silkworm disease – muscardine – was parasitical; it was also known that the disease trichinosis was related to micro-organisms in pigs and humans.[6]

Yet it was Pasteur who is most usually remembered as the father of the 'germ theory' of disease. One reason for this is that the diseases he went on to elucidate were either economically significant – like anthrax and fowl cholera – or dramatic and widely feared, like rabies. As a scientist, Pasteur also had an unrivalled knowledge of the structure of micro-organisms and of their nutritional requirements. This gave his pronouncements an air of authority that many predecessors lacked. He was politically astute too, and adroitly exploited the press to popularize his discoveries. At Pouilly-le-Fort he invited the press to witness his vaccination of farm animals against anthrax, for example. By so doing, he managed quickly to convince several crucial sections of the medical profession and the lay public that his theories were useful to them, and it was for the practical dimensions of his work that Pasteur is deservedly famous. In addition to the anthrax vaccine, he developed vaccines for fowl cholera, swine erysipelas and rabies. Pasteur's technique was to inject a small quantity of micro-organisms that had been made less virulent; the attenuated organisms produced just enough reaction to trigger immunity without producing the symptoms of full-blown disease.[7]

The other main architect of 'germ theory' was the German doctor Robert Koch (1843–1910). As well as discovering the causal organisms of important diseases like tuberculosis and cholera, Koch developed the procedures and techniques that gave shape to the emerging discipline of bacteriology. He grew micro-organisms on plates of culture medium rather than in flasks, as Pasteur had done – a method that was both easier and cheaper. The agar-agar culture medium is still used today to grow bacteria, as are the small dishes named after one of Koch's assistants, Petri. But it is for his 'Postulates' that Koch is better known. These were a series of rules that needed to be followed if the causal organism of a disease was to be determined beyond reasonable doubt. The organism had to be shown to be present constantly in diseased tissue; it had to be capable of being isolated and grown in pure culture; and the pure culture had to induce the disease experimentally in animals. These postulates were implicit in some earlier experimental work by Jacob Henle (1809–95) and were formulated more clearly by Koch's pupil Friedrich Löffler (1852–1915) after his discovery of the diphtheria germ. Nevertheless, it is as 'Koch's Postulates' that the procedures are generally known, and this owes much to the stature that Koch had acquired by the 1880s, after his work on tuberculosis and cholera.[8]

Koch and Pasteur received the enthusiastic backing of their respective countries' governments, in the hope that their research would provide solutions to the health problems caused by urbanization and imperial expansion. A Pasteur Institute was founded in Paris, and in Berlin an Institute for Infectious Diseases was established under Koch's direction. These two great institutes had rather different characters, and bequeathed different scientific legacies. The Pasteur Institute was more pluralist in organization and more flexible in its relations with other institutes; Koch's was more centralist and hierarchical. Although Pasteur was a very much revered figure, he worked only briefly at his own institute, and the style of research there remained individualistic. At Koch's institute research was highly co-ordinated and more influenced by the priorities of the state, especially the army and navy. All the most important staff at Koch's institute were military and naval medical officers.[9]

We will look more closely at the work of these institutes in a moment, but it is important to note that other germ theories and practices were developing alongside those of Koch and Pasteur. One important example was the work of the British surgeon Joseph Lister (1827–1912), who became famous as the pioneer of antiseptic surgery. In a seminal paper of 1867 entitled 'On the Antiseptic Principle in the Practice of Surgery', Lister explained wound infections as a form of chemical poisoning, using analogies similar to those of Pasteur. Unlike many surgeons, who believed that infection developed spontaneously within the body, Lister claimed that it came from without, from particles floating in the air. He favoured carbolic acid as a means of preventing infection from reaching the wound and destroying any germs that might already have entered. Initially, this involved dipping surgical instruments in carbolic acid and applying dressings soaked in carbolic acid directly to the wound; later, in the 1870s, Lister perfected an antiseptic spray.[10]

Lister taught his methods at Edinburgh University, and later in London, after he moved to King's College Hospital to become professor of surgery in 1877. This gave him the opportunity to influence a generation of surgeons, many of whom adopted his techniques. But some of those who tried antiseptic surgery regarded the procedure as too complicated, and were not favourably impressed with the results; others believed that sepsis was beyond the control of surgeons. It was better, they argued, to help the patient's body withstand the spread of infection.

On the whole, Listerism was more popular in Germany than it was in Britain, where general cleanliness was often preferred to specific antiseptic measures – a legacy of the sanitary reform movement and the hospital and nursing reforms inspired by Florence Nightingale. But though Lister did not always accept the claims of bacteriologists, some of his disciples, like William Watson Cheyne (1852–1932) and Alexander Ogston (1844–1929), conducted research similar to that of Koch. Ogston, for example, investigated the role of streptococci and staphylococci in abscesses, whereas it took some years for Lister himself to accept that they had a pathogenic role.[11]

By the end of the century, what had hitherto been a distinct surgical practice – Listerian antisepsis – began to merge into what was known as 'asepsis', which aimed to keep the entire surgical environment free from germs. Rather than using chemicals, asepsis made use of sterilization by heat and steam. Although the Listerians claimed that they had effected a revolution in surgical procedure, antisepsis in the strict sense had only a limited impact on surgery, and the sterile operating theatres of the 1900s owed as much to the movement for cleanliness and newer bacteriological theories as to Listerian methods.[12] But Listerism had helped to demonstrate the need for better hygiene, and it had encouraged surgeons to become less fatalistic than before.[13]

The new germ theories were also connected with changes taking place in the realm of public health, though not in any simple causal way. In the era of Edwin Chadwick, public health had been the domain of engineers and civil servants, but from the 1850s, the medical profession began to make its influence felt. Doctors were beginning to coalesce as a professional group, as surgeon-apothecaries turned into the general practitioners we know today. Although divisions between surgical specialists and physicians still existed, doctors were increasingly required to train in both disciplines in order to practise. The advent of medical registration from the middle of the century did much to improve the public image of doctors, who became more respected and more active in the societies in which they lived.[14] One avenue to social respectability was involvement in local government, and those doctors who were elected to local bodies began to play an important role in sanitary reform. A few also found employment as health officers with municipalities.[15]

At the national level, too, doctors were being appointed to take charge of public health. A famous example is Dr John Simon who, in 1858, became the first medical officer of the United Kingdom's Privy Council (and to the Local Government Board after 1871). Simon's tenure of office typified a more general shift in public health work, from sanitary engineering to a more scientific programme under the direction of medical experts.[16] 'State medicine', as it came to be known, made extensive use of epidemiological surveys and vital statistics, in order to devise more effective means of controlling disease.[17] The battery of control measures was also expanded as the state began to regulate more areas of life in the name of public health. In most developed countries, from the middle of the nineteenth century, a succession of laws was passed making vaccination against smallpox compulsory, securing the purity of water and foodstuffs, and regulating atmospheric pollution, housing and noxious trades.[18] Local authorities were also beginning to take pride in sanitation, and new legislation enabled them to take over many functions formerly conducted by private companies, including refuse removal and the provision of drinking water.

Some of the measures taken were of a very specific nature, especially from the 1890s. Bacteriological diagnosis allowed the early detection and isolation of those suffering from a number of infectious diseases. In 1896 a French clinician, Ferdinand Widal, developed an agglutination test for typhoid, and in 1907 August von Wasserman developed a test for syphilis.[19] The identification of the bacillus causing diphtheria in 1883–4 also had important implications for public health. It took some time for the discovery to be accepted; but, by the 1890s, laboratory techniques were being used to diagnose the disease. Even more important was the work conducted at the Pasteur and Koch institutes to produce a diphtheria antitoxin. By 1894 the large-scale production of sera was possible, and clinical trials were carried out in children's hospitals. Soon, diphtheria antitoxin was being used prophylactically and curatively,[20] and its success did much to win public confidence in hospitals, which had often been regarded as custodial institutions with dubious medical reputations.[21] Diphtheria antitoxin also did much to establish bacteriology as an important element in public health.[22]

From consumption to tuberculosis

Of all the advances made at the end of the nineteenth century, Koch's discovery of the bacillus causing tuberculosis was potentially the most important. Tuberculosis was responsible for more deaths in industrialized countries than any other disease. Mortality rates could be as high as 500 per 100,000, though in most cases they were nearer to 300 per 100,000. In England and Wales, for example, tuberculosis was responsible for 54,231 out of a total of 515,229 deaths during 1870. This normally exceeded the mortality caused by epidemic diseases like cholera, which even in its worst year – 1849 – claimed only 53,293 deaths in England and Wales.[23] The mortality rate for those who developed active symptoms of tuberculosis was around 80 per cent at this time, but many more were infected without developing symptoms. Only about 10 per cent of those infected with the bacterium went on to suffer from tuberculosis, and it is probable that nearly all people in large cities were exposed to the infection.[24] But, unlike cholera, tuberculosis barely figured as a public health problem until the last two decades of the nineteenth century. As two famous chroniclers of tuberculosis observed, the disease 'appeared to be so constantly and universally present that there was a tendency to regard it as an act of God . . . against which little action was possible'.[25]

For most of the nineteenth century, pulmonary tuberculosis was generally known as consumption, or phthisis, in the English-speaking world. It was the most common form of a wide range of tubercular infections, which manifested themselves in the bones, lymphatic glands (scrofula) and other internal organs. The received wisdom was that consumption was a constitutional disease: sufferers were thought to possess a 'diathesis', or predisposition, to develop tuberculosis, and carried the stigma of a hereditary 'taint'. However, it was generally believed that this 'proclivity' was activated under certain conditions, and that an individual's constitution could be altered by life-style and environmental influences. Laënnec, who conducted the classic study that established a connection between the different varieties of tuberculosis, believed that 'sorrowful passions' and sexual vice were among the most important causes of the disease.[26] His views dominated French medicine until the 1860s, and similar ideas circulated throughout Europe.

Consumption had a romantic quality, and was widely associated with etiolated young women and delicate, artistic young men. The poet Keats famously died from consumption at the tender age of twenty-three, and the disease also claimed the life of the German dramatist Friedrich von Schiller. The close association between consumption and genius meant that it was a common theme in the arts: Hugo's *Les Misérables*, Dickens's *Nicholas Nickleby*, Brontë's *Wuthering Heights* and Verdi's *La Traviata* are among the many contemporary works that depict death from consumption. Tuberculosis symbolized frailty, innocence and unworldliness; its victims had what Edgar Allen Poe described as a 'morbidly angelic quality'. This perception owed much to the anaemia that was a symptom of tuberculosis, and the pallid countenance of consumptives led to the disease being dubbed the 'white plague', or 'white death'.[27]

The belief that consumption was a constitutional disease went largely unchallenged until the late nineteenth century, although a few heretics such as the British physician William Budd (1811–80) and the Frenchman Jean Antoine Villemin (1827–92) ventured that it was contagious.[28] But epidemiological studies such as those conducted by the French social hygienist Villermé, tended to reinforce the dominant view. It seemed that tubercular diseases did not affect the population indiscriminately. Consumption was particularly common among tradesmen who worked in confined and dusty conditions, and it was more common among the poor than the rich, notwithstanding a few prominent victims among the socially exalted. Slowly, the romantic images surrounding the disease disappeared; consumption was no longer associated with heightened sensibilities, but with poverty and urban squalor.[29]

Consumption was thus transformed from a disease of individuals into a social disease, a shift that was accelerated by the discovery of the bacterium causing tuberculosis. Robert Koch announced his discovery at a meeting of the Physiological Society of Berlin in March 1882. Reactions were initially mixed: many doctors were convinced that tubercular disease was hereditary, as there was still no strong evidence of it being spread from person to person. Nor had there been any successful attempt to replicate transmission in animals. The existence of the tubercle bacillus was not itself an issue, but many doubted that it had a causal role: some thought that its presence was merely a symptom or a consequence of the disease. Koch was to experience a similar reaction when he claimed, two years later, to have discovered the germ causing cholera.[30] But in the case of tuberculosis there was a complicating factor: the fact that comparatively few of those exposed to infection went on to develop the disease. Doctors could accept that a bacillus caused tuberculosis, but its course appeared to depend upon the body's response to infection.

Although the profession gradually came to accept that tuberculosis was a contagious disease, the peculiarities of an individual's response to infection meant that it remained, to some extent, a constitutional disorder. It now seemed more capricious in its choice of victims, but all the factors that had formerly been supposed to affect consumption – poverty, intemperance and poor climate – still seemed to affect it. Yet Koch's discovery did lead to some important innovations in the management and treatment of tuberculosis. Most importantly, it persuaded doctors that tuberculosis was curable, or at least that its progress could be arrested. Some tried to kill the bacillus using antisepsis after the manner of Lister's surgical practice. Antiseptics like creosote, for example, were inhaled as vapour, or sometimes given rectally in suppositories. There was even more excitement when Koch announced, in 1890, that he had discovered a cure for tuberculosis in the form of 'tuberculin', a product derived from killed bacilli. But most trials with the vaccine were disappointing, and although a few claimed good results, most doctors doubted that it had any beneficial effect. Nevertheless, humans and animals with latent infection reacted positively when inoculated with small quantities of tuberculin, so it became an important diagnostic tool.[31]

The failure of tuberculin as a treatment led most doctors to concentrate on boosting the body's resistance to infection. Doctors were heartened by the fact that some tubercular lesions healed spontaneously, which suggested that nature could be assisted to achieve a cure, and of the many factors affecting resistance, fresh climates and clean air seemed to be the most important. It had long been fashionable for the wealthy to seek relief from tuberculosis in mountain resorts, which offered an antidote to the conditions in which consumption was thought to thrive, and in the early 1880s some German doctors began to popularize the treatment, extolling the virtues of fresh air and sunlight. Provision for the free circulation of air and exposure to sunlight were the guiding factors in the design of the new tuberculosis hospitals, or 'sanatoria' as they were generally known: fresh air was deemed vital, not only to satisfy the needs of the body, but to kill harmful bacteria. 'Aerial sewage', as one manual described microbes, 'must . . . be entirely got rid of. There must be no stagnant areas in corners or ceilings; and the ventilation currents must sweep away all impurity.'[32]

Sanatoria spread rapidly across the world and provided many tuberculosis sufferers with their first experience of treatment in hospital.[33] Before 1880 there were very few hospitals devoted to respiratory ailments. In Great Britain, for example, there were only four, all of which were in London. Most other charitable institutions refused to admit patients with consumption, because hospitals could not afford to provide beds for chronic patients who had little chance of recovery.[34] Therapeutic optimism also transformed relationships between doctors and their patients. Although tuberculosis sufferers had always visited doctors and dispensaries, they had enjoyed a large measure of personal freedom. Even those who voluntarily confined themselves in mountain resorts possessed some measure of control over their lives and saw themselves as invalids rather than patients. With the advent of sanatorium therapy all that changed. Patients were far more circumscribed than before: in the new sanatoria, they were obliged to conduct themselves according to rigidly prescribed rules and to take prescriptions as the doctor ordered. A manual of the 1910s emphasized that 'A characteristic feature of modern sanatorium treatment is constant medical supervision. By this means the daily life of each individual patient is so regulated that the greatest possible benefit from treatment is obtained.'[35]

Tuberculosis patients saw themselves very differently from the consumptives of old. They often referred to themselves as 'TBs' or 'lungers', as though they were not fully human; they were simply cases, rather than sick people. Those diagnosed with the disease usually feared their removal to a sanatorium, but the experiences of patients in sanatoria varied considerably. Discipline tended to be harshest in public institutions, rather than in private sanatoria – the kind of institution that Thomas Mann wrote about in his novel *The Magic Mountain*. In these private hospitals, patients and their families retained some measure of control over their lives, and most enjoyed a pampered existence. But many patients in public sanatoria told stories of humiliation and degradation, of how they had sacrificed their dignity for the promise of better health.[36]

From the 1890s, the promotion of sanatorium treatment began to be absorbed into a wider movement to control tuberculosis. National associations were formed, first in France in 1891, and within a few years in most other industrialized countries. As well as promoting sanatoria, the associations aimed to educate the public about prevention, and to remove the threat posed to humans by tuberculosis in cattle. The discovery of the tuberculosis germ in cattle gave added impetus to the attempts of municipal medical officers to improve the quality of food and drink. By the end of the nineteenth century, several municipalities had made regulations to prevent the sale of milk from infected herds. However, in 1901 the movement received a set-back when Koch cast doubt on the link between bovine and human tuberculosis. Although most veterinary and public health officials were convinced of the connection, it took further research before most governments were prepared to introduce legislation, and in most cases it was not passed until after the First World War.[37]

The national associations had more immediate success in their campaigns against spitting. The discovery of the tuberculosis germ strengthened the hand of those who had long claimed that spitting was unhygienic. By the turn of the twentieth century, notices prohibiting spitting had been posted in many public places like railway stations. Some local authorities, like New York City, had also made spitting a punishable offence. It was through such campaigns that the new germ theory of disease was communicated from the laboratory to the general public.[38]

Efforts to prevent tuberculosis coincided with a decline in mortality in most industrialized countries. Mortality from tuberculosis in England and Wales reached its peak around 1870, but by 1921 had fallen by nearly one-half.[39] Mortality in Paris also reached its peak around 1870, though it came somewhat later in other large cities such as Le Havre; in France as a whole, deaths from tuberculosis peaked around 1890, and fell off steadily in the coming decades.[40] Most contemporaries attributed the decline in deaths from tuberculosis to public health regulations and the construction of sanatoria. The retreat of tuberculosis thus seemed to validate sanitary reform and the isolation of sufferers, but in many cases it began before the establishment of sanatoria and before the introduction of specific measures to combat the disease. This has led some historians to argue that the decline in tuberculosis mortality must have been due to rising standards of living, rather than medical intervention or public health reforms.[41] But several recent studies have once again emphasized the role of public health reforms and the isolation of those suffering from the disease – an issue to which we shall return at the end of the chapter.[42]

Another possibility is that the decline of tuberculosis was due to factors that were not influenced greatly by either diet or human action. When suddenly exposed, a population that has had little contact with tuberculosis typically suffers very high rates of infection, but inherited immunity builds up gradually in the survivors, and only the most susceptible die, sometimes without offspring. This pattern occurred in most industrializing countries, with mortality increasing in Ireland, for example, just as it was beginning to decline in England and Wales, which had industrialized earlier.[43] The effect of tuberculosis on non-immune populations was also widely reported by medical officers working in parts of Africa and the Pacific Islands.[44] Some, like the British medical officer S. Lyle Cummings, concluded that tuberculosis was the quintessential 'disease of civilization,' a veritable rite of passage to modernity.[45]

The third plague pandemic: an imperial crisis

The plague pandemic that originated in China at the end of the nineteenth century left some 13 million victims in its wake. This pales by comparison with the Black Death, or the influenza pandemic of 1918–19, but it was still sufficient to provoke a major international crisis. The localities most affected by plague were the colonies of the British, French and German empires. In all these contexts, but especially in India, the disease heightened tensions latent within the imperial order, providing a spur to nationalist movements and eliciting a powerful and often draconian response from the authorities. The third plague pandemic was also the first major disease crisis of what Rosen has termed the 'bacteriological era'.[46] Scientific commissions of various nationalities raced to the main foci of the pandemic, eager to outshine their competitors. In the process, plague was transformed from a medieval bogeyman into a disease that could be readily understood and prevented using modern scientific techniques.

The plague probably originated in the Yunnan province of China in the middle of the nineteenth century, and was one of several diseases that erupted amidst the suppression of a Muslim insurrection in Yunnan.[47] This civil war destroyed the region's prosperity, and brought to an end the isolation of this formerly prosperous and fertile plateau. The first European observer in the region – Émile Rocher – attributed the outbreak to a miasma arising from the soil, affecting underground animals like the rat before other animals and humans. Since many of the animal deaths occurred among domesticated cattle, sheep and fowl (species not affected by bubonic plague), it is likely that epizootics of rinderpest and fowl cholera accompanied whatever diseases were afflicting the human population. The outbreak is reminiscent of the complex mortality crises of the medieval and early modern periods, in which plague was probably mixed with other diseases.

By 1867, plague had spread to Pakhoi on the South China coast, where it became endemic until disappearing in 1884. The disease returned a decade later, and spread to other provinces like Canton. By March 1894, the outbreak had turned into a serious epidemic that had killed 40,000 people. The mortality rate was extremely high for plague – around 80 per cent – which again suggests that plague may have been accompanied by other diseases. Alternatively, some of the cases may have been the pneumonic rather than the bubonic variety of plague, which is both more infectious and more fatal. By May 1894, the disease had appeared in Hong Kong. Compared with the number of deaths in Yunnan and Canton, fatalities in Hong Kong were comparatively few – around 3,000. But the epidemic there was to have momentous consequences. Sitting at the hub of an Asian–Pacific trading network, Hong Kong became the point from which plague was disseminated around the world, turning a serious epidemic into a pandemic of horrific proportions.[48]

It was in Hong Kong, in 1894, that two investigators, Shibasaburo Kitasato and Alexandre Yersin independently discovered the bacterium causing plague. These two researchers represented the rival traditions of Koch and Pasteur, respectively. Kitasato had trained at Koch's laboratory, whereas Yersin, a Swiss by birth but now a naturalized Frenchman, followed the methods prescribed by Pasteur. Neither collaborated in any way with the other, but what each aimed to do was essentially the same. Both were attempting to transform plague from a diffuse condition, defined largely by its symptoms, to one that possessed a more definite identity, predicated on the existence of a causal organism. In so doing, they wished to heap glory on themselves, their countries and their respective schools of scientific research. Before the year was out, both men had identi-fied a micro-organism in the bodies of humans and animals diagnosed with plague, and had subjected this organism to the various labora-tory tests associated with their respective schools. The bacteria, for example, could be cultivated and used to reproduce the disease in animals, fulfilling Koch's Postulates. Although many medical practi-tioners continued to stress the role of the environment in the prop-agation of the bacillus, most soon came to accept that plague was a bacterial disease, and that the ultimate arbiter of its presence was the laboratory.[49]

The discoveries of Yersin and Kitasato preceded another major outbreak of plague in Asia, this time originating in the Indian port of Bombay. The initial reaction to the appearance of suspected cases in the summer of 1896 was to deny that plague had broken out at all. The city's authorities did their best to reassure the local population and the international community that the disease was not 'true plague' – as defined by Kitasato and Yersin – but a form of 'bubonic fever'. Hardly anyone was convinced, and by October it was clear that the disease was plague, as it had appeared in Hong Kong. Bombay had extensive trading links with the West, and was the main port from which Muslim pilgrims embarked from India on the Haj, so countries likely to be infected lost no time in imposing quarantine against Indian vessels. Some of the measures, like an embargo on hides and skins (materials thought to harbour plague), had a detrimental effect upon the economy of India, and the disruption of trade brought Bombay to a standstill. The British government of India had to do something to bring plague under control and do it quickly, or else substantial parts of the Indian economy were likely to be ruined for years.

The response, when it came, was powerful. In 1897 the Government of India passed an Epidemic Diseases Act, which made provision for the segregation of plague suspects, the medical inspection and deten-tion of passengers, house-to-house searches, and so on. A 'Plague Committee' chaired by General Gatacre of the Indian Army wrested control of preventive measures from Bombay's municipal council, and set about applying the new legislation with vigour. J. A. Lowson, a colonial medical service officer from Hong Kong, was brought in to oversee the operations. He had enlisted the help of the army in enforcing hospitalization and segregation in Hong Kong, and was determined to take an equally robust approach in Bombay and its hinterland. Some medical officers in India resented the 'interference' of an outsider, but others welcomed the opportunity that the epidemic presented. The suspension of normal municipal arrangements in major cities like Bombay permitted the reassertion of European control after a period in which Indians had enjoyed municipal self-government. Sanitary reformers felt that 'plague operations . . . properly undertaken present some of the best opportunities for riveting our rule in India . . . [and] for showing the superiority of our Western science and thoroughness'.[50]

Together with a ban on the Muslim pilgrimage, the measures taken in the Bombay Presidency of India were sufficient to satisfy most of India's critics. An international sanitary conference held in Venice in May 1897 relaxed the quarantine against India, and this led to a modest revival of Indian exports. But these concessions were won at enormous cost, and it became clear that an authoritarian response was no longer sustainable in India, where nationalist grievances were being more openly expressed. The backlash came first in Bombay, where there were several violent assaults even before the passage of the Epidemic Diseases Act. The focus of the attacks was initially the Arthur Road Infectious Diseases Hospital, which came under attack in October 1896, when mill-workers protested against the enforced hospitalization of a woman suspected of having plague. Despite growing attendance at hospitals over the preceding decades, these institutions were still unfamiliar to most Indians, and all forms of segregation were unpopular because they deprived people of contact with loved ones. At the beginning of the epidemic, those in charge of hospitals and segregation camps also paid little attention to religious sensibilities, and there was fear of ritual pollution among the higher castes.

A similar pattern of events unfolded in other towns. After the isolation of victims and suspects, the most common grievance was against the physical examination of female travellers. 'Native ladies' were said to 'prefer death to the humiliation of having their groins examined by male doctors who are utter strangers to them.'[51] The examination of women on the streets and relentless house-to-house searches eventually provoked the murder of W. C. Rand, the Plague Commissioner of Pune, near Bombay. These episodes of violence were accompanied by strikes and the mass flight of thousands of people from cities afflicted with plague. More than 100,000 people fled Bombay, in fear not so much of plague but of the measures used to prevent it.

As the plague spread throughout western and northern India, so did incidents of the kind seen in Pune and Bombay. The British began to fear a 'second Mutiny', and the draconian measures of the early plague years were soon modified or repealed. In Calcutta in 1898, compulsory segregation was abandoned after rioting and a mass exodus from the city; in Karachi, the authorities had to promise the city's majority Muslim population that no such orders would be issued so as to ensure its compliance with other measures, like the temporary ban on the pilgrimage to Mecca.[52] From 1898 to 1900, the authorities began to enter into a dialogue with community leaders in order to bring anti-plague measures into line with the requirements of caste and religion. Voluntary segregation, female medical inspectors, and caste hospitals became the rule.

One important dimension of the plague epidemic in India was the arrival of foreign plague commissions, which saw the outbreak as an opportunity to conduct path-breaking research. Although the causal organism had already been identified, there was still much to be explained, including how it entered the body and under what conditions it was infective. There was also a drive to develop treatments and preventatives using insights from bacteriology. In addition to the Plague Research Committee formed by the Government of India, there were commissions sent from Egypt, Germany, Russia and France. Among the members of the German commission was Robert Koch, himself no stranger to India, having isolated the causal organism of cholera in Calcutta in 1883–4. With the spotlight of the world upon it, the Government of India had no choice but to tolerate these commissions, but their presence was deeply resented. It seemed that India was incapable of looking after its own affairs, and that it lacked sufficient scientific expertise.[53] Yet among the many things investigated by the commissions was a major innovation pioneered in India itself – an inoculation against plague.

The inoculation had been developed towards the end of 1896 by the Armenian bacteriologist Waldemar Haffkine (1860–1930). The Government of India had invited Haffkine to work on the plague vaccine because of his apparent success in developing a cholera vaccine two years previously. Towards the end of 1896, Haffkine announced that tests with the plague inoculation in one of Bombay's prisons had proved successful, and he was allowed to extend inoculation on a voluntary, experimental basis in several nearby towns. As a foreigner and a Jew, Haffkine was disliked by many in the Indian Medical Service, some of whom saw inoculation as a distraction from more 'useful' measures like segregation and sanitation. But some of the more scientifically inclined medical officers greeted Haffkine's announcement with enthusiasm: here was a means of demonstrating the potential of medical science and the importance of their profession.[54]

The advocates of inoculation finally got their chance to prove its efficacy when plague spread to the Punjab. During 1901–2 the disease spread rapidly in the countryside, killing hundreds of thousands of people, and the governor of the province decided that inoculation offered the only means of preventing further devastation. Haffkine was asked to turn his small laboratory in Bombay into a factory, where the vaccine could be mass-produced. The Government of India endorsed the scheme, and provided the funds necessary to convert the laboratory. Due to a massive increase in output, around one million people were inoculated in the Punjab during 1902–3, which was a considerable achievement, especially considering that many were initially reluctant to accept inoculation.[55] But inoculation received a serious set-back in 1902, when a batch of vaccine contaminated with tetanus killed nineteen villagers in Malkowal. Although operations did not cease altogether, the incident did tremendous damage to the inoculation campaign, and was deeply embarrassing to the colonial authorities, which tried to pin the blame on Haffkine and his laboratory. Haffkine was forced to take 'unpaid leave' for three years, during which he and influential friends like Ronald Ross cleared his name. He eventually returned to the laboratory, though broken in spirit. In all likelihood the vaccine had been contaminated in the field.[56]

Tropical diseases

Plague spread to many regions of the globe, but with the exception of some Australian cities and small outbreaks in ports such as San Francisco, it did not affect the developed world. This, and the decline of cholera in the West (the last epidemic was in 1892), reinforced the growing impression that the warmer nations, and especially the tropics, were epidemiologically distinct. Plague and cholera were increasingly regarded as tropical diseases, alongside malaria and yellow fever. The idea of 'tropical diseases' was not entirely new: the term had been used in the title of medical works as early as the 1780s, amidst numerous references to diseases of 'hot' and 'warm' climates. These diseases seemed to behave differently, and to warrant different forms of treatment than those in temperate latitudes. But the concept of tropical disease that emerged at the end of the nineteenth century was quite different from that of previous generations. It rested on new epistemological foundations – on the sciences of bacteriology and parasitology; it also had an institutional presence, in the form of special teaching and research institutes such as the Liverpool and London Schools of Tropical Medicine (founded in 1898 and 1899 respectively). Tropical medicine had its own journals too, like the British *Journal of Tropical Medicine*, founded in 1898.[57]

The 'father' of this new tropical medicine was Sir Patrick Manson (1844–1922). Manson began to study exotic diseases while a customs medical officer in the treaty port of Amoy in south-east China. It was here that he did the research that led to his discovery of the cause of elephantiasis, a nematode worm that he named *Filaria*. Although elephantiasis was already known to be distinct from leprosy, with which it had formerly been confused, there was no agreement about its causes. Bad water, the consumption of rotting fish, and a host of other explanations were put forward to explain this distressing condition. Manson's identification of the causal organism was thus a major breakthrough, as was his discovery that the filarial worm entered the human body through the bite of a mosquito. He conducted his experiment in a ramshackle shed, in which a Chinese volunteer – whose blood teemed with filaria – lay exposed to the bites of mosquitoes let in from outside. Over the course of six days, Manson and a servant examined the worms in blood extracted from the mosquitoes. They showed the gradual development of the filarial embryos into larvae.[58]

The course of Manson's research shows him moving gradually from the traditional natural-historical framework in which most physicians worked in the middle of the century, to one where attention focused primarily – though not exclusively – on parasites and their vectors.[59] This approach was institutionalized in the London School of Tropical Medicine, which Manson helped to found, and was outlined in his landmark study, *Tropical Diseases: A Manual of the Diseases of Warm Climates* (1898). The book marked the founding of a new discipline, quite different from the 'tropical medicine' of old: climate was no longer seen as a cause of disease, but merely as a factor that affected the distribution of germs, parasites and their hosts. Manson also took account of the role of organisms competing and preying on vectors, like larvae-eating fish.[60] Yet he was well aware that the term 'tropical' was 'more convenient than accurate' when applied to most of the diseases he was writing about. Manson made it clear that he was referring to diseases that were especially prevalent in the tropics, rather than those that occurred only in tropical regions. This qualification allowed him to embrace malarial fevers, which were still common in some parts of Europe.[61]

Malaria was the most widespread of all 'tropical' diseases, and the main cause of death in most of Europe's colonies. The new tropical medicine offered the prospect of bringing to an end what many thought to be simply a fact of life in the tropics. For centuries, malarial fevers were regarded as environmental diseases. They were prevalent in marshy areas and were to be found from the fens of northern Europe to tropical parts of Asia, Africa and the Americas. Although they seemed to vary in severity and periodicity, they were thought to have essentially the same cause: bad air. Bad air was said to have a depressing effect upon the nervous system, which, in turn, affected other parts of the body such as the vascular system, causing the familiar symptoms of fever, vomiting and anaemia. Poverty, an intemperate life-style and other factors helped to explain why some individuals or groups seemed to be more susceptible than others. Concepts of race also began to enter into explanations of susceptibility from the early 1800s, although in most developed countries, the emphasis came to be placed on man-made causes such as filth and the detritus of industrial cities.[62]

The first step towards a different conception of malaria came in 1880, when the French military doctor Alphonse Laveran isolated its causal organism, the *Plasmodium* parasite.[63] The meaning of the term 'malaria' now changed from a description of the atmosphere (meaning literally 'bad air') to the name of a specific disease. At first Laveran's discovery met with scepticism, and in some cases with great hostility, as the link between malaria and marshes had become an article of faith for many doctors. But following confirmation by Italian and American scientists in the 1880s, the concept of a 'specific factor' began to gain acceptance.[64] One of those who quickly accepted Laveran's claim was Patrick Manson, who was instrumental in convincing other doctors that *Plasmodium* was the cause of malaria and that, like filariasis, it might be transmitted by the bite of a mosquito.

One of those influenced by Manson was Ronald Ross, an Indian Medical Service officer on leave in London. On returning to India in 1895, Ross set about trying to prove Manson's hypothesis. While Ross conducted his experiments in India, he maintained a regular correspondence with Manson, who provided encouragement and advice, and arranged for the publication of Ross's results in important medical journals. By 1898 Ross had shown that malaria was transmitted by the *Anopheles* mosquito. At about the same time, and quite independently, two Italian scientists, Giovanni Grassi (1854–1925) and Amico Bignami (1862–1929), also demonstrated that mosquitoes became infected with *Plasmodium* as a result of feeding on the blood of a person suffering from malaria. This independent discovery did much to lend credibility to the mosquito vector theory, but it sparked off a bitter and lengthy dispute over priority, which was aggravated by the decision in 1902 to award the Nobel prize for physiology to Ross alone.[65]

It is hard to overstate the potential significance of the discovery of the mosquito vector. When Ross left the Indian Medical Service to take up a post as a lecturer at the Liverpool School of Tropical Medicine, he declared in his inaugural lecture that the only solution to the problem of malaria was to eradicate mosquitoes. In the same month he also wrote to Manson urging that 'We must be first in with the practical side of the mosquito theory or else Grassi will develop it.'[66] Such personal and imperial rivalries spurred a rapid drive to develop an effective solution to the problem of malaria, although the practical dimensions of malaria research were more evident in the case of the Liverpool than the London School, which was more exclusively committed to laboratory research and instruction. Ross tried to gain support for his idea of mosquito brigades during a series of expeditions organized by the Liverpool School to West Africa, but colonial medical officers displayed little interest. Ross proposed that the brigades would destroy larvae and breeding sites through such means as the drainage of stagnant water, the oiling of pools, and the introduction of larvae-eating fish. In tropical West Africa, there was simply too much stagnant water to make this feasible.[67]

Ironically, Ross's work had a more enthusiastic reception in India, which he had left in 1899 feeling frustrated with the government's refusal to provide practical support. Barely a year later, the Royal Society sent R. S. Christophers and J. W. W. Stephens to India to conduct experiments on mosquito eradication and other methods of malaria prevention at the military station of Mian Mir, in the malarious province of Punjab. Shortly afterwards, an imperial malaria conference was held at Nagpur, in India, at which several delegates became excited at the prospect of eradication campaigns of the kind suggested by Ross. Others were more sceptical and preferred to try to prevent malaria using mass prophylaxis with the drug quinine, as was currently recommended by Robert Koch for the German colonies. Disappointing results from the experiments at Mian Mir meant that there was quite a lot of interest in quinine as an alternative; but quinine had problems of its own. Mass distribution was expensive, and the drug was not always effective; it also had unpleasant side-effects like nausea. Until the end of the First World War, the medical profession working in the tropical colonies was split fairly evenly between those who favoured quinine and those who tried to implement elements of Ross's scheme.[68] For the most part, however, malaria prevention continued much as it had before Ross's discovery; in India it was barely distinguishable from everyday sanitary measures, although special initiatives like drainage schemes were occasionally justified as a means of reducing the incidence of malaria.[69]

The other chief tropical disease at the end of the nineteenth century was yellow fever, which had become endemic in tropical parts of Africa, the Caribbean, and Central and Southern America, as well as in southern parts of the USA. Occasionally, the disease erupted in epidemic form, taking a terrible toll in human life. Some 20,000 people died in the notorious 1878 epidemic in the Mississippi and Ohio valleys of the USA.[70] It was in the Caribbean, however, that the long-running controversy over the transmissibility of the disease was eventually resolved. For some years, a Cuban doctor, Carlos Finlay (1833–1915), had been attempting to prove his theory that yellow fever was carried by mosquitoes. To this end, he had subjected healthy volunteers to the bites of mosquitoes that had previously fed on victims of yellow fever. He found that these volunteers regularly contracted the disease. But Finlay had used no controls, and had not taken precautions to prevent his volunteers being infected from other possible sources. He also laboured under a further disadvantage. Unlike Manson and Ross, Finlay had no idea of the actual organism causing yellow fever, and he was uncertain whether it was a bacterium or a parasite. The true cause – a virus – was not discovered until 1929.[71]

Nevertheless, other researchers attempted to prove the mosquito theory. The Spanish–American War of 1898 brought to the island of Cuba an American Yellow Fever Commission, headed by Walter Reed (1851–1902) of the US Army. The Commission had the co-operation of Finlay and the chief sanitary officer in Havana, the American military doctor William Gorgas (1845–1920). The Commission took Finlay's hypothesis seriously, and eventually proved that it was correct: yellow fever was transmitted to man by the bite of the *Aedes aegypti* mosquito. Gorgas went on to attempt mosquito eradication of the kind advocated by Ronald Ross, making water receptacles mosquito-proof, oiling breeding pools, dusting with pyrethrum insecticide powder, and isolating victims with mosquito screens. The measures proved a great success: whereas there had been 310 deaths from yellow fever in Havana in 1900, there were only eighteen in 1902. His experience in Havana also enabled Gorgas to devise effective measures to prevent yellow fever and malaria during a second, and ultimately successful, attempt to build the Panama Canal. The first had to be abandoned because of the great loss of life from both diseases.[72]

But for some historians, the most remarkable thing about the research on yellow fever was that it represented a major epistemological shift.[73] Medicine now had new objects of study (parasites, bacteria, arthropod vectors) and new disciplines such as parasitology and medical entomology. All over the world, medical scientists began to turn their attention to these things and to structure their research in new ways and in new institutions; not only in Europe and the USA, but also in the less prosperous, but proudly independent, nations of South America. Here, too, a predominantly climatic framework of research was giving way to a new one, in which scientists began to search for causal organisms and vectors. Several South American scientists like the Brazilian Carlos Chagas (1879–1934) made remarkable discoveries: in Chagas's case, isolating the parasite causing 'New World Trypanosomiasis' and its arthropod vector within the space of two years (1907–9). The discovery was made in a new institute devoted to research in tropical medicine in Rio de Janeiro, directed by Dr Oswaldo Cruz.[74]

These developments were, indeed, revolutionary, but as with most of the diseases considered in this chapter, a holistic view was not wholly obliterated. The natural-historical bent of doctors such as Manson was simply reconfigured to embrace the relationships between man, parasites, vectors and their competitors. Although specific measures were developed to diagnose and prevent some diseases, in many cases they did not wholly eclipse a more comprehensive sanitary approach. For all his work in the laboratory, Ross remained essentially a sanitarian, interested in practical measures. There were other continuities, too. Despite its emphasis on vectors and parasites, the new tropical medicine still carried a good deal of the racist baggage accumulated by Western medicine during the colonial period. Previously, the climates of Africa and Asia had been blamed for the foul miasmas causing cholera and malaria, whereas now the people themselves were regarded as reservoirs of germs and parasites.[75] As a consequence, more attention began to be paid to the cultural habits of indigenous peoples with the aim of inculcating Western standards of hygiene.[76]

Microbes and migrants

The late nineteenth century and the early years of the twentieth century saw unprecedented levels of migration, principally from Europe and Asia to North America and, to a lesser extent, South America and Australia. Steamships made the voyage to far-away continents less forbidding, while the economic attractions and greater freedom to be found in these 'new' lands encouraged millions to emigrate every year. Between 1880 and 1924, the United States alone received 23.5 million immigrants, largely from southern and eastern Europe, but also smaller numbers from China, Japan and Mexico.[77] Some were economic migrants, seeking relief from near poverty in the countryside of Italy or Greece, and many were Jews fleeing from persecution in Russia. The assassination of Tsar Alexander II had sparked a series of pogroms and restrictions on Jewish people. These intolerable conditions led as many as 2.5 million Jews to leave eastern Europe between 1880 and 1914, 2 million of whom headed for the United States.[78]

In the United States the massive influx of immigrants from southern and eastern Europe was viewed with alarm in some quarters. There had been concerns over immigration before – especially when Irish Catholics arrived in what was then a predominantly Protestant country – but the scale of immigration and the unfamiliar habits and cultures of the immigrants who arrived at the end of the century led many to believe that American culture was threatened.[79] Immigrants were prepared to work long hours for low wages, and threatened to undermine the wages of native-born workers; they were also deemed a threat to public health. They were blamed for the importation of Old World infections like cholera, typhus and even plague, and it was claimed that they were predisposed for racial and cultural reasons to diseases such as trachoma, an eye infection that causes blindness. If allowed into the country, they would become reservoirs of disease and undermine the racial purity of American stock. In an age of social Darwinism, where the theory of natural selection was applied crudely to explain the rise and fall of peoples and nations, nativist demagogues found it easy to mobilize opposition to immigration on precisely these grounds, and the prevention of infection from without became a proxy for controls on immigration.[80]

It was not the first time that immigrants had been blamed for bringing disease into America. During the cholera epidemics of 1832 and 1849, the Irish had been singled out as carriers of contagion, because Protestants claimed that Catholicism bred poverty, corruption and disease. By the time of the 1866 cholera epidemic, such claims were rare, and the emphasis was not so much on spiritual corruption as on practical sanitary action.[81] Yet the growing acceptance of germ theories in the last two decades of the century made it possible to make a more direct connection between immigration and the importation of disease. Though vestiges of an older, more holistic view survived, immigration and infection became virtually synonymous. What appeared to be needed was a new form of quarantine that did not screen out all immigrants, but which appeared to discriminate objectively on the basis of science.[82]

The job of screening immigrants was given to the Marine Hospital Service (MHS, renamed the Public Health Service in 1912), a body that had been established originally to provide medical care for merchant seamen. In 1891 a federal law was passed forbidding entry into the USA of criminals and 'all idiots, insane persons, paupers or persons likely to become public charges, persons suffering from a loathsome or dangerous contagious disease'. The MHS was charged with identifying all those who were 'idiots', insane or diseased; they saw themselves, in the words of one official, as 'watchdogs at the gate'.[83] Although the inspection purported to be impartial, better-off immigrants were treated much more favourably than the poor. First- and second-class passengers on steamers arriving at New York were examined in the privacy of their own cabins, whilst those in steerage proceeded to the new immigration depot at Ellis Island (founded in 1892), which became the gateway to America for millions of immigrants over the coming years. In 1907 – the peak year for immigration into the USA – 1,285,000 immigrants entered the country, 866,660 (67.4 per cent) of whom arrived at Ellis Island.[84]

The massive number of immigrants meant that medical inspections were usually superficial. MHS officials would first check for physical disabilities, signs of heart trouble, or difficulty in breathing, then each immigrant faced an inspection of their eyes, throat, hands and scalp. The scalp was examined for signs of lice or scabs – the symptom of the contagious skin condition, fauvus – and the eyes for signs of trachoma.[85] These two diseases, especially trachoma, provided the focus for a great deal of anti-immigrant agitation around the turn of the century. Trachoma was known to be prevalent in the parts of Russia and Poland from which many Jewish refugees had fled, and was commonly seen as a predominantly Jewish disease. But the number of immigrants arriving with trachoma was probably very small. Medical inspections at European ports and the fairly rapid passage to America (seven to ten days by steamer) meant that it was rare for anyone to develop recognizable symptoms by the time they reached America. Only those with acute trachoma, contracted just before leaving or *en route*, normally appeared at Ellis Island. At this point, the symptoms would have been indistinguishable from many other common and less harmful eye infections like conjunctivitis.[86]

As an instrument of nativist policy, medical inspection proved less than successful. In 1911, a fairly typical year in terms of immigration, 749,642 aliens were examined on arrival in the USA, of whom 16,910 were certified for physical or mental defects. Of these, only 1,363 had 'loathsome or contagious diseases', the vast majority of which were said to be cases of trachoma. From 1890 to 1924, never more than 3 per cent of immigrants were returned to their ports of origin on medical grounds, and the average for the entire period was less than 1 per cent.[87] Although a few inspectors treated immigrants contemptuously, most were compassionate individuals who tried to perform their task in a professional and unbiased manner. The inspecting physicians always insisted that their medical assessments were kept separate from the final decision about whether to admit or deport an immigrant. The authorities were also keen that immigration depots be kept free from corruption, and officials pretending to be immigrants would occasionally pass through Ellis Island to see that all was in order.[88]

The system of medical inspection was an awkward compromise between nativist sentiment and modern scientific detachment. These ambiguities were also present in responses to outbreaks of disease among immigrant populations in American cities. Two cases show clearly the difference that race could make to official responses and public reactions. One was the death in 1900 of the Chinese immigrant Chick Gin from plague; the other was that of Mary Mallon ('Typhoid Mary'), an asymptomatic carrier of typhoid. The death of Chick Gin – one of several cases of bubonic plague among Chinese living in San Francisco – caused great alarm, and resulted in a quarantine being imposed around Chinatown. There appears to have been a consensus that the Chinese posed a special danger to Caucasian inhabitants on account of their connections with sources of infection and their allegedly unclean habits. Racial distinctiveness and residential segregation, sometimes voluntary, sometimes not, made the Chinese easy targets, and served to engender suspicion and fear.

When William Randolph Hearst's *New York American* magazine ran a story in 1909 entitled 'Typhoid Mary – The Most Harmless and yet the Most Dangerous Woman in America', it elicited a very different reaction. Mary Mallon, who was of Irish origin, had worked as a servant for several wealthy New York families, and had unwittingly spread typhoid in some of their households. Mary's role in the outbreaks was traced by the epidemiologist Dr George A. Soper, who recommended to his superiors at the city's Health Department that Mallon be arrested, so that her excreta could be subjected to laboratory analysis. She was kept in isolation at the Willard Parker Hospital for several months, during which she underwent bacteriological tests, and was afterwards sent to Riverside Hospital on North Border Island. Here, she was allowed to live alone, in some comfort, in a small bungalow. Sympathetic press coverage and offers of support emboldened Mary to sue for her release, which was eventually granted. Afterwards she went underground using an assumed name. Several more outbreaks of typhoid were traced to her before she was captured and compelled to spend the rest of her life in detention. Unlike

Chick Gin, Mary was an Irish Catholic, a group that now played an influential role in American life. On the whole, she elicited pity rather than fear.[89]

Mortality decline

At the end of the nineteenth century, mortality in the developed world began to decline, and, apart from the 1918–19 influenza pandemic, the trend has not been reversed. This transition in mortality raised life expectancy in many countries by more than ten years in only three decades, coinciding with a parallel increase in fertility. The 'mortality revolution' was most evident among children aged between one and fourteen years. Mortality among adults also fell, as did infant mortality, although the latter occurred somewhat later.[90] It is generally acknowledged that this decline in mortality was due primarily to the decline in infectious diseases. In some European countries, half the gains in life expectancy between 1871 and 1911 were due to the decline of infectious diseases, especially respiratory tuberculosis. Decreases in other respiratory ailments and in the prevalence of intestinal diseases also help to account for this decline, although the pattern varies from place to place and among different social groups.[91]

The fall in mortality from infectious diseases has often been referred to as the modern 'epidemiological transition' – a shift away from infectious diseases and towards death from chronic and degenerative diseases like heart disease and cancer. This seems to have coincided, in some countries, with changes in the incidence and duration of sickness. Although fewer people now died of respiratory diseases, for example, just as many were falling sick and living for longer with their complaints. In other words, the decline in mortality in the developed world was accompanied by an increase in the amount of time spent in sickness.[92] There was also a reversal of what demographers have termed the 'urban penalty'. Towns had hitherto been more unhealthy places than the countryside, but during the late nineteenth century, death rates fell more quickly in urban than in rural areas. The normal disadvantages of urban life were offset by sanitary improvements and a better standard of living.[93] Many rural areas were still untouched by sanitary reforms, and the eminent British hygienist E. A. Parkes likened the sanitary conditions of English villages to those in Africa and India.[94]

On most of these matters there is general agreement; what is far more contentious is *why* this decline in mortality occurred. Broadly speaking, historians are divided between those who support the position of Thomas McKeown and those who do not. McKeown observed that reductions in air-borne diseases such as tuberculosis accounted for most of the mortality decline between 1848 and 1971; mortality from water- and food-borne diseases showed the next largest reductions. He argued that medical advances could have contributed little to the decline of any of these categories, as mortality from most diseases, with the exception of smallpox and diphtheria, began to decline long before effective therapy or prophylactics became available. He acknowledged that sanitary and public health measures had some effect after the middle of the nineteenth century, but surmised that some diseases had begun to fall even before these measures were introduced. In any case, he argued, sanitary measures could account only for the fall in water-borne diseases, which constituted a comparatively small proportion of total mortality. And, as most people living in cities were still exposed to respiratory infections like tuberculosis, some other factor like resistance to infection must have accounted for the fall in mortality attributed to them. Economic and nutritional factors therefore seemed to be central to the question of mortality decline.[95]

Many historians nevertheless defend the traditional position that the chief cause of mortality decline was growing state involvement in public health: a view compatible with the recent experience of many who have worked in the developing world, where in some cases mortality reductions have occurred despite no substantial increase in the standard of living.[96] But McKeown's chief opponents in recent years have been the British historians Simon Szreter and Anne Hardy, who point to inconsistencies in his argument and make a strong case for the importance of sanitary and other public health measures. They argue that knowledge derived from bacteriology was used to redirect and improve the efficacy of public health, especially after 1895, when laboratories began to play a more significant role in diagnosis.[97]

Studies of other countries, such as imperial Germany, have also acknowledged the role of public health intervention, though stressing that nutritional improvements – brought about by rising wages and better-quality food – probably played a part in mortality decline. Reinhard Spree, for example, has shown that such benefits accrued chiefly to the 'new middle class' and the skilled working class, which suggests that income levels and standards of living had an important role.[98] Sumit Guha has also emphasized the role of nutritional factors in accounting for mortality decline, finding little evidence for

Szreter's contention that it was due primarily to social intervention. However, some of Guha's most recent work – on the British Army in India – suggests that better nutrition had no significant role in the reduction of death rates that occurred among British soldiers.[99]

The picture is rather a confusing one. On the one hand, there are few data to support McKeown's contention that nutrition was the chief factor in mortality decline before the second half of the nineteenth century, and he ignores the probable role played by vaccination against smallpox. Nor can we be certain that nutrition improved consistently between 1700 and 1850; indeed, most areas undergoing industrialization probably experienced a decline in nutritional standards in the short term, before reaping the long-term gains of higher real incomes. On the other hand, most of the convincing statistical evidence for the role of public health in lowering mortality exists for the twentieth century only. Recent studies showing the lengthening duration of sickness during the mortality transition also suggest that many respiratory ailments remained common, despite falling mortality. In view of the absence of effective treatment, it seems likely that better nutrition enabled people to live for longer with diseases that formerly would have killed them within a short space of time.[100] The debate is likely to continue, although these positions are far from exclusive. Better nutrition, for example, depends at least in part on better public health provision, such as measures to prevent the adulteration of food and drink. Nutrition and public health are influenced by such an array of common factors – income levels, work-place management, public policy, and so forth – that separation for the purposes of analysis can only be partial. All must be taken into account if we are to understand patterns of disease and mortality.[101]

7

Disease, War and Modernity

Health and medicine in an age of total war

By 1914 the mortality transition was well under way in most industrialized nations, with a substantial decline in deaths from infectious
diseases. The pattern in poorer countries is less easy to discern, but
there is little evidence to suggest any real improvement in the health
of the Asian or African colonies, for example. It was proving difficult
to export Western technologies of health to countries that lacked sufficient resources;[1] cultural differences, technical problems and vested
interests also served to frustrate developments of the kind that had
occurred in the West.[2] But after 1918 the health problems of these
colonies were viewed in a different light. Organizations such as the
League of Nations made available statistics with which to compare
the health status of different countries, and health became an index
of comparative development. This proved to be somewhat embarrassing to the colonial powers, which professed to bestow the benefits of civilization on the peoples over whom they ruled. The
Communist R. Palme Dutt complained that in India 'provision for
the most elementary needs of public hygiene, sanitation or health is
so low, in respect of the working masses in the towns or in the villages, as to be practically non-existent'.[3]

Like many others of his generation, Dutt looked to the socialized
health care system of the Soviet Union, which provided a model of
equity and social justice. The Soviet Union was also applauded by the
historian of medicine Henry Sigerist, a professor of medicine at Johns
Hopkins University. Sigerist spent two summers in the USSR, and

travelled widely; although he recognized the technological superiority of American medicine, he praised the efforts of the Soviet Union in bringing free health care to the people and in taking a more active role in the prevention of disease. Although the Soviet Union was still afflicted by epidemics of typhus, for example, considerable progress had been made in the prevention of other diseases such as smallpox, vaccination against which was made compulsory in 1919.[4]

But the main driving force behind health care provisions in nearly all countries was the conviction that health and efficiency were closely related. The reduction of disease and the promotion of better health were elements of a modernizing ideology shared by all industrialized nations, regardless of political complexion. All recognized that medicine and public health had a vital role to play in the rational management of the state's human resources.[5] Although they differed over how best to organize public health and on questions of entitlement, all countries began to take a more active interest in preserving the health of their populations. Insurance schemes were established with state aid, to ensure that at least some working people had access to health care, and in most countries provisions were made for maternal and infant welfare.[6] Proponents of scientific management promoted mental and physical health in the name of efficiency, leading to greater emphasis on health and safety in the work place. The rapid expansion in literacy from the late nineteenth century also meant that education had a greater role to play in the prevention of disease. Schools, news media and posters loudly proclaimed that the maintenance of health was one of the most important duties of the patriotic citizen.[7] Indeed, one of the main reasons for the rapid expansion in health provisions in many countries was the threat and, ultimately, the reality of war. This has led some to suggest that health policy was determined largely by the demands of twentieth-century warfare. As Richard Titmuss commented, rather sardonically, 'The aims and content of social policy, both in peace and war, are . . . determined – at least to a substantial extent – by how far the cooperation of the masses is essential to the prosecution of war.'[8] The total wars of 1914–18 and 1939–45 required the participation of the entire adult population, either as service personnel or as workers. It was not only soldiers who needed to keep 'fighting fit', but every man and woman who participated in the war effort.[9]

One of the greatest problems facing the armed forces during the two world wars was disease. In all the major wars of the eighteenth and nineteenth centuries, disease had claimed far more lives than injuries in battle. The First World War was the first major conflict in which this ratio was reversed, and in which deaths from battle injuries exceeded those from disease. This was due in part to the greater destructive power of modern weapons, but even more to measures taken to check the spread of infectious disease. On the Western Front, disease was effectively controlled through sanitary discipline and a battery of modern technologies including mobile laboratories, inoculation against typhoid, and tetanus antitoxin. Outside Western Europe it was quite a different story: typhus ravaged armies and civilian populations on the Eastern Front, while malaria, dysentery and other diseases took a deadly toll in Macedonia, East Africa and the Middle East. The movement of troops and refugees at the end of the war was also one of the reasons for the pandemic of influenza that killed in excess of 30 million people around the globe.

Wartime experiences helped to determine the ways in which disease was controlled during the next few decades. In the European colonies, and also in many parts of the developed world, certain infectious diseases were tackled in great, military-style campaigns. One such was the campaign to rid the Belgian Congo of sleeping sickness. Stung by widespread criticism of their misgovernment of the Congo, Belgian colonial officials came to regard medical and public health programmes as a kind of compensation for the hardships caused by colonization. But rather than attempt to improve health as a whole, the colonial administration settled on a single disease – sleeping sickness – that caused a great deal of suffering and economic disruption. Using a combination of public health measures, chemotherapy and resettlement, the Belgian authorities seem to have made some impact upon sleeping sickness, which began to decline by the 1930s. But it was a campaign that created a good deal of resentment. Many Congolese were reluctant to come forward for what they regarded as intrusive and painful therapies, and were particularly angry about forced resettlement. This was typical of many of the disease 'campaigns' conducted in the African colonies, which often failed to enlist the support of indigenous peoples.[10]

In many colonies, as well as in independent countries, the fight against disease was now assisted by the Rockefeller Foundation (RF). A philanthropic body established by the American oil magnate John D. Rockefeller, the RF pumped vast amounts of money into medical research and the reform of public health and medicine. Some critics claim that its intentions were not entirely benevolent, and that it regarded support for scientific medicine as an investment in the economic and moral order of Western capitalism.[11] Its activities, especially in the developing world, have thus been viewed as imperialistic. The RF began its involvement in disease prevention with a programme against hookworm in the southern USA, but it was not long before it began to look beyond America. In 1913 an International Health Division, or 'Health Commission', was established to carry the work of the RF into Latin America and the colonies of the European empires. At first, the Health Commission concentrated on hookworm, and had notable successes in Mexico and the West Indies, for example;[12] but by the 1920s it had extended its purview to include malaria and yellow fever. For instance, the RF co-operated with officials in Rio de Janeiro to drain and oil the breeding sites of mosquitoes, producing a marked drop in the incidence of malaria. The RF also sponsored research into diseases such as yellow fever – its general approach being to tackle the problem of disease using the latest and best technologies.

This type of health care, based on Western models and provided by Western or Western-trained physicians, sometimes displaced broader-based notions of health care delivered by personnel with less formal training.[13] Critics have therefore claimed that these 'vertical' health programmes were pursued to the detriment of many poor people, whose basic needs were ignored.[14] And what of the RF's imperialistic ambitions? There was almost certainly a desire to represent America and American capitalism in the best possible light, but the connection was often a loose one. As well as areas like Latin America with which the USA had close economic ties, the RF supported projects in areas like West Africa in which the USA had little economic interest.[15] Also, in many of the European colonies, RF initiatives were left to wither due to lack of financial support or were subsumed into the existing infrastructure, losing their distinctive identity.[16]

The very idea of a 'campaign' against disease suggests that disease prevention took the form of a war between man and microbe. In a sense this is true, but the militaristic language employed by doctors was more often a way of drawing attention to their work than an accurate description of it. Disease prevention was, in many respects, more sophisticated than this. It was increasingly recognized that many diseases had complex transmission cycles, and that it was necessary to view disease ecologically. This was evident in the case of parasitic diseases from an early stage, especially those for which an insect vector had been identified. Between the wars, research on diseases such as malaria revealed even more about the nature of the life cycle of parasites and their hosts, and the conditions under which they thrived. This new information made it possible to target preventive efforts more effectively, and measures increasingly aimed to break the transmission cycle of disease.[17] New ideas also entered medicine from population ecology: concepts of 'equilibrium', dynamics, evolution and 'webs of causation' all affecting thinking on the prevention of disease.[18]

Bacteriologists were also beginning to acknowledge the complexity of epidemics. Faced with the challenge of new and unpredictable epidemics like the outbreaks of cerebro-spinal fever that occurred among new recruits in the First World War, they began to distrust knowledge obtained solely from 'artificial' environments such as the laboratory. It became evident that an epidemic amounted to more than just the 'invasion' of germs, and that the spread of an illness depended heavily on such factors as population density and resistance to disease. Bacteriologists thus came to think of epidemics as disturbances of a natural equilibrium. In the case of cerebro-spinal fever or even cholera, for example, there seemed to be a balance between host and pathogen, with epidemics occurring only when it was disturbed.[19] The restoration of equilibrium, rather than complete eradication, therefore became the goal of many of those working in public health between the wars.

However, by the end of the Second World War, the eradication of disease once again seemed like a real possibility. Disease was a major problem during the war, just as in previous conflicts, but it was managed far more effectively than before. Not only were there fewer deaths from disease than from battle injuries, but fewer admissions to hospital. Better understanding of disease causation and more attention to medicine on the part of combatant officers were probably the key factors. Many commanders who entered the armed forces between the wars had imbibed ideas of man management then current in business and public administration, and these uniformly emphasized the importance of maintaining a healthy work-force. Greater efforts were also made to train combatant officers and NCOs in the rudiments of hygiene and sanitation. But there were significant differences between – and sometimes within – the opposing forces. In the Western Desert of Egypt, for example, British-led forces were able to keep infectious disease to a level three times lower than among the Germans and Italians. Far more attention was paid to sanitation in the Allied armies than in the Afrika Korps, which disdained such matters as beneath its dignity.[20]

But Rommel, the commander of the Afrika Korps, was not typical of German commanders. Like most of their Allied counterparts, they acknowledged the threat from disease, and for the most part were aware of the best means of preventing it. Doctors were now equipped with a modern therapeutic arsenal that included sulphonamide drugs, which were effective against a range of bacterial diseases, as well as new, more effective antimalarials; the antibiotic penicillin was also widely available from 1944. Penicillin revolutionized the treatment of many common infectious diseases, as well as the management of wound infections and burns. The fact that it was developed and used exclusively by the Allies meant that they had a significant advantage over their Axis counterparts, who suffered severely from wound infections. The insecticide DDT was also used from the winter of 1943, with devastating effect in the case of arthropod-borne diseases like typhus and malaria.[21] Once again, doctors began to dream of conquering disease.[22] We shall now look in more detail at several diseases – including malaria – whose history was closely intertwined with that of the two world wars.

The influenza pandemic of 1918–1919

Outbreaks of influenza are normal occurrences in most parts of the world and, though often fatal among the more vulnerable sections of society, rarely result in many fatalities. But some strains of the influenza virus – like the 'A' strain – are far more deadly, and are responsible for most of the major epidemics. This virus normally exists in non-human hosts such as birds, and spreads only occasionally to humans.[23] But when it does, the result is often catastrophic, as in the case of the influenza pandemic of 1918–19. The pandemic began in early 1918, possibly in the Midwestern United States, and from there it spread rapidly to Europe, with a serious early outbreak in Spain – hence the epithet 'Spanish Flu'.[24] By May, influenza had reached Asia and North Africa, and had appeared in Australia by July. A second, more deadly wave began in August, possibly originating in France, and spread rapidly around the world, carried by armies returning from the Western Front. A third, less virulent wave occurred in the winter of 1918 and spring of 1919. The true number of deaths due to the pandemic can never be known, as most occurred in countries where the reporting of deaths was rudimentary. But it has recently been estimated that the total is close to 30 million, making the pandemic the most deadly since the Black Death.[25]

When the flu arrived in Europe, conditions were ideal for the rapid transmission of the disease. On the Western Front, soldiers were crowded together in cramped trenches, and their immune systems were lowered by exposure to the elements and hard fighting. Although the armies had been very successful in preventing the spread of disease, the measures normally taken to check diseases like dysentery failed in the case of a far more contagious disease like influenza. In the British Army alone there were 138,782 admissions to hospital from influenza on the Western Front, compared with

28,980 the year before. Around 5 per cent of cases admitted in 1918 were fatal, most of the deaths being due to pneumonic complications. Influenza was also rife among British troops in Macedonia and Egypt, to which it was probably carried from France. In Mesopotamia, the disease broke out in June among a group of men returning from leave in India. Even though influenza victims were isolated from other sick patients, they would probably have spread the disease before they were diagnosed and confined. Diagnosis itself was a problem, as the causal organism had not been identified, and it proved difficult to distinguish the early symptoms of influenza from those of the common cold.[26]

The mortality in some of the countries affected by influenza is truly staggering. In India the death toll exceeded 17 million: a mortality rate of around sixty per thousand, which was substantially higher than the plague epidemics of the 1890s. But compared with its response to plague, the government's response to influenza was muted. Influenza was already widely disseminated in the West, and there was no international pressure upon the British administration to take measures to control the disease, as had been the case with plague. Perhaps stunned by the lack of success which other countries had had in tackling the disease, the government viewed the outbreak with a degree of fatalism, and was heavily criticized by nationalists for its inaction.[27]

But in some cases prompt action saved many lives. In the Caribbean, for example, some islands of the British West Indies escaped with comparatively few deaths from influenza. Here, the imposition of quarantine may have played a part, as well as the depressing effects of the war upon maritime trade. The islands may also have been infected by a less virulent strain of the disease. But poverty also appears to have been a factor in mortality in the Caribbean islands, as most deaths occurred among the very poor, especially among immigrant labourers from the East Indies.[28] Widespread poverty and its effects upon the immune system may also explain the massive death toll in India and among refugees in war-torn areas. The mixture of pathogens was another common problem. Influenza claimed many lives among refugees in northern Persia at the end of the war, partly because the population was already weakened by malaria.[29] Less easy to explain is the age/sex profile of the victims, which included an unusually high number of men aged between fifteen and forty. The overcrowded and confined conditions endured by conscript soldiers and workers may go some way to accounting for this, although the same pattern seems to have been evident in many countries not mobilized for war.

The medical response to the epidemic in all countries was desperate. Many assumed, falsely, that the disease was caused by a bacterium, and urged the use of antiseptics to prevent the spread of germs. Another simple precaution taken by health personnel was the wearing of gauze masks. This was a sensible measure, but it probably had little effect, because the influenza virus is so small that it can easily spread through fabric. Using the same bacteriological model, there were also numerous attempts to develop vaccines against the disease. One of the most famous was the vaccine developed by Dr Timothy Leary of Tufts Medical College near Boston. It was distributed free to physicians in badly affected localities such as San Francisco, and by November as many as 18,000 people in the city had been inoculated. The vaccination programme coincided with a decline in the disease, and this led many to believe that the vaccine was beneficial. But neither this vaccine, nor the many others that were developed in the USA and other countries, actually had any positive effect.[30]

The popular response to influenza varied enormously from one country to another, and within countries too. Some fascinating insights into how the epidemic was interpreted by quite different cultures are to be found in Terence Ranger's study of the influenza epidemic in the British colony of Southern Rhodesia. Existing belief systems proved remarkably resilient, despite the initial shock. European mission stations recovered sufficiently to send out 'salted' converts to provide care and relief, as they would normally at times of crisis, and some believed that the epidemic might win future converts. Europeans also continued to have faith in traditional remedies like castor oil and mustard powder, as well as patent medicines, even though there was little objective evidence that they worked. Most Africans, too, believed that the epidemic could be comprehended and controlled by traditional means, and consequently there were few new converts for the missionaries. Some believed that they had saved themselves by using traditional African medicines, while others resorted to witchcraft or flocked to newly established 'spirit churches'. On the whole, Africans seem to have relied rather more on spiritual measures than on medicines, especially those of the European variety.[31]

The influenza epidemic thus revealed the inherent difficulties of popularizing Western medicine. If Western medicine had little effect in treating a powerful disease like influenza, then confidence in the entire system could easily be shaken. It is worth bearing this in mind when considering the spread of Western medicine and disease concepts around the world, for virtually nowhere was Western medicine's dominance complete. The pattern in nearly all countries into which Western medicine was introduced was the emergence of a pluralistic system of medicine and of multiple ways of conceptualizing disease, including the persistence of spiritual ideas.

Typhus

By the late nineteenth century, typhus was confined largely to the east of Europe, the Middle East and North Africa. Countries like Germany, which had formerly had many cases of typhus, now had very few cases indigenous to the country, and typhus was seen almost exclusively as a disease of immigrants, and specifically as a Jewish disease.[32] But until 1909, fear of importation rested on little more than circumstantial evidence. In that year Charles Nicolle, Director of the Pasteur Institute in Tunis, demonstrated that the body louse was the vector of typhus. In 1910, during an epidemic of typhus in Mexico, Howard Taylor Ricketts found small bacteria in the blood of typhus victims, as well as in lice and their faeces. But before he could confirm his observations, he was taken ill with typhus and died; as a mark of respect, the genus of the typhus germ was named after him.[33]

These new discoveries raised interest in typhus to a new pitch, which coincided with the outbreak of the First World War. Germany and the central European nations feared that typhus would spread from its endemic centres in the East. Typhus was rife in other theatres of the war too, such as the Balkans and the Middle East, and posed a danger to the European troops who were stationed there. It also seemed likely that the disease would be imported with colonial troops and labour detachments to the Western Front. Conditions on the Western Front were, indeed, very favourable to the spread of typhus, as the trenches dug from the end of 1914 were infested with lice. The response of most of the armies was broadly similar, and followed precedents laid down before the war, such as the medical screening of migrants from suspect areas and the isolation and disinfection regimes established by medical volunteers during the Balkan Wars of 1912 and 1913.[34] In Germany, one of the main concerns was typhus among prisoners from the Eastern Front. By March 1915 there were 500,000 Russian POWs in Germany, 27,500 of whom had contracted typhus. There were epidemics in twenty-five of the forty-one POW camps, and the prisoners were sealed off as far as possible to prevent the disease from spreading to German soldiers and civilians. The high death toll among POWs was widely criticized outside Germany, but the Germans protested that the epidemics were not the result of conditions at the camps but of high rates of infection among Russian soldiers prior to capture. Nevertheless, the outbreaks roused the German authorities to action, and a strict regime of delousing was instituted at the camps: new inmates were bathed, disinfected and kept under observation for twenty-one days.[35]

It has been suggested that German precautions against typhus were more authoritarian and more oriented to mass delousing than those of the British, for example.[36] But this does not hold true in all cases. The British war effort in the Middle East depended heavily on local workers in the form of Native Labour Detachments, and many thousands were employed (often against their will) in the construction of water pipes stretching from the Canal Zone of Egypt through the Sinai Peninsula to Palestine. Having arrived from Egypt, the labourers were put through what resembled an industrial assembly line, where they were shaved, washed and fumigated, along with their possessions. There was a good deal of resentment among the labourers, but the measures did help to prevent a serious epidemic of typhus.[37] Most soldiers, however, needed little encouragement to take precautions against the disease, and willingly took advantage of mobile laundries and steam-baths where they were available and rubbed anti-lice powder into their clothing. Ridding one's undergarments of lice became one of the daily rituals of life in several theatres of the war.[38]

After the war, typhus came under the scrutiny of the Health Organization of the newly established League of Nations (LNHO), the Rockefeller Foundation and the League of Red Cross Societies.[39] The LNHO saw the prevention of epidemic disease as a vital precondition of economic regeneration, and aimed to create a permanent system of 'sanitary defence' against Poland and Russia, where the number of typhus cases was rising alarmingly. The British statesman Lord Balfour warned of 'a calamity which, following hard on war, seems almost worse than war itself'.[40] The calamity was to be averted using the same techniques as in wartime. Delousing was still the dominant strategy, and the League's office in Warsaw was concerned almost exclusively with the disinfection of refugees, rather than the provision of protection and assistance. Yet organizations like the RF also poured large sums of money into research in eastern Europe, helping countries to construct hospitals and bacteriological institutes in cities such as Warsaw and Lvov. The latter institute, under Rudolf Weigl, became a major centre of research on typhus, and attracted scientists from all over the world. However, the RF's work in eastern Europe stood in marked contrast to its attitude to Soviet Russia, which received no money for research, or for relief during the famine and typhus epidemic of 1921. The RF, which sought to foster

American capitalism, was disinclined to give any money to a Communist country like the Soviet Union.[41]

The measures taken against typhus were part and parcel of international efforts to create and maintain homogenous nation-states. Sanitary policing provided a means of reinforcing their borders and of restricting the movement of populations. But in Nazi Germany, medical inspection and delousing began to be used as a pretext for exclusion of Jews and other 'undesirable' ethnic groups. Exclusion soon turned to eradication, as the control of insect parasites became intertwined with the regime's genocidal ambitions. It was said that typhus was transmitted by 'nomadic' races like Gypsies and Jews, and the eradication of parasites provided a justification for the eradication of these racial groups. The sedentary populations of lands to Germany's east were also said to harbour lice and disease, and Nazi doctors such as Heinz Zeiss argued that if Germany was to fulfil its 'racial destiny' and obtain *Lebensraum*, it would have to eradicate these sources of infection.

The rise in cases of typhus in Germany during the war provided all the justification that was needed to put such a policy into action. In 1939 there were virtually no cases in Germany, but typhus soon became as prevalent as in the previous war. Following the invasion of Poland, there were a number of outbreaks among POWs and civilians captured for forced labour. These groups were blamed for importing the disease into Germany, and became the targets of coercive delousing measures; fear of infection became a pretext for isolating Jews and for subjecting them to humiliating disinfections. The German army also employed mass delousing to protect itself from typhus after the invasion of Russia in 1941, although it became increasingly difficult to sustain because of technical and organizational problems.[42] A simpler solution was at hand: the SS leader Heinrich Himmler declared that 'Anti-semitism is exactly the same as delousing. Getting rid of lice is not a question of ideology, it is a matter of cleanliness.'[43] Indeed, the same gas – Zyklon (hydrocyanic acid) – was used both as a disinfectant and as a poison in the gas chambers of camps such as Auschwitz.[44]

The inmates of the concentration camps were also used to test new vaccines against typhus. The development of a vaccine had been hampered for many years by the fact that Rickettsial organisms could not be grown in sufficient quantities outside living cells. In 1937 Harold R. Cox of the US Public Health Service found that the organisms grew easily in the yolks of hen's eggs, which simplified vaccine production and made it commercially feasible for the first time. The League of Nations soon came to see vaccination as the only effective means by which typhus could be controlled in regions such as eastern

Europe.[45] Vaccine production was accorded a great deal of importance in Germany because of its fear of infection from the East. The invasion of the Soviet Union increased the sense of urgency, and trials with the vaccine began at Buchenwald concentration camp. Of every twenty people forced to receive vaccinations, six died.[46] The vaccine was not widely available in the German army until 1943, too late for the campaign in North Africa, but of some use for the remainder of the war on the Eastern Front. In the USA, clinical trials and mass production proceeded more quickly. By 1940 the Rockefeller Institute had produced a vaccine that was roughly 90 per cent effective, and most Allied soldiers received it from 1942.[47]

But vaccination was not the only means used to control typhus during the war. Most forces employed a combination of measures, which included vaccination and mass delousing of civilians and POWs. Disinfection of POWs proceeded in much the same way as in the First World War, with all new inmates being stripped, bathed and fumigated before admission to the camps. With Allied armies, however, these measures lacked the sinister overtones of typhus prevention on the Eastern Front. With the exception of Vichy North Africa, the Allies encountered little resistance to delousing, and normally sought the co-operation of civilians. In Italy, where an epidemic of typhus broke out in Naples in December 1943, there was actually great enthusiasm for delousing measures. The Naples outbreak was the first occasion on which the insecticide DDT was used on a large scale. Such was the fear of typhus that the people of Naples formed long queues at disinfecting stations, and armed guards had to be posted to prevent the stations from being mobbed.[48]

During the final phase of the war in the West, there were fears that typhus might spread from eastern to western Europe. The sharp rise in typhus in Germany during the war, and the revelation that it was rife in German POW and concentration camps, suggested the strong possibility that typhus might spread with refugees and released POWs. Measures for the prevention of typhus were directed by a representative of the US Typhus Control Commission, which had guided measures in Naples and other areas under Allied control. On his orders, all surviving inmates of POW and concentration camps were deloused and subjected to quarantine until all cases had been detected and isolated. A cordon sanitaire was also established along Germany's western border to prevent the spread of typhus and other infectious diseases from reaching uninfected parts of the continent. With the exception of a few isolated cases, these measures proved successful. Once the war was over, mass delousing with DDT in Germany and eastern Europe brought typhus quickly under control.[49]

Malaria

Ronald Ross once remarked that the history of war and the history of malaria were inseparable.[50] War favours the spread of malaria in several ways. The movement of large numbers of troops and civilians introduces parasites and vectors into areas formerly free of them; the destruction of dams and levies causes low-lying areas to be flooded, providing ideal breeding grounds for mosquitoes. These factors were evident to some degree during the two world wars, and in some cases had lasting consequences for the regions concerned.[51] Malaria was also one of the greatest causes of sickness in campaigns fought in the Mediterranean and in tropical regions, and in some cases had a devastating effect upon military operations.

During the First World War, malaria was a major problem during campaigns in Macedonia, East Africa, Mesopotamia and Palestine. Anti-malaria measures in these theatres ranged from large-scale drainage to localized mosquito destruction and quinine prophylaxis. The British and French armies undertook extensive drainage works in parts of Macedonia, the Egyptian Canal Zone and Mesopotamia, for example. In the latter, the drainage of cities like Basra was linked to Britain's imperial ambitions, the aim being to make the city habitable for Europeans once the war had ended. These drainage schemes were moderately successful, but their contribution to malaria prevention was limited. They offered no solution to malaria on mobile campaigns – such as in Palestine – or in mountainous areas like Macedonia. In 1918, when British forces pushed the Turks into the malarious Jordan valley, half the British force, which numbered some 40,000, was admitted to hospital with malaria; in the same year, 25,000 malaria cases were sent back to Britain from Macedonia.[52] A similar state of affairs existed in the French army, which, following public criticism, dispatched a 'Mission Anti-Paludique' to Macedonia.[53] Part of the problem was that quinine was very unpopular with the troops, owing to the nausea that it sometimes induced and rumours that it caused sexual impotence.

Nevertheless, the French mission was determined to make quinine prophylaxis a priority. Up to 1916 it had not been strictly enforced, but the tighter discipline imposed by the Mission brought about a great reduction in malaria. Admissions to hospital fell from 390 per thousand troops in 1916 to 157 per thousand in 1917 and to 63 per thousand in 1918.[54] The remarkable difference between French and British rates of infection may be explained by the fact that the British were deployed in a more heavily infected area than the French;

however, the French figures should be regarded with some scepticism, and may possibly have been exaggerated. The Germans – who had used quinine prophylaxis with some success in their colonies before the war – found it of little use in theatres such as East Africa, for example.[55] The British experience with quinine was also disappointing: some officers in Macedonia observed that soldiers fell sick despite having taken quinine, and declared that it was an 'absolute failure'. A report by the Medical Research Committee in 1917 concluded that there was no strong evidence that quinine had lessened the incidence of malaria. This represented a major professional victory for Ross, whose much vaunted mosquito brigades were to form the basis of malaria control in the British army for the remainder of the war, and for long afterwards in many British colonies.[56]

In British India, where opinion had previously been divided over the use of quinine, the focus of anti-malaria work after the end of the war was largely on mosquito destruction and drainage.[57] In colonial Malaya, too, the British continued and extended their pre-war policy of controlling malaria primarily through environmental management. Quinine was distributed at schools, police stations and dispensaries, but was regarded as subsidiary to measures such as drainage, the concreting of channels, the spraying of larvicides, and the introduction of larvae-eating fish. These measures were said to be the main reason for the falling death rate, which dropped from just over fifty-one per thousand in 1902 to just below twenty per thousand by 1933. Running alongside these expensive environmental measures was a campaign of education, which aimed to encourage individuals to take precautions against malaria, including mosquito nets and screens over windows and doors.[58]

Singapore was one of the few success stories in the colonies: in Bengal, Mauritius and Ceylon, there were devastating epidemics of malaria that led to criticism from nationalists.[59] The Ceylonese epidemic was probably the most serious of these, affecting some 1.5 million people out of a total population of only 5.5 million. The epidemic occurred largely as a result of the failure of the south-west and north-east monsoons, which decreased the flow of water to the normally fast-flowing waters of the wet zone. Water began to stagnate, making ideal breeding conditions for malaria-bearing mosquitoes. The immunity of the population had also been lowered by the impact of the world-wide economic depression. However, the government was blamed not so much for causing the epidemic as for the inadequacy of its response. Some critics felt that it had failed to act early enough to provide medical care and other relief. These criticisms were not wholly fair, but they led to a major shift in colonial health policy. Expenditure on health increased markedly after 1935, with due attention to primary health care as well as to sanitary and anti-epidemic measures.

The persistence of malaria in many areas scotched all hopes of eradicating the disease, and malariologists came to think in more complex ways, which borrowed ideas from the new discipline of ecology. They began to think of controlling malaria by tilting the ecological balance away from parasites and their vectors, in favour of human beings. These principles underlay the successful campaign against malaria in Italy between the wars. Italy posed a real challenge, as malaria was present in approximately one-third of municipal districts, despite some earlier success in controlling the disease with quinine. Post-war measures against malaria in Italy owed a good deal to the influence of Dr L. W. Hackett, head of the RF's Malaria Experimental Station in Rome. Established in 1924, the station was run jointly by the RF and the Italian Department of Public Health. Hackett worked closely with an Italian malariologist named Alberto Missiroli, and both took an experimental attitude towards malaria control, informed by findings from local studies. Hackett saw malaria as 'protean in its character' and 'diverse in its local manifestations'. He and Missiroli thus recommended a variety of measures to tip the ecological balance, including drainage, land reclamation, quinine prophylaxis, and the destruction of mosquitoes, making extensive use of the new insecticide 'Paris Green'. As a result, malaria mortality fell considerably.[60]

During the Second World War mosquito destruction was still a common means of controlling malaria, but it was a realistic option only around encampments, and was of little use to armies on the move. Most of the combatant nations therefore began to turn their attention to prophylaxis, which was made considerably more difficult as the main source of quinine was closed to the Allies at least after the Japanese invaded Java. The Allies therefore had an incentive to develop synthetic substitutes for quinine, one such being the drug Atebrin, also known as Mepacrine. German chemists had synthesized the drug in the early 1930s, but the Germans had sold the formula to the Americans. Although they had omitted vital details, it had enabled the Americans and the British to synthesize small quantities of Mepacrine before the start of the war. After the fall of Java, the drug went into mass production, and it was made available to front-line units from 1942.

At first, Mepacrine was just as unpopular as quinine. Medical officers admitted that it sometimes had mild side-effects, but the real problem was that few could be bothered to take it regularly. Mepacrine also suffered from the same stigma as quinine, in that it was thought to cause sexual impotence. Such reservations were not easily overcome, despite a concerted effort to popularize the drug and to give instructions on its use. Special 'Atrebrin days' were organized in theatres like North Africa in 1943, when troops were bombarded with leaflets, broadcasts and lectures. Ultimately, the key factor in preventing malaria – as in the case of many other diseases – was discipline. The fate of the British-led Fourteenth Army in Burma provides an excellent example. After their long retreat from Burma in 1942, British and Indian forces were dispirited and riddled with malaria. Subsequent operations in the Arakan region of Burma in 1943 also produced heavy malaria casualties, with infection rates nearing 100 per cent. In the last three months of that year, no fewer than 18,000 British malaria cases were evacuated from India. The commander of Fourteenth Army, Field Marshal William Slim, was determined that the disease should be brought under control. Having seen that Australian forces had successfully used Mepacrine while fighting the Japanese in New Guinea, he instituted a strict regime of anti-malaria discipline, sacking any commander who refused to enforce it. Refusing to take Mepacrine soon became a military offence. Treatment units for malaria were also established near the front line, enabling many men to be treated quickly and returned to battle. The result was a sharp decline in the number of malaria casualties, with admissions to hospital falling from 60 per cent of total strength in 1943 to around 10 per cent in 1945. The death rate was also greatly reduced, and from May 1944 to November 1945 there were only six deaths out of around 14,000 cases. This gave Slim's army an advantage over the Japanese, whose own discipline and drug supplies were collapsing as they retreated. Blood samples taken from Japanese POWs at the end of the campaign showed an infection rate as high as 50 per cent.[61]

But the control of malaria in Burma and other theatres of war was not due entirely to chemo-prophylaxis. DDT also played a major role, just as it had in the case of typhus in Italy. In Burma and Italy it was used extensively from the malaria season of 1944, being sprayed from the ground, as troops advanced, as well as from the air. One important discovery was that buildings sprayed with DDT remained lethal to mosquitoes for up to two months, which drastically cut the time it took to fumigate forward areas. Thanks to DDT, the Allies managed to prevent a major epidemic of malaria in Italy. As the Germans retreated, they had deliberately flooded low-lying areas to impede the Allies' progress, leading some to fear a serious epidemic. But confidence in DDT was such, according to one report, that it would 'convert a hopelessly insanitary area into a health resort'.[62] As we shall see in the next chapter, this excitement did not abate with the end of hostilities, and for many malariologists it offered the first real prospect of eradicating the disease.

Sexually transmitted diseases

'War breeds vice and venereal', observed one British general in 1930.[63] It was taken for granted that the onset of war – particularly a large war – would lead to a rise in what were then termed 'venereal diseases', principally gonorrhoea and syphilis. The rise in venereal infection that normally accompanied wars – both among soldiers and civilians – was well known, and VD had been a constant drain on the armed forces of all nations whether in peace or war. But public concern over VD was not simply an expression of fears about military fitness – VD symbolized wider threats to what was perceived as the 'natural order'. Soldiers and prostitutes had always been regarded as dangers to society, even in times of peace, and during the nineteenth century there were numerous attempts to confine them within well-regulated enclaves. The soldier's regiment aspired to take the place of his family, and to become a self-contained unit.[64] At the same time, beginning with regulations imposed in France, a wave of controversial legislation was passed across Europe and in the colonies to regulate prostitution.[65] In Britain and its colonies the notorious and short-lived Contagious Diseases Acts of the 1860s concentrated solely on the regulation of prostitution in military towns.[66] In France, regulation was more widespread, with all prostitutes being forced to ply their trade in brothels known as *maisons de tolérance*, where they were medically inspected and forcibly treated if necessary. The aim was to prevent prostitutes from walking the streets and corrupting the rest of society.[67]

The First World War threatened to throw these arrangements into chaos. Troops would be removed from the confines of their military encampments and, in the eyes of the military, would be 'exposed' to infection from 'unclean' women. Soldiers were also widely regarded as carriers of venereal and other infections, and their morals, if they had any, were deemed to be of a low order. Women were said to be at risk whenever an army passed through, and prostitutes, who had perhaps been confined to licensed houses, would walk the streets looking for business. It was also feared that soldiers, having contracted disease from prostitutes, would spread it to their families, and that it would be passed down – in the case of congenital syphilis – to subsequent generations. The race would thus become degenerate and enfeebled.[68]

Such anxieties were present in all countries touched by the war, but the way in which each dealt with venereal disease depended greatly on national traditions and political circumstances. The French continued to maintain a system of licensed brothels that received periodic medical inspection. There is no evidence that this had any effect on the incidence of venereal diseases, and by the end of the war there had been almost one million admissions to hospital for VD in the French army.[69] But the system kept prostitutes off the streets, and allayed anxieties about public decency. Many within the armed forces also favoured this system because troops were confined to areas that could easily be policed. If they attended regulated brothels, they were less likely to contract disease and fall into bad company. The same line of reasoning existed in imperial Germany, which also had a tradition of registering prostitutes. During the war, as VD increased, the regulation of prostitutes became more stringent, and their medical examination became the responsibility of military physicians. A system of regulated brothels was also to be found in German-occupied France and Belgium.[70]

Britain and the United States approached the problem rather differently. The British army used regulated brothels overseas, but not at home, as the purity lobby and women's groups were strongly opposed to a system that degraded and oppressed women, and which seemed to encourage immorality.[71] By 1918 such organizations had also brought about a shift in policy in some overseas theatres of war. Much to the chagrin of the French authorities, the tolerated houses were placed out of bounds to British troops. In Egypt, British and Islamic purity campaigners joined forces in an extraordinary campaign to close all brothels, drug dens and drinking houses. The 'purification' of Alexandria and Cairo resulted in so many arrests that new prisons had to be built to accommodate thousands of prostitutes, pimps and drug-dealers.[72] The US army was also forbidden to use brothels in France. American Progressives linked modern ideas of efficiency with older ideals of morality and cleanliness. The American government was thus determined that their army would be the cleanest in France and a beacon of light amidst the corruption of the Old World.[73]

The regulation of prostitution was not the only means by which the authorities attempted to control VD. Church leaders, purity organizations and even some within the armed forces continued to recommend chastity as the only sure way of preventing venereal infection.[74] After all, control over mind and body was deemed an essential preparation for the battlefield.[75] But these appeals to chastity sat uneasily beside more technical solutions to the problem of VD. Syphilis could now be treated effectively with the drug Salvarsan, an arsenical compound developed by Paul Ehrlich in 1909; an improved version, Neosalvarsan, appeared in 1912. In 1906 the Paris-based bacteriologists Elie Metchnikoff and Émile Roux claimed that VD could be prevented by applying calomel ointment to the sexual organs after intercourse.[76] The Germans began to use chemical prophylaxis well before the start of the war, and credited it with bringing down the rate of venereal infection. The official policy during the war was to make prophylaxis freely available, but not officially to sanction it, for fear of offending public opinion: the distribution of prophylactics from vending machines had been denounced in some quarters as a 'moral, religious and national threat'.[77] The French, New Zealand, Australian, Canadian and American armies also embraced prophylaxis, but in Britain there was more resistance. Both the Anglican Church and the National Council for the Combatting of Venereal Disease were firmly opposed to the measure. Chemical prophylaxis was also unpopular with soldiers, as the apparatus was installed in urinals, and disinfection had to be performed in full view of other men. The system was also poorly enforced, although it probably made little difference, as there is no hard evidence to suggest that disinfection was effective.[78] The only truly effective prophylactics were condoms, but their use was limited because of moral considerations.

After the end of the First World War, debates over the prevention of VD continued along much the same lines, with a clear divide between 'moralists' and 'pragmatists'. In Weimar Germany, for example, the chief opponents of prophylaxis were the Catholic and Protestant churches, social purity organizations and the conservative wing of the women's movement. These organizations maintained that chastity and early marriage were the only sure means of preventing VD. But health educators criticized their approach as unworldly and ineffective. Although most proponents of prophylaxis did not approve of sexual license, they saw themselves as realists who recognized that many people would not abstain from sex before marriage. During the 1920s they had the ear of government, which in 1927 abolished all remaining restrictions on the sale of prophylactics. The Weimar government openly endorsed prophylaxis, and many more vending machines were installed in public toilets. The 1927 Act also abolished state-regulated prostitution, and replaced it with the requirement that all persons, regardless of gender, would be subject to medical inspection. Hitherto only prostitutes had been required to undergo compulsory treatment, although sickness insurance funds had made it obligatory for workers suffering from VD to be treated in hospitals.[79] After 1927 anyone identified as having VD was compelled to undergo treatment by a recognized medical practitioner.[80] The law no longer discriminated on grounds of gender, but the state had extended its purview to include all men and women – an approach that stood in marked contrast to the situation in Britain, where there was no compulsion of any kind.[81]

It is often said that the Second World War brought more liberal attitudes to sexual behaviour, as well as greater frankness in the discussion of venereal diseases. This is generally true, but some qualification is necessary. In most countries, rising VD rates and concerns over national efficiency led governments to take a more 'scientific' approach towards its prevention. The facts about sexually transmitted diseases were disseminated widely in an effort to dispel the stigma surrounding them. VD was regarded as a public health hazard just like any other disease. Even in Britain, which had been one of the most traditionally minded nations in its attitudes towards VD, the subject was deemed fit for a radio broadcast. But most countries continued to display a 'double standard' by introducing compulsory treatment for women but not for men.

The same combination of regulation and education was evident in armies stationed abroad. The Germans maintained a system of regulated brothels in all the countries they occupied, and, by the end of 1942 the Wehrmacht was running as many as 500 such establishments, and each prostitute carried a card to prove that she had been examined medically. Sexual intercourse was widely regarded as essential to morale, and the provision of brothels appeared to be necessary lest frustrated troops turn to 'unnatural' forms of vice like homosexuality. The racial ideology that underpinned Nazi Germany was no barrier to sexual contact between races, however, and German brothels contained women from all over the occupied territories, most of whom had been forced into prostitution.[82] A similar system of 'comfort women' – women forced to work as prostitutes for the military – existed in the Japanese forces.[83]

British and American armies also used regulated brothels to control VD, though seemingly without much success. VD rates in most of the expeditionary forces were high, and showed no sign of declining despite a continual barrage of education and propaganda. Soldiers in the Allied armies were told that they had a duty to avoid venereal infection, and that they let their comrades, countries and families down badly if they did not. Duty to the state had replaced duty to God.[84] But the chief factor governing the incidence of VD seems to have been opportunity. When troops were stationed close to large civilian centres, there were ample opportunities to find sexual partners in the brothels and among so-called amateurs who plied their trade on the streets. But when troops were on active service, especially in remote locations like the jungles of Burma, the VD rate was far lower.[85] In the Allied armies, VD rates were highest in India and Italy, and it was noticed that rates of infection were indicative of low morale. Towards the end of the war – when British VD rates rose to seventy and eighty per thousand in Italy and India – many troops had been away from their wives and sweethearts for several years, and some had seen their relationships break down. Although the war was going well for the Allies, most soldiers were longing to go home.[86]

Had there not been an effective treatment for VD, the Allied armies would have been severely incapacitated. Sulphonamide drugs had been used to treat gonorrhoea since the 1930s, and by 1944 a more effective drug in the form of penicillin had become available. Just before the war, a team of scientists working at Oxford University – Howard Florey, Ernst Chain and Norman Heatley – had investigated the antibacterial properties of the mould that Alexander Fleming had called 'penicillin'.[87] During the war, Florey supervised a number of field trials with penicillin, and showed that it was effective against a wide range of micro-organisms, including many that sulphonamide drugs could not kill. These ranged from the germs causing wound infection, to many common bacterial infections, including syphilis and gonorrhoea. By 1943, large-scale manufacture of penicillin was under way in the United States, and it was soon being used to treat burns and wound infections.[88] By the summer of 1944 it was also being used to treat VD, which proved timely in view of the fact that some strains of gonorrhoea had become resistant to sulphonamides. A series of intramuscular injections with penicillin could cure gonorrhoea in just a few days, and syphilis in around a week, instead of the forty to fifty days it took with arsenical drugs.[89] A revolution in therapeutics had begun.

8

Health for All?
Affluence, Poverty and
Disease since 1945

The world is now both more united and more divided by the experience of disease than at any time in its history. It is more united in the sense that there are few geographical barriers to infection: air travel means that disease can spread from one continent to another in a matter of hours. The entire world is potentially at risk, and yet diseases remain very unequally distributed between countries, and between rich and poor. In the prosperous countries of what is sometimes called the 'developed world', few die from infectious diseases, and most people live past seventy years of age. In the poor countries of the 'undeveloped' or 'Third' world, or what is now sometimes called 'the South', infectious diseases remain the main cause of death, claiming more than one in ten lives during infancy. Cholera, which once ravaged the richest countries on Earth, is now largely confined to South Asia and the poorest nations; tuberculosis, once the scourge of all industrial countries, now kills a relatively tiny number in the affluent world compared with the high mortality suffered in South Asia, China and sub-Saharan Africa.[1] This, the final chapter of the book, examines these two contrasting experiences of disease and investigates their causes.

Disease in affluent societies

As the Western world moved into the second half of the twentieth century, the age of epidemics was long past. Improved nutrition, together with sanitation and better personal hygiene, had reduced many common infections, and had prevented the return of major epidemic diseases like cholera. By the 1940s, most developed countries had also introduced immunization against diseases like tuberculosis, diphtheria, whooping cough and smallpox. But one infectious disease was still regarded with terror: poliomyelitis. Epidemics of the 'summer plague' struck periodically throughout the twentieth century, claiming many victims in Europe and the Americas, including the future American president, Franklin D. Roosevelt. Polio is a viral disease that attacks the nerves in the spine, cutting off impulses from the brain to the limbs, and causing their muscles to shrivel. The legs are more affected than other parts of the body, so polio often leaves its victims, most famously President Roosevelt, crippled. In some cases the virus also affects the lungs and can be fatal, but many of those afflicted were able to survive with the assistance of an artificial respirator like the 'iron lung', which was developed at the Harvard School of Medicine in 1928.[2]

During the 1940s and 1950s, several severe epidemics of polio caused great alarm across the Western world. Parents kept their children inside for fear that they would encounter the 'crippler' as it was known in the USA. But as the disease reached its peak, salvation was close at hand. In 1953 the American doctor Jonas Salk became a national hero when he announced that he had developed a vaccine against the disease. Salk's vaccine, the IPV, was an 'inactivated vaccine', so called because it was made from killed viruses. Later in the decade, A. B. Sabin announced that he had produced a vaccine from attenuated viruses that could be given orally, usually in the form of an impregnated sugar lump. This oral (OPV) vaccine had many advantages over an injected vaccine as it was cheaper and could be given without medical supervision. However, OPV had disadvantages too: three separate doses were required, and heat reduced its effectiveness. In about one in a million cases, the vaccination can also produce polio. These disadvantages have meant that OPV has encountered problems in warmer countries, especially those that have been unable to afford refrigeration facilities. For this reason, many poorer countries in the tropics have preferred to use the inactive vaccine. But while the disease has been reduced to negligible proportions in prosperous countries, in many poor nations immunization rates are still below 50 per cent, and hopes of eradicating the disease are fading fast.[3]

In the coming decades the polio vaccine was joined by a range of other immunizations, against childhood diseases like measles, mumps, rubella and chicken-pox. For many children born during or after the 1960s, these diseases were no longer an inevitable part of growing up.

But scares over the safety of vaccines like those for whooping cough and MMR (the combined mumps, measles and rubella injection) have deterred parents from bringing their children for vaccination, and pools of non-immune children have given rise to localized epidemics. In 2002–3 the number of measles cases in the United Kingdom, for example, quadrupled as a growing number of parents shunned the controversial MMR vaccination and immunization rates for two-year-olds fell to 78.9 per cent. Many parents had always been cautious about vaccinations, but the scares of the 1960s onwards were rather different. Fears about brain damage or other disabilities as a result of adverse reactions to vaccination loomed larger as the spectre of serious childhood illness became more remote. A growing sense of individualism also began to outweigh the feeling that public health was a matter of collective responsibility. At the same time, people became less trusting of scientists and governments, and came to doubt reassurances that vaccines were safe.

The great breakthroughs made in the prevention of disease were more than matched by those in therapeutics. From the 1930s the advent of sulphonamide drugs had a major impact on the treatment of some infectious diseases, most notably puerperal fever, which declined more than 80 per cent between 1934, when mortality was at its peak, and 1940.[4] Sulphonamides were followed in the early 1940s by the 'wonder drug', penicillin, which became available for civilian use soon after the end of the war. Penicillin enabled doctors to treat infections like bacterial meningitis that were sometimes lethal, as well as many non-fatal conditions, like impetigo, that were unsightly or painful. Penicillin could also be used to prevent surgical infections, and permitted major innovations such as organ transplantation and heart surgery.[5] Spurred by the success of penicillin, drug companies soon began to develop other antibiotics, including streptomycin, the first effective treatment for tuberculosis.[6] But drug-resistant strains soon appeared. Tuberculosis bacteria resistant to streptomycin were identified as early as 1946, and by 1948 the Hammersmith Hospital in London reported that 60 per cent of staphylococci found in the hospital were resistant to penicillin.[7] Since then, pharmaceutical companies have been involved in a constant struggle to overcome drug-resistant strains of bacteria, a problem which has been compounded by the tendency to prescribe drugs unnecessarily and the failure of some patients to take the prescribed dosage for a sufficient time.[8]

Another important breakthrough in treatment was the realization that a steroid – the naturally occurring hormone, cortisone – could relieve rheumatoid arthritis and rheumatic fever. But unfortunately, it was soon recognized that cortisone produced severe side-effects, called 'rebound', in which patients experienced fever or an aggravation of their condition.[9] Though steroids proved to be a mixed blessing in rheumatic cases, it became apparent that they provided relief for a range of other conditions such as eczema, asthma, allergic reactions and meningitis. By the 1990s, more than eighty disorders were said to respond favourably to treatment with steroids.[10] The new generation of steroid drugs included some that treated rheumatism, without producing unpleasant side-effects. Yet rheumatoid arthritis remains a lamentably intractable condition, and the only hope of a complete cure probably lies with molecular science and the control of the inflammatory proteins that damage joints.[11]

The treatment of mental illness was also transformed by the greater intensity of pharmacological research after the Second World War. For some years previously, psychiatry had been dominated by Freudian psychoanalysis, with its talk of repression and instinctive drives. Such ideas gained respectability after psychoanalysis was used to treat some 'shell-shocked' soldiers during the First World War.[12] But psychoanalysis was not the only therapy available to treat mental disorders, and electro-convulsive therapy (ECT), surgical procedures such as lobotomy, and drug treatments were all used with some evidence of success. During the 1930s, for instance, a few asylum doctors began to experiment with insulin to induce comas in their patients, a technique that continued to be used in some hospitals during the Second World War.[13] Barbiturates such as Pentothal were also widely used in wartime to aid sleep, and in some cases to assist psychotherapy. But the biggest breakthrough came after the end of the war when Henri Laborit, a French naval surgeon, noted that the drug antihistamine promethiazine had a calming effect on patients whom he was treating for shock. He began to try the drug on some psychiatric cases with impressive results.

Other chemically synthesized drugs were also found to be useful in the treatment of mental disorders. Chlorpromazine, for example, dramatically improved the condition of schizophrenic patients. Since then, an enormous range of psychotropic drugs has been synthesized, leading to a revolution in the treatment of the mentally ill and in ideas about mental illness. The efficacy of these drugs led psychiatrists away from psychoanalysis and towards biological models of treatment, and by the 1970s these ideas had filtered down to the general public. As David Healy comments, 'Where once lay people had gone to psychiatrists expecting to hear about sexual repression, they now came knowing that something might be wrong with their amines or with some brain chemical.'[14] People now expected specific cures for specific disorders, almost as if they were suffering from a bacterial infection. As new drugs like the tranquillizer Valium became available in the 1960s, and the antidepressant Prozac in the 1990s, people also became less tolerant of sadness and anxiety, and more inclined to think they were suffering from an illness. 'Depression', which was all but unknown as a clinical diagnosis before the 1960s, became commonplace; tolerance thresholds for emotional pain plummeted, while addiction and drug abuse became rife.[15] Or, to look at it more positively, disorders that were once regarded as failures of character came to be regarded as illnesses, and hence lost much of their stigma.[16]

But the therapeutic revolution in psychiatry did not go unchallenged. The backlash started in the 1960s, when psychiatry was branded an instrument of capitalist and patriarchal oppression. In 1960 the Hungarian-born psychoanalyst Thomas Szasz claimed that mental illness was a 'myth'. He argued that most individuals diagnosed with mental illness simply had problems in adjusting to society, and that psychiatrists were little better than witch-doctors. Another former analyst, the British psychiatrist R. D. Laing, claimed in his book *The Divided Self* (1960) that the condition schizophrenia was not a disease but a creative state: the response of a sane mind to a mad society. In the coming years, Laing backed up his own insights with the historical observations of Michel Foucault, who proclaimed that madness was an invention of the Enlightenment, and that it was merely a label given to behaviour that society was unwilling to tolerate.

If all mental illness was a myth, there seemed to be little justification for the incarceration of the 'insane' – an opinion shared by the sociologist Erving Goffman, whose influential book *Asylums* (1961) claimed that such institutions were dehumanizing. In the antiauthoritarian climate of the 1960s, these ideas quickly caught on, and came to a wider public in the form of novels and films, like Ken Kesey's 1962 novel *One Flew Over the Cuckoo's Nest*. Formerly intended as refuges for the insane, asylums were now seen as wicked and oppressive, as part of a conspiracy to control social deviance.[17] Antipsychiatrists believed unshakeably that biological psychiatry in some way violated the 'spiritual essence' of human beings, in spite of evidence that treatments such as ECT, antidepressants and tranquillizers were in some cases beneficial.[18]

Keeping patients in asylums also cost a good deal of money, and some politicians seized on the new public mood to justify their closure on economic grounds. By the 1970s, the watchword had become 'care in the community'. In the United States, for example, the number of patients in public mental hospitals fell from a high of 559,000 in 1955, to 338,000 in 1970 and 107,000 in 1988. Drug therapy, if prescribed, was supposed to take place on an outpatient basis, but all too often, patients failed to take their medication. Many drifted into a life of homelessness and crime; there were several well-publicized cases of violent assaults, including killings, committed by the mentally ill. Beginning in the late 1980s, there was a backlash: public hospitals began once again to admit psychiatric cases as in-patients, and the number of psychiatric hospitals began to increase. As the historian Edward Shorter comments, 'though worthy in spirit', the antipsychiatry movement had failed.

During the 1960s and 1970s the only really serious threat from infectious disease in the world's richer countries was the possibility that a deadly strain of influenza would sweep the world before scientists had time to develop a vaccine. But periodic scares did little to shake the general mood of optimism that had resulted from medical progress. The attention of the medical profession and the general public began to turn instead to diseases like cancer and coronary heart disease which were now the main causes of death in affluent countries. These diseases had formerly been regarded as the inevitable consequences of ageing; they had also been less 'visible', in the sense that fewer individuals lived to old age than was now the case. As these diseases began to attract more attention, the dread and social stigma surrounding them increased, particularly in the case of cancer – the 'big "C"'. A host of myths grew up about the disease and those who contracted it. Fear of cancer was such that people could scarcely utter its name; cancer patients and their families were condemned to suffer in silence. It was these experiences that led Susan Sontag to write her best-selling book, *Illness as Metaphor*, in which she likened the mythologies of cancer to those surrounding tuberculosis during the nineteenth century. Like tuberculosis, cancer seemed to be a disease of the personality, associated with certain traits of character and appearance, and generally regarded as fatal.[19]

But as Sontag put pen to paper, there were hopeful signs that cancer was losing some of its stigma. Surgery and radiotherapy (first developed during the 1920s) were increasingly supplemented or replaced by chemotherapy. Many American pharmaceutical firms – spurred by President Nixon's 'crusade' against cancer – began to develop drugs that were effective against certain cancers, such as childhood lymphoblastic leukaemia, though others – like lung cancer – proved less tractable. Cancer sufferers were also more involved in their own treatment than before.[20] As a result, some of the fear surrounding cancer began to diminish, but it is unrealistic to suppose that cancer can be divested entirely of myths or metaphorical allusions. All diseases have social meanings, although they are clearly amenable to change.

Indeed, cancer has taken the place of tuberculosis as the focus of many social concerns. The process began in 1947 when the British Medical Research Council commissioned an inquiry into the causes of lung cancer, which was then one of the largest causes of death. Austin Bradford Hill (1897–1991), a statistician, and Richard Doll (b. 1912), a physician, conducted a detailed analysis of lung cancer patients at twenty London hospitals. Their study, published in 1951, concluded that smoking was an important cause of lung cancer, and five years later, they showed that mortality from the disease dropped rapidly if individuals stopped smoking. These findings were of tremendous significance, as the prevention of smoking now became one of the main thrusts of public health policy in many developed nations. In Britain and North America smoking was dramatically reduced as a result of public health education and taxation on cigarettes. Smoking in many public places, in restaurants, and on transport was banned. But around one in three adult men in the UK still smokes, and the figure is far higher in Mediterranean countries and the developing world, where there are few injunctions against smoking. In these countries the prevalence of lung cancer is far higher and increasing. In richer nations, too, there is also a trend towards smoking amongst young women, among whom smoking has become fashionable despite – or perhaps because of – incessant warnings in schools. It is well known that nicotine is an appetite suppressant, and this is a powerful incentive to smoke in cultures that value thinness. Indeed, it is one of the paradoxes of very affluent societies that the denial of consumption is accorded aesthetic and moral value. Health education is thus a necessary, but not always a sufficient, preventative measure.

The clear statistical link between smoking and lung cancer has led to a good deal of speculation about the links between cancer and other aspects of modern life. There has long been unease about the link between certain cancers and radiation, for example, and it is currently thought that around 3 per cent of cancers are caused by ionizing radiation, some of which is naturally occurring. Other cancers have been shown to be due to exposure to radioactive substances in the work place: radon gas causes cancer among uranium miners, for example. Anxieties over nuclear power have also led many to attribute 'clusters' of childhood leukaemia to radiation emitted from nearby power stations, and some cancers have even been blamed on electricity pylons and substations. There is no proof of any causal link in these cases, but official pronouncements have done little to reassure a public wary of nuclear power and distrustful of government information. But in recent years, scares over food have tended to be more common than scares over sources of power, and there are certainly significant correlations between some cancers and dietary habits. Colorectal cancer, for example, is closely associated with a diet low in fresh fruit and vegetables, while the increase in obesity in many affluent countries has been linked with common malignancies such as breast cancer.[21]

Cardiovascular diseases like arteriosclerosis – the thickening and hardening of the arteries – have never elicited the same kind of dread as cancer, despite the fact that they are the most common causes of death in affluent countries. Heart disease has generally been seen as a mechanical failure, rather than a failure of character or the expression of some pathological trait of personality. Nevertheless, there has been a profound change in the ways in which these diseases have been understood during the last fifty years. Until the 1950s coronary heart disease was thought to be a chronic, degenerative disease that was part of the ageing process; as such, it did not seem to lend itself to specific preventative measures. But coronary heart disease is now viewed less fatalistically, as growing evidence of 'risk factors' has emerged. As with many cancers, doctors have been able to identify several modifiable risks, including smoking, high blood pressure, and high cholesterol. To a great extent, the individual is now recognized as the master of his or her biological destiny: a message that has harmonized with the individualism of most affluent societies. Risk factors have become part and parcel of a new, life-style consumerism, in which informed choices are made about diet and exercise on the basis of medical advice.[22]

The evangelical fervour of risk-factor advocates has alienated many who stood to benefit from some modification of their life-style, but public health education has contributed to a substantial reduction in mortality. In the United States, the death rate from heart-related disorders reached its peak in 1963 and has declined continuously ever since.[23] But while much of this improvement was due to preventive medicine, better means of treatment and diagnosis have played an important part too. From the 1960s the electrocardiograph, which detects rhythmic abnormalities, has been widely used in conjunction with other diagnostic methods to detect heart disorders. Over the same period heart bypass and open-heart surgery have become common, as has the use of drugs to reduce cholesterol and to dilate blood vessels. In some cases, heart transplants – pioneered in 1967 by Christian Barnard at the Groote Schuur Hospital in Cape Town – have also saved the lives of those suffering from life-threatening complaints.[24]

Among the risk factors that have been identified for cancers and heart diseases is our genetic inheritance. Certain diseases have long been regarded as hereditary, but it is only comparatively recently that they have been linked to defective genes. One such disease is Duchenne muscular dystrophy, a disease in which the membrane of muscle fibres breaks down, causing debility and death from respiratory failure, usually in the late teens. Muscular dystrophy was recognized as a distinct disorder during the 1830s, and was easily linked to inheritance because it affects only boys. But in 1959 it became apparent that the disease was inherited through female carriers, and statistical analyses were used to calculate the probability of a woman having a child with muscular dystrophy. To begin with, risks were calculated using information about a mother's antecedents and siblings, but during the 1960s Professor Edmond Murphy at Johns Hopkins University, in the USA, developed a method of calculating probability based on clinical findings and test results. A search also began for the gene responsible for muscular dystrophy. The breakthrough came in 1985, when two separate teams of researchers in the USA and Canada isolated the gene responsible for the disease.

Once the gene had been isolated, attention turned to improving methods of prevention and to the possibility of gene therapy. A few years after the gene was identified, it became apparent that the genetic abnormality associated with muscular dystrophy caused a deficiency of a protein known as a dystrophin in the membranes of muscle fibres. This deficiency can be detected, and can serve as a diagnostic test during pregnancy, allowing the mother to terminate the pregnancy if she chooses to. However, the test is not totally reliable. No form of effective treatment has yet been developed, but the most direct approach would be to reverse the mutation that causes muscular dystrophy. Presently there is no notion of how this might be achieved, though it would require the upgrading of defective genes, possibly by the addition of a compensatory protein or a normal gene. The difficulty in achieving this lies partly in the difficulty of introducing the normal gene into patients' muscles, and success seems a very long way off.[25] The best hope for the future may lie with stem cell therapy, and the introduction of young, healthy cells into the body to supply the necessary proteins.

Muscular dystrophy is just one of many diseases that have been affected by the genetic revolution in medicine. Another is diabetes – a growing problem in many affluent societies – which can now be treated with genetically engineered 'human' insulin rather than insulin produced from pigs or cows, as was formerly the case. The suggestion that hormones like insulin could be manufactured by genetic manipulation was first made by Hebert Boyer of the University of Southern California, who teamed up with a young venture capitalist named Robert Swanson to form a new company, Genetec. In 1977, a year after the company was founded, the insulin gene was discovered, as Boyer had predicted. The following year, he reported that he had been able to manufacture small amounts of 'human' insulin after inserting the insulin gene into the bacterium *E. coli*. Shortly afterwards, Boyer and Swanson signed a contract with the pharmaceutical firm Eli Lilly to enable its mass production. The biotech industry was born, and in the coming years human insulin entirely replaced insulin obtained from animals. Numerous other biotech products followed and were in widespread use by the mid-1990s. These included alpha Interferon, which is used to treat leukemia, and Interferon beta, which is used to relieve the symptoms of multiple sclerosis.

The potential for the 'new genetics' to treat or alleviate disease has led some physicians to compare its impact to that of the bacteriological revolution of the late nineteenth century. Genetics has certainly come to affect clinical practice in significant ways,[26] but its potential is still uncertain. Some products of the biotech industry – such as Interferon beta – are extremely expensive, and it is sometimes difficult to justify their mass usage in view of competing claims on resources. Biotechnology is also constrained by the fact that genes can only make proteins, thus limiting their use to conditions where a protein is deficient or needs to be replaced. What, then, of screening for genetic disease? By 1995, the genes of forty-two of the 5,000 or so genetic diseases affecting humans had been identified, raising the possibility that foetuses could be screened during pregnancy to detect genetic defects, as well as those whose family history suggests a strong possibility of contracting a disease. But mass screening would be enormously costly and time consuming, which again raises the question of whether money could be better directed elsewhere. Widespread testing of children or adults is also likely to be unpopular, because the identification of defective genes could increase the cost of life or health insurance.[27] Compulsory screening, of course, raises the spectre of eugenics and a genetic underclass. Clearly, the potential of genetics will be severely circumscribed by these ethical and political considerations.

Amidst feverish speculation over the future of genetic medicine, it is sobering to remind ourselves of the continuing danger posed by infectious diseases. The Western world was left in no doubt about its continuing vulnerability to epidemics by the outbreak of a mysterious new disease in the late 1970s. The disease first came to light in Los Angeles, when several cases of a strange syndrome appeared among the gay community. Sufferers had a range of symptoms that seemed to suggest a dysfunction of their immune system. Between 1979 and 1981 there were also rumours that a new disease was spreading among gay men in New York City and San Francisco. The victims – mostly young men – appeared to have a particularly malignant form of Kaposi's cancer, which is a chronic disorder normally affecting much older people. The cancer was sometimes accompanied by infections like pneumocystis pneumonia. By 1982 the number of such cases had increased to more than 200, and there were reports of a similar disease appearing among young homosexual men in Europe. Still lacking a scientific name, the media dubbed the disease the 'gay plague'.[28] As Susan Sontag pointed out, the term 'plague' came readily to those who sought to stigmatize homosexuals, implying, as 'plagues' normally did, that the disease was a punishment for transgression of the natural or spiritual order.[29]

There was general agreement among doctors that they were observing a distinct clinical entity – an entity that was given the name 'AIDS' (Acquired Immunity Deficiency Syndrome) in the summer of 1982. Most suspected that the disease was viral in origin, but a pathogen had still to be detected. In early 1983, a team of researchers led by Luc Montagnier in Paris claimed to have identified the causal organism, although its discovery was not publicized until May. At around the same time, researchers at the USA's National Cancer Institute, led by Robert Gallo, announced that they had discovered a similar virus. A bitter dispute between the two teams ended only when it became clear that the two organisms were identical, and in 1986 it was decided to refer to the virus as the 'human immunodeficiency virus' or 'HIV'.[30]

But very little was known about how the disease was spread. By 1982 it was clearly no longer confined to gay men, because it had affected intravenous drug-users and some other groups. Already marginal to society, most of these groups were stigmatized further as a result of their association with AIDS, which had become almost synonymous with moral degeneracy. The disease also had a racial dimension. One group singled out as scapegoats in the United States were Haitian immigrants, who were blamed for bringing the disease into the country. From the very beginning, most doctors were resolutely opposed to a simple 'racial' explanation of why this group was affected, but it did not stop some from attributing the disease to bad hygienic practices, drug abuse or even voodoo. It subsequently became clear that the disease had become widespread in Haiti because of burgeoning sex tourism, which fed off the dire poverty in which most Haitians lived.[31]

Haemophiliacs, however, were treated differently. In 1982 a number of heterosexual haemophiliacs were diagnosed as having AIDS, which immediately raised the possibility that the disease could be transmitted in blood and its products. Like others who had received infected blood during transfusion, haemophiliacs were regarded as 'innocent' victims, unlike gays and intravenous drug-users. At first, the medical profession was reluctant to admit that HIV could be transmitted through blood, lest public confidence in transfusion was lost. But the implications of the growing number of haemophiliac AIDS cases could not be avoided, and from 1983 most countries began to screen donated blood for HIV.[32] Not all health authorities were equally scrupulous, however. In 1992 a trial took place in Paris, which indicted four ministers of state and their medical advisers for permitting infected blood to be used for transfusion between 1983, when the threat first became apparent, and 1985. More than 2,000 persons, around half of whom were haemophiliacs, had been infected with HIV as a result of ministers' inaction. The trial led to the closure of many transfusion centres and to much stricter supervision.[33]

In the course of 1983 there was also mounting evidence that HIV could be transmitted by heterosexual intercourse. The first cases were detected among the partners of bisexual men and intravenous drug-users with AIDS; AIDS was also diagnosed in the wife of a haemophiliac. Cases came to light simultaneously among prostitutes in Europe and North America, and the possibility that HIV could be transmitted from mothers to infants was also raised when several cases of AIDS appeared among babies. But in these cases no one was yet sure whether the virus was transmitted *in utero* or after birth. People began to speculate whether the disease could be transmitted in other ways, too, including as a droplet infection. There were dire predictions of millions of AIDS cases in Western countries by the end of the decade – predictions that were not entirely unfounded. The disease had spread rapidly during the first few years after its discovery. In the USA, for example, the number of recorded cases rose from 750 at the end of 1982 to 3,000 by the end of 1983 and 8,000 at the end of 1984.[34] A wave of hysteria passed through the Western media. Rabble-rousers, unscrupulous politicians and religious bigots began to call for draconian measures to curtail the disease; mandatory testing, detention, quarantine and deportation were among the measures suggested.[35] Health workers were also concerned that they lacked adequate provisions to protect themselves from infection, and came to demand routine testing of workers and inmates in public institutions, as well as compulsory notification and isolation in special hospitals or wards.[36]

However, most governments were wary of being labelled authoritarian. The Conservative government of Margaret Thatcher in the UK rejected calls for compulsory notification and screening, and for the most part AIDS was treated in the UK and other Western countries much as any other infectious disease.[37] At this juncture, historical arguments had an important impact upon policy. Historians pointed out that the 'policeman' approach to the control of infectious diseases had failed in the past, because it had led to the concealment of cases. Such arguments helped to construct what has subsequently been described as a 'liberal consensus' surrounding AIDS.[38] At the heart of this new consensus was the belief that a campaign against AIDS could be successful only if it enlisted the support of the populations most at risk from it, such as the gay community and intravenous drug-users. This led some to argue that AIDS had legitimated homosexuality; it had brought the gay community into the open, making it part of the new liberal consensus.[39]

Most countries decided to fight AIDS by encouraging individuals to modify their behaviour, and they embarked on a campaign of mass health education, the likes of which had not been seen since the Second World War. In the case of the gay community, this meant popularizing 'safe sex', especially the use of condoms – advice that was soon directed at heterosexuals too. In the case of intravenous drug-users, the emphasis was placed upon clean needles. But, as some cautioned, there was a fine line between education and control, and some homosexuals saw public health messages as an unwelcome intrusion.[40] However, resistance began to diminish as the extent of infection became more widely known, and as AIDS claimed several prominent victims such as the film star Rock Hudson.

Two additional things need to be noted about this stage of the epidemic. The first is that there were some exceptions to the liberal approach taken by Western governments. In 1987, for example, the US Senate passed a bill making infection with HIV grounds for refusing entry to would-be immigrants. The action was considered an extraordinary breach of the principle that such decisions should always be made by the Department of Health and Human Services. In the early 1990s, it resulted in the detention of around 200 Haitian refugees at the US naval facility of Guantánamo Bay in Cuba, which was later to house prisoners from the war in Afghanistan. The refugees were kept for two years in conditions regarded by some as unhygienic, and with inadequate medical treatment, before they were finally released following a judicial decision.[41]

A second qualification to the notion of a 'liberal consensus' is the slowness with which the medical authorities recognized the problem of HIV/AIDS among women. Despite the fact that cases among women were recorded from an early stage, many people, including some doctors, AIDS activists and the media, believed that the disease posed little risk to women. In 1985 a popular American science magazine, *Discover*, declared that women had little to fear as long as they did not indulge in anal sex.[42] By the late 1980s, however, it was clear that AIDS was declining among gay men and increasing among heterosexuals, which led to an increasing awareness of the problem among women. Ahead of government and public opinion, prostitutes formed self-help groups to raise awareness of the problem and to urge the practice of safe sex.[43] But the publication of books such as *The Myth of Heterosexual AIDS* in 1991 (a second edition appeared in 1993) showed that some still refused to believe mounting epidemiological and clinical evidence.[44]

The growing recognition of AIDS among women contributed to a more general change in public perception of the disease. AIDS in North America and Europe was viewed against the backdrop of the burgeoning epidemic in poor countries, particularly in sub-Saharan Africa. Here, heterosexual sex and *in utero* transmission (which was now well established) were the main ways in which the disease spread. It was therefore clear that AIDS was potentially a threat to all, not just to minorities. But the disease had settled into a rather different pattern in Western societies than in the developing world. The millions of cases predicted in the early and mid-1980s had failed to materialize, probably as a result of concerted health education. AIDS was now regarded more as a chronic condition, as the passage of time revealed that the virus could take many years to develop into the disease itself. Biomedical intervention also altered public perception of AIDS: in 1986 the drug azidothymidine (AZT) was shown to prolong the period in which the virus remained latent, and it was approved for use soon afterwards.[45]

Although the threat of wholesale devastation subsided in the West, AIDS remained at the centre of medical controversies, not least the question of its origins. In the early 1980s, Africa was identified as the most likely source of the HIV virus. Physicians from the French AIDS Task Force noted in 1982–3 that several cases had occurred among heterosexual Europeans who had visited Central Africa. The cases included both men and women. At around the same time, Belgian physicians began to note cases of an AIDS-like illness among immigrants from the former Belgian Congo; most were neither homosexuals nor drug-users. Although they had only the barest notion at the time of the epidemiological situation in Africa, European doctors began to suspect that a virus – new or previously dormant – had begun to spread in Zaire, Rwanda, Chad and Uganda during the late 1970s. Subsequently, it became clear that the disease had been present since at least the early 1960s.[46] The most widely held view was that it had jumped the species barrier, and that the HIV virus had descended from retroviruses found in certain species of monkeys and apes. But the 'African hypothesis', as it came to be known, was little more than racist speculation according to some critics: the latest version of 'Africa, the dark continent', a land of untamed nature and disease. In the late 1980s, some even argued that

European doctors had exaggerated the number of AIDS cases in Africa.[47]

Such views were well received by the liberal Western media. A reviewer in the UK's *Guardian* newspaper declared that the number of AIDS cases in Africa had been 'grossly overstated', and that 'Western medical research teams and the media bear a grave burden of responsibility'. In the *New York Native*, American and European epidemiology was denounced as 'shoddy'.[48] But it later became evident that Western doctors had *under-* rather than over-estimated the extent of HIV infection in Africa.[49] The 'African hypothesis' came to be generally accepted, although new explanations of the emergence of the virus were offered. The most controversial was Edward Hooper's claim in his book *The River* (1999), that the virus had been able to jump the species barrier because cells taken from African primates had been used to culture the first polio vaccines in the 1950s. He pointed out that some of these early vaccines had been contaminated by simian viruses, some of which were not identified at the time of their use in Africa. He argued that the most likely source of AIDS was the chimpanzee, which suffers from a virus very similar to HIV. Chimpanzees had also been used in experiments to perfect some of the early polio vaccines.[50] However, as Hooper acknowledged, there was no hard evidence to substantiate his claim that tissues from chimps used in these experiments were subsequently used to culture vaccines; nor had any polio vaccine ever been found contaminated with HIV. Recent research has also shown that the HIV virus has a very similar molecular structure to that of viruses causing simian immune diseases. This makes it likely that the disease was passed on to humans by the consumption of bush meat and that HIV is a variant of kinds found in chimpanzees and macaques.

The AIDS epidemic of the 1980s does not fit easily with our conventional views of epidemics. It was an epidemic played out more than ever before in the media, which had a crucially important role in shaping social responses to the disease. At the same time, media representations and other responses to the epidemic were monitored by academics, doctors, bureaucrats and various interest groups, not least those infected with HIV.[51] For the first time, disease prevention was seen as much in terms of human rights as of public health.[52] Unlike previous epidemics, too, no single drama was enacted during the AIDS epidemic, but rather a series of dramas unfolding at different times, reflecting the rich social fabric that now existed in most Western countries and the progressive revelation that AIDS was a disease that affected groups other than homosexual men and intravenous drug-users.

Disease, poverty and environment in the developing world

In the first decades after the Second World War, there were good reasons to hope that the crushing burden of disease in poorer countries would be lifted. Mortality rates for infants and under-fives fell consistently, raising hopes that developing countries would soon achieve levels of life expectancy similar to those in the West. But from the 1980s, the economic systems on which many newly independent countries had pinned their faith began to falter. Over-reliance on state planning and regulation, together with endemic corruption and wasteful expenditure, caused their economies to stagnate. Development aid tended increasingly to be squandered and to result in little benefit for the people as a whole. At the same time, tariff barriers and other constraints prevented these emergent nations from trading on an equal footing with many Western countries. Economic stagnation led to growing indebtedness, as many developing countries were unable to repay enormous loans. The international financial community demanded economic reforms that included cuts in public spending. The net result was a serious deterioration in the health of most developing countries and growing inequalities between rich and poor nations.

The mortality decline that occurred in the first three decades after 1945 gave rise to confident expectations that were never fully realized. Sulphonamide drugs, penicillin and other antibiotics enabled doctors to combat a wide range of common but deadly infections. DDT, which had been used with such dramatic effect against typhus and malaria during the war, led many to believe that insect-borne diseases could be eradicated anywhere in the world. In tropical Africa, India and parts of the Americas, vector-borne diseases like malaria claimed the majority of lives. If this burden could be removed, the full economic potential of the population could be tapped.[53]

Confidence in the power of science was matched by the idealism of new international organizations such as the World Health Organization, which was founded in 1948. The WHO was a direct descendant of the health organization of the League of Nations, and its chief aims were to promote international co-operation in the field of health and to supply expert guidance. It was no accident that the first major project undertaken by the WHO was the eradication of malaria on a global scale. This was a truly enormous undertaking, but such was the confidence in the power of DDT that many experts believed it to be possible. Early success in southern Europe, North America and some parts of South America and the Western Pacific showed that this optimism was not unfounded. By 1968, it was estimated that as many as 1.1 billion people had been protected against malaria as a result of the eradication campaign. This was a fantastic achievement, but hopes of global eradication proved premature. Some species of mosquito began to develop resistance to DDT, and the poorest countries, lacking a basic health infrastructure, found it difficult to organize regular spraying of mosquitoes and breeding pools, especially in rural areas. There were also indications that the insecticide had damaged the environment. Many harmless insects died as a result of its use, and with them perished birds and mammals higher up the food chain. The harmful effects of DDT came to prominence with the publication of Rachel Carson's powerful book, *The Silent Spring* (1965), which led to public clamour against its use.

The net result of these developments was the scaling down of the WHO's malaria eradication programme and its replacement with the less ambitious objective of malaria 'control'. The failure of eradication also prompted the WHO to look closely at the way in which it conducted its campaigns. The malaria eradication campaign – like many similar projects in the former colonies – was a 'vertical' programme. It possessed its own funds, equipment and health workers that were not integrated with other health services. When eradication had been achieved in one area, the team moved on to another, seldom leaving structures in place to continue its work. In a large country like India, where there was no possibility of eradicating all vectors simultaneously, it was not long before mosquitoes returned to formerly treated areas.

This realization was one of the reasons why the WHO began to shift its emphasis to primary care, although the move also took into account growing dissatisfaction among people in poorer countries with the health services available to them. It was clear that many people felt helpless in the face of disease, because most did not have access to medicines or other health services. The most basic care now taken for granted in richer countries was absent in the vast majority of nations. In seeking to remedy this situation, the WHO took its cue from a number of countries that had already experimented with primary health programmes. These included Communist countries such as China and Cuba and some Third World countries such as Guatemala and Tanzania. Tanzania established a system of village dispensaries and health workers in the late 1960s, just a few years after securing independence from Great Britain. But the greatest inspiration was the Barefoot Doctor scheme launched in China following the Cultural Revolution of 1966–9. The success with which the

scheme tackled the major endemic diseases of the countryside lay in the symbiotic relationship that existed between the health workers and the communities they served. Concentrating on primary care, and working closely with the people of rural areas, the Barefoot Doctor scheme helped to secure a substantial increase in life expectancy from forty-seven years in 1960 to sixty-seven by 1980. Over the same period, infant mortality rates also fell to Western levels.

Inspired by these initiatives, the WHO came to demand 'Health for All by the Year 2000'. The proposal, made in 1975, was fleshed out three years later at an International Conference on Primary Health Care in Alma-Ata, in the Soviet Union. The declaration, backed by both UNICEF (the United Nations Children's Fund) and the WHO, outlined the importance of primary health care in achieving this goal – that is, 'essential health care based on practical, scientifically sound and socially acceptable methods and technology made universally accessible to individuals and families in the community'.[54] The declaration marked a substantial break with the vertical health programmes of old and the inauguration of a new model, based firmly on the principles of equality and community participation.

But at least one of the WHO's vertical programmes had resulted in very real benefits for the world's poor. The greatest triumph was the global eradication of smallpox, a disease that regularly appeared in epidemic form in many developing countries. By the 1950s, most Western nations had succeeded in eradicating the disease through vaccination, but most poor countries lacked the resources to fund an adequate vaccine regime. In tropical areas, heat had also reduced the potency of vaccine lymph, but the development of freeze-drying techniques and mass production of vaccine in the 1940s and 1950s had solved that problem. The crucial step was the WHO's call in 1966 for the global eradication of smallpox, which led to the provision of funds and technical assistance to developing countries. In 1967, the first year of the campaign, an estimated 10–15 million people contracted the disease every year, and it was present in every continent except North America and Europe. By 1972, as a result of mass vaccination campaigns, the disease was eradicated from South America, and by the end of 1973 it was restricted to the horn of Africa and the Indian subcontinent. The WHO then altered its strategy from mass vaccination to the targeting of outbreaks, which succeeded in removing smallpox from Africa and Asia. The last naturally occurring case of smallpox was recorded in Somalia in October 1977, and in 1979 the disease was officially declared eradicated.[55]

The campaign, which was co-ordinated by the WHO official Donald A. Henderson, ranks as one of the great public health achievements of all time. But its conduct was not without controversy.

In India, for example, questionable tactics were used in the early 1970s to compel individuals to undergo vaccination. Military-style operations were mounted, in which villages were surrounded in the middle of the night and their inhabitants pinned to the ground by armed police and forced to undergo vaccination.[56] It is also a little-known fact that the success of the eradication campaign owed a good deal to rivalry between the Soviet Union and the USA. Assistance with smallpox prevention and other humanitarian projects was used to gain political influence during the Cold War, with the USA providing expert assistance from the Centers for Disease Control and the Soviet Union much of the vaccine.[57]

Set against the only successful attempt to eradicate a major disease, the results of primary health proved less dramatic. From the outset, there was disagreement over how best to implement the WHO's new strategy. Scarcely a year after the Alma-Ata declaration, two specialists in tropical medicine, Julia Walsh and Kenneth Warren, argued that it was far too idealistic, and that few countries could afford to provide health care for all. They recommended a more selective approach, whereby countries would identify their most common diseases and concentrate resources on treating and preventing them. Malaria was one of the diseases singled out as requiring a major concentration of resources. But many advocates of primary health care regarded this as a betrayal of the original ideals, and argued that selective health care did nothing to widen participation.

Being cheaper and easier to implement, as well as easier to assess, selective primary health care came to dominate in most developing countries. Typically, the emphasis has been placed on the health of the young, with mechanisms put in place to enable the monitoring of growth, and oral rehydration following bouts of intestinal disease, the promotion of breast-feeding (which helps to prevent diarrhoeal diseases), and immunization. Some of these objectives have been easier to meet than others. The promotion of breast-feeding, for example, was difficult in the face of the aggressive marketing of breast-milk substitutes. The WHO was itself accused of enjoying a cosy relationship with the manufacturers of baby food and of stifling criticism from health workers in the field.[58]

Immunization, though, made considerable progress. In the mid-1970s, around 5 million children were dying needlessly every year from infectious diseases like measles, tetanus, whooping cough, diphtheria, tuberculosis and polio. Vaccines were available for all these diseases, but only around 5 per cent of children in poor and middle-income countries were protected in this way. By the end of the 1980s, following immunization campaigns in most developing countries, more than 80 per cent of children were fully immunized by the time

they were one year old – a higher proportion than in some developed countries. Great progress was also made in some specialized areas of therapeutics, notably in the case of leprosy. The advent of Dapsone therapy in the 1950s, championed by the WHO, had reduced the number of cases in many countries where leprosy was endemic. But the use of multi-drug therapy from the early 1980s brought more dramatic results, and was successful in curing many cases that were resistant to Dapsone. By the 1990s some countries in which leprosy was endemic, like Myanmar (formerly Burma), were well on the road to the WHO's target of elimination, the incidence of leprosy having been lowered to one case in 10,000. Some critics have argued that these campaigns diverted resources from other important areas. That may be true, but the savings in human life and misery were tangible.[59]

Yet these successes need to be seen against the backdrop of a general deterioration in the health of people in many developing countries. When the initiative in primary health care was launched in the late 1970s, the mood was generally optimistic. Many newly independent countries in Africa and elsewhere had enjoyed an increase in resources during the 1970s, and had assumed, mistakenly, that primary health care would be inexpensive. They had been further encouraged by the generosity of international donors and by the assistance of countries as ideologically diverse as the USA and the USSR. But within a few years, the political environment changed radically. Although East and South-East Asia continued to prosper, economic growth in many parts of Africa and Latin America slowed or reversed. Growing indebtedness prompted financial institutions such as the World Bank and the International Monetary Fund to seek 'structural adjustment' as a condition for rescheduling repayment of loans. Structural adjustment usually entailed currency devaluation, the withdrawal of subsidies on foodstuffs, and cuts in public spending. This began to affect health in two ways. First, job losses, rising inflation and the withdrawal of subsidies had a devastating effect upon standards of living and nutrition. Second, cuts in health spending, higher charges and lower incomes left many unable to afford health care.

The effects of structural adjustment meant that many poorer countries were unable to cope with new menaces such as HIV/AIDS, and with resurgent infections of malaria, yellow fever and tuberculosis. The history of HIV/AIDS dramatically illustrates the inequalities that exist between rich and poor nations, though not all such inequalities can be attributed to wealth or poverty alone. By the year 2000, around 33 million people were living with the HIV virus, while AIDS killed nearly a million people per year, making it the world's third biggest killer, and the second biggest if deaths from AIDS-related infections are included.[60] Ninety-five per cent of these cases occurred in developing countries. The problem was particularly acute in sub-Saharan Africa, where between 20 and 50 per cent of all pregnant women carried the disease. Life expectancy at birth in the southern African nation of Botswana, for example, fell from seventy to fifty years. HIV infection also began to rise alarmingly in many Asian countries like India, which at the turn of the century had one-quarter of the people diagnosed as HIV-positive.[61] In these and other poor countries, it made little sense to speak of 'risk groups', as the virus was far more widely disseminated than in the West. The main factors affecting the spread of the disease were poverty, the low status of women, and political turmoil. What was most striking was the vulnerability of the poorest in society, particularly those forced to find employment in the sex trade.[62]

Because the overwhelming majority of cases occurred in developing countries, the international community was slow to recognize HIV as a global problem. In the early years of the epidemic in the West, the tendency, as we have seen, was to regard Africa as the source of the disease rather than its victim. It was not until 1987 that the WHO founded the Global Programme on AIDS and began to fund initiatives in poorer countries. One of its few success stories was Uganda, which was one of the first countries to take advantage of WHO funds to launch a national campaign. A state-sponsored campaign against AIDS was inaugurated in 1986, and government efforts were assisted by a number of self-help groups like the Ugandan AIDS Support Organisation, which provided counselling, medical care and material assistance to the afflicted. One particularly important measure was the use of the drug Nevirapine to prevent the transmission of AIDS from mothers to babies. The drug was relatively cheap, and was provided free of charge to expectant mothers.[63] Although it proved difficult to overcome deeply ingrained prejudices, particularly about the role of women,[64] Uganda proved far more successful in controlling the spread of HIV infection than other sub-Saharan countries. From a peak of 10,235 new cases per year in 1991, the number fell to a low of 1,149 in 1999, with a slight increase the year after.[65] Uganda's success provided proof that political will was the key to successful health initiatives, and that even the poorest countries could do much to better the lives of their population.

The response of some richer countries was highly negligent by comparison. The conduct of the South African president, Thabo Mbeki, was singled out for particular criticism for his refusal to admit that AIDS is caused by a virus. Mbeki insisted that AIDS was primarily an auto-immune disease caused by poverty and malnutrition, a ploy that aimed to deflect public criticism from his government's refusal to tackle the problem. Mbeki's standpoint rested partly on the observation that many AIDS victims died from diseases – such as tuberculosis – that were commonly associated with poverty. In 1993 the WHO had declared tuberculosis a 'global emergency', noting that 8 million new cases occurred every year. This increase was attributed to the combined effects of AIDS on the immune system, poor nutrition, cuts in treatment facilities, and the emergence of drug-resistant strains. But Mbeki's refusal to accept that AIDS was a sexually transmitted disease, and to take the necessary medical and educational steps to prevent it, led to mounting criticism within and outside South Africa. AIDS activists and doctors in South Africa, and even the Ministry of Health, saw the president's stance as incompatible with human rights. They pointed out that the drug Nevirapine, as used in Uganda, was safe, effective and affordable.[66]

But in one sense AIDS was very much a disease of poverty. From the late 1980s, most people who had contracted the disease in the West could avail themselves of treatment with AZT or other drugs, with the result that the disease was transformed into a long-term, chronic condition. The vast majority of those infected with HIV in the developing world, however, had no access to the drugs needed to manage HIV- and AIDS-related diseases. The AIDS-related infection cryptococcal meningitis, for example, can be treated effectively with the drug Flucanzole, but the first two weeks of treatment alone cost the equivalent of $800 in most countries – a sum well beyond the means of most people in the developing world. Patent law protected the rights of pharmaceutical companies to manufacture and retail these drugs, so cheaper generic alternatives could not be used. At the beginning of the twenty-first century, there were signs that this straitjacket was beginning to loosen in the face of adverse publicity. The American company that manufactured Flucanzole donated the drug free of charge to AIDS patients in South Africa. However, this gesture may have served only to highlight the absence of an ethical policy on the production and marketing of drugs. Notable too is the silence of international health agencies on this issue. As Paul Farmer comments, 'In Geneva and Paris and Bethesda, few have made anything of the fact that Africa is the continent that could benefit most from these drugs,'[67] while others claim that the WHO is now dominated more than ever before by the interests of powerful donor states.[68]

But the perspective from poor countries was sometimes very different. Some regarded it as inevitable that pharmaceutical companies would protect their patents in order to recover the large sums invested in research and development. Others blamed their own governments for their failure to purchase drugs on behalf of their populations, claiming that many African countries had squandered funds through corruption and needless wars. There was a growing feeling in developing countries that they needed to put their own house in order before seeking more assistance from the West.[69]

At the beginning of the twenty-first century, HIV/AIDS stood out as the major threat to the health of the developing world, whereas it played a relatively minor role in mortality in more prosperous countries. But it was not the only disease to cause alarm. Many familiar infections like malaria and yellow fever were beginning to creep back into areas from which they had once been eradicated. Some apparently new diseases were also emerging as a consequence of ecological disruption and changing patterns of settlement. The world watched with horror as previously unknown diseases erupted in parts of Africa and some other tropical regions, arousing apocalyptic fears of a deadly new pestilence.[70]

The most infamous of these diseases were the haemorrhagic fevers, Marburg, Ebola and Lassa fever. All are viral diseases and cause massive internal and external bleeding. The Marburg virus was first identified when thirty-one people died of a mysterious disease in what was then West Germany. Eventually, the outbreak was traced to a shipment of African green monkeys imported from Uganda. Since then, the disease has struck in the West only twice, in 1976 and again in 1990. All the individuals involved had contracted the disease during travels to Africa, but despite extensive searches in Africa, scientists were unable to identify the main vector of the disease. The high mortality among monkeys suggested that they were not the natural carrier, as mortality is greatest in hosts that have never been exposed to the virus.

A closely related viral disease, Ebola, was identified in the Sudan and Zaire in 1976. The outbreaks appear to have been caused by two strains of the same virus: the former with a mortality rate of 50 per cent, the latter, more deadly, strain with a lethality of 90 per cent. In 1989 there was further alarm when the disease was identified in monkeys imported into the USA for scientific research. The monkeys came from the Philippines rather than Africa, but died from a virus very similar to that which killed humans in Africa. Fortunately, the disease did not claim any human lives in this instance, although the episode caused a great panic. The Hazelton Research facility in Virginia, where the outbreak occurred, was completely scrubbed and fumigated, and the entire consignment of monkeys destroyed.[71]

At around the same time, there were several other outbreaks of rare tropical fevers in the West, resulting in the death of one man from Lassa fever in Chicago in 1989. Media coverage of these events was lurid, and the incident inspired several fictional accounts, such as the film *Outbreak*. The outbreaks also formed the subject of Paul Preston's best-selling book, *The Hot Zone* (1994), which conjured up familiar metaphors of tropical Africa as a dark factory of disease. But the attention given to these diseases, as Preston himself admitted, was out of all proportion to the threat they posed to humanity, in either Africa or the West. They were so deadly that they effectively burned themselves out, destroying their hosts with a rapidity that beggared belief. Despite the well-publicized images of doctors in protective 'space-suits', the viruses causing Marburg and Ebola fevers were also found to be less contagious than originally thought. It became evident that they could not be transmitted easily by air or human contact, and that many previous outbreaks had been aggravated by placing victims and suspects in hospital, where they were in close proximity with one another. The natural hosts of Ebola, like Marburg, continued to elude scientists, but in the case of Lassa fever, it was found that the most common route of infection was the urine of infected rats.

Compared with the heavy burden of diseases like AIDS and malaria, the threat posed by these exotic fevers pales into insignificance. Nevertheless, they have continued to attract a disproportionate amount of attention, perhaps because they have come to epitomize the dangers of ecological disruption. These 'emerging diseases', as they are often termed, have been seen as Nature's retribution for environmental degradation.[72] Such apocalyptic interpretations contain a grain of truth, as many diseases have arisen as a result of changes in human settlement and agricultural practices. The extension of rice cultivation in some areas of Asia, for example, has brought humans into contact with the mouse vector of the Hanta virus, the cause of another haemorrhagic fever. Changing agricultural practices in Argentina and Bolivia have been linked to the emergence of the diseases Junin and Machupo, again both haemorrhagic fevers.[73] However, the most deadly threat to humanity continues to be the highly contagious influenza virus, which emerges from long-settled agricultural areas in southern China. Pandemics normally arise when two strains of the virus existing among fowl come together to produce a new strain that can infect humans. The reason why China appears to be the source of influenza pandemics is probably the prevalence of duck rearing alongside that of pigs. Ducks appear to be the main reservoirs of influenza, and pigs serve as 'mixing vessels' for new mammalian strains.[74]

This is not to suggest that environmental degradation has had a trivial effect upon the health of developing countries – far from it. The scale and pace of change have been staggering, and have had a detrimental effect upon health. In the Brazilian state of Rondonia in the western Amazon, between 400,000 and 800,000 new cases of malaria annually have been attributed to the construction of Highway 364, which necessitated the clearance of 20 per cent of forest in the state in less than five years. Clearance of the woodland allowed pools of water to form in which mosquitoes could breed.[75] Indeed, by the 1990s, more than a million acres of tropical rain forest had been lost as a result of logging, causing soil erosion and possibly climatic change. It is now known that many diseases have a close relationship with climate change, malaria being an obvious example, because climate affects the distribution of its mosquito vectors. But even diseases like cholera appear to be affected by climate change, possibly because the warming of water provides a better habitat for the bacterium.[76] Cholera and malaria are also closely linked in some Asian countries to fluctuations in the monsoon, which in turn may be linked to climate change.[77]

An even more widespread problem in developing countries stems from rapid urbanization, itself partly a function of devastating droughts and crop failures in already impoverished regions. At the beginning of the twenty-first century, more than 80 per cent of the world's population lived in cities, and between 30 and 60 per cent of those in poor countries lived in slums or slept rough. Conditions in the shanty towns were similar to those in the new industrial cities of the nineteenth century, in that they lacked sewerage, refuse disposal and clean water. But the comparison is not exact, as new hazards like the exhaust fumes of motor vehicles have replaced smoke from railways and factories, for example. The economic context is also rather different, in that it is more international: toxic chemicals have been pumped into and dumped extensively in poor countries unable to withstand the pressure of multinational companies. The combined result is an increasing rate of respiratory and water-borne diseases, and of vector-borne diseases like malaria and dengue, as mosquitoes find breeding sites in badly drained land.[78] An unregulated market in drugs has made matters worse. In many developing countries, drugs are available at pharmacists without prescription, and people often fail to take them properly, or cease taking them too quickly because they cannot afford to complete their course of treatment. This has contributed to the emergence of drug-resistant strains of malaria and tuberculosis, for example – a situation aggravated by the lack of proper treatment centres in poor areas.[79] Slum and squatter communities have not been passive, however. Many have taken steps to provide their communities with paved roads, sewers, water supplies and refuse collection, sometimes, as in the case of Brazil, with support from government.

Epilogue

Despite the remarkable medical advances of the last half-century or so, the vast majority of human beings still die as a result of infectious diseases that are both preventable and treatable. Around 4 million deaths per year are due to acute respiratory infections, and around 3 million to diarrhoeal diseases, which often claim their victims at an early age.[80] Modernization has thus occurred unevenly, bringing economic change and social dislocation, often without the compensation of better health and material prosperity. The failure of many poor countries to develop in the ways that they and policy analysts predicted is a complex problem, and beyond the scope of this book. Explanations have ranged from economic exploitation by Western nations and transnational companies, to socialist policies that stifled enterprise and initiative. In more recent years, attention has also focused on unequal terms of trade, and particularly on the tariffs imposed by the North American Free Trade Agreement and the European Union. None of these explanations seems sufficient in itself, but all contain a grain of truth. The odds have been stacked against developing countries, but their destiny lies partly in their own hands. Corruption, privilege and poor economic management have served to compound whatever structural inequalities exist between the poorest and the richest nations.

There is little prospect that these inequalities will be addressed in the near future, and the burden of disease will continue to fall hardest upon the poor. But this should not be a counsel for despair. The last chapters of this book have shown that improvements in health can be achieved without major structural changes provided there is political will on both the part of the countries concerned and the international community. The global eradication of smallpox and the near eradication of polio and leprosy stand as testaments to what can be achieved with international co-operation, even though the immediate prospects look bleak. The success of a poor nation like Uganda in tackling AIDS by comparison with some of its richer neighbours shows that health depends on more than money alone. We already possess the knowledge and the technology to prevent and treat many of the world's major diseases; all that is currently lacking is the will.

Glossary

acclimatization The belief that humans, plants and animals could be transplanted to different climates.

Actor Network Theory Theory originally developed by Bruno Latour to analyse the formation of scientific knowledge. It states that both human beings and material objects acquire their identities as a result of their relation to one another.

acute Term used to describe an illness of short duration with severe symptoms.

agglutination The adherence of small bodies in fluid, e.g. blood corpuscles. Used as a test for certain infections.

alchemy The transformation of base metals into gold, silver or substances deemed to have magical properties; often practised as a branch of occult philosophy.

amine A compound derived from ammonia, or amino acids, which plays an important part in the working of the body, e.g. adrenaline.

anthrax A deadly bacterial disease of sheep and cattle, capable of being transmitted to man.

antibiotic Term used to describe any antibacterial agent derived from micro-organisms.

antibody A protein produced by the body to combat toxins (antigens).

antihistamine Substance that counteracts the production of the amine, histamine; used mainly to relieve allergic reactions.

antipsychiatry Term used to describe the movement that developed in the 1960s which questioned the legitimacy of psychiatric authority and the reality of mental illness. It was particularly opposed to the biomedical treatment of madness in asylums.

antisepsis Method devised by Joseph Lister to kill germs during surgical operations, usually entailing the application of chemicals to the body.

antiseptic Term used originally to describe substances thought to prevent putrefaction; later to describe substances that killed germs.

antitoxin Preparation containing antibodies that neutralize a particular toxin released into the bloodstream by bacteria, e.g. tetanus, diphtheria.

apothecary Type of druggist or pharmacist, existing from medieval times.

Aristotelianism Pertaining to the philosophy of Aristotle (d. 322 BC); in medicine, generally characterized by the use of the deductive method and ideas of purpose in nature.

arthropod Animal of the phylum Arthropoda, with segmented body and jointed limbs, e.g. insects, spiders, crustaceans.

asepsis The attempt to make surgical operating theatres germ-free.

attenuation The process of reducing the potency of bacteria and viruses to enable them to be used for inoculation.

auto-immune The natural response of the body to infection, causing the production of antibodies.

bacillus Rod-shaped bacterium.

bacteria Microscopic, unicellular organisms, sometimes a cause of disease.

bacteriology Science of bacteria.

barbiturates Sedative drug.

bedside medicine Term used to describe system of medicine resting on close observation of patients' symptoms.

Benthamism see **utilitarianism**.

biomedical Term sometimes used to refer to modern medicine, especially its most technocratic aspects; denotes a form of medicine that concentrates on clinical entities rather than the whole person.

blood-letting A form of depletive therapy originally based on the humoral system; blood was drawn using leeches, cupping and venesection.

cameralism Germanic variant of mercantilism, which held that the size and welfare of the population were of vital political importance.

cardiovascular Pertaining to the heart and blood vessels.

cellular pathology A form of pathology pioneered by Rudolf Virchow in which the cell is the primary site of disease.

chemotherapy A form of therapy using chemicals.

cholera Term used from at least the sixteenth century to describe a serious, acute bowel disorder, now used specifically for the disease caused by the *Vibrio cholerae*.

chronic   Term used to describe a persistent or recurring condition.

classical   In medicine, it normally refers to ideas and practices developed in ancient Greece and Rome, or to their revival during the Renaissance.

clinical medicine   Medicine practised within a modern hospital setting; following the work of Michel Foucault, associated with new ways of seeing the body and disease, and new forms of doctor–patient relationship emerging in Revolutionary Paris.

Columbian   Pertaining to the voyage of Columbus to the Americas in 1492; specifically to the 'exchange' of diseases that followed contact with Europeans.

constitution   In humoral medicine, the peculiar balance of humours that makes up each human body; sometimes refers to an innate predisposition to disease (diathesis); also peculiar atmospherical conditions conducive to certain diseases (epidemic constitutions).

constructionism   see **social construction**.

consumption   Pulmonary wasting disease, often identified with tuberculosis.

contagion   In its most general sense, any corrupting influence or contamination; used more specifically to refer to the transfer of disease-causing matter directly from person to person, or to poisons produced by the body rather than the environment.

cordon sanitaire   Form of land quarantine or barrier to prevent movement of peoples suspected of carrying disease.

Dapsone   An antibacterial drug effective in the treatment of leprosy (Hansen's disease).

demography   The study of populations, especially population statistics.

depletion   A form of therapy that involves expelling corrupt or excessive humours from the body, e.g. by bleeding, vomiting or purging.

diagnosis   Traditionally, the identification of disease by examination of patients' symptoms; now includes the use of laboratory tests, radiography, etc.

diathesis   see **constitution**.

disorder   In medicine, the disturbance of the normal state of the body.

dispensary   Public or charitable institution where medicines are dispensed and where medical advice is given; has sometimes performed public health functions, e.g. as centres for vaccination.

electro-convulsive therapy (ECT)   Controversial, though sometimes effective, treatment for severe depression and psychoses.

emetic   Medicine that causes vomiting.

empiric Unqualified medical practitioner whose practice is based on knowledge gained entirely from experience.

endemic Term used to describe a disease that is normally present in a particular locality.

Enlightenment Wide-ranging movement occurring in the wake of the Scientific Revolution of the late seventeenth century and lasting until the French Revolution of 1789. Normally associated with the attempt to dispel ignorance, superstition, and political and religious tyranny. The Enlightenment was truly an international movement, but it was also geographically diverse.

entomology The study of insects.

epidemic Term given to a disease that affects a large number of people in a particular locality at a given time.

epidemiology The study of disease as it affects groups of people.

epistemology The theory of the method, or of the grounds of knowledge, determining what can be known and how.

eugenics The attempt to improve the biological condition of a population; can be 'positive' in the sense of ameliorating conditions affecting life chances, or 'negative' in the sense of discouraging or preventing those deemed 'unfit' from breeding.

Evangelicalism A form of Protestantism that maintains that salvation can be achieved only through atonement for one's sins. In the course of the nineteenth century, some Evangelicals became less individualistic and saw social action as part of their Christian duty.

fermentation Process of change induced by an enzyme like yeast.

framing Term used by the historian Charles Rosenberg to describe the recognition and explanation of disease by society.

Galenic Pertaining to the medical writings of Galen, a Greek physician of the second century AD.

germ theory Term often used to describe the theory that diseases are caused by specific micro-organisms, usually bacteria, viruses or parasites. In recent years, historians have stressed that there is more than one way of thinking about the action of 'germs'; hence it may be more accurate to speak of 'germ theories'.

haemorrhagic fever Fevers such as Ebola, which typically cause severe loss of blood from the blood vessels, internally and externally.

Hellenists Renaissance physicians and others who attempted to imitate the ancient Greeks.

Hippocratic Referring to the works of Hippocrates of Cos and his followers, and to later medical writers and practitioners who developed certain aspects of the Hippocratic writings, e.g. the relationship between disease and environment, the study of epidemics, and bedside medicine.

historicism   The attempt to see historical periods in their own terms; specifically, in this book, the attempt to understand disease and medicine in the same way as people living in the past.

humanism   Renaissance movement aroused by the rediscovery of ancient Greek and Roman literature, typified by devotion to human interests (rather than supernatural matters) and with man's progress as an intellectual being.

humoral system   System of medicine based on the supposition that the body is composed of four fluid substances called humours, i.e. black bile (associated with melancholy), yellow bile (with choler), phlegm and blood. Good health required that all four humours be kept in balance. The system was, and is, common throughout Europe and Asia, forming the basis of Hippocratic and Galenic medicine, Islamic medicine and Ayurvedic medicine.

hygiene   A branch of medicine devoted to the prevention of disease.

impetigo   Infectious skin disease that is caused by species of *Staphylococcus*.

incidence   The frequency with which a particular disease appears in a given interval.

infection   A term probably arising in the Middle Ages referring generally to corruption, contamination and affliction with disease; both people and places were described as 'infected'. The term was sometimes used in distinction to 'contagion', which from time to time was used to denote direct contamination from person to person. Today the terms 'infection' and 'infectious' are normally used to describe the transmission of pathogens from one person or place to another.

inflammation   Swelling of the tissues in response to disease or injury.

inoculation   Process by which infective material is brought into the body through a puncture of the skin or in a mucous membrane; the term is now practically synonymous with vaccination, but historically was used to distinguish between different ways of protecting against smallpox. Inoculation (or 'variolation') was the name usually given to the practice of inserting matter from dried smallpox scabs, whereas vaccination was the name given to the practice of using cowpox lymph, pioneered by Edward Jenner in 1796.

insulin   A hormone produced by the pancreas which helps the body to regulate the metabolism of carbohydrates, fats and proteins; its deficiency leads to the disease diabetis mellitus.

iron lung   Rigid case fitted over a patient's body, used as an artificial respirator in cases of polio.

isolation   The act of keeping a person suffering from a disease, or suspected of suffering from a disease, from contact with others. Isolation has been enforced by preventing the afflicted from leaving their homes, by quarantines, and by the use of special buildings or hospitals.

lazaretto A term originating in medieval Italy to describe a hospital for the diseased poor, initially for lepers and later for persons suffering from plague. Later, the term was used to refer to places of quarantine.

leper Term used to describe an 'unclean' person, usually afflicted with the disease leprosy. In medieval times, what was understood by the term 'leprosy' was very different from today, and 'lepers' may have suffered from a range of conditions. Because of its associations with moral corruption, the term is now considered inappropriate to describe persons suffering from leprosy (Hansen's disease).

leprosy Historically, a term given to a condition marked by severe skin conditions, loss or deformation of fingers and toes, bone changes, impaired vision and hoarseness of voice. Historical descriptions may or may not have been referring to leprosy as understood today, i.e. Hansen's disease, which is caused by the *Mycobacterium leprae*.

leukemia An umbrella term for several malignant disorders caused by an excess of white blood cells; the condition may be acute (lymphoblastic or myeloid) or chronic.

lobotomy Sometimes referred to as a leucotomy, a surgical procedure that cuts fibres in the frontal lobe of the brain to treat severe mental illness. The practice is now largely discredited and rarely practised.

Lutheran Follower of the German Protestant theologian Martin Luther (1483–1546).

malaria Historically, an Italian term meaning literally 'bad air', commonly used to refer to the air above marshy ground. Malaria in this sense was thought to produce fevers, especially what were known as 'intermittent fevers', in which symptoms occurred cyclically. After the discovery of the *Plasmodium* parasite by A. Laveran in 1880, the term 'malaria' was applied to a specific disease. Malaria as it is understood today encompasses four diseases caused by different species of the *Plasmodium* parasite: *P. falciparum*, *P. vivax*, *P. ovale* and *P. malariae*. The parasites are transmitted to human beings by the bite of the female *Anopheles* mosquito.

malignant Meaning virulent or infectious; also cancerous, tending to recur after removal.

Malthusian Pertaining to the doctrines of Thomas Malthus, whose *Essay on the Principle of Population* (1798) argued that population, if left unchecked, increased exponentially, doubling every 25 years, while food production increased much more slowly. Malthus advocated late marriage and sexual restraint to keep population growth in line with food production, and opposed all measures of artificial assistance such as poor relief.

materialism   The opinion that nothing exists except matter.

mechanism   A set of medical ideas and practices fashionable in late seventeenth- and early eighteenth-century Europe, in which medical practitioners attempted to reform their discipline in line with the physical sciences.

medicament   A substance used in the treatment of disease.

melancholy   One of the four humours (see above), an excess of which predisposed the individual to bouts of sadness.

mercantilism   An economic system, originating in the seventeenth century, based on the belief that the wealth of the nation depended on a surplus of exports over imports, and which recommended the accumulation of high reserves of bullion, together with aggressive action by the state to secure export markets and monopolies.

metropolis   A term used in colonial history to denote the main centre of power. The term is sometimes used to describe dominant nations, e.g. Great Britain in the nineteenth century, or cities in which power is concentrated. See **periphery**.

miasma   An infectious or noxious emanation, usually from rotting animal or vegetable matter.

molecular science   The science of molecules, minute groups of atoms whose role in bodily processes such as respiration was elucidated during the twentieth century.

morbid anatomy   Name given to the attempt to discern causes of death and the nature of disease by post-mortem dissections of the human body. Morbid anatomy played an increasingly important part in elucidating disease from the time of the Renaissance, but did not really come into its own until the eighteenth century. It is also known as pathological anatomy. Morbid anatomy led practitioners to think about diseases as if they were distinct entities, often localized in particular organs or tissues.

morbidity   Sickness, illness, disease or rates of sickness.

mortality   Death, or rates of death.

mortality transition   The name given to the change in mortality patterns experienced by many advanced industrial nations. It consists of falling general death rates, the main component of which was a fall in deaths from infectious disease. Following the transition, most deaths occur from long-term, degenerative conditions such as cancer and heart disease.

nativism   Xenophobic political philosophy which aims to deter immigration and promote the birth rate of native-born peoples.

natural-historical   In medicine, an approach that sees disease in terms of the environmental factors affecting its development. It is also a historical method that seeks to understand fluctuations and changes in disease over time.

natural philosophy A branch of classical philosophy concerned with the principles governing the material universe, embracing much of what is now thought of as 'science' but within a broader philosophical and, sometimes, theological framework.

nosology The classification of disease.

ontological A conception of disease that sees it as a distinct entity or thing, as opposed to a generalized disorder of the body.

paleopathology A science that aims to detect signs of disease from bodily remains, usually bones.

Paludism French name for malaria, also used in some other countries in the nineteenth and early twentieth century; now obsolete.

pandemic An epidemic that affects several different countries or, in some cases, most of the world.

Paracelsian Pertaining to the writings of Paracelsus and his followers during the sixteenth and seventeenth centuries. The term connotes the rejection of classical learned medicine, and the adoption of a more empirical approach based largely upon chemical remedies.

parasite An organism that lives in or on another organism, known as the host; it often damages bodily functions and causes disease.

paternalism A form of government or management that limits the freedom of the individual with the aim of improving the welfare of the whole.

pathological anatomy see **morbid anatomy**.

pathology The science dealing with the causes of, and changes produced in the body by, disease.

penicillin An antibiotic produced naturally on moulds; its discovery marked the beginning of a therapeutic revolution in medicine.

periphery A term in colonial history used to denote a nation or region that is exploited by, or is dependent on, the imperial core or metropolis.

pharmacology The science of the action of drugs upon the body.

phthisis Term formerly used to describe pulmonary wasting disease, which in many cases was probably tuberculosis.

physic The art of healing.

physician One who practises the healing art, normally after having completed a degree in medicine. Physicians were formerly the only practitioners to receive a university education, and were at the top of the medical hierarchy. The term is now used specifically to denote specialist practitioners of internal medicine.

physiology The science of the functions of living organisms and their parts.

plague　Originally a general term given to many forms of affliction and infestation but often used specifically for epidemics of contagious disease. The term is now most often used to denote the disease caused by the bacterium *Yersinia pestis*, which appears most commonly in its bubonic form and occasionally as pneumonic or septicaemic plague.

pneumonia　Inflammation of the lung tissue caused by an infection.

pneumonic　Pertaining to the lungs.

pogrom　Russian name given to an organized massacre of Jews.

poliomyelitis　Disease caused by a viral infection, involving the brain and the spinal cord.

Poor Laws　Laws relating to the support of the poor, often involving measures of control and discipline as well as pecuniary relief.

prevalence　A term used to indicate the proportion of a population afflicted by a disease at a given point in time.

prophylaxis　A treatment or other measure intended to prevent disease.

psychoanalysis　A form of psychotherapy derived from the theory and practice of Sigmund Freud, and later of Carl Jung and others. It is based on the theory that mental disorders arise from a repression in the subconscious of painful memories or conflicting instincts.

psychotherapy　The psychological, as opposed to physical, treatment of mental disorders.

psychotropic drugs　Drugs affecting mental states, e.g. hallucinogens, hypnotics, sedatives and tranquillizers.

public health　Originally a nineteenth-century term used to describe various aspects of state medicine designed to prevent disease. Initially, public health focused upon sanitary reform, smallpox vaccination and quarantine measures, but it was expanded in the late nineteenth and twentieth centuries to embrace the regulation of food and drink, trades, buildings and so forth; it also placed increasing emphasis on health education and measures to promote individual cleanliness. The focus of public health also moved during the twentieth century from the prevention of disease to the promotion of optimal health.

puerperal fever　An infection beginning in the genital tract after childbirth, miscarriage or abortion, often fatal before the advent of effective treatment in the 1930s; formerly known as 'childbed fever', now most often known as 'puerperal sepsis'.

purging　A treatment originating in humoral medicine designed to expel noxious matter from the bowels.

putrefaction　The decomposition of animal or vegetable matter.

quarantine　Originally a period of forty days in which a person, ship or thing was detained to prevent the spread of disease; later the period became more flexible. Quarantine was first imposed against plague in Italian states during the Renaissance, and later became more widespread.

radiotherapy The treatment of disease, mainly cancer, with penetrating radiation.

rationalization A term used by the German sociologist Max Weber to denote the application of scientific measurement to the management of human affairs.

realism A doctrine which holds that objects of perception have a real existence, independent of the person who perceives them. The term has been applied to those historians and others who hold that diseases have an irreducible biological reality that does not depend upon individual or social perceptions.

Reformation The sixteenth-century movement for the reform of the doctrines and practices of the Roman Catholic Church, culminating in the establishment of the Reformed and Protestant churches.

Renaissance The revival of art and literature under the influence of classical models between the fourteenth and sixteenth centuries.

retrospective diagnosis The attempt to identify, according to modern standards of medical knowledge, the diseases of the past.

retrovirus A virus containing ribonucleic acid, which is able to change its genetic material into DNA. This conversion allows the virus to become integrated into the host cell's DNA. HIV is a retrovirus.

rheumatic fever An acute febrile disease usually affecting children, often following a streptococcal infection.

rheumatism A term formerly used to describe many painful conditions of the muscles and joints, now considered obsolete.

rheumatoid arthritis A chronic inflammation of the synovial lining of the joints.

sanitarianism A term used to describe the movement for sanitary reform initiated by Edwin Chadwick and others in the mid-nineteenth century. The term was often used to refer to those who focused chiefly on the removal of filth as a means of preventing disease. Some of those described as sanitarians, such as Florence Nightingale, were opposed to the germ theory of disease.

schizophrenia The term given to a group of psychiatric disorders affecting cognition, behaviour and emotional responses, often involving delusions and hallucinations.

Scientific Revolution A term used to describe developments in natural philosophy during the seventeenth century; it is associated particularly with the rise of experimentation and mathematical descriptions of nature. The appropriateness of the term has recently been questioned by those who claim that these developments were too disparate and gradual to be described as revolutionary.

scurvy   A disease characterized by debility, soreness and bleeding of the gums, subcutaneous bleeding, and limb pains. The term was formerly used to describe a range of conditions with these symptoms, and was thought to arise from the putrefaction of bodily humours. It is now used to denote the condition caused by deficiency of vitamin C.

seasoning   A term formerly used to describe the gradual acclimatization of a person transported from one climate to another, during which protection against local diseases was conferred.

septicaemia   Blood-poisoning caused by bacterial infection.

serum   A clear, yellowish fluid that separates from blood and other bodily fluids when clotting occurs, e.g. plasma.

shell-shock   A label given to mental disorders occuring on the Western Front during the First World War. It was initially thought that these disorders arose as a result of exposure to exploding shells, but they were later attributed to psychological trauma and conflicting emotions. The term had enduring popular appeal despite being replaced by other labels such as 'war neuroses'.

social construction   The term often used to describe the theory that medical and scientific knowledge, including conceptions of disease, are affected by the social context in which they are produced. This position was first developed by sociologists of science at Edinburgh University, and is sometimes referred to as the Sociology of Scientific Knowledge (SSK). It contrasts with the realist position, described above. Many historians and sociologists now prefer the term 'constructionist', partly because social constructionism has been closely associated with a Marxist political agenda, and because everything is in some sense 'social'.

staphylococci   A genus of bacteria which appear in clusters resembling a bunch of grapes. One of the commonest micro-organisms, it is found in pus.

stem cells   Cells that develop a few days after an egg is fertilized by a sperm and begins to develop into an embryo. They contain an enzyme that enables them to divide indefinitely into specialized cells like those that comprise blood, skin, bone and nervous tissue. This has raised the possibility of regenerative therapy for a range of presently incurable diseases, including Parkinson's disease.

steroid   The name given to a group of compounds including adrenal and sex hormones. They play an important role in the normal functioning of the body. Natural and synthetic steroids can be used in the treatment of many diseases.

streptococci Bacteria that appear in clusters resembling a string of beads. Species of this bacteria cause many common diseases, including scarlet fever and pneumonia.

streptomycin An antibacterial substance derived from soil mould, it was the first effective treatment for tuberculosis.

sulphonamides Chemically synthesized drugs which became the first effective antibacterial agents.

surgery A branch of medical practice which treats injuries, deformities and diseases by means of physical operations or manipulation. Surgery originally had the status of a trade, and was commonly performed by barbers, hence the term 'barber-surgeon'. In some Italian states during the Renaissance, surgeons began to receive a university education, and their art was increasingly founded on a good knowledge of anatomy. Surgery was later practised alongside other forms of medicine, leading to the emergence of general practitioners in the nineteenth century.

sweating sickness The name given to a mysterious fever that occurred in many parts of Europe in the late fifteenth and sixteenth centuries, it was characterized by profuse sweating and was frequently fatal.

therapeutics A part of medical practice that aims to cure or ameliorate disease.

trypanosomiasis A group of parasitic infections endemic in west, east, central and south Africa, characterized by fever, anaemia and lethargy; popularly known as sleeping sickness.

tuberculosis A disease resulting from infection with *Mycobacterium tuberculosis*, most commonly affecting the lungs, but also the lymph nodes, bones and gastro-intestinal tract.

utilitarianism A social philosophy associated with Jeremy Bentham, James Mill and J. S. Mill, it places the satisfaction of the individual's wants at its core. Utilitarianism defines the goal of social policy as producing the greatest happiness of the greatest number; it was an important influence on the movement for sanitary reform.

vaccination The act of introducing a vaccine into the body. The term originated in the use of cowpox as a preventative against smallpox, but is now used to describe similar measures taken against all diseases.

vaccine The name given to dead or attenuated infectious material introduced into the body with the object of increasing its power to resist disease.

vaccinnifer A person, normally a child, who was used as a reservoir for vaccination when it was conducted on an arm-to-arm basis.

variolation see **inoculation**.

vector An animal that is the carrier of an infectious disease.

venesection   The puncturing of blood vessels in order to let blood for therapeutic reasons.

virulence   The severity of a disease or capacity of a micro-organism to cause disease.

virus   The name given to a group of very small infective agents causing many diseases, including the common cold, influenza, AIDS and chickenpox.

vitalism   The belief that life originates in, and is sustained by, a vital principle, such as a soul or spirit, as distinct from a chemical or physical force.

Notes

INTRODUCTION

1 Agnes Heller, *A Theory of Modernity* (Blackwell, Oxford, 1999), p. 52.
2 Max Weber, *Economy and Society*, ed. G. Roth and C. Wittich (University of California Press, Berkeley, 1978[1922]), vol. 1, chs 3 and 7; vol. 2, ch. 11; *idem, The Protestant Ethic and the Spirit of Capitalism*, tr. T. Parsons (HarperCollins Academic, London, 1991[1930]).
3 Heller, *Theory of Modernity*, pp. 1–18.
4 Fernand Braudel, *Capitalism and Material Life 1400–1800* (Fontana, London, 1979), p. 1.
5 Recent surveys include Philip D. Curtin, *The World and the West: The European Challenge and the Overseas Response in the Age of Empire* (Cambridge University Press, Cambridge, 2000); A. G. Hopkins (ed.), *Globalization in World History* (Pimlico, London, 2002).
6 Immanuel Wallerstein, *The Modern World System* (3 vols, Academic Press, New York, 1974–80).
7 The classic studies are Paul Baran, *The Political Economy of Growth* (Penguin, London, 1973[1957]); A. G. Frank, 'The Development of Underdevelopment', *Monthly Review*, 24 (1966), pp. 17–31. A good recent study is Robert Biel, *The New Imperialism: Crisis and Contradiction in North/South Relations* (Zed Books, London, 2000).
8 See John V. Pickstone, *Ways of Knowing: A New History of Science, Technology and Medicine* (Manchester University Press, Manchester, 2000).
9 David Healy, *The Antidepressant Era* (Harvard University Press, Cambridge, Mass., and London, 1997).
10 A useful introduction is provided in Andrew Cunningham and Bridie Andrews (eds), *Western Medicine as Contested Knowledge* (Manchester University Press, Manchester, 1997).

11   See Arthur A. Caplan, 'The Concepts of Health, Illness and Disease', in *Companion Encyclopedia of the History of Medicine*, ed. W. F. Bynum and R. Porter (Routledge, London, 1993), pp. 233–48; Robert P. Hudson, 'Concepts of Disease in the West', in *The Cambridge World History of Human Disease*, ed. K. Kiple (Cambridge University Press, Cambridge, 1993), pp. 45–52.

12   Christopher Boorse, 'On the Distinction between Disease and Illness', *Philosophy and Public Affairs*, 5 (1975), pp. 49–68; *idem*, 'What a Theory of Mental Health Should Be', *Philosophy of Science*, 44 (1976), pp. 542–73.

13   A. L. Caplan, H. T. Engelhardt Jr and J. M. McCartney (eds), *Concepts of Health and Illness: Interdisciplinary Perspectives* (Addison-Wesley, Reading, Mass., 1981); C. Currer and M. Stacey (eds), *Concepts of Health and Illness and Disease: A Comparative Perspective* (Berg, Leamington Spa, 1986).

14   P. Atkinson, *Medical Talk and Medical Work: The Liturgy of the Clinic* (Sage, London, 1995). See also Robert Dingwall, *Aspects of Illness* (Martin Robertson, London, 1976), ch. 6.

15   Ludwik Fleck, *The Genesis and Development of a Scientific Fact*, trs. F. Bradley and T. J. Trenn, ed. T. J. Trenn and R. K. Merton (University of Chicago Press, Chicago, 1979).

16   Owsei Temkin, *The Falling Sickness: A History of Epilepsy from the Greeks to the Beginnings of Modern Neurology* (Johns Hopkins University Press, Baltimore, 1945).

17   e.g. F. A. Hirst, *The Conquest of Plague: A Study of the Evolution of Epidemiology* (Oxford University Press, Oxford, 1953).

18   The classic early studies include Barry Barnes, *Scientific Knowledge and Sociological Theory* (Routledge and Kegan Paul, London, 1974); *idem, Interests and the Growth of Knowledge* (Routledge and Kegan Paul, London, 1977); Barry Barnes and Steven Shapin (eds), *Natural Order: Historical Studies of Scientific Culture* (Cambridge University Press, Cambridge, 1979).

19   Karl Figlio, 'Chlorosis and Chronic Disease in Nineteenth-Century Britain: The Social Construction of Somatic Illness in a Capitalist Society', *Social History*, 3 (1978), pp. 167–97.

20   The new agenda was most clearly expressed in P. Wright and A. Treacher (eds), *The Problem of Medical Knowledge* (Edinburgh University Press, Edinburgh, 1982). A classic study in this vein is Christopher Lawrence, '"Definite and Material": Coronary Thrombosis and Cardiologists in the 1920s', in C. E. Rosenberg and J. Golden (eds), *Framing Disease: Studies in Cultural History* (Rutgers University Press, New Brunswick, NJ, 1992), pp. 51–82.

21   François Delaporte, *Disease and Civilization: The Cholera in Paris, 1832*, trs. A. Goldhammer (MIT Press, Cambridge, Mass., and London, 1986), p. 6.

22   See, e.g., Christopher Lawrence, 'Disciplining Disease: Scurvy, the Navy, and Imperial Expansion, 1750–1825', in *Visions of Empire: Voyages, Botany, and Representations of Nature*, ed. D. P. Miller and

P. H. Reill (Cambridge University Press, Cambridge, 1998), pp. 80–106; Christopher Hamlin, *Public Health and Social Justice in the Age of Chadwick: Britain, 1800–1854* (Cambridge University Press, Cambridge, 1998).

23 Alison Bashford and Claire Hooker, 'Introduction: Contagion, Modernity and Postmodernity', in *Contagion: Historical and Cultural Studies*, ed. A. Bashford and C. Hooker (Routledge, London, 2001), p. 7.

24 Mary Douglas, *Purity and Danger: An Analysis of the Concepts of Pollution and Taboo* (Routledge, London, 1991[1966]), p. 35. Some of these ideas are explored further in Douglas's *Natural Symbols: Explorations in Cosmology* (Penguin, Harmondsworth, 1978[1970]).

25 See Alison Bashford, *Purity and Pollution: Gender, Embodiment and Victorian Medicine* (Macmillan, London, 2000).

26 Ludmilla Jordanova, 'The Social Construction of Medical Knowledge', *Social History of Medicine*, 8 (1995), pp. 361–82.

27 Bruno Latour, *The Pasteurization of France* (Harvard University Press, Cambridge, Mass., 1988), p. 159. See also Latour's 'Give me a Laboratory and I will Raise the World', in *Science Observed: Perspectives on the Social Study of Science*, ed. K. Knorr-Cetina and M. Mulkay (Sage, London, 1983), pp. 141–70.

28 Simon Schaffer, 'The Eighteenth Brumaire of Bruno Latour', *Studies in History and Philosophy of Science*, 22 (1991), pp. 174–92.

29 See Steve Sturdy, 'The Germs of a New Enlightenment', *Studies in the History and Philosophy of Science*, 22 (1991), pp. 163–73.

30 See Jan Golinski, *Making Natural Knowledge: Constructivism and the History of Science* (Cambridge University Press, New York and Cambridge, 1998); Michael Worboys, *Spreading Germs: Disease Theories and Medical Practice in Britain, 1865–1900* (Cambridge University Press, Cambridge and New York, 2000), pp. 12–13.

31 Charles Rosenberg, 'Introduction – Framing Disease: Illness, Society and History', in *Framing Disease*, ed. Rosenberg and Golden, pp. xii–xxvi. This essay is reprinted in Charles Rosenberg, *Explaining Epidemics and Other Studies in the History of Medicine* (Cambridge University Press, New York and Cambridge, 1992), pp. 305–18. All citations below refer to the latter.

32 Rosenberg, 'Framing Disease', p. 307.

33 Adrian Wilson, 'On the History of Disease-Concepts: The Case of Pleurisy', *History of Science*, 38 (2000), p. 282.

34 See Alfred W. Crosby, *The Columbian Exchange: Biological and Cultural Consequences of 1492* (Greenwood Press, Westport, Conn., 1972); *idem, Ecological Imperialism: The Biological Expansion of Europe, 900–1900* (Cambridge University Press, New York, 1986), William H. McNeill, *Plagues and Peoples* (Anchor Press, Doubleday, Garden City, NY, 1976). See notes to ch. 5 for a fuller set of references.

35 See Keith Manchester, *The Archaeology of Disease* (University of Bradford Press, Bradford, 1983); Charles L. Greenblatt (ed.), *Digging for Pathogens: Ancient Emerging Diseases – Their Evolutionary,*

Anthropological and Archaeological Context (Balaban Publishers, Rehovot, 1998).

CHAPTER 1   DISEASE AND MEDICINE BEFORE 1500

1   See Wilfrid Bosner, *The Medical Background of Anglo-Saxon England* (Wellcome Historical Library, London, 1963), pp. 59–63; J.-N. Biraben and Jacques Le Goff, 'The Plague in the Early Middle Ages', in *Biology of Man in History: Selections from the Annales*, ed. R. Foster and O. Ranum (Johns Hopkins University Press, Baltimore and London, 1975), pp. 48–80.

2   Lawrence I. Conrad, 'The Arab-Islamic Medical Tradition', in L. I. Conrad, M. Neve, V. Nutton, R. Porter and A. Wear, *The Western Medical Tradition 800 BC to AD 1800* (Cambridge University Press, Cambridge, 1995), pp. 93–138.

3   Michael McVaugh, *Medicine before the Plague* (Cambridge University Press, Cambridge, 1993); L. Garcia-Ballester et al. (eds), *Practical Medicine from Salerno to the Black Death* (Cambridge University Press, Cambridge, 1994); V. Nutton, 'Medicine in Medieval Western Europe, 1000–1500', in Conrad et al., *Western Medical Tradition*, pp. 139–206.

4   G. E. R. Lloyd (ed.), *Hippocratic Writings* (Penguin, London, 1983); Owsei Temkin, *Hippocrates in a World of Pagans and Christians* (Johns Hopkins University Press, Baltimore, 1991); V. Nutton, 'Medicine in the Greek World, 800–50 BC', in Conrad et al., *Western Medical Tradition*, pp. 11–38.

5   Nutton, 'Medicine in Medieval Western Europe', p. 177.

6   Carole Rawcliffe, *Medicine and Society in Later Medieval England* (Sutton, Stroud, 1997), chs 5–7; Nutton, 'Medicine in Medieval Western Europe', pp. 164–8.

7   Miri Rubin, *Charity and Community in Medieval Cambridge* (Cambridge University Press, Cambridge, 1987), pp. 99–147; *idem*, 'Development and Change in English Hospitals, 1150–1500', in *The Hospital in History*, ed. L. Granshaw and R. Porter (Routledge, London, 1989), pp. 41–60; *idem*, 'Imagining Medieval Hospitals: Considerations on the Cultural Meaning of Institutional Change', in *Medicine and Charity before the Welfare State*, ed. J. Barry and C. Jones (Routledge, London, 1991), pp. 14–26; John Henderson, *Piety and Charity in Late Medieval Florence* (Clarendon Press, Oxford, 1994); Guenter B. Risse, *Mending Bodies, Saving Souls: A History of Hospitals* (Oxford University Press, New York, 1999), pp. 87–166.

8   Risse, *Mending Bodies, Saving Souls*, pp. 167–190; Nutton, 'Medicine in Medieval Western Europe', p. 189.

9   Michel Foucault, *Madness and Civilization: A History of Insanity in the Age of Reason*, tr. R. Howard (Tavistock, London, 1967); P. Richards,

The Medieval Leper and his Northern Heirs (D. S. Brewer, Cambridge, 1977); R. I. Moore, *The Formation of a Persecuting Society: Power and Deviance in Western Europe, 950–1250* (Basil Blackwell, Oxford, 1987).

10 F-O. Touati, 'Contagion and Leprosy: Myths, Ideas and Evolution in Medieval Minds and Societies', in *Contagion: Perspectives from Pre-Modern Societies*, ed. L. I. Conrad and D. Wujastyk (Ashgate, Aldershot, 2000), pp. 179–202.

11 Martha Carlin, 'Medieval English Hospitals', in *Hospital in History*, ed. Granshaw and Porter, p. 23; Nutton, 'Medicine in Medieval Western Europe', p. 189.

12 Norman F. Cantor, *In the Wake of the Plague: The Black Death and the World it Made* (Simon and Shuster, London, 2001), pp. 6–7.

13 Graham Twigg, *The Black Death: A Biological Reappraisal* (Schocken, New York, 1984).

14 Cantor, *In the Wake of the Plague*, pp. 15–16.

15 See Philip Ziegler, *The Black Death* (Collins, London, 1969), pp. 87–8; Norman Cohn, *The Pursuit of the Millennium* (Secker and Warburg, New York, 1962), pp. 127–47; William Naphy and Andrew Spicer, *The Black Death: A History of Plagues 1345–1730* (Tempus, Stroud, 2000), pp. 63–74; Suzanne E. Hatty and James Hatty, *The Disordered Body* (State University of New York Press, Albany, 1999).

16 Michael W. Dols, *The Black Death in the Middle East* (Princeton University Press, Princeton, 1977), pp. 296–8.

17 Philippe Ariès, *The Hour of Our Death* (Peregrine, London, 1987[1977]), p. 116.

18 John Hatcher, *Plague, Population and the English Economy 1348–1530* (Macmillan, London, 1987); J. M. W. Bean, 'The Black Death: The Crisis and its Social and Economic Consequences', in *The Black Death: The Impact of the Fourteenth Century Plague: Papers of the Eleventh Annual Conference of the Center for Medieval and Early Renaissance Studies* (CMERS, Binghampton, NY, 1982); G. Huppert, *After the Black Death* (University of Indiana Press, Bloomington, 1986); David Herlihy, *The Black Death and the Transformation of the West* (Harvard University Press, Cambridge, Mass., 1997).

19 Ann G. Carmichael, 'Epidemics and State Medicine in Fifteenth-Century Milan', in *Medicine from the Black Death to the French Disease*, ed. R. French et al. (Ashgate, Aldershot, 1998), pp. 221–47.

20 Robert S. Gottfried, *The Black Death: Natural and Human Disaster in Medieval Europe* (Free Press, New York, 1983), pp. 110–14.

21 See Robert Parker, *Miasma: Pollution and Purification in Early Greek Religion* (Clarendon Press, Oxford, 1983); Mirko D. Grmek, *Diseases in the Ancient Greek World*, tr. M. Muellner and L. Muellner (Johns Hopkins University Press, Baltimore, 1989); Conrad and Wujastyk (eds), *Contagion*; Valerie M. Hope and Eireann Marshall (eds), *Death and Disease in the Ancient City* (Routledge London, 2000).

22 Naphy and Spicer, *Black Death*, pp. 66–7.

23 Carlo M. Cipolla, *Public Health and the Medical Profession in the*

Renaissance (Cambridge University Press, Cambridge, 1976), pp. 11–16.

24 Nutton, 'Medicine in Medieval Western Europe', pp. 196–7.

CHAPTER 2 EARLY MODERN EUROPE

1   William H. McNeill, *Plagues and Peoples* (Blackwell, Oxford, 1977), pp. 221–2; Paul Slack, 'Mortality Crises and Epidemic Disease in England 1485–1610', in *Health, Medicine and Mortality*, ed. C. Webster (Cambridge University Press, Cambridge, 1979), pp. 9–61. The most recent hypothesis is that the disease was an arbovirus which possibly became epidemic due to environmental changes produced by agriculture. See Alan Dyer, 'The English Sweating Sickness of 1551: An Epidemic Anatomized', *Medical History*, 41 (1997), pp. 362–84.

2   Andrew Cunningham and Ole P. Grell, *The Four Horsemen of the Apocalypse: Religion, War, Famine and Death in Reformation Europe* (Cambridge University Press, Cambridge, 2000); Laurence Brockliss and Colin Jones, *The Medical World of Early Modern France* (Clarendon Press, Oxford, 1997), pp. 55–7; Slack, 'Mortality Crises'.

3   Charles Carlton, *Going to the Wars: The Experience of the British Civil Wars, 1638–1651* (Routledge, London, 1992), pp. 209–12; E. A. Eckert, *The Structure of Plagues and Pestilences in Early Modern Europe: Central Europe, 1560–1640* (Karger, Basel, 1996); Quentin Outram, 'The Socio-Economic Relations of Warfare and the Military Mortality Crisis of the Thirty Years War', *Medical History*, 45 (2001), pp. 151–84.

4   E. A. Wrigley, 'No Death without Birth: The Implications of English Mortality in the Early Modern Period', in *Problems and Methods in the History of Medicine*, ed. R. Porter and A. Wear (Croom Helm, London, 1987), pp. 137–8.

5   Mary Dobson, *Contours of Death and Disease in Early Modern England* (Cambridge University Press, Cambridge, 1997), pp. 287–367.

6   Philippe Ariès, *Centuries of Childhood*, tr. R. Baldick (Pimlico, London, 1996), pp. 36–7; Lawrence Stone, *The Family, Sex and Marriage in England, 1500–1800* (Weidenfeld and Nicolson, London, 1977), p. 81.

7   Colin Heywood, *A History of Childhood* (Polity, Cambridge, 2001); Eamon Duffy, *The Voices of Morebath: Reformation and Rebellion in an English Village* (Yale University Press, London, 2001), pp. 13–14.

8   E. A. Wrigley and R. S. Schofield, *The Population History of England 1541–1871* (Edward Arnold, London, 1981), pp. 250–3; *idem*, 'Infant and Child Mortality in England in the late-Tudor and early Stuart Period', in *Health, Medicine and Mortality*, ed. Webster, pp. 61–97.

9   Michael Neill, *Issues of Death: Mortality and Identity in English Renaissance Tragedy* (Clarendon Press, Oxford, 1987), p. 22.

10 R. A. Houston, *The Population History of Britain and Ireland 1500–1750* (Macmillan, London, 1992), p. 50; R. A. Finlay, *Population*

and Metropolis: The Demography of London, 1580–1650 (Cambridge University Press, Cambridge, 1981), pp. 107–8, 168–71.

11 Andrew Wear, *Knowledge and Practice in English Medicine, 1550–1680* (Cambridge University Press, Cambridge, 2000), p. 11.

12 See Barbara Howard Traister, *The Notorious Astrological Physician of London: Works and Days of Simon Forman* (University of Chicago Press, Chicago, 2001).

13 Andrew Wear, 'Medicine in Early Modern Europe, 1500–1700', in L. I. Conrad, M. Neve, V. Nutton, R. Porter and A. Wear, *The Western Medical Tradition 800 BC to AD 1800* (Cambridge University Press, Cambridge, 1995), p. 293.

14 Lucinda McCray Beier, *Sufferers and Healers: The Experience of Illness in Seventeenth-Century England* (Routledge and Kegan Paul, London, 1978); David Gentilcore, *Healers and Healing in Early Modern Italy* (Manchester University Press, Manchester, 1998), pp. 1–28; Margaret Pelling, *The Common Lot: Sickness, Medical Occupations and the Urban Poor in Early Modern England* (Longman, London, 1998).

15 Jerome J. Bylebyl, 'The School of Padua: Humanistic Medicine in the Sixteenth Century', in *Health, Medicine and Mortality*, ed. Webster, pp. 335–70; Nancy Sirasi, *Medieval and Early Renaissance Medicine* (University of Chicago Press, Chicago, 1990); Katharine Park, *Doctors and Medicine in Early Renaissance Florence* (Princeton University Press, Princeton, 1995); Ian Maclean, *Logic, Signs and Nature in the Renaissance* (Cambridge University Press, Cambridge, 2002).

16 Owsei Temkin, *Galenism: Rise and Decline of a Medical Philosophy* (Cornell University Press, Ithaca, NY, 1973), pp. 160–1.

17 Maclean, *Logic, Signs and Nature*.

18 Recent works include Andrew Wear, Roger French and Iain Lonie (eds), *The Medical Renaissance of the Sixteenth Century* (Cambridge University Press, Cambridge, 1985); Jonathan Sawday, *The Body Emblazoned: Dissection and the Human Body in Renaissance Culture* (Routledge, London, 1995); Roger French, *Dissection and Vivisection in the European Renaissance* (Ashgate, Aldershot, 1999).

19 Ole Peter Grell and Andrew Cunningham, 'Introduction', and Vivian Nutton, 'Wittenberg Anatomy', both in *Medicine and the Reformation*, ed. Grell and Cunningham (London: Routledge, 1993), pp. 1–11, 12–33.

20 Andrew Cunningham, 'Fabricius and the "Aristotle Project" in Anatomical Teaching and Research at Padua', in *Medical Renaissance of the Sixteenth Century*, ed. Wear, French and Lonie, pp. 195–222.

21 The best studies of Harvey are Gweneth Whitteridge, *William Harvey and the Circulation of the Blood* (Macdonald, London, 1971); Robert G. Frank, *Harvey and the Oxford Physiologists: Scientific Ideas and Social Interaction* (University of California Press, Berkeley, 1978); Roger French, *William Harvey's Natural Philosophy* (Cambridge University Press, Cambridge, 1994).

22 Classic studies include Walter Pagel, *Paracelsus: An Introduction to Philosophical Medicine in the Era of the Renaissance* (Karger, Basel,

1958); Allen Debus, *The Chemical Philosophy: Paracelsian Science and Medicine in the Sixteenth and Seventeenth Centuries* (Science History Publications, New York, 1977); Charles Webster, 'Alchemical and Paracelsian Medicine', in *Health, Medicine and Mortality*, ed. Webster, pp. 301–34; *idem, From Paracelsus to Newton: Magic and the Making of Modern Science* (Cambridge University Press, Cambridge, 1982); *idem*, 'Paracelsus: Medicine as Popular Protest', in *Medicine and the Reformation*, ed. Grell and Cunningham, pp. 57–77; *idem*, 'Paracelsus Confronts the Saints: Miracles, Healing and the Secularization of Magic', *Social History of Medicine*, 8 (1995), pp. 403–22; *idem*, 'Paracelsus, Paracelsianism, and the Secularization of the Worldview', *Science in Context*, 15 (2002), pp. 9–29.

23   Claude Quétel, *History of Syphilis* (Polity, Cambridge, 1990; Johns Hopkins University Press, Baltimore, 1992), p. 10.

24   R. S. Morton, *Venereal Diseases* (Penguin, Harmondsworth, 1974), pp. 24–5.

25   Jon Arrizabalaga, John Henderson and Roger French, *The Great Pox: The French Disease in Renaissance Europe* (Yale University Press, New Haven, Conn., 1997), pp. 84–5.

26   Ibid., p. 11.

27   Keith Manchester, *The Archaeology of Disease* (Bradford University Press, Bradford, 1982), p. 49; Srboljub Zivanovic, *Ancient Diseases: The Elements of Palaeopathology*, tr. L. F. Edwards (Methuen, London, 1982), pp. 232–4.

28   Hugh Miller, *Secrets of the Dead* (Macmillan, London, 2000), pp. 183–4.

29   Quétel, *History of Syphilis*.

30   Arrizabalaga et al., *Great Pox*, p. 126.

31   Ibid., p. 88.

32   Ibid., pp. 35–6.

33   Gentilcore, *Healers and Healing*, pp. 126–8.

34   Arrizabalaga et al., *Great Pox*, pp. 243–4.

35   Ibid., pp. 99–103.

36   Webster, 'Alchemical and Paracelsian Medicine'.

37   Mary Lindemann, *Medicine and Society in Early Modern Europe* (Cambridge University Press, New York and Cambridge, 1999), p. 57.

38   J. F. D. Shrewsbury, *A History of the Bubonic Plague in the British Isles* (Cambridge University Press, Cambridge, 1971); Paul Slack, *The Impact of Plague in Tudor and Stuart England* (Clarendon Press, Oxford, 1985).

39   Pneumonic plague was present in several late medieval outbreaks. See J.-N. Biraben, *Les Hommes et la peste en France et dans les pays Européens et Méditerranéens* (Mouton, Paris, 1975–6), vol. 1, pp. 9–18, 86; E. Carpentier, *Une Ville devant la peste: Orvieto et la Peste Noir de 1348* (SEVPEN, Paris, 1962), pp. 79–82; R. S. Gottfried, *Epidemic Disease in Fifteenth Century England* (Leicester University Press, Leicester, 1978), pp. 50–1; *idem, The Black Death: Natural and Human Disaster in Medieval Europe* (Free Press, New York, 1983), pp. 51–5.

40 Slack, *Impact of Plague*, p. 9; Ann G. Carmichael, *Plague and the Poor in Renaissance Florence* (Cambridge University Press, Cambridge and New York, 1986), pp. 86–7.

41 Slack, *Impact of Plague*, p. 16; Cipolla, *Fighting the Plague in Seventeenth-Century Italy* (University of Wisconsin Press, Madison, 1981).

42 F. A. Hirst, *The Conquest of Plague: A Study of the Evolution of Epidemiology* (Oxford University Press, Oxford, 1953), pp. 310–28.

43 Shrewsbury, *History of the Bubonic Plague*, p. 206.

44 Slack, *Impact of Plague*, p. 12.

45 Giulia Calvi, *Histories of a Plague Year: The Social and the Imaginary in Baroque Florence* (University of California Press, Berkeley, 1989), pp. 21–58.

46 Gentilcore, *Healers and Healing*, pp. 12–13; Margaret Pelling, 'The Meaning of Contagion: Reproduction, Medicine and Metaphor', in *Contagion: Historical and Cultural Studies*, ed. A. Bashford and C. Hooker (Routledge, London, 2001), pp. 15–39.

47 See Slack, *Impact of Plague*, pp. 26–8.

48 Wear, *Knowledge and Practice in English Medicine*, pp. 280, 286–8.

49 Slack, *Impact of Plague*, p. 29.

50 Ibid., pp. 29–30.

51 Brian Pullan, 'Plague and Perceptions of the Poor in Early Modern Italy', in *Epidemics and Ideas: Essays on the Historical Perception of Pestilence*, ed. T. Ranger and P. Slack (Cambridge University Press, Cambridge, 1992), pp. 101–24.

52 Shrewsbury, *History of the Bubonic Plague*, p. 327.

53 Lindemann, *Medicine and Society*, p. 45.

54 Slack, *Impact of Plague*, p. 32.

55 Biraben, *Les Hommes et la peste*, vol. 2, pp. 86–9, 102–5, 139–41; Carlo M. Cipolla, *Public Health and the Medical Profession in the Renaissance* (Cambridge University Press, Cambridge, 1976), pp. 11–15; Philippe Ariès, *The Hour of Our Death* (Peregrine, London, 1987 [1977]), pp. 56–8.

56 Paul Slack, 'Introduction' to *Epidemics and Ideas*, ed. Ranger and Slack, p. 18.

57 Michael Dols, *The Black Death in the Middle East* (Princeton University Press, Princeton, 1977), pp. 285–98; Lawrence I. Conrad, 'Epidemic Disease in Formal and Popular Thought in Early Islamic Society', in *Epidemics and Ideas*, ed. Ranger and Slack, pp. 77–100.

58 Pullan, 'Plague and Perceptions of the Poor', p. 119.

59 Ann G. Carmichael, 'Plague Legislation in the Italian Renaissance', *Bulletin of the History of Medicine*, 57 (1983), pp. 519–25.

60 Biraben, *Les Hommes et la peste*, vol. 1, pp. 198, 205–6.

61 Cipolla, *Public Health*, p. 59.

62 Hirst, *Conquest of Plague*, pp. 14–49.

63 Carmichael, *Plague and the Poor*.

64 Thomas More, *Utopia*, tr. P. Turner (Penguin, Harmondsworth, 1965), p. 81.

65 Shrewsbury, *History of the Bubonic Plague*, pp. 194, 259.

66   Wear, *Knowledge and Practice in English Medicine*, p. 317.
67   Norbert Elias, *The Civilizing Process*, tr. E. Jephcott (Blackwell, Oxford, 1994 [1939]).
68   Pelling, 'Illness among the Poor', in M. Pelling, *The Common Lot: Sickness, Medical Occupations, and the Urban Poor in Early Modern England* (Longman, London, 1998), pp. 64–5.
69   Pullan, 'Plague and Perceptions of the Poor', p. 117.
70   William G. Naphy, *Plagues, Poisons and Potions: Plague-Spreading Conspiracies in the Western Alps, c.1530–1640* (Manchester University Press, Manchester, 2002).
71   Suzanne E. Hatty and James Hatty, *The Disordered Body: Epidemic Disease and Cultural Transformation* (State University of New York Press, Albany, 1998).
72   Slack, *Impact of Plague*, pp. 295–300.
73   Ibid., p. 300.
74   Stephen Porter, *The Great Plague* (Sutton, Stroud, 1999), pp. 124–6.
75   John Henderson, 'Epidemics in Renaissance Florence: Medical Theory and Government Response', in *Maladies et société (XIIe–XVIIIe siècles)*, ed. N. Bulst and R. Delort (CNRS, Paris, 1989), pp. 165–86.
76   Wear, *Knowledge and Practice in English Medicine*, pp. 336–42.
77   Walter Pagel, *Joan Baptista Van Helmont: Reformer of Science and Medicine* (Cambridge University Press, Cambridge, 1982).
78   Wear, *Knowledge and Practice in English Medicine*, pp. 305–13.
79   Kenneth Dewhurst (ed.), *Dr Thomas Sydenham (1624–1689): His Life and Original Writings* (Berkeley: University of California Press, 1966).
80   Recent surveys include John Henry, *The Scientific Revolution and the Origins of Modern Science* (Macmillan, Basingstoke, 1997), and Steven Shapin, *The Scientific Revolution* (University of Chicago Press, Chicago, 1996).
81   On Puritanism and medicine, see Charles Webster, *The Great Instauration: Science, Medicine and Reform 1626–1660* (Duckworth, London, 1975).
82   Harold J. Cook, *The Decline of the Old Medical Regime in Stuart London* (Cornell University Press, Ithaca, NY, 1986); *idem*, 'The New Philosophy and Medicine in Seventeenth-Century England', in *Reappraisals of the Scientific Revolution*, ed. D. Lindberg and R. Westman (Cambridge University Press, Cambridge, 1990), pp. 397–436; Steven Shapin, *A Social History of Truth: Civility and Science in Seventeenth-Century England* (University of Chicago Press, Chicago, 1994), ch. 4.
83   R. French and A. Wear (eds), *The Medical Revolution of the Seventeenth Century* (Cambridge University Press, Cambridge, 1989); Lester S. King, *The Road to Medical Enlightenment 1650–1695* (Macdonald, London, 1970).
84   R. B. Carter, *Descartes' Medical Philosophy: The Organic Solution to the Mind-Body Problem* (Johns Hopkins University Press, Baltimore, 1983); Brockliss and Jones, *Medical World of Early Modern France*, pp. 418–32.

CHAPTER 3   DISEASE AND SOCIAL ORDER

1   See Theodore M. Brown, 'The College of Physicians and the Acceptance of Iatromechanism in England, 1665–1695', *Bulletin of the History of Medicine*, 44 (1970), pp. 12–30; Anita Guerrini, 'Isaac Newton, George Cheyne and the *Principia Medicinae*', in *The Medical Revolution of the Seventeenth Century*, ed. R. French and A. Wear (Cambridge University Press, Cambridge, 1989), pp. 222–45.
2   Benjamin Moseley, *A Treatise on Tropical Diseases* (T. Cadell, London, 1789), p. viii.
3   Lester S. King, *The Medical World of the Eighteenth Century* (University of Chicago Press, Chicago, 1958), pp. 59–93; *idem*, 'Medical Theory and Practice at the Beginning of the 18th Century', *Bulletin of the History of Medicine*, 46 (1972), pp. 1–15; G. A. Lindeboom, *Hermann Boerhaave: The Man and his Work* (Methuen, London, 1968).
4   Guenter Risse, 'Medicine in the Age of Enlightenment', in *Medicine in Society: Historical Essays*, ed. A. Wear (Cambridge University Press, Cambridge, 1992), pp. 159–60.
5   G. Rath, 'Neural Pathology: A Pathogenetic Concept of the Eighteenth and Nineteenth Centuries', *Bulletin of the History of Medicine*, 33 (1959), pp. 526–41; H. Buess, 'Albrecht von Haller and his *Elementia Physiologiae* as the Beginnings of Pathological Physiology', *Medical History*, 3 (1959), pp. 123–31.
6   E. A. Underwood, *Boerhaave's Men at Leyden and After* (Edinburgh University Press, Edinburgh, 1976); Andrew Cunningham, 'Medicine to Calm the Mind: Boerhaave's Medical System and Why it was Adopted in Edinburgh', in *The Medical Enlightenment of the Eighteenth Century*, ed. A. Cunningham and R. K. French (Cambridge University Press, Cambridge, 1990), pp. 40–66.
7   On Cullen see Inci A. Bowman, 'William Cullen (1710–90) and the Primacy of the Nervous System' (University of Indiana Ph.D. thesis, 1975); R. Stott, 'Health and Virtue: Or How to Keep out of Harm's Way: Lectures on Pathology and Therapeutics by William Cullen, *c*.1770', *Medical History*, 31 (1987), pp. 123–42.
8   E. Fischer-Homberger, 'Eighteenth-Century Nosology and its Survivors', *Medical History*, 14 (1970), pp. 397–403; King, *Medical World*, pp. 193–226; *idem*, 'Boissier de Sauvages and 18th Century Nosology', *Bulletin of the History of Medicine*, 40 (1966), pp. 43–51.
9   W. F. Bynum, 'Cullen and the Study of Fevers in Britain, 1760–1820', in *Theories of Fever from Antiquity to the Enlightenment*, ed. W. F. Bynum and V. Nutton, Medical History, Supplement no. 1 (Wellcome Institute for the History of Medicine, London, 1981), p. 137.
10   Michel Foucault, *The Order of Things* (Random House, New York, 1970), ch. 5.
11   Risse, 'Medicine in the Age of Enlightenment', pp. 164–5.

12   See W. F. Bynum and Roy Porter (eds), *Brunonianism in Britain and Europe*, Medical History Supplement no. 8 (Wellcome Institute for the History of Medicine, London, 1988).
13   Bynum, 'Cullen and the Study of Fevers', pp. 138–40.
14   'Lectures on Fevers', *c*.1770, Cullen Papers, 29, Royal College of Physicians of Edinburgh.
15   For Sydenham, see Roy Porter, *The Greatest Benefit to Mankind: A Medical History of Humanity from Antiquity to the Present* (Harper Collins, London, 1997), p. 269. Andrew Cunningham, 'Thomas Sydenham: Epidemics, Experiment and the "Good Old Cause"', in *Medical Revolution*, ed. French and Wear, pp. 164–90. Sydenham was indebted to Robert Boyle for his experimental methodology and his notion that the air was a source of fevers.
16   See John Arbuthnot, *An Essay Concerning the Effects of Air on Human Bodies* (J. Tonson, London, 1733); Baron de Montesquieu, *The Spirit of the Laws*, tr. T. Nugent (Hafner Press, New York, 1949), bks XIV–XVIII; Clarence Glacken, *Traces on the Rhodian Shore: Nature and Culture in Western Thought from Ancient Times to the End of the Eighteenth Century* (University of California Press, Berkeley, 1967).
17   Bynum, 'Cullen and the Study of Fevers', pp. 140–2.
18   Ludmilla Jordanova, 'Earth Science and Environmental Medicine: The Synthesis of the Late Enlightenment', in *Images of the Earth: Essays in the History of the Environmental Sciences*, ed. L. J. Jordanova and R. S. Porter (British Society for the History of Science, Chalfont St Giles, 1979), pp. 119–46.
19   Mark Harrison, 'From Medical Astrology to Medical Astronomy: Sol-Lunar and Planetary Theories of Disease in British Medicine, *c*.1700–1850', *British Journal for the History of Science*, 33 (2000), pp. 25–48; Anna Marie Roos, 'Luminaries in Medicine: Richard Mead, James Gibbs, and Solar and Lunar Effects on the Human Body in Early Modern England', *Bulletin of the History of Medicine*, 74 (2000), pp. 433–57.
20   David Harley, 'Political Post-mortems and Morbid Anatomy in Seventeenth-Century England', *Social History of Medicine*, 7 (1994), pp. 1–29.
21   Porter, *Greatest Benefit to Mankind*, p. 263.
22   See Othmar Keel, 'The Politics of Health and the Institutionalisation of Clinical Practices in Europe in the Second Half of the Eighteenth Century', in *William Hunter and the Eighteenth-Century Medical World*, ed. W. F. Bynum and R. Porter (Cambridge University Press, Cambridge, 1985), pp. 207–58; Malcolm Nicholson, 'Giovanni Battista Morgagni and Eighteenth-Century Physical Examination', in *Medical Theory, Surgical Practice*, ed. C. Lawrence (Routledge, London, 1992), pp. 101–34; Susan Lawrence, *Charitable Knowledge: Hospital Pupils and Practitioners in Eighteenth-Century London* (Cambridge University Press, Cambridge, 1996), pp. 306–10.
23   See Mary Fissell, *Patients, Power, and the Poor in Eighteenth-Century Bristol* (Cambridge University Press, Cambridge, 1991).

24 Post-mortems were common from the 1750s. See Papers of Sir John Pringle, vol. 5, f. 430, Royal College of Physicians of Edinburgh.

25 Elizabeth Haigh, *Xavier Bichat and the Medical Thought of the Eighteenth Century* (Wellcome Institute for the History of Medicine, London, 1984); John Pickstone, 'Bureaucracy, Liberalism and the Body in Post-Revolutionary France: Bichat's Physiology and the Paris School of Medicine', *History of Science*, 19 (1981), pp. 117–42.

26 Michel Foucault, *The Birth of the Clinic*, tr. A. M. Sheridan (Routledge, London, 1997 [1963]), p. 129.

27 N. D. Jewson, 'The Disappearance of the Sick-Man from Medical Cosmology, 1770–1870', *Sociology*, 10 (1976), pp. 225–44; Erwin Ackerknecht, *Medicine at the Paris Hospital, 1794–1848* (Johns Hopkins University Press, Baltimore, 1967); Toby Gelfand, 'Professionalizing Modern Medicine: Paris Surgeons and Medical Science and Institutions in the Eighteenth Century', in *Constructing Paris Medicine*, ed. C. Hannaway and A. La Berge (Rodopi Press, Amsterdam and Atlanta, 1998).

28 Keel, 'Politics of Health'.

29 L. W. B. Brockliss, 'Before the Clinic: French Medical Teaching in the Eighteenth Century', in *Constructing Paris Medicine*, ed. Hannaway and La Berge, pp. 71–115.

30 Laurence Brockliss and Colin Jones, *The Medical World of Early Modern France* (Clarendon Press, Oxford, 1997), pp. 689–700.

31 Jacalyn Duffin, 'The Medical Philosophy of R. T. H. Laënnec (1781–1826)', *History and Philosophy of the Life Sciences*, 8 (1986), pp. 209–10; Ackerknecht, *Medicine at the Paris Hospital*, pp. 101–13; George Weisz, 'Creating the Posthumous Laënnec', *Bulletin of the History of Medicine*, 61 (1987), pp. 541–62.

32 Russell C. Maulitz, *Morbid Appearances: The Anatomy of Pathology in the Early Nineteenth Century* (Cambridge University Press, Cambridge, 1987); Thomas Neville Bonner, *Becoming a Physician: Medical Education in Britain, France, Germany and the United States* (Oxford University Press, New York, 1995); John Harley Warner, *Against the Spirit of System: The French Impulse in Nineteenth-Century American Medicine* (Princeton University Press, Princeton, 1988).

33 Ackerknecht, *Medicine at the Paris Hospital*; W. F. Bynum, *Science and the Practice of Medicine in the Nineteenth Century* (Cambridge University Press, Cambridge, 1994), ch. 2.

34 Michel Foucault, 'The Politics of Health in the Eighteenth Century', in *Michel Foucault, Power/Knowledge: Selected Interviews and Other Writings 1972–1977*, ed. C. Gordon (Harvester Press, London, 1988), p. 171.

35 George Rosen, 'Cameralism and the Concept of Medical Police', *Bulletin of the History of Medicine*, 27 (1953), pp. 21–42; Risse, 'Medicine in the Age of Enlightenment', pp. 172–3.

36 George Rosen, 'The Fate of the Concept of Medical Police, 1780–1890', *Centaurus*, 5 (1957), pp. 97–113.

37 Dorothy Porter, *Health, Civilization and the State: A History of Public Health from Ancient to Modern Times* (Routledge, London, 1999), p. 55; Mary Lindemann, *Health and Healing in Eighteenth-Century Germany* (Johns Hopkins University Press, Baltimore, 1996).

38 Alfred Perrenoud, 'The Attenuation of Mortality Crises and the Decline of Mortality', in *The Decline of Mortality in Europe*, ed. R. Schofield, D. Reher and A. Bideau (Clarendon Press, Oxford, 1991), p. 21.

39 Alex Mercer, *Disease, Mortality and Population in Transition* (Leicester University Press, Leicester, 1990), p. 27.

40 Paul Slack, *The Impact of Plague in Tudor and Stuart England* (Clarendon Press, Oxford, 1985), pp. 323–6.

41 Caroline Hannaway, 'The *Société Royale de Médecine* and Epidemics in the Ancien Régime', *Bulletin of the History of Medicine*, 46 (1972), pp. 257–73; Mathew Ramsey, 'Public Health in France', in *The History of Public Health and the Modern State*, ed. D. Porter (Rodopi Press, Amsterdam and Atlanta, 1994), pp. 45–118.

42 C. Huygelen, 'The Immunization of Cattle against Rinderpest in Eighteenth-Century Europe', *Medical History*, 41 (1997), pp. 182–96.

43 Beatrice Moring, 'Motherhood, Milk, and Money: Infant Mortality in Pre-Industrial Finland', *Social History of Medicine*, 11 (1998), pp. 177–196.

44 Foucault, 'Politics of Health', p. 173.

45 Risse, 'Medicine in the Age of Enlightenment', p. 175.

46 George Rosen, *From Medical Police to Social Medicine: Essays on the History of Health Care* (Science History Publications, New York, 1974), pp. 159–75.

47 Courtney Dainton, *The Story of England's Hospitals* (Museum Press, London, 1961); H. C. Cameron, *Mr Guy's Hospital, 1726–1948* (Longman, London, 1977); Archibald Clark-Kennedy, *London Pride: The Story of a Voluntary Hospital* (Hutchinson Benham, London, 1979).

48 Lindsay Granshaw and Roy Porter (eds), *The Hospital in History* (Routledge, London, 1989); Anne Borsay, *Medicine and Charity in Georgian Bath: A Social History of the General Infirmary, c.1739–1830* (Ashgate, Aldershot, 1999).

49 Risse, 'Medicine in the Age of Enlightenment', pp. 176–7.

50 Ibid., p. 190.

51 J. R. Smith, *The Speckled Monster: Smallpox in England, 1670–1970, with Particular Reference to Essex* (Essex Record Office, Chelmsford, 1987), pp. 30–3.

52 G. Miller, 'Putting Lady Mary in her Place: A Discussion of Historical Causation', *Bulletin of the History of Medicine*, 55 (1981), pp. 2–16.

53 Risse, 'Medicine in the Age of Enlightenment', p. 191.

54 Ibid., p. 192; Peter Razzell, *The Conquest of Smallpox* (Caliban Press, Firle, Sussex, 1975).

55 Pierre Darmon, *La Longue Traque de la variole: les pionniers de la médecine préventive* (Perrin, Paris, 1986), pp. 116–18.

56 Genevieve Miller, *The Adoption of Inoculation for Smallpox in England and France* (Oxford University Press, London, 1957), chs 7–8.
57 Razzell, *Conquest of Smallpox.*
58 Donald R. Hopkins, *The Greatest Killer: Smallpox in History* (University of Chicago Press, Chicago, 2002), pp. 77–81.
59 Richard B. Fisher, *Edward Jenner 1749–1823* (André Deutsch, London, 1991), pp. 81–4.
60 See Michael Roberts, *The Military Revolution, 1560–1660* (Marjory Boyd, Belfast, 1956); Geoffrey Parker, *The Military Revolution: Military Innovation and the Rise of the West 1500–1800* (Cambridge University Press, Cambridge, 1996); Jeremy M. Black, *A Military Revolution? Military Change and European Society 1550–1800* (Macmillan, London, 1991).
61 Neil Cantlie, *A History of the Army Medical Department*, vol. 1 (Churchill Livingstone, Edinburgh, 1974), p. 69; Jeremy Black, *European Warfare 1660–1815* (Yale University Press, New Haven and London, 1994), p. 112.
62 Stephen F. Gradish, *The Manning of the British Navy during the Seven Years' War* (Royal Historical Society, London, 1980), pp. 38–9.
63 Richard Brocklesby, *Œconomical and Medical Observations* (T. Beckett and P. A. De Hondt, London, 1764), pp. 27–8.
64 Donald Monro, *An Account of the Diseases which were the most Frequent in the British Military Hospitals in Germany, from January 1761 to the Return of the Troops to England in March 1763* (A. Millar, D. Wilson and T. Durham, London, 1764), p. ix.
65 Gilbert Blane, *Observations on the Diseases Incident to Seamen* (Joseph Cooper, London, 1785), p. 207; Elliot Arthy, *The Seaman's Medical Advocate* (Richardson and Egerton, London, 1798), p. i.
66 Friedrich Ring, *Zur Geschichte der Militämedizin in Deutschland* (Deutscher Verlag, Berlin, 1962); H. Müller-Dietz, *Der russische Militärtz im 18 Jahrhundert* (Osteuropa Institut, Berlin, 1970); Joachim Moerchel, *Das Österreichische Militärsanitätswesen im Zeitalter des aufgeklärten Absolutismus* (Peter Lang, Frankfurt, 1984); Mark Harrison, 'Medicine and the Management of Modern Warfare', *History of Science*, 34 (1996), pp. 379–410.
67 Colin Jones, *The Charitable Imperative: Hospitals and Nursing in Ancien Regime and Revolutionary France* (Routledge, London, 1989), p. 210.
68 Ibid., pp. 217–18.
69 Geoffrey L. Hudson, 'Disabled Veterans and the State in Early Modern England', in *Disabled Veterans in History*, ed. D. A. Gerber (University of Michigan Press, Ann Arbor, 2000), pp. 117–44.
70 N. A. M. Rodger, *The Wooden World: An Anatomy of the Georgian Navy* (Fontana, London, 1986), pp. 109–12.
71 Gradish, *Manning of the British Navy*, p. 196.
72 Michel Foucault, *Discipline and Punish: The Birth of the Prison*, tr. A. Sheridan (Penguin, Harmondsworth, 1991), pp. 144–5.

73   Cantlie, *History of the Army Medical Department*, vol. 1, pp. 38, 108.
74   Monro, *Account*, pp. x–xi.
75   Peter Mathias, 'Swords and Ploughshares: The Armed Forces, Medicine and Public Health in the Late Eighteenth Century', in *War and Economic Development: Essays in Memory of David Joslin*, ed. J. Winter (Cambridge University Press, Cambridge, 1975), p. 75; Kenneth J. Carpenter, *The History of Scurvy and Vitamin C* (Cambridge University Press, Cambridge, 1988), ch. 3; Glyn Williams, *The Prize of the Oceans: The Triumph and Tragedy of Anson's Voyage Round the World* (Harper Collins, London, 1999), pp. 44–5, 56–8, 134–40.
76   Christopher Lawrence, 'Disciplining Disease: Scurvy, the Navy, and Imperial Expansion, 1750–1825', in *Visions of Empire: Voyages, Botany, and Representations of Nature*, ed. D. P. Miller and P. H. Reill (Cambridge University Press, Cambridge, 1996), pp. 80–106.
77   Blane, *Observations*, pp. 245–6.
78   Gilbert Blane, 'On the Comparative Health of the British Navy, from the Year 1779 to the Year 1814, with Proposals for its Further Improvement', in his *Select Observations on Several Subjects of Medical Science* (Thomas and George Underwood, London, 1822), p. 40.
79   John Walter and Roger Schofield, 'Famine, Disease and Crisis Mortality in Early Modern Society', in *Famine, Disease and the Social Order in Early Modern Society*, ed. J. Walter and R. Schofield (Cambridge University Press, Cambridge, 1989), pp. 57–8; Perrenoud, 'Attenuation of Mortality Crises'.
80   Michael W. Flinn, 'The Stabilization of Mortality in Preindustrial Western Europe', *Journal of European Economic History*, 3 (1974), pp. 285–318.
81   E. A. Wrigley and R. S. Schofield, *The Population History of England 1541–1871* (Edward Arnold, London, 1981), p. 650.
82   Most of the Italian states, e.g., experienced a rise in mortality crises during the second half of the eighteenth century. See Lorenzo Del Panta, *Le Epidemie nella Storia Demografica Italiana (Secoli XIV–XIX)* (Loescher Editore, Turin, 1986), pp. 195–8.
83   J.-N. Biraben, *Les Hommes et la peste en France et dans les pays Européens et Méditerranéens*, vol. 1 (Mouton, Paris, 1975), pp. 230ff.
84   Jean Deumeau and Yves Lequin, *Les Malheurs des temps: histoire des fléaux et calamités en France* (Librairie Larousse, Paris, 1987); John D. Post, *Food Shortages, Climatic Variability, and Epidemic Disease in Preindustrial Europe: The Mortality Peak in the Early 1740s* (Cornell University Press, Ithaca, NY, 1985).
85   Michael Anderson, 'Population Change in North-Western Europe, 1750–1850', in *British Population History*, ed. M. Anderson (Cambridge University Press, Cambridge, 1996), p. 246.
86   Vicente Pérez Moreda, *Las Crisis de Mortalidad en la España Interior (Siglos XVI–XIX)* (Siglo Veintuno de Espana, Madrid, 1980), pp. 327–74; François Lebrun, *Les Hommes et la mort en Anjou aux 17e et 18e siècles* (Mouton, Paris, 1971), pp. 329–87.

87 Jacques Vallin, 'Mortality in Europe from 1720 to 1914: Long-Term Trends and Changes in Patterns by Age and Sex', in *Decline of Mortality in Europe*, ed. Schofield et al., p. 42.

88 Flinn, 'Stabilization of Mortality'; Anderson, 'Population Change in North-Western Europe'; E. A. Wrigley, *People, Cities and Wealth: The Transformation of Traditional Society* (Blackwell, Oxford, 1987).

89 Flinn, 'Stabilization of Mortality'.

90 Roger Schofield and David Reher, 'The Decline of Mortality in Europe', in *Decline of Mortality in Europe*, ed. Schofield et al., p. 3; Wrigley and Schofield, *Population History*, pp. 230–1.

91 Alfred Perrenoud, 'The Mortality Decline in a Long-Term Perspective', in *Pre-Industrial Population Change: The Mortality Decline and Short-Term Population Movements*, ed. T. Bengtsson, G. Fridlizius and R. Ohlsson (Almquist & Wiksell, Stockholm, 1984), pp. 41–61; Vallin, 'Mortality in Europe from 1720 to 1914'.

92 John Landers, *Death and the Metropolis: Studies in the Demographic History of London 1670–1830* (Cambridge University Press, Cambridge, 1993).

93 Schofield and Reher, 'Decline of Mortality in Europe', p. 4.

94 John D. Post, *Food Shortage, Climatic Variability, and Epidemic Disease in Preindustrial Europe: The Mortality Peaks of the 1740s* (Cornell University Press, Ithaca, NY, 1985).

95 Steve King, 'Dying with Style: Infant Death and its Context in a Rural Industrial Township 1650–1830', *Social History of Medicine*, 10 (1997), pp. 3–24.

96 Wrigley and Schofield, *Population History*, pp. 384–94.

97 Post, *Food Shortage*.

98 Richard Grove, *Ecology, Climate and Empire: Colonialism and Global Environmental History, 1400–1940* (White Horse, Cambridge, 1997); J. P. Desaive, J.-P. Goubert, E. Le Roy Ladurie, J. Meyer, O. Muller and J.-P. Peter, *Médecins, climat et épidémies à la fin du XVIIIe siècle* (Mouton, Paris, 1972); Lebrun, *Les Hommes et la mort*, pp. 373–87.

99 Perrenoud, 'Attenuation of Mortality Crises', pp. 36–7.

100 Stephen J. Kunitz, 'Speculations on the European Mortality Decline', *Economic History Review*, 36 (1983), pp. 349–64.

101 Max Byrd, *London Transformed: Images of the City in the Eighteenth Century* (Yale University Press, New Haven, Conn., 1978).

102 Peter Borsay, 'The English Urban Renaissance: The Development of Provincial Urban Culture, *c.*1680–*c.*1760', in *The Eighteenth Century Town: A Reader in English Urban History 1688–1820*, ed. P. Borsay (Longman, London, 1990), p. 152; J. C. Riley, 'Insects and the European Mortality Decline', *American Historical Review*, 91 (1986), pp. 833–58; Landers, *Death and the Metropolis*, pp. 354–6.

103 J. D. Chambers, *Population, Economy and Society in Pre-Industrial England* (Oxford University Press, Oxford, 1972), p. 162.

CHAPTER 4   THE WORLD BEYOND EUROPE

1   On early European expansion see G. V. Scammel, *The First Imperial Age: European Overseas Expansion c.1400–1715* (Routledge, London, 1989); C. R. Boxer, *The Dutch Seaborne Empire* (Hutchinson, London, 1965); *idem*, *The Portuguese Seaborne Empire 1415–1825* (Penguin, Harmondsworth, 1973); A. J. R. Russell-Wood, *The Portuguese Empire, 1415–1808* (Johns Hopkins University Press, Baltimore, 1992); Nicholas Canny (ed.), *The Oxford History of the British Empire*, vol. 1: *The Origins of Empire* (Oxford University Press, Oxford, 1998).
2   Emmanuel Le Roy Ladurie, 'A Concept: The Unification of the Globe by Disease', in his *Mind and Method of the Historian* (Harvester, Brighton, 1981), pp. 28–83.
3   Jared Diamond, *Guns, Germs and Steel: A Short History of Everybody for the Last 13,000 Years* (London: Vintage, 1998).
4   Woodrow Borah and Sherburne F. Cook, *Essays in Population History* (3 vols, University of California Press, Berkeley, 1971–9).
5   Alfred W. Crosby, *The Columbian Exchange: Biological and Cultural Consequences of 1492* (Greenwood Press, Westport, Conn., 1972).
6   Alfred W. Crosby, *Ecological Imperialism: The Biological Expansion of Europe, 900–1900* (Cambridge University Press, New York, 1986).
7   The importation of smallpox remains a matter of some controversy. See George W. Lovell, 'Disease and Depopulation in Early Colonial Guatemala', in *The Secret Judgments of God: Native Peoples and Old World Disease in Colonial Spanish America*, ed. D. N. Cook and W. G. Lovell (University of Oklahoma Press, Norman, 1992), pp. 51–85.
8   T. M. Whitmore, *Disease and Death in Early Colonial Mexico: Simulating Amerindian Depopulation* (Westview Press, Boulder, Colo., 1991).
9   Virginia DeJohn Anderson, 'New England in the Seventeenth Century', in *Oxford History of the British Empire*, vol. 1, ed. Canny, pp. 193–217. See also John Duffy, 'Smallpox and the Indians in the American Colonies', *Bulletin of the History of Medicine*, 25 (1951), pp. 324–41; *idem*, *Epidemics in Colonial America* (Louisiana State University Press, Baton Rouge, 1953); Henry F. Dobyns, *Their Number become Thinned: Native American Population Dynamics in Eastern North America* (University of Tennessee Press, Knoxville, 1983); Russell Thornton, *American Indian Holocaust and Survival: A Population History since 1492* (University of Oklahoma Press, Norman, 1987).
10 Crosby, *Columbian Exchange*, p. 49.
11 William H. McNeill, *Plagues and Peoples* (Blackwell, Oxford, 1977), p. 207; Crosby, *Columbian Exchange*, pp. 55–6.
12 McNeill, *Plagues and Peoples*, pp. 208–9.
13 See David E. Stannard, *American Holocaust: Columbus and the Conquest of the New World* (Oxford University Press, New York, 1992);

Ronald Wright, *Stolen Continents: The Americas through Indian Eyes since 1492* (Houghton Mifflin, Boston, 1992).

14 Francis J. Brooks, 'Revising the Conquest of Mexico: Smallpox, Sources, and Populations', *Journal of Interdisciplinary History*, 24 (1993), pp. 15–28.

15 Robert McCaa, 'Spanish and Nahuatl Views on Smallpox and Demographic Catastrophe in Mexico', in *Health and Disease in Human History: A Journal of Interdisciplinary History Reader*, ed. R. I. Rotberg (MIT Press, Cambridge, Mass., 2000), pp. 167–202.

16 In addition to the literature cited above, see Francisco Guerra, 'The Earliest American Epidemic: The Influenza of 1493', *Social Science History*, 12 (1988), pp. 305–25; Cook and Lovell (eds), *Secret Judgments of God*.

17 David Noble Cook, *Born to Die: Disease and the New World Conquest, 1492–1650* (Cambridge University Press, New York, 1998), p. 13.

18 Ibid., p. 100.

19 Hans Zinnser, *Rats, Lice, and History* (Penguin, Harmondsworth, 2000 [1935]), p. 256.

20 McNeill, *Plagues and Peoples*, p. 209; Henry F. Dobyns, 'An Outline of Andean Epidemic History to 1720', *Bulletin of the History of Medicine*, 37 (1963), p. 499.

21 Hans J. Prem, 'Disease Outbreaks in Central Mexico during the Sixteenth Century', in *Secret Judgments of God*, ed. Cook and Lovell, p. 34.

22 Cook, *Born to Die*, p. 101.

23 Ibid., p. 102.

24 Crosby, *Columbian Exchange*, p. 57; Cook, *Born to Die*, pp. 72–83.

25 See David Henige, 'When did Smallpox Reach the New World (And Why does it Matter)?', in *Africans in Bondage: Studies in Slavery and the Slave Trade*, ed. P. Lovejoy (University of Wisconsin Press, Madison, 1986), pp. 11–26.

26 Hence Adrian Wilson's call for a history of 'disease concepts' rather than a history of diseases. See ch. 1.

27 Alan Moorehead, *The Fatal Impact* (Harper and Row, New York, 1966).

28 *The Journals of Captain Cook*, ed. P. Edwards (Penguin Books, Harmondsworth, 1999), 3 June 1773.

29 Ibid., 1 July 1774.

30 A. W. Crosby, 'Hawaiian Depopulation as a Model for the Amerindian Experience', in *Epidemics and Ideas: Essays on the Historical Perception of Pestilence*, ed. T. Ranger and P. Slack (Cambridge University Press, Cambridge, 1992), pp. 175–202.

31 Ibid., p. 189.

32 Stephen J. Kunitz, *Disease and Social Diversity: The European Impact on the Health of Non-Europeans* (Oxford University Press, New York, 1994), esp. ch. 3.

33 Ibid.; O. A. Bushnell, *The Gifts of Civilization: Germs and Genocide in Hawai'i* (University of Hawaii Press, Honolulu, 1993).

34   Kunitz, *Disease and Social Diversity*, p. 48.
35   See K. F. Kiple and S. V. Beck (eds), *The Biological Consequences of European Expansion, 1450–1800* (Variorum, Aldershot, 1997); Donald Denoon, 'Pacific Island Depopulation: Natural or Unnatural History?', in *New Countries and Old Medicine*, ed. L. Bryder and D. A. Dow (Pyramid Press, Auckland, 1995), pp. 324–39.
36   For recent studies of the Atlantic slave trade, see Johannes M. Postma, *The Dutch in the Atlantic Slave Trade* (Cambridge University Press, Cambridge, 1990); Robin Law, *The Slave Coast of West Africa* (Clarendon Press, Oxford, 1991); Hugh Thomas, *The Slave Trade: The History of the Atlantic Slave Trade 1440–1870* (Picador, London, 1997). Estimates of the number of slaves transported from Africa to the Americas vary from 9,566,100 – the estimate made by Philip Curtin – to 11,345,000, calculated by Rawley. See Philip D. Curtin, *The Atlantic Slave Trade: A Census* (University of Wisconsin Press, Madison, 1969) and J. A. Rawley, *The Transatlantic Slave Trade* (Norton, New York, 1981).
37   Sheldon Watts, *Epidemics and History: Disease, Power and Imperialism* (Yale University Press, New Haven, Conn., and London, 1997), p. 222.
38   Kenneth F. Kiple, *The Caribbean Slave: A Biological History* (Cambridge University Press, Cambridge, 1984); *idem* (ed.), *The African Exchange: Towards a Biological History of Black People* (Duke University Press, Durham, NC, 1987).
39   James D. Goodyear, 'The Sugar Connection: A New Perspective on the History of Yellow Fever in West Africa', *Bulletin of the History of Medicine*, 52 (1978), pp. 5–21.
40   Richard B. Sheridan, *Doctors and Slaves: A Medical and Demographic History of Slavery in the British West Indies, 1680–1834* (Cambridge University Press, New York and Cambridge, 1985).
41   Curtin, *Atlantic Slave Trade*; Kiple and Beck (eds), *Biological Consequences of European Expansion*.
42   Roy M. Anderson and Robert M. May, *Infectious Diseases in Humans* (Oxford University Press, Oxford, 1991), pp. 374–418.
43   Crosby, *Columbian Exchange*, pp. 48–9.
44   Dauril Alden and Joseph C. Miller, 'Out of Africa: The Slave Trade and the Transmission of Smallpox to Brazil, 1560–1831', in *Health and Disease in Human History*, ed. Rotberg, pp. 204–30.
45   Kenneth F. Kiple and Virginia H. Kiple, 'Deficiency Diseases in the Caribbean', in ibid., pp. 231–48.
46   Todd L. Savitt, *Medicine and Slavery: The Diseases and Health Care of Blacks in Antebellum Virginia* (University of Illinois Press, Urbana, 1978).
47   Thomas, *Slave Trade*, pp. 420–1.
48   Curtin, *Atlantic Slave Trade*, table 81.
49   David Northrup, 'African Mortality in the Suppression of the Slave Trade: The Case of the Bight of Biafra', in *Health and Disease in Human History*, ed. Rotberg, pp. 275–92.

50   H. S. Klein and S. L. Engermann, 'A Note on Mortality in the French Slave Trade in the Eighteenth Century', in *The Uncommon Market: Essays on the Economic History of the Atlantic Slave Trade*, ed. H. A. Gemery and J. S. Hogendorn (Academic Press, New York, 1979), pp. 261–72.

51   Curtin, *Atlantic Slave Trade*, pp. 280–2.

52   Northrup, 'African Mortality', pp. 288–92.

53   Thomas, *Slave Trade*, p. 716.

54   Ibid., p. 717.

55   Eugenia W. Herbert, 'Smallpox Inoculation in Africa', *Journal of African History*, 16 (1975), pp. 539–59.

56   Genevieve Miller, *The Adoption of Inoculation for Smallpox in England and France* (University of Pennsylvania Press, Philadelphia, 1957).

57   Herbert S. Klein and Stanley L. Engerman, 'A Note on Mortality in the French Slave Trade in the Eighteenth Century', in *Uncommon Market*, ed. Gemery and Hogendorn, p. 271; L. Stewart, 'The Edge of Utility: Slaves and Smallpox in the Early Eighteenth Century', *Medical History*, 29 (1985), pp. 54–70.

58   Sheridan, *Doctors and Slaves*, pp. 252–6; Megan Vaughan, 'Slavery, Smallpox and Revolution: 1792 in Île de France (Mauritius)', *Social History of Medicine*, 13 (2000), pp. 1–28.

59   Alden and Miller, 'Out of Africa', pp. 218–19.

60   Crosby, *Ecological Imperialism*, p. 215.

61   Philip D. Curtin, 'The White Man's Grave: Image and Reality, 1780–1850', *Journal of British Studies*, 1 (1961), pp. 64–110; *idem*, *The Image of Africa: British Ideas and Action, 1780–1850* (2 vols, University of Wisconsin Press, Madison, 1964), esp. chs 3 and 14.

62   David Geggus, 'Yellow Fever in the 1790s: The British Army in Occupied Saint Dominique', *Medical History*, 23 (1979), pp. 38–58; *idem*, *Slavery, War, and Revolution: The British Occupation of Saint Domingue 1793–1798* (Clarendon Press, Oxford, 1982); Douglas Leach, *Roots of Conflict: British Armed Forces and Colonial Americans, 1677–1763* (University of North Carolina Press, Chapel Hill, 1986), pp. 55–61; Kenneth Kiple, 'Race, War and Tropical Medicine in the Eighteenth-Century Caribbean', in *Warm Climates and Western Medicine*, ed. David Arnold (Rodopi Press, Amsterdam and Atlanta, 1996), pp. 65–79.

63   J. R. McNeill, 'The Ecological Basis of Warfare in the Caribbean, 1700–1804', in *Adapting to Conditions*, ed. M. Utlee (University of Alabama Press, Tuscaloosa, 1986), pp. 26–42.

64   See Alan Bewell, *Romanticism and Colonial Disease* (Johns Hopkins University Press, Baltimore and London, 1999), pp. 80–1.

65   James Lind, *An Essay on Diseases Incidental to Europeans in Hot Climates, with the Method of Preventing their Consequences* (J. & J. Richardson, London, 1808 [1768]), p. 8.

66   Bewell, *Romanticism and Colonial Disease*, ch. 2.

67   Thomas Trotter, *A Practicable Plan for Manning the Royal Navy, and Preserving our Maritime Ascendency, without Impressment* (Longman, Hurst, Ress, Orme and Brown, Newcastle, 1819).

68   Thomas Trotter, *Medicina Nautica: An Essay on the Diseases of Seamen* (T. Cadell and W. Davies, London, 1797), pp. 9, 322.

69   Thomas Trotter, *A View of the Nervous Temperament* (Longman, Hurst, Rees and Orme, London, 1807), pp. 143–4.

70   There was a marked contrast between the health and welfare of the British seaman and his American counterpart. See Harold D. Langley, *A History of Medicine in the Early U.S. Navy* (Johns Hopkins University Press, Baltimore, 1995).

71   See David Arnold, 'Introduction' to *Warm Climates*, pp. 1–19.

72   See Richard Towne, *A Treatise of the Diseases most Frequent in the West Indies, and herein more Particularly those which Occur in Barbadoes* (John Clarke, London, 1776), pp. 8–9; John Hunter, *Observations on the Diseases of the Army in Jamaica; and on the Best Means of Preserving the Health of Europeans in that Climate* (G. Nicol, London, 1788), p. 24.

73   See the essays in *Warm Climates*, ed. Arnold.

74   Copy of a letter from Mr Wigram, merchant, to Mr W. Richardson, East India Company House, undated (probably 1784), Western MS 7226, Wellcome Library for the History and Understanding of Medicine, London.

75   See Nancy Stepan, *The Idea of Race in Science: Great Britain 1800–1960* (Macmillan, London, 1982); *idem*, 'Biology and Degeneration: Races and Proper Places', in *Degeneration: The Dark Side of Progress*, ed. S. L. Gilman and J. E. Chamberlain (Columbia University Press, New York, 1985), pp. 97–120; Seymour Drescher, 'The Ending of the Slave Trade and the Evolution of European Scientific Racism', in *The Atlantic Slave Trade: Effects on Economies, Societies, and Peoples in Africa, the Americas and Europe*, ed. J. E. Inikori and S. L. Engerman (Duke University Press, Durham, NC, 1992), pp. 361–96.

76   Mark Harrison, '"The Tender Frame of Man": Disease, Climate and Racial Difference in India and the West Indies, 1760–1860', *Bulletin of the History of Medicine*, 70 (1996), pp. 68–93; Norris Saakwa-Mante, 'Western Medicine and Racial Constitutions: Surgeon John Atkins' Theory of Polygenism and Sleepy Distemper in the 1730s', in *Race, Science and Medicine, 1700–1960*, ed. W. Ernst and B. Harris (Routledge, London, 1999), pp. 29–57.

77   See Kenneth F. Kiple and Brian T. Higgins, 'Yellow Fever and the Africanization of the Caribbean', in *Disease and Demography in the Americas*, ed. J. W. Verano and D. H. Ubelaker (Smithsonian Institution Press, Washington, DC, 1992), pp. 237–48; Kiple, *Caribbean Slave*, pp. 12–22, 161–76; Kenneth F. Kiple and V. H. King, *Another Dimension to the Black Diaspora* (Cambridge University Press, Cambridge, 1981), pp. 29–49; Donald B. Cooper and Kenneth F. Kiple, 'Yellow Fever', in *The Cambridge World History of Disease*, ed. K. F. Kiple (Cambridge University Press, Cambridge, 1993), p. 1102.

78   Watts, *Epidemics and History*, p. 232.
79   Stepan, 'Biology and Degeneration'; Curtin, *Image of Africa*, vol. 1, pp. 84–5.
80   Curtin, *Image of Africa*, pp. 80–1.
81   Ibid., p. 80.
82   Bewell, *Romanticism and Colonial Disease*, pp. 39–40.
83   See Richard Grove, *Green Imperialism: Colonial Expansion, Tropical Island Edens and the Origins of Environmentalism, 1600–1860* (Cambridge University Press, Cambridge, 1995).
84   By stressing the distinctive development of environmental and medical ideas in India, this account differs in emphasis somewhat from that given by David Arnold in 'India's Place in the Tropical World, 1770–1930', *Journal of Imperial and Commonwealth History*, 26 (1998), pp. 1–21.
85   Mark Harrison, *Climates and Constitutions: Health, Race, Environment and British Imperialism in India 1600–1850* (Oxford University Press, New Delhi, 1999), chs 1–3.
86   Ibid., pp. 118–21.
87   On the Indian cholera epidemics, see David Arnold, 'The Indian Ocean as a Disease Zone, 1500–1950', *South Asia*, 14 (1991), pp. 1–22; *idem, Colonizing the Body: State Medicine and Epidemic Disease in Nineteenth-Century India* (University of California Press, Berkeley, 1993), ch. 4; Harrison, *Climates and Constitutions*, pp. 177–91; *idem, Public Health in British India: Anglo-Indian Preventive Medicine 1859–1914* (Cambridge University Press, Cambridge, 1994), chs 4 and 5.
88   Harrison, *Climates and Constitutions*, pp. 114–24.
89   Arnold, *Colonizing the Body, passim*; Harrison, *Climates and Constitutions*, ch. 4; *idem, Public Health, passim*.
90   Dane Kennedy, *The Magic Mountains: Hill Stations and the British Raj* (University of California Press, Berkeley, 1996).
91   J. Kukla, 'Kentish Agues and American Distempers: The Transmission of Malaria from England to Virginia in the Seventeenth Century', *Southern Studies*, 25 (1986), pp. 135–47.
92   Darrett B. Rutman and Anita H. Rutman, ' "Of Agues and Fevers": Malaria in the Early Chesapeake', *William and Mary Quarterly*, 33 (1976), pp. 31–60.
93   Karen Kupperman, 'Fear of Hot Climates in the Anglo-American Experience', *William and Mary Quarterly*, 41 (1984), pp. 213–40; John Duffy, 'The Impact of Malaria on the South', in *Disease and Distinctiveness in the American South*, ed. T. L. Savitt and J. H. Young (University of Tennessee Press, Knoxville, 1988).
94   Quoted in Rutman and Rutman, ' "Of Agues and Fevers" ', p. 44. See also Karen Kupperman, 'Apathy and Death in Early Jamestown', *Journal of American History*, 66 (1979), pp. 24–40.
95   Daniel Blake Smith, 'Mortality and Family in the Colonial Chesapeake', in *Health and Disease*, ed. Rotberg, pp. 249–73. See also M. Vinovskis, 'Mortality Rates and Trends in Massachusetts before 1860', *Journal of Economic History*, 32 (1972), pp. 184–213.

96   J. Gallman, 'Mortality among White Males: Colonial North Carolina', *Social Science History*, 4 (1980), pp. 295–316.

97   Jill Dubisch, 'Low Country Fevers: Cultural Adaptations to Malaria in Antebellum South Carolina', *Social Science and Medicine*, 21 (1985), pp. 641–2.

98   Mary J. Dobson, 'Mortality Gradients and Disease Exchanges: Comparisons from Old England and Colonial America', *Social History of Medicine*, 2 (1989), pp. 259–98.

99   H. Roy Merrens and George D. Terry, 'Dying in Paradise: Malaria, Mortality, and the Perceptual Environment in Colonial South Carolina', *Journal of Southern History*, 50 (1984), pp. 533–50.

100 Andrew Wear, 'Perceptions of Health and New Environments in the Early English Settlement of North America: Ideals and Reality', in *The Great Maritime Discoveries and World Health*, ed. M. G. Marques and J. Cule (Escola Nacional de Saude Publica, Lisbon, 1991), pp. 273–8.

101 Philip D. Curtin, *Death by Migration: Europe's Encounter with the Tropical World in the Nineteenth Century* (Cambridge University Press, New York, 1989).

102 Philip D. Curtin, *Disease and Empire: The Health of European Troops in the Conquest of Africa* (Cambridge University Press, New York, 1998).

103 Harrison, *Public Health*, pp. 68–9.

CHAPTER 5   DISEASE IN AN AGE OF COMMERCE AND INDUSTRY

1   See E. A. Wrigley, *Continuity, Chance, and Change: The Character of the Industrial Revolution in England* (Cambridge University Press, Cambridge, 1988); N. F. R. Crafts, *British Economic Growth during the Industrial Revolution* (Clarendon Press, Oxford, 1985); Peter Mathias, *The First Industrial Nation: An Economic History of Britain, 1700–1914*, 2nd edn (Methuen, London, 1983).

2   Roger Schofield and David Reher, 'The Decline of Mortality in Europe', in *The Decline of Mortality in Europe*, ed. R. Schofield, D. Reher and A. Bideau (Clarendon Press, Oxford, 1991), pp. 5–6.

3   Claudia Heurkamp, 'The History of Smallpox Vaccination in Germany: A First Step in the Medicalisation of the General Public', *Journal of Contemporary History*, 20 (1985), p. 623; E. P. Hennock, 'Vaccination Policy against Smallpox, 1835–1914: A Comparison of England with Prussia and Imperial Germany', *Social History of Medicine*, 11 (1998), pp. 51–2; Peter Baldwin, *Contagion and the State in Europe 1830–1930* (Cambridge University Press, New York, 1999), pp. 254–73.

4   Hennock, 'Vaccination Policy', pp. 54–8, 65.

5   Matthew Smallman-Raynor and Andrew D. Cliff, 'The Geographical Transmission of Smallpox in the Franco–Prussian War: Prisoner of War Camps and their Impact upon Epidemic Diffusion Processes in the

Civil Settlement System of Prussia, 1870–71', *Medical History*, 46 (2002), pp. 241–64.

6 Baldwin, *Contagion*, pp. 265–7.

7 D. Porter and R. Porter, 'The Politics of Prevention: Anti-Vaccinationism and Public Health in Nineteenth-Century England', *Medical History*, 32 (1988), pp. 231–52; Nadja Durbach, ' "They Might as Well Brand Us": Working-Class Resistance to Compulsory Vaccination in Victorian England', *Social History of Medicine*, 13 (2000), pp. 45–62.

8 Porter and Porter, 'Politics of Prevention'; Baldwin, *Contagion*, p. 288.

9 Hennock, 'Vaccination Policy', p. 61; Baldwin, *Contagion*, pp. 301–2.

10 Baldwin, *Contagion*, pp. 303–4.

11 E. Wolff, 'Medizinkritik der Impfgegner im Spannungsfeld zwischen Lebenswelt- und Wissenschaftsorientierung', in *Medizinkritische Bewegungen im Deutschen Reich*, ed. M. Dinges (Franz Steiner, Stuttgart, 1996), pp. 79–108.

12 Hennock, 'Vaccination Policy', pp. 61–2; Baldwin, *Contagion*, p. 316.

13 Hennock, 'Vaccination Policy', p. 71; Graham Mooney, ' "A Tissue of the Most Flagrant Anomalies": Smallpox Vaccination and the Centralization of Sanitary Administration in Nineteenth-Century London', *Medical History*, 41 (1997), pp. 261–90.

14 David Arnold, *Colonizing the Body: State Medicine and Epidemic Disease in Nineteenth-Century India* (University of California Press, Berkeley, 1993), ch. 3.

15 Sanjoy Bhattacharya, Mark Harrison and Michael Worboys, *Expunging Variola: The Control and Eradication of Smallpox in India, 1850–1977* (Orient Longman, Hyderabad, forthcoming).

16 Baldwin, *Contagion*, p. 551.

17 Paul Slack, *The Impact of Plague in Tudor and Stuart England* (Clarendon Press, Oxford, 1985), pp. 326–37.

18 Margaret Pelling, 'The Meaning of Contagion: Reproduction, Medicine and Metaphor', in *Contagion: Historical and Cultural Studies*, ed. A. Bashford and C. Hooker (Routledge, London and New York, 2001), p. 25.

19 J. H. Powell, *Bring Out Your Dead: The Great Plague of Yellow Fever in Philadelphia in 1793* (University of Pennsylvania Press, Philadelphia, 1949), pp. 13–14; Lisbeth Haakonssen, *Medicine and Morals in the Enlightenment: John Gregory, Thomas Percival and Benjamin Rush* (Rodopi Press, Amsterdam and Atlanta, 1997), pp. 214–16, 229 n. 50.

20 Powell, *Bring Out Your Dead*, pp. 281–2.

21 Ibid., p. v.

22 Benjamin Rush, *An Account of the Bilious Remitting Yellow Fever* (Thomas Dobson, Philadelphia, 1794), p. 313.

23 Martin S. Pernick, 'Politics, Parties and Pestilence: Epidemic Yellow Fever in Philadelphia and the Rise of the First Party System', in *Sickness and Health in America: Readings in the History of Medicine and Public Health*, ed. J. Walzer Leavitt and R. L. Numbers (University of Wisconsin Press, Madison, 1985), pp. 356–71.

24   John Duffy, *A History of Public Health in New York City 1625–1866*
     (Russell Sage Foundation, New York, 1968), pp. 97–150; William
     Coleman, *Yellow Fever in the North: The Methods of Early Epidemiol-
     ogy* (University of Wisconsin Press, Madison, 1987).

25   E. A. Heaman, 'The Rise and Fall of Anticontagionism in France',
     Canadian Bulletin of the History of Medicine, 12 (1995), pp.
     5–6.

26   Ibid., pp. 10–11; E. H. Ackerknecht, 'Anticontagionism between 1821
     and 1861', *Bulletin of the History of Medicine*, 22 (1948), pp. 561–93;
     Ann F. La Berge, *Mission and Method: The Early Nineteenth-Century
     French Public Health Movement* (Cambridge University Press, Cam-
     bridge, 1992), pp. 90–4; Matthew Ramsey, 'Public Health in France', in
     The History of Public Health and the Modern State, ed. D. Porter
     (Rodopi Press, Amsterdam and Atlanta, 1994), pp. 56, 58.

27   Heaman, 'Rise and Fall of Anticontagionism', pp. 3–25.

28   Ibid., p. 11.

29   David Arnold, 'The Indian Ocean as a Disease Zone, 1500–1950', *South
     Asia*, 14 (1991), pp. 1–22.

30   Roderick E. McGrew, *Russia and the Cholera 1823–1832* (University
     of Wisconsin Press, Madison, 1965).

31   Mark Harrison, *Climates and Constitutions: Health, Race, Environment
     and British Imperialism in India 1600–1850* (Oxford University Press,
     New Delhi, 1999), pp. 177–91.

32   R. J. Morris, *Cholera 1832* (Holmes and Meier, New York, 1976), p. 24.

33   François Delaporte, *Disease and Civilization: The Cholera in Paris,
     1832* (MIT Press, Cambridge, Mass., 1986), pp. 24–6.

34   Ackerknecht, 'Anticontagionism'.

35   Roger Cooter, 'Anticontagionism and History's Medical Record', in
     The Problem of Medical Knowledge, ed. P. Wright and A. Treacher
     (Edinburgh University Press, Edinburgh, 1983), pp. 87–108.

36   Baldwin, *Contagion*, p. 120.

37   Ibid., pp. 123–5.

38   See *Correspondence Respecting the Quarantine Laws since the Corre-
     spondence Last Presented to Parliament: Presented by Command to the
     House of Commons, in Pursuance to their Address of 19 May 1846*
     (T. R. Harrison, London, 1846).

39   Sir W. M. G. Colebrook, governor of Barbados, to Rt.-Hon. Sir John
     Packington, MP, 15 January 1853, F.552, Gloucestershire County
     Record Office.

40   Neville M. Goodman, *International Health Organizations and their
     Work* (J. & A. Churchill, London, 1952), p. 5.

41   Baldwin, *Contagion*, p. 141.

42   Richard J. Evans, *Death in Hamburg: Society and Politics in the Cholera
     Years 1830–1910* (Clarendon Press, Oxford, 1987), pp. 260–4.

43   John Snow, *On the Mode of Communication of Cholera* (John
     Churchill, London, 1855).

44   Margaret Pelling, *Cholera, Fever, and English Medicine 1825–1865*
     (Clarendon Press, Oxford, 1978), pp. 203–49.

45 Royston Lambert, *Sir John Simon, 1816–1904 and English Social Administration* (MacGibbon and Kee, London, 1963).

46 Baldwin, *Contagion*, pp. 242–3.

47 Mark Harrison, *Public Health in British India: Anglo-Indian Preventive Medicine 1859–1914* (Cambridge University Press, Cambridge, 1994), pp. 117–38.

48 Delaporte, *Disease and Civilization*, pp. 59–60.

49 Michael Durey, *The Return of the Plague: British Society and the Cholera, 1831–2* (Macmillan, London, 1979), p. 150.

50 Geoffrey Bilson, *A Darkened House: Cholera in Nineteenth-Century Canada* (Toronto University Press, Toronto, 1980).

51 Charles E. Rosenberg, *The Cholera Years: The United States in 1832, 1849, and 1866* (University of Chicago Press, Chicago, 1987), pp. 13–64.

52 R. Baehrel, 'Épidemie et terreur: histoire et sociologie', *Annales historiques de la Révolution française*, 23 (1951), pp. 113–14; Morris, *Cholera 1832*, p. 112.

53 Louis Chevalier, *Le Choléra, la première épidémie du xix siècle* (Impr. Centrale de l'Ouest, La Roche, 1958).

54 Ruth Richardson, *Death, Dissection and the Destitute* (Phoenix Press, London, 2001).

55 Jonathan Sawday, *The Body Emblazoned: Dissection and the Human Body in Renaissance Culture* (Routledge, London, 1995).

56 Quoted in Richardson, *Death and Dissection*, p. 163.

57 Ibid., p. 170; Morris, *Cholera 1832*, p. 112.

58 Evans, *Death in Hamburg*, p. 244.

59 McGrew, *Russia and the Cholera*.

60 Rosenberg, *Cholera Years*, pp. 60, 95.

61 Norman Longmate, *King Cholera: The Biography of a Disease* (London: Hamish Hamilton, 1966), pp. 76–7.

62 Rosenberg, *Cholera Years*, pp. 68–72.

63 Ian Inkster, '"Marginal Men": Aspects of the Social Role of the Medical Community in Sheffield, 1790–1850', in *Health Care and Popular Medicine in Nineteenth-Century England*, ed. D. Richards and J. Woodward (Holmes and Meier, New York, 1977), pp. 128–52; M. J. Peterson, *The Medical Profession in Mid-Victorian London* (University of California Press, Berkeley, 1978); Irvine Loudon, *Medical Care and the General Practitioner, 1750–1850* (Clarendon Press, Oxford, 1986).

64 Durey, *Return of the Plague*, pp. 163–4.

65 Delaporte, *Disease and Civilization*, p. 42.

66 Morris, *Cholera 1832*, p. 111.

67 Chevalier, *Le Choléra*; McGrew, *Russia and the Cholera*.

68 Morris, *Cholera 1832*, pp. 112–13, 122–5; Durey, *Return of the* Plague, pp. 183–200.

69 Rosenberg, *Cholera Years*.

70 Pelling, *Cholera, Fever and English Medicine*, pp. 4–6; Morris, *Cholera*, pp. 204–5.

71 Pelling, *Cholera, Fever and English Medicine*, pp. 50–1.

72   Mary Douglas, *Purity and Danger: An Analysis of the Concepts of Pollution and Taboo* (Routledge, London, 1991[1966]).

73   S. E. Finer, *The Life and Times of Sir Edwin Chadwick* (Methuen, London, 1952); R. A. Lewis, *Edwin Chadwick and the Public Health Movement, 1832–1854* (Longmans, Green, London, 1952); Christopher Hamlin, *Public Health and Social Justice in the Age of Chadwick: Britain, 1800–1854* (Cambridge University Press, Cambridge and New York, 1998).

74   Anthony S. Wohl, *Endangered Lives: Public Health in Victorian Britain* (Methuen, London, 1983), pp. 175–7; Boyd Hilton, *The Age of Atonement: The Influence of Evangelicalism on Social and Economic Thought, 1785–1865* (Clarendon Press, Oxford, 1988); Hamlin, *Public Health*, pp. 74–6.

75   E.g. Edwin Chadwick, *Report on the Sanitary Condition of the Labouring Population of Great Britain* (Edinburgh University Press, Edinburgh, 1965[1842]), pp. 228–31.

76   Pelling, *Cholera, Fever and English Medicine*, pp. 1–33.

77   Ibid., pp. 41–6; Hamlin, *Public Health*, pp. 78–82.

78   John Ferriar, 'Epidemic Fever of 1789 and 1790', quoted in Hamlin, *Public Health*, p. 66; John V. Pickstone, 'Ferriar's Fever to Kay's Cholera: Disease and Social Structure in Cottonopolis', *History of Science*, 22 (1984), pp. 401–19.

79   James Johnson, *A Practical Treatise on the Derangements of the Liver, Digestive Organs and Nervous System* (for the author, London, 1818); idem, *An Essay on the Morbid Sensibility of the Stomach and Bowels* (T. and G. Unwin, London, 1827).

80   John V. Pickstone, 'Dearth, Dirt and Fever Epidemics: Rewriting the History of British "Public Health", 1780–1850', in *Epidemics and Ideas: Essays on the Historical Perception of Pestilence*, ed. T. Ranger and P. Slack (Cambridge University Press, Cambridge, 1992), pp. 125–48; Hamlin, *Public Health*, pp. 78–82.

81   Pickstone, 'Dearth, Dirt and Fever Epidemics', p. 146.

82   Christopher Hamlin, 'Providence and Putrefaction: Victorian Sanitarians and the Natural Theology of Health and Disease', in *Energy and Entropy: Essays from Victorian Studies*, ed. P. Brantlinger (University of Indiana Press, Bloomington, 1989), pp. 93–123.

83   Hamlin, *Public Health*, chs 7–8; George Rosen, *A History of Public Health* (Johns Hopkins University Press, Baltimore, 1993[1958]), pp. 196–7.

84   Donald Reid, *Paris Sewers and Sewermen: Realities and Representations* (Harvard University Press, Cambridge, Mass., 1991), p. 27.

85   La Berge, *Mission and Method*; Ramsey, 'Public Health in France', pp. 51–69.

86   Reid, *Paris Sewers*, p. 28.

87   Ibid., pp. 18–24.

88   Ibid., pp. 37–52.

89   Rosen, *History of Public Health*, pp. 230–3.

90   Harrison, *Public Health in British India*, pp. 202–26.

91   Abram de Swaan, *In Care of the State Health Care, Education and Welfare in Europe and the USA in the Modern Era* (Polity, Cambridge, 1988), pp. 124–8.

CHAPTER 6   THE INDIVIDUAL AND THE STATE

1   See A. Youngson, *The Scientific Revolution in Victorian Medicine* (Croom Helm, London, 1979); A. Cunningham and P. Williams (eds), *The Laboratory Revolution in Medicine* (Cambridge University Press, Cambridge, 1992).
2   K. Codell Carter, *The Rise of Causal Concepts of Disease: Case Histories* (Ashgate, Aldershot, 2003).
3   W. F. Bynum, *Science and the Practice of Medicine in the Nineteenth Century* (Cambridge University Press, Cambridge, 1994), pp. 123–7.
4   Rudolf Virchow, 'Cellular Pathology', in *Disease, Life and Man: Selected Essays by Rudolf Virchow*, tr. and ed. L. J. Rather (Stanford University Press, Stanford, Calif., 1958), p. 100.
5   Margaret Pelling, *Cholera, Fever and English Medicine 1825–1865* (Clarendon Press, Oxford, 1978), pp. 113–45; J. B. Morrell, 'The Chemist Breeders: The Research Schools of Liebig and Thomas Thompson', *Ambix*, 19 (1972), pp. 1–46.
6   George Rosen, *A History of Public Health* (Johns Hopkins University Press, Baltimore, 1993 edn), pp. 272–6.
7   Gerald L. Geison, *The Private Science of Louis Pasteur* (Princeton University Press, Princeton, 1995); René Dubos, *Louis Pasteur: Freelance of Science* (Scribner, New York, 1986); Bynum, *Science and the Practice of Medicine*, pp. 127–9; Bruno Latour, *Les Microbes: guerre et paix suivi de irréductions* (Pandore, Paris, 1984).
8   Bynum, *Science and the Practice of Medicine*, pp. 130–3; William Coleman, 'Koch's Comma Bacillus: The First Year', *Bulletin of the History of Medicine*, 61 (1987), pp. 315–42; K. Codell Carter, 'Koch's Postulates in Relation to the Work of Jacob Henle and Edwin Klebs', *Medical History*, 29 (1985), pp. 353–74.
9   Paul Weindling, 'Scientific Elites and Laboratory Organisation in *Fin de Siècle* Paris and Berlin: The Pasteur Institute and Robert Koch's Institute for Infectious Diseases Compared', in *Laboratory Revolution*, ed. Cunningham and Williams, pp. 170–88.
10   C. Lawrence and R. Dixey, 'Practising on Principle: Joseph Lister and the Germ Theories of Disease', in *Medical Theory: Surgical Practice*, ed. C. Lawrence (Routledge, London, 1992), pp. 153–215; L. Granshaw, '"Upon this principle I have based a practice": The Development of Antisepsis in Britain, 1867–90', in *Medical Innovation in Historical Perspective* , ed. J. V. Pickstone (Macmillan, London, 1992), pp. 17–46; Michael Worboys, *Spreading Germs: Disease Theories and Medical*

Practice in Britain, 1865–1900 (Cambridge University Press, Cambridge and New York, 2000), chs 3 and 5.

11   Bynum, *Science and the Practice of Medicine*, p. 136; Worboys, *Spreading Germs*, pp. 172–4.

12   Alison Bashford, *Purity and Pollution: Gender, Embodiment and Victorian Medicine* (Macmillan, London, 2000), pp. 128–33.

13   Worboys, *Spreading Germs*, pp. 191–2.

14   Thomas Neville Bonner, *Becoming a Physician: Medical Education in Britain, France, Germany, and the United States, 1750–1945* (Johns Hopkins University Press, Baltimore, 1995); M. J. Peterson, *The Medical Profession in Mid-Victorian London* (University of California Press, Berkeley, 1978).

15   Simon Szreter, *Fertility, Class and Gender in Britain, 1860–1940* (Cambridge University Press, Cambridge, 1996), pp. 190–237; Jeane L. Brand, *Doctors and the State: The Medical Profession and Government Action in Public Health, 1870–1912* (Johns Hopkins University Press, Baltimore, 1965).

16   Royston Lambert, *Sir John Simon, 1816–1904 and English Social Administration* (MacGibbon and Kee, London, 1963).

17   John M. Eyler, 'Mortality Statistics and Victorian Health Policy: Program and Criticism', *Bulletin of the History of Medicine*, 50 (1976), pp. 335–55.

18   Christopher Hamlin, *A Science of Impurity: Water Analysis in Nineteenth-Century England* (Adam Hilger, Bristol, 1990); Anthony S. Wohl, *Endangered Lives: Public Health in Victorian Britain* (Methuen, London, 1983).

19   Rosen, *History of Public Health*, p. 307.

20   Worboys, *Spreading Germs*, pp. 254–65; Paul Weindling, 'Émile Roux et la diphtérie', in *L'Institut Pasteur: contributions à son histoire*, ed. M. Morange (Éditions la Découverte, Paris, 1991), pp. 137–43.

21   Paul Weindling, 'From Isolation to Therapy: Children's Hospitals and Diphtheria in *Fin de Siècle* Paris, London and Berlin', in *In the Name of the Child: Health and Welfare 1880–1940*, ed. R. Cooter (Routledge, London, 1992), pp. 124–45.

22   J. M. Eyler, *Sir Arthur Newsholme and State Medicine, 1885–1935* (Cambridge University Press, Cambridge, 1997); Dorothy Porter, *Health, Civilization and the State: A History of Public Health from Ancient to Modern Times* (Routledge, London, 1999), pp. 139–46.

23   J. N. Hays, *The Burdens of Disease: Epidemics and Human Response in Western History* (Rutgers University Press, New Brunswick, NJ, 2000), p. 159; F. B. Smith, *The Retreat of Tuberculosis 1850–1950* (Croom Helm, London, 1986), p. 7; Worboys, *Spreading Germs*, p. 194.

24   David S. Barnes, *The Making of a Social Disease: Tuberculosis in Nineteenth-Century France* (University of California Press, Berkeley, 1995), p. 4.

25   René Dubos and Jean Dubos, *The White Plague: Tuberculosis, Man and Society* (Victor Gollancz, London, 1953), p. 210.

26   Barnes, *Making of a Social Disease*, p. 25.

27 Thomas Dormandy, *The White Death: A History of Tuberculosis* (Hambledon, London, 1999), pp. 85–100.

28 S. Lyle Cummins, *Tuberculosis in History: From the 17ᵗʰ Century to our own Times* (Baillière, Tindall and Cox, London, 1949), pp. 133–66; Barnes, *Making of a Social Disease*, pp. 42–3; Dormandy, *White Death*, pp. 50–9; Worboys, *Spreading Germs*, pp. 195–200.

29 Worboys, *Spreading Germs*, pp. 195–6.

30 Mark Harrison, *Public Health in British India: Anglo-Indian Preventive Medicine 1859–1914* (Cambridge University Press, Cambridge, 1994), pp. 111–15.

31 Cristoph Gradmann, 'Robert Koch and the Pressures of Scientific Research: Tuberculosis and Tuberculin', *Medical History*, 45 (2001), pp. 1–32; Smith, *Retreat of Tuberculosis*, pp. 56–62.

32 Arthur Ransome, *The Principles of 'Open-Air' Treatment of Phthisis and of Sanatorium Construction* (Smith, Elder & Co., London, 1903), p. 9.

33 Michael Worboys, 'The Sanatorium Treatment for Consumption in Britain, 1890–1914', in *Medical Innovation*, ed. Pickstone, pp. 47–71; Barnes, *Making of a Social Disease*; A. J. Proust, 'Evolution of Treatment', in *History of Tuberculosis in Australia, New Zealand and Papua New Guinea*, ed. A. J. Proust (Brolga Press, Canberra, 1991), pp. 147–70.

34 Smith, *Retreat of Tuberculosis*, pp. 62–4.

35 H. Hyslop Thomson, *Consumption in General Practice* (Oxford University Press, Oxford, 1912), p. 230.

36 Sheila M. Rothman, *Living in the Shadow of Death: Tuberculosis and the Social Experience of Illness in American History* (Johns Hopkins University Press, Baltimore, 1994), pp. 194–246; Katherine Ott, *Fevered Lives: Tuberculosis in American Culture since 1870* (Harvard University Press, Cambridge, Mass., 1996); Linda Bryder, *Below the Magic Mountain: A Social History of Tuberculosis in Twentieth-Century Britain* (Clarendon Press, Oxford, 1988); Smith, *Retreat of Tuberculosis*.

37 J. Arthur Myers, *Man's Greatest Victory over Tuberculosis* (Charles C. Thomas, Springfield, Ill., 1940), pp. 243–83; Deborah Dwork, *War is Good for Babies and Other Young Children: A History of the Infant Welfare Movement in England 1898–1918* (Tavistock, London, 1987); Jim Philips and Michael French, 'State Regulation and the Hazards of Milk, 1900–1939', *Social History of Medicine*, 12 (1999), pp. 371–88.

38 Nancy Tomes, *The Gospel of Germs: Men, Women, and the Microbe in American Life* (Harvard University Press, Cambridge, Mass., 1998), pp. 113–35; Bryder, *Below the Magic Mountain*, pp. 17–18.

39 Smith, *Retreat of Tuberculosis*, p. 5.

40 Barnes, *Making of a Social Disease*, pp. 6–8.

41 Thomas McKeown, *The Modern Rise of Population* (Edward Arnold, London, 1976). McKeown's thesis is partially endorsed in Smith's *Retreat of Tuberculosis*.

42 See Simon Szreter, 'The Importance of Social Intervention in Britain's Mortality Decline, 1850–1914: A Re-interpretation of the Role of

Public Health', *Social History of Medicine*, 1 (1988), pp. 1–37; Allan Mitchell, 'An Inexact Science: The Statistics of Tuberculosis in Late Nineteenth-Century France', *Social History of Medicine*, 3 (1990), pp. 387–403; Leonard G. Wilson, 'The Historical Decline of Tuberculosis in Europe and America: Its Causes and Significance', *Journal of the History of Medicine*, 45 (1990), pp. 366–96; Anne Hardy, *The Epidemic Streets: The Rise of Preventive Medicine in London, 1850–1910* (Oxford: Oxford University Press, 1993).

43   Greta Jones, *'Captain of all these men of death': The History of Tuberculosis in Nineteenth and Twentieth Century Ireland* (Rodopi Press, Amsterdam and Atlanta, 2001).

44   Proust (ed.), *History of Tuberculosis in Australia, New Zealand and Papua New Guinea*.

45   Mark Harrison and Michael Worboys, 'A Disease of Civilization: Tuberculosis in Britain, Africa and India, 1900–39', in *Migrants, Minorities and Health: Historical and Contemporary Studies*, ed. L. Marks and M. Worboys (Routledge, London, 1997), pp. 93–124; Randall M. Packard, *White Plague, Black Labor: Tuberculosis and the Political Economy of Health and Disease in South Africa* (University of California Press, Berkeley, 1989).

46   Rosen, *History of Public Health*, pp. 270–472.

47   Carol Benedict, *Bubonic Plague in Nineteenth-Century China* (Stanford University Press, Stanford, Calif., 1996).

48   Molly Preston Sutphen, 'Rumoured Power: Hong Kong, 1894 and Cape Town, 1901', in *Western Medicine as Contested Knowledge*, ed. A. Cunningham and B. Andrews (Manchester University Press, Manchester, 1997), pp. 241–61; L. Fabian Hirst, *The Conquest of Plague: A Study of the Evolution of Epidemiology* (Clarendon Press, Oxford, 1953), pp. 101–3.

49   Edward Marriot, *The Plague Race: A Tale of Fear, Science and Heroism* (Picador, London, 2002); Andrew Cunningham, 'Transforming Plague: The Laboratory and the Identity of Infectious Disease', in *Laboratory Revolution*, ed. Cunningham and Williams, pp. 209–44.

50   Major W. L. Reade of the Army Medical Service, quoted in Harrison, *Public Health in British India*, p. 143.

51   Quoted in David Arnold, *Colonizing the Body: State Medicine and Epidemic Disease in Nineteenth-Century British India* (University of California Press, Berkeley, 1993), p. 214.

52   Harrison, *Public Health in British India*, p. 146.

53   Ibid., pp. 152–6.

54   Ibid., p. 144.

55   Arnold, *Colonizing the Body*, p. 221; Rajnarayan Chandavarkar, 'Plague Panic and Epidemic Politics in India, 1896–1914', in *Epidemics and Ideas: Essays on the Historical Perception of Pestilence*, ed. T. Ranger and P. Slack (Cambridge University Press, Cambridge, 1992), pp. 203–40.

56 Ian Catanach, 'Plague and the Tensions of Empire', in *Imperial Medicine and Indigenous Societies*, ed. D. Arnold (Manchester University Press, Manchester, 1988), pp. 159–61.

57 Helen J. Power, *Tropical Medicine in the Twentieth-Century: A History of the Liverpool School of Tropical Medicine, 1898–1990* (Kegan Paul International, London, 1999); Lise Wilkinson and Anne Hardy, *The London School of Hygiene and Public Health: A Twentieth-Century Quest for Global Public Health* (Kegan Paul, London, 1998); Gordon C. Cook, *From the Greenwich Hulks to Old St Pancras: A History of Tropical Disease in London* (Athlone, London, 1992); Michael Worboys, 'Germs, Malaria and the Invention of Mansonian Tropical Medicine: From "Diseases in the Tropics" to "Tropical Diseases"', in *Warm Climates and Western Medicine*, ed. D. Arnold (Rodopi Press, Amsterdam and Atlanta, 1996), pp. 181–207.

58 Douglas M. Haynes, *Imperial Medicine: Patrick Manson and the Conquest of Tropical Disease* (University of Pennsylvania Press, Philadelphia, 2001), pp. 13–56.

59 Shang-Jen Li, 'British Imperial Medicine in Late Nineteenth-Century China and the Early Career of Patrick Manson' (University of London Ph.D. thesis, 1999).

60 Patrick Manson, *Tropical Diseases: A Manual of the Diseases of Warm Climates* (London: Cassell & Co., 1907 edn), p. xvii.

61 L. J. Bruce-Chwatt and J. de Zulueta, *The Rise and Fall of Malaria in Europe: A Historico-Epidemiological Study* (Oxford University Press, Oxford, 1980).

62 Mark Harrison, *Climates and Constitutions: Health, Race, Environment and British Imperialism in India 1600–1850* (Oxford University Press, New Delhi, 1999), pp. 154–77.

63 On Laveran's career see L. Parrot, *La Découverte de Laveran* (Masson, Paris, 1929).

64 Opposition was especially strong in India, where climatic explanations of disease were still deeply entrenched. See Harrison, *Public Health in British India,* p. 57; Gordon Harrison, *Mosquitoes, Malaria and Man: A History of the Hostilities since 1880* (John Murray, London, 1978), pp. 12–16.

65 Ronald Ross, *Studies on Malaria* (John Murray, London, 1928), pp. 1–40; Bynum, *Science and the Practice of Medicine*, pp. 150–1; W. F. Bynum and Caroline Overy (eds), *The Beast in the Mosquito: The Correspondence of Ronald Ross and Patrick Manson* (Rodopi Press, Amsterdam and Atlanta, 1998); Edwin R. Nye and Mary E. Gibson, *Ronald Ross, Malariologist and Polymath: A Biography* (Macmillan, Basingstoke, 1997); Haynes, *Imperial Medicine*, pp. 86–124.

66 Michael Worboys, 'Manson, Ross and Colonial Medical Policy: Tropical Medicine in London and Liverpool, 1899–1914', in *Disease, Medicine, and Empire: Perspectives on Western Medicine and the Experience of European Expansion*, ed. Roy MacLeod and Milton Lewis (Routledge, London, 1988), pp. 21–37, p. 27.

67   Ibid., p. 31.
68   Harrison, *Public Health in British India*, pp. 158–64; Wolfgang U. Eckart, *Medizin und Kolonialimperialismus: Deutschland 1884–1945* (Ferdinand Schöningh, Paderbon, 1997), pp. 221–4.
69   Arabinda Samanta, *Malarial Fever in Colonial Bengal 1820–1939* (Firma KLM, Kolkata, 2002), pp. 142–3; Harrison, *Public Health in British India*, p. 163.
70   Margaret Humphreys, *Yellow Fever and the South* (Rutgers University Press, New Brunswick, NJ, 1992).
71   Donald B. Cooper, 'Yellow Fever', in *The Cambridge World History of Human Disease*, ed. K. F. Kiple (Cambridge University Press, Cambridge, 1993), pp. 1100–7.
72   L. G. Goodwin and C. E. Gordon Smith, 'Yellow Fever', in *The Wellcome Trust Illustrated History of Tropical Diseases*, ed. F. E. G. Cox (The Wellcome Trust, London, 1996), pp. 142–7; Bynum, *Science and the Practice of Medicine*, p. 151.
73   F. Delaporte, *The History of Yellow Fever: An Essay on the Birth of Tropical Medicine* (MIT Press, Cambridge, Mass., 1991).
74   Julyan G. Peard, *Race, Place, and Medicine: The Idea of the Tropics in Nineteenth-Century Brazilian Medicine* (Duke University Press, Durham, NC, 1999); Jaime Larry Benchimol, *Dos Micróbios aos Mosquitos: Febre amarela e a Revolução Pasteuriana no Brasil* (Editora Fiocruz, Rio de Janeiro, 1999).
75   Harish Naraindas, 'Poisons, Putrescence and the Weather: A Genealogy of the Advent of Tropical Medicine', in *Médecines et santé*, vol. 4: *Les Sciences hors d'Occident au XXe siècle*, ed. A.-M. Moulin (Orstrom, Paris, 1996), pp. 31–56.
76   Megan Vaughan, *Curing their Ills: Colonial Power and African Illness* (Polity, Cambridge, 1991), p. 35.
77   Alan M. Kraut, 'Silent Travelers: Germs, Genes, and American Efficiency, 1890–1924', *Social Science History*, 12 (1988), p. 378.
78   V. D. Lipman, *A History of the Jews in Britain since 1858* (Leicester University Press, Leicester, 1990), p. 41.
79   John Higham, *Strangers in the Land: Patterns of American Nativism 1860–1925* (Rutgers University Press, New Brunswick, NJ, 1988).
80   Alan M. Kraut, *Silent Travelers: Germs, Genes, and the 'Immigrant Menace'* (Basic Books, New York, 1994), chs 3–6; Howard Markel, *Quarantine! East European Jewish Immigrants and the New York City Epidemics of 1892* (Johns Hopkins University Press, Baltimore, 1997).
81   Charles Rosenberg, *The Cholera Years: The United States in 1832, 1849 and 1866* (University of Chicago Press, Chicago, 1987); Kraut, *Silent Travelers*, ch. 2.
82   Anne-Emmanuelle Birn, 'Six Seconds per Eyelid: The Medical Inspection of Immigrants at Ellis Island, 1892–1914', *Dynamis*, 17 (1997), pp. 281–316.
83   John Parascandola, 'Doctors at the Gate: PHS at Ellis Island', *Public Health Service Chronicles*, 113 (1998), pp. 83–4.
84   Kraut, *Silent Travelers*, p. 379.

85   Parascandola, 'Doctors at the Gate', p. 84.
86   Howard Markel, '"The Eyes Have It": Trachoma, the Perception of Disease, the United States Public Health Service, and the American Jewish Immigration Experience, 1897–1924', *Bulletin of Medical History*, 74 (2000), pp. 525–60.
87   Kraut, *Silent Travelers*, pp. 383–4.
88   Birn, 'Six-Seconds per Eyelid'.
89   Kraut, *Silent Travelers*, ch. 4.
90   Robert I. Woods, P. A. Watterson and J. H. Woodward, 'The Causes of Rapid Infant Mortality Decline in England and Wales', pt 1, *Population Studies*, 42 (1988), pp. 343–66, and pt 2, *Population Studies*, 43 (1989), pp. 113–32; Jaques Vallin, 'Mortality in Europe from 1720 to 1914: Long-Term Trends and Changes in Patterns by Age and Sex', in *The Decline of Mortality in Europe*, ed. R. Schofield, D. Reher and A. Bideau (Clarendon Press, Oxford, 1991), pp. 38–67.
91   Vallin, 'Mortality in Europe'; Graziella Caselli, 'Health Transition and Cause-Specific Mortality', in *Decline of Mortality in Europe*, ed. Schofield et al., pp. 68–96. On differences according to age-group, see F. B. Smith, *The People's Health: 1830–1910* (Croom Helm, London, 1979); on social class, see Reinhard Spree, *Health and Social Class in Imperial Germany*, tr. S. McKinnon-Evans (Berg, Oxford, 1988).
92   James C. Riley, *Sick, not Dead: The Health of British Working-men during the Mortality Decline* (Johns Hopkins University Press, Baltimore, 1997).
93   Jörg P. Vögele, 'Urban Infant Mortality in Imperial Germany', *Social History of Medicine*, 3 (1994), pp. 401–26.
94   E. A. Parkes, *Public Health* (J. Churchill, London, 1876).
95   McKeown, *Modern Rise of Population*.
96   Samuel H. Preston, 'Causes and Consequences of Mortality Decline in Less Developed Countries during the Twentieth Century', in *Population and Economic Change in Developing Countries*, ed. R. E. Easterlin (University of Chicago Press, Chicago, 1980), pp. 289–360; John C. Caldwell, 'Routes to Low Mortality in Poor Countries', *Population and Development Review*, 12 (1986), pp. 171–220; P. G. K. Panikar and C. R. Soman, *Health Status of Kerala: Paradox of Economic Backwardness and Health Development* (Centre for Development Studies, Tivandrum, 1984).
97   Szreter, 'Importance of Social Intervention'; *idem*, 'Mortality in England in the Eighteenth and Nineteenth Centuries: A Reply to Sumit Guha', *Social History of Medicine*, 7 (1994), pp. 269–82; Hardy, *Epidemic Streets*, pp. 289–94.
98   Spree, *Health and Social Class*, pp. 151–3.
99   Sumit Guha, 'The Importance of Social Intervention in England's Mortality Decline: The Evidence Reviewed', *Social History of Medicine*, 7 (1994), pp. 89–113; *idem*, 'Nutrition, Sanitation, Hygiene, and the Likelihood of Death: The British Army in India c.1870–1920', in his *Health and Population in South Asia: From Earliest Times to the Present* (Hurst and Co., London, 2001), pp. 110–39.

100 Riley, *Sick, not Dead*.
101 Roger Schofield and David Reher, 'The Decline of Mortality in Europe', in *Decline of Mortality in Europe*, ed. Schofield et al., pp. 9–10.

CHAPTER 7 DISEASE, WAR AND MODERNITY

1 Daniel Headrick, *The Tentacles of Progress: Technology Transfer in the Age of Imperialism* (Oxford University Press, New York, 1988).
2 See, e.g., Mark Harrison, *Public Health in British India: Anglo-Indian Preventive Medicine 1859–1914* (Cambridge University Press, Cambridge, 1994).
3 R. Palme Dutt, *India Today* (Gollancz, London, 1940), p. 79.
4 Henry E. Sigerist, *Socialised Medicine in the Soviet Union* (Gollancz, London, 1937).
5 Abram de Swaan, *In Care of the State: Health Care, Education and Welfare in Europe and the USA in the Modern Era* (Polity, Cambridge, 1988); Theda Skocpol, *Protecting Soldiers and Mothers: The Political Origins of Social Policy in the United States* (Belknap Press, Harvard University Press, Cambridge, Mass., 1992); John Pickstone, 'Production, Community and Consumption: The Political Economy of Twentieth-Century Medicine', in *Medicine in the 20th Century*, ed. R. Cooter and J. V. Pickstone (Harwood Academic Publishers, Amsterdam, 2000), pp. 1–20.
6 See, e.g., Deborah Dwork, *War is Good for Babies and Other Young Children: A History of the Infant and Child Welfare Movement in England, 1898–1918* (Tavistock, London, 1987); Richard A. Meckel, *Save the Babies: American Public Health Reform and the Prevention of Infant Mortality, 1850–1929* (Johns Hopkins University Press, Baltimore, 1990); Lara Marks and Hilary Marland (eds), *Women and Children First: International Maternal and Infant Welfare, 1800–1950* (Routledge, London, 1992); Roger Cooter (ed.), *In the Name of the Child: Health and Welfare 1880–1940* (Routledge, London, 1992).
7 E. Fee and D. Porter, 'Public Health, Preventive Medicine and Professionalization: England and America in the Nineteenth Century', in *Medicine in Society: Historical Essays*, ed. A. Wear (Cambridge University Press, Cambridge, 1992), pp. 249–76; David Armstrong, *The Political Anatomy of the Body: Medical Knowledge in Britain in the Twentieth Century* (Cambridge University Press, Cambridge, 1993), pp. 10–13.
8 Richard Titmuss, 'War and Social Policy', in his *Essays on 'The Welfare State'* (George Allen & Unwin, London, 1958), p. 86.
9 See S. Andreski, *Military Organisation and Society* (Routledge and Kegan Paul, London, 1968).

10 Maryinez Lyons, *The Colonial Disease: A Social History of Sleeping Sickness in Northern Zaire, 1900–1940* (Cambridge University Press, Cambridge, 1992).

11 E. Richard Brown, *Rockefeller Medicine Men: Medicine and Capitalism in America* (University of California Press, Berkeley, 1979).

12 Anne-Emmanuel Birn and Armando Solórzano, 'The Hook of the Hookworm: Public Health and the Politics of Eradication in Mexico', in *Western Medicine as Contested Knowledge*, ed. A. Cunningham and B. Andrews (Manchester University Press, Manchester, 1997), pp. 147–72.

13 Ilana Löwy, 'What/Who should be Controlled? Opposition to Yellow Fever Campaigns in Brazil, 1900–39', in *Western Medicine as Contested Knowledge*, ed. Cunningham and Andrews, pp. 124–46.

14 See John Farley, 'The International Health Division of the Rockefeller Foundation: The Russell Years, 1920–1934', in *International Health Organisations and Movements 1918–1939*, ed. P. Weindling (Cambridge University Press, Cambridge, 1995), pp. 203–22; Marcos Cueto, 'The Cycles of Eradication: The Rockefeller Foundation and Latin American Public Health, 1918–1940', in ibid., pp. 222–43.

15 Marisa Chambers, 'The Socio-Economic Impact of Tropical Diseases in West Africa, 1900–1948' (University of Liverpool Ph.D. thesis, 2000).

16 Margaret Jones, 'British Colonial Health Policy 1900–1940: Ceylon and the Asian Colonies' (University of Bristol Ph.D. thesis, 2000).

17 Heather Bell, *Frontiers of Medicine in the Anglo-Egyptian Sudan 1899–1940* (Clarendon Press, Oxford, 1999), pp. 101–4.

18 Helen Tilley, 'Africa as a "Living Laboratory": The African Research Survey and the British Colonial Empire: Consolidating Environmental, Medical, and Anthropological Debates, 1920–1940' (University of Oxford D.Phil. thesis, 2001), pp. 181–97.

19 J. Andrew Mendelsohn, 'From Eradication to Equilibrium: How Epidemics became Complex after World War I', in *Greater than the Parts: Holism in Biomedicine 1920–1950*, ed. C. Lawrence and G. Weisz (Oxford University Press, New York, 1998), pp. 303–34.

20 F. A. E. Crew (ed.), *The Army Medical Services: Campaigns*, vol. 1 (HMSO, London, 1956), pp. 359, 362, 365; H. Fischer, *Der deutsche Sanitätsdienst 1921–1945* (Biblio Verlag, Osnabrück, 1984), pp. 1517, 1535; Mark Harrison, *Medicine and Victory: British Military Medicine in the Second World War* (Oxford University Press, Oxford, forthcoming, 2004), ch. 3.

21 Harrison, *Medicine and Victory*.

22 Mark Harrison, 'Medicine', in *The Oxford Companion to the Second World War*, ed. M. R. D. Foot and I. C. B. Dear (Oxford University Press, Oxford, 1995), pp. 723–31; Albert E. Cowdrey, *Fighting for Life: American Military Medicine in World War II* (Free Press, New York, 1994).

23 Alfred J. Crosby, 'Influenza', in *The Cambridge World History of Human Disease*, ed. K. F. Kiple (Cambridge University Press, Cambridge, 1995), pp. 807–10.

24   Alfred W. Crosby, *America's Forgotten Pandemic: The Influenza of 1918* (Cambridge University Press, New York and Cambridge, 1989), p. 25; Edwin D. Kilbouvne, 'A virologist's perspective on the 1918–19 Pandemic', in *The Spanish Influenza Pandemic of 1918–19: New Perspectives* (Routledge, London, 2003), ed. Howard Phillips and David Killingray, pp. 29–38.

25   K. D. Patterson and G. Fyle, 'The Geography and Mortality of the 1918 Influenza Pandemic', *Bulletin of the History of Medicine*, 65 (1991), pp. 4–21; Howard Phillips and David Killingray, 'Introduction', in *Spanish Influenza Pandemic*, pp. 1–26.

26   W. G. MacPherson, W. P. Herringham, T. R. Elliott and A. Balfour (eds), *History of the Great War Based on Official Documents: Medical Services: Diseases of the War*, vol. 1 (HMSO, London, 1923), pp. 174–211.

27   I. D. Mills, 'The Influenza Pandemic: The Indian Experience', *Indian Economic and Social History Review*, 23 (1988), pp. 1–40; Mridula Ramanna, 'Coping with the Influenza Pandemic: The Bombay Experience', in *Spanish Influenza Pandemic*, ed. Phillips and Killingray, pp. 86–98.

28   David Killingray, 'The Influenza Pandemic of 1918–1919 in the British Caribbean', *Social History of Medicine*, 7 (1994), pp. 59–88.

29   W. H. Willcox, *Mesopotamia (1916–1919)* (Morton and Burt, London, 1919), p. 20.

30   Crosby, *America's Forgotten Pandemic*, pp. 100–1.

31   Terence Ranger, 'The Influenza Pandemic in Southern Rhodesia: A Crisis of Comprehension', in *Imperial Medicine and Indigenous Societies*, ed. D. Arnold (Manchester University Press, Manchester, 1988), pp. 172–89.

32   Paul Weindling, *Epidemics and Genocide in Eastern Europe, 1890–1945* (Oxford University Press, Oxford, 2000), pp. 60–72.

33   Victoria A. Harden, 'Epidemic Typhus', in *Cambridge World History of Human Disease*, ed. Kiple, pp. 1080–4.

34   Weindling, *Epidemics and Genocide*, pp. 75–6.

35   Ibid., pp. 79–80.

36   Paul Weindling, 'The First World War and the Campaigns against Lice: Comparing British and German Sanitary Measures', in *Die Medizin und der Erste Weltkrieg*, ed. W. U. Eckart and C. Gradmann (Centaurus, Pfaffenweiler, 1996), pp. 227–41.

37   Serjeant-Major R.A.M.C. [pseud.], *With the R.A.M.C. in Egypt* (Cassell, London, 1918), pp. 187–9, 297–300; Diary of W. Knott, 31 October 1917, p. 305, Imperial War Museum.

38   G. H. Edington, *With the 1/1st Lowland Field Ambulance in Gallipoli* (Alex MacDougall, Glasgow, 1920), p. 30.

39   See John F. Hutchinson, *Champions of Charity: War and the Rise of the Red Cross* (Boulder, Colo.: Westview Press, 1996); Martin David Dubin, 'The League of Nations Health Organisation', in *International Health Organisations*, ed. Weindling, pp. 56–80.

40 Quoted in Marta Aleksandra Balinska, 'Assistance and Not Mere Relief: The Epidemic Commission of the League of Nations', in *International Health Organisations*, ed. Weindling, p. 82.

41 Weindling, *Epidemics and Genocide*, ch. 6.

42 Karl-Heinz Leven, 'Fleckfieber beim deutschen Heer während des Krieges gegen die Sowjetunion (1941–1945)', in *Sanitätswesen im Zweiten Weltkrieg*, ed. E. Guth (E. S. Mittler, Herford and Bonn, 1990), pp. 127–66.

43 Quoted in Weindling, *Epidemics and Genocide*, p. 296.

44 Ibid, pp. 298–312.

45 Ibid., p. 216.

46 Leven, 'Fleckfieber'.

47 Crew (ed.), *Army Medical Services: Campaigns*, vol. 2, p. 369; Lt.-Col. H. D. Chalke, 'Typhus Prophylaxis, Winter 1942–3', RAMC Collection, Wellcome Library for the History and Understanding of Medicine, London.

48 Harrison, *Medicine and Victory*, chs 3 and 4.

49 Weindling, *Epidemics and Genocide*, pp. 399–400.

50 Imperial War Museum 77/1119/1, Maj. J. C. MacKillop, 'Anti-Malaria Campaign, British North African Force 1943–1944', p. 1.

51 See Nancy E. Gallagher, *Egypt's Other Wars: Epidemics and the Politics of Public Health* (Syracuse University Press, Syracuse, NY, 1990).

52 Mark Harrison, 'Medicine and the Culture of Command: The Case of Malaria Control in the British Army during the Two World Wars', *Medical History*, 40 (1996), pp. 440–2.

53 Edmond Sergent and Étienne Sergent, *L'Armée d'Orient deliverée du Paludisme* (Librairie de l'Académie de Médicine, Paris, 1932).

54 Ibid., pp. 41–5, 59, 77; Bernadino Fantini, 'Malaria and the First World War', in *Die Medizin und der Erste Weltkrieg*, ed. Eckart and Gradmann, pp. 241–73.

55 L. J. Bruce-Chwatt and J. de Zuleta, *The Rise and Fall of Malaria in Europe: A Historico-Epidemiological Study* (Oxford University Press, Oxford, 1980), p. 85.

56 Harrison, 'Medicine and the Culture of Command', pp. 441–2.

57 Gordon Covell, *Anti-Mosquito Measures with Special Reference to India* (Govt of India Publications, Calcutta, 1931).

58 Lenore Manderson, *Sickness and the State: Health and Illness in Colonial Malaya, 1870–1940* (Cambridge University Press, Cambridge, 1996), pp. 87–8.

59 Andrew Balfour, *Health Problems of the Empire: Past, Present and Future* (W. Collins Sons & Co., London, 1924), p. 222; Margaret Jones, 'The Ceylon Malaria Epidemic of 1934–35: A Case Study in Colonial Medicine', *Social History of Medicine*, 13 (2000), pp. 87–111; Arabinda Samanta, *Malarial Fever in Colonial Bengal 1820–1939* (Firma KLM, Kolkata, 2002).

60 Bruce-Chwatt and Zuleta, *Rise and Fall of Malaria in Europe*, pp. 94–7.

61 Harrison, 'Medicine and the Culture of Command', p. 448.

62   Ibid., pp. 449–50.
63   Lesley Hall, '"War always brings it on": War, STDs, the Military, and the Civilian Population in Britain, 1850–1950', in *Medicine and Modern Warfare*, ed. R. Cooter, M. Harrison and S. Sturdy (Rodopi Press, Amsterdam and Atlanta, 1999), p. 205.
64   A. R. Skelley, *The Victorian Army at Home: The Recruitment and Terms and Conditions of the British Regular, 1859–1899* (Croom Helm, London, 1977); Myna Trustram, *Women of the Regiment: Marriage and the Victorian Army* (Cambridge University Press, Cambridge, 1994).
65   See, e.g., Annet Mooj, *Out of Otherness: Characters and Narrators in the Dutch Venereal Disease Debates 1850–1990* (Rodopi Press, Amsterdam and Atlanta, 1998), pp. 19–79; Roger Davidson and Lesley A. Hall (eds), *Sex, Sin and Suffering: Venereal Disease and European Society since 1870* (Routledge, London, 2001).
66   F. B. Smith, 'Ethics and Disease in the Late-Nineteenth Century: The Contagious Diseases Acts', *Historical Studies*, 15 (1971), pp. 118–35; *idem*, 'The Contagious Diseases Acts Reconsidered', *Social History of Medicine*, 3 (1990), pp. 197–215; Edward J. Bristow, *Vice and Vigilance: Purity Movements in Britain since 1700* (Gill and Macmillan, Dublin, 1979), pp. 78–84; Judith R. Walkowitz, *Prostitution and Victorian Society: Women, Class and the State* (Cambridge University Press, Cambridge, 1980), pp. 48–76; Ronald Hyam, *Empire and Sexuality: The British Experience* (Manchester University Press, Manchester, 1991), ch. 6; Philippa Levine, 'Venereal Disease, Prostitution, and the Politics of Empire: The Case of British India', *Journal of the History of Sexuality*, 4 (1994), pp. 579–602; *idem*, 'Public Health, Venereal Disease and Colonial Medicine in the Later Nineteenth Century', in *Sex, Sin and Suffering*, ed. Davidson and Hall, pp. 160–72; Mary Spongberg, *Feminizing Venereal Disease: The Body of the Prostitute in Nineteenth-Century Medical Discourse* (Macmillan, London, 1996).
67   Alain Corbin, *Women for Hire: Prostitution and Sexuality in France after 1850*, tr. A. Sheridan (Harvard University Press, Cambridge, Mass., 1990); Peter Baldwin, *Contagion and the State in Europe 1830–1930* (Cambridge University Press, New York, 1999), ch. 6.
68   Robert Nye, *Crime, Madness and Politics in Modern France: The Medical Concept of National Decline* (Princeton University Press, Princeton, 1984); Paul Weindling, *Health, Race and German Politics between National Unification and Nazism 1870–1945* (Cambridge University Press, Cambridge, 1989); Daniel Pick, *Faces of Degeneration: A European Disorder, c.1848–c.1918* (Cambridge University Press, Cambridge, 1989); Claude Quétel, *History of Syphilis*, tr. J. Braddock and B. Pike (Polity, Cambridge, 1990; Johns Hopkins University Press, Baltimore, 1992), pp. 176–210.
69   Corbin, *Women for Hire*, pp. 334–5.
70   Lutz D. H. Sauerteig, 'Sex, Medicine and Morality during the First World War', in *War, Medicine and Modernity*, ed. R. Cooter, M. Harrison and S. Sturdy (Stroud, Sutton, 1998), pp. 167–88.

71 Suzann Buckley, 'The Failure to Resolve the Problem of Venereal Disease among the Troops in Britain during the First World War', in *War and Society: A Yearbook of Military History*, vol. 2, ed. B. Bond and I. Roy (Croom Helm, London, 1977), pp. 65–85.

72 Hyam, *Empire and Sexuality*; Mark Harrison, 'The British Army and the Problem of Venereal Disease in France and Egypt during the First World War', *Medical History*, 39 (1995), pp. 133–58.

73 Edward H. Beardsley, 'Allied against Sin: American and British Responses to Venereal Disease in World War I', *Medical History*, 20 (1976), pp. 189–202; Allan Brandt, *No Magic Bullet: A Social History of Venereal Disease in the United States since 1880* (Oxford University Press, New York, 1985), pp. 52–115.

74 Bridget A. Towers, 'Health Education Policy 1916–1926: Venereal Disease and the Prophylaxis Dilemma', *Medical History*, 24 (1980), pp. 70–87.

75 Frank Mort, *Dangerous Sexualities: Medico-Moral Politics in England since 1830* (Routledge and Kegan Paul, London, 1987), p. 194.

76 S. M. Tomkins, 'Palminate or Permanganate: The Venereal Prophylaxis Debate in Britain, 1916–1926', *Medical History*, 37 (1993), pp. 382–98.

77 Sauerteig, 'Sex, Medicine and Morality'.

78 Harrison, 'British Army and the Problem of Venereal Disease', pp. 146–9.

79 Gunnar Stollberg, 'Health and Illness in German Workers' Autobiographies from the Nineteenth and Early Twentieth Centuries', *Social History of Medicine*, 6 (1993), p. 272.

80 Lutz D. H. Sauerteig, '"The Fatherland is in Danger, Save the Fatherland!": Venereal Disease, Sexuality and Gender in Imperial and Weimar Germany', in *Sex, Sin and Suffering*, ed. Davidson and Hall, pp. 76–93.

81 Towers, 'Health Education Policy'; Roger Davidson, '"A Scourge to be firmly gripped": The Campaign for VD Controls in Interwar Scotland', *Social History of Medicine*, 6 (1993), pp. 213–36.

82 Franz Seidler, *Prostitution, Homosexualität, Selbstverstümmelung: Problem der deutschen Sanitätsführung 1939–1945* (Kurt Vowinkel, Neckardemünd, 1977); Christa Paul, *Zwangs Prostitution: Staatlich Errichte Bordelle im Nationalsozialismus* (Hentrich, Berlin, 1994).

83 'Comfort Women', in *Oxford Companion to the Second World War*, ed. Foot and Dear, p. 257.

84 Mark Harrison, 'Sex and the Citizen Soldier: Health, Morals and Discipline in the British Army during the Second World War', in *Medicine and Modern Warfare*, ed. Cooter, Harrison and Sturdy, pp. 225–50.

85 L. D. Heaton, *Medical Department U.S. Army: Preventive Medicine in World War II*, vol. 5: *Communicable Disease* (Office of the Surgeon General, Department of the Army, Washington, DC, 1960), pp. 260–8; Harrison, 'Sex and the Citizen Soldier'.

86 Harrison, *Medicine and Victory*, chs 4 and 5.

87 Trevor L. Williams, *Howard Florey: Penicillin and After* (Oxford University Press, New York, 1984).

88   Peter Neushul, 'Science, Government, and the Mass Production of Penicillin', *Journal of the History of Medicine and Allied Sciences*, 48 (1993), pp. 373–95; *idem*, 'Fighting Research: Army Participation in Clinical Testing and Mass Production of Penicillin during the Second World War', in *War, Medicine and Modernity*, ed. Cooter, Harrison and Sturdy, pp. 203–24.

89   *British Medical Journal*, 25 March 1944, pp. 428–9; Maj. Herbert Bell, 'Gonorrhoea in Italy', *Journal of the Royal Army Medical Corps*, 84 (1945), pp. 21–6.

CHAPTER 8   HEALTH FOR ALL?

1   Brent Hoff and Carter Smith III, *Mapping Epidemics: A Historical Atlas of Disease* (Franklin Watts, New York, 2000), pp. 21, 93.

2   John R. Paul, *A History of Poliomyelitis* (Yale University Press, New Haven, Conn., 1971); Tony Gould, *A Summer Plague: Polio and its Survivors* (Yale University Press, New Haven, Conn., and London, 1995); Naomi Rogers, 'A Disease of Cleanliness: Polio in New York City, 1900–1990', in *Hives of Sickness: Public Health and Epidemics in New York City*, ed. D. Rosner (Rutgers University Press, Brunswick, NJ, 1995), pp. 114–30.

3   H. V. Wyatt, 'Poliomyelitis', in *The Cambridge World History of Human Disease*, ed. K. F. Kiple (Cambridge University Press, Cambridge, 1993), pp. 942–50.

4   Irvine Loudon, *Death in Childbirth: An International Study of Maternal Care and Maternal Mortality 1800–1950* (Clarendon Press, Oxford, 1992), pp. 258–61.

5   Milton Wainwright, *Miracle Cure* (Blackwell, Cambridge, Mass., 1990).

6   James Le Fanu, *The Rise and Fall of Modern Medicine* (Abacus, London, 2000), pp. 14–15.

7   Anne Hardy, *Health and Medicine in Britain since 1860* (Palgrave, Basingstoke, 2001), pp. 154–5.

8   David Weatherall, *Science and the Quiet Art: Medical Research and Patient Care* (Oxford University Press, Oxford, 1995), p. 185.

9   Peter C. English, *Rheumatic Fever in America and Britain* (Rutgers University Press, Brunswick, NJ, 1999), p. 149.

10   Le Fanu, *Rise and Fall of Modern Medicine*, p. 25.

11   Weatherall, *Science and the Quiet Art*, p. 294.

12   The literature on the history of war-related psychiatric disorders is extensive. An accessible, critical overview is presented in Ben Shephard, *A War of Nerves: Soldiers and Psychiatrists 1914–1994* (Jonathan Cape, London, 2000). For a survey that includes the non-Anglophone world, see Hans Binneveld, *From Shellshock to Combat Stress: A Comparative History of Military Psychiatry* (Amsterdam University Press, Amsterdam, 1997).

13   Edward Shorter, *A History of Psychiatry: From the Era of the Asylum to the Age of Prozac* (James Wiley and Sons, New York, 1997), pp. 208–15; Jack D. Pressman, *The Last Resort: Psychosurgery and the Limits of Medicine* (Cambridge University Press, Cambridge, 1998).

14   David Healy, *The Antidepressant Era* (Harvard University Press, Cambridge, Mass., 1997), p. 161.

15   Ibid., p. 4.

16   Shorter, *History of Psychiatry*, p. 324.

17   Ibid., pp. 272–81.

18   Healy, *Antidepressant Era*, p. 221.

19   Susan Sontag, *Illness as Metaphor* (Farrar, Straus and Giroux, New York, 1977).

20   Patrice Pinel, 'Cancer', in *Medicine in the 20th Century*, ed. R. Cooter and J. V. Pickstone (Harwood Academic Publishers, Amsterdam, 2000), pp. 671–86.

21   Richard Doll and Richard Peto, *The Causes of Cancer* (Oxford University Press, Oxford, 1981); C. J. Williams, 'Cancer', in *The Health of the Nation: The BMJ View*, ed. R. Smith (British Medical Journal, London, 1991), pp. 71–5.

22   Robert A. Aronowitz, 'The Social Construction of Coronary Heart Disease Risk Factors', in his *Making Sense of Illness: Science, Society, and Disease* (Cambridge University Press, New York, 1998), pp. 111–44.

23   Joel D. Howell, 'Concepts of Heart-Related Diseases', in *Cambridge World History of Human Disease*, ed. Kiple, p. 93.

24   J. O. Leibowitz, *The History of Coronary Heart Disease* (Wellcome Institute for the History of Medicine, London, 1970); W. F. Bynum, C. Lawrence and V. Nutton (eds), *The Emergence of Modern Cardiology*, Medical History Supplement no. 5 (Wellcome Institute for the History of Medicine, London, 1985).

25   Alan E. H. Emery and Marcia L. H. Emery, *The History of a Genetic Disease: Duchenne Muscular Dystrophy or Meryon's Disease* (Royal Society of Medicine Press, London, 1995).

26   See D. J. Weatherall, *The New Genetics and Clinical Practice* (Oxford University Press, Oxford, 1991).

27   Le Fanu, *Rise and Fall of Modern Medicine*, pp. 285–300; Jon Turney and Brian Balmer, 'The Genetic Body', in *Medicine in the 20th Century*, ed. Cooter and Pickstone, pp. 399–415.

28   Mirko D. Grmek, *History of AIDS: Emergence and Origin of a Modern Pandemic* (Princeton University Press, Princeton, 1990), pp. 1–12.

29   Susan Sontag, *AIDS and its Metaphors* (Penguin, London, 1990), p. 131.

30   Grmek, *History of AIDS*, ch. 6.

31   Ibid., pp. 34–6; Paul Farmer, *Infections and Inequalities: The Modern Plagues* (University of California Press, Berkeley, 1999), pp. 127–49.

32   Virginia Berridge, *AIDS in the UK: The Making of Policy, 1981–1994* (Oxford University Press, Oxford, 1996), pp. 37–54.

33   Anne Marie Moulin, 'Blood Transfusion and AIDS in France', in *AIDS and the Public Debate: Historical and Contemporary Perspectives*, ed.

C. Hannaway, V. A. Arden and J. Parascandola (IOS Press, Amsterdam, 1995), pp. 170–86.

34   Grmek, *History of AIDS*, p. 41.

35   C. Everett Koop, 'The Early Days of AIDS as I Remember Them', in *AIDS and the Public Debate*, ed. Hannaway et al., pp. 9–18.

36   Berridge, *AIDS in the UK*, pp. 55–66.

37   Ibid., p. 69.

38   Elizabeth Fee and Daniel M. Fox, 'Introduction: AIDS, Public Policy, and Historical Inquiry', in *AIDS: The Burdens of History*, ed. E. Fee and D. M. Fox (University of California Press, Berkeley, 1988); Virginia Berridge, 'AIDS and Contemporary History', in *AIDS and Contemporary History*, ed. V. Berridge and P. Strong (Cambridge University Press, Cambridge, 1993), pp. 2–3; Allan M. Brandt, 'AIDS: From Public History to Public Policy', in *AIDS and the Public Debate*, ed. Hannaway et al., pp. 124–31.

39   Berridge, *AIDS in the UK*, p. 56. See also Jeffrey Weeks, 'AIDS and the Regulation of Sexuality', in *AIDS and Contemporary History*, ed. Berridge and Strong, pp. 17–36.

40   Dennis Altman, *AIDS in the Mind of America* (Anchor Press, Garden City, NY, 1986).

41   Paul Farmer, 'Pestilence and Restraint: Haitians, Guantánamo, and the Logic of Quarantine', in *AIDS and the Public Debate*, ed. Harraway et al., pp. 139–52.

42   Quoted in Farmer, *Infections and Inequalities*, p. 61.

43   On women and AIDS, see Cindy Patton, *Last Served? Gendering the HIV Pandemic* (Taylor and Francis, London, 1994); Ruth Fadden, Gail Geller and Madison Powers (eds), *AIDS, Women and the Next Generation: Towards a Morally Acceptable Public Policy for HIV Testing of Pregnant Women and Newborns* (Oxford University Press, Oxford, 1991).

44   M. Fumento, *The Myth of Heterosexual AIDS* (Regnery Gateway, Washington, DC, 1993).

45   Daniel M. Fox, 'The Politics of HIV Infection: 1989–1990 as Years of Change', in *AIDS: The Making of a Chronic Disease*, ed. E. Fee and D. M. Fox, (University of California Press, Berkeley, 1992), pp. 125–43.

46   Grmek, *History of AIDS*, pp. 27–30.

47   e.g. Richard Chirimuuta and Rosalind Chirumuuta, *AIDS, Africa and Racism* (Free Association Books, London, 1989).

48   See excerpts from reviews on cover of ibid.

49   K. Keersmaekers and A. Meheus, 'Epidemiology of Sexually Transmitted Infections and AIDS in Developing Countries', in *Sexually Transmitted Infections and AIDS in the Tropics*, ed. O. P. Arya and C. A. Hart (CAB Publishing, New York, 1998), pp. 3–30.

50   Edward Hooper, *The River: A Journey Back to the Source of HIV and AIDS* (Allen Lane, London, 1999).

51   Charles Rosenberg, 'What is an Epidemic? AIDS in Historical Perspective', in his *Explaining Epidemics and Other Studies in the*

History of Medicine (Cambridge University Press, Cambridge and New York, 1992), pp. 278–92.

52 Renée Danziger, 'The HIV/AIDS Epidemic: Public Policies and Possessive Individualism', in *The Politics of Emerging and Resurgent Infectious Diseases*, ed. J. Whitman (Macmillan, London, 2000), pp. 110–29.

53 Randall M. Packard, 'Malaria Dreams: Postwar Visions of Health and Development in the Third World', *Medical Anthropology*, 17 (1997), pp. 279–96.

54 Quoted in Gill Walt, 'Health Care in the Developing World, 1974 to 2001', in *Caring for Health: History and Diversity*, ed. C. Webster (Open University Press, Buckingham, 2001), p. 265.

55 F. Fenner et al., *Smallpox and its Eradication* (WHO, Geneva, 1988); Donald A. Henderson, *Smallpox Eradication* (WHO, Geneva, 1988); A. W. Crosby, 'Smallpox', in *Cambridge World History of Human Disease*, ed. Kiple, pp. 1008–13.

56 Paul Greenough, 'Intimidation, Coercion and Resistance in the Final Stages of the South Asian Smallpox Eradication Campaign, 1973–1975', *Social Science and Medicine*, 41 (1982), pp. 633–45.

57 S. Bhattacharya, M. Harrison and M. Worboys, *Expunging Variola: The Control and Eradication of Smallpox in India, 1850–1977* (Orient Longman, Hyderbad, forthcoming).

58 Walt, 'Health Care', p. 278.

59 Ibid., p. 279.

60 Barry E. Zimmerman and David J. Zimmerman, *Killer Germs: Microbes and Diseases that Threaten Humanity* (Contemporary Books, Chicago, 2003), p. 148.

61 Walt, 'Health Care', p. 285.

62 Farmer, *Infections and Inequalities*, p. 128; M. Lewis, S. Bamber and M. Waugh (eds), *Sex, Disease, and Society: A Comparative History of Sexually Transmitted Diseases and HIV/AIDS in Asia and the Pacific* (Greenwood Press, Westport, Conn., 1997); D. Bloom and P. Godwin (eds), *The Economics of HIV and AIDS: The Case of South and South East Asia* (Oxford University Press, New Delhi, 1997).

63 'Africa hope after Uganda Aids "Breakthrough"', *http://bbc.co.uk/1/hi/world/africa/433517.stm*.

64 Maryinez Lyons, 'Women's Destiny and AIDS in Uganda', in *AIDS and the Public Debate*, ed. Harraway et al., pp. 187–201.

65 Uganda Aids Commission: National Aids Documentation Center, *www.aidsuganda.org*.

66 See 'South Africa Sued over Aids Drugs', *http://bbc.co.uk/1/hi/world/africa/1502518.stm*, and 'Ministry Attacks Mbeki Aids Stance', *http://bbc.co.uk/1/hi/world/africa/1556715.stm*.

67 Farmer, *Infections and Inequalities*, p. 267.

68 Javed Siddiqi, *World Health and World Politics: The World Health Organization and the U.N. System* (Hurst and Co., London, 1995).

69 See contributions to the debate on pharmaceuticals in 'Essential Drugs: Out of Reach of Africa', *http://bbc.co.uk/1/hi/talking_point/debates/african/1166793.stm*.

70   Joshua Lederberg, Robert E. Shope and Stanley C. Oaks (eds), *Emerging Infections: Microbial Threats to Health in the United States* (National Academy Press, Washington, DC, 1992).

71   Wilbur G. Downs, 'Ebola Virus Disease', in *Cambridge World History of Human Disease*, ed. Kiple, pp. 699–703.

72   A classic exposition is to be found in Laurie Garrett, *The Coming Plague: Newly Emerging Diseases in a World out of Balance* (Virago Press, London, 1994).

73   Stephen J. Morse, 'Examining the Origins of Emerging Viruses', in *Emerging Viruses*, ed. S. J. Morse (Oxford University Press, New York, 1993), pp. 13–14.

74   Robert C. Webster, 'Influenza', in *Emerging Viruses*, ed. Morse, pp. 37–45.

75   Thomas E. Lovejoy, 'Global Change and Epidemiology: Nasty Synergies', in *Emerging Viruses*, ed. Morse, p. 265.

76   Xavier Rodo, Mercedes Pascal, George Fuchs and A. S. G. Faruque, 'ENSO and Cholera: A Nonstationary Link related to Climate Change?', *Proceedings of the National Academy of Sciences of the United States of America*, 99 (1 October 2002), pp. 12901–6.

77   Elizabeth Whitcombe, 'Uses of History: India's Contribution to the Study of Climate and Disease', in *Thinking Social Science in India: Essays in Honour of Alice Turner*, ed. S. Patel, J. Bagchi and K. Raj (Sage, New Delhi, 2002), pp. 69–83.

78   Morse, 'Examining the Origins of Emerging Viruses', p. 14.

79   See, e.g., A. K. Chakraborty, 'Tuberculosis Program in India: Current Operational Issues'; Yogesh Jain, 'Disturbing Trends in the Treatment of Malaria'; Anand Zacharia, 'Public Health in Vellore: Experiences with Malaria and Cholera'; all in *Public Health and the Poverty of Reforms: The South Asian Predicament*, ed. I. Qadeer, K. Sen and K. R. Nayar (Sage, New Delhi, 2001), pp. 339–60, 436–8, 439–48.

80   Christopher J. L. Murray and Alan D. Lopez, 'Quantifying the Burden of Disease and Injury Attributable to Ten Major Risk Factors', in *The Global Burden of Disease*, ed. C. J. L. Murray and A. D. Lopez (Harvard University Press, Cambridge, Mass., 1996), p. 311.

Select Bibliography

Ackerknecht, Erwin, 'Anticontagionism between 1821 and 1861', *Bulletin of the History of Medicine*, 22 (1948), pp. 561–93.

Ackerknecht, Erwin, *Medicine at the Paris Hospital, 1794–1848* (Johns Hopkins University Press, Baltimore, 1967).

Andrews, Bridie and Cunningham, Andrew (eds), *Western Medicine as Contested Knowledge* (Manchester University Press, Manchester, 1997).

Arnold, David, 'The Indian Ocean as a Disease Zone, 1500–1950', *South Asia*, 14 (1991), pp. 1–22.

Arnold, David, *Colonizing the Body: State Medicine and Epidemic Disease in Nineteenth-Century British India* (University of California Press, Berkeley, 1993).

Arnold, David (ed.), *Imperial Medicine and Indigenous Societies* (Manchester University Press, Manchester, 1988).

Aronowitz, Robert A., *Making Sense of Illness: Science, Society, and Disease* (Cambridge University Press, New York, 1998).

Arrizabalaga, Jon, Henderson, John and French, Roger, *The Great Pox: The French Disease in Renaissance Europe* (Yale University Press, New Haven, Conn., 1997).

Baldwin, Peter, *Contagion and the State in Europe 1830–1930* (Cambridge University Press, New York, 1999).

Barnes, David S., *The Making of a Social Disease: Tuberculosis in Nineteenth-Century France* (University of California Press, Berkeley, 1995).

Bashford, Alison, *Purity and Pollution: Gender, Embodiment and Victorian Medicine* (Macmillan, London, 2000).

Bashford, Alison and Hooker, Claire (eds), *Contagion: Historical and Cultural Studies* (Routledge, London and New York, 2001).

Bell, Heather, *Frontiers of Medicine in the Anglo-Egyptian Sudan 1899–1940* (Clarendon Press, Oxford, 1999).

Benedict, Carol, *Bubonic Plague in Nineteenth-Century China* (Stanford University Press, Stanford, Calif., 1996).

Berridge, Virginia, *AIDS in the UK: The Making of Policy, 1981–1994* (Oxford University Press, Oxford, 1996).

Berridge, V. and Strong, P. (eds), *AIDS and Contemporary History* (Cambridge University Press, Cambridge, 1993).

Bewell, Alan, *Romanticism and Colonial Disease* (Johns Hopkins University Press, Baltimore and London, 1999).

Bilson, Geoffrey, *A Darkened House: Cholera in Nineteenth-Century Canada* (Toronto University Press, Toronto, 1980).

Biraben, J.-N., *Les Hommes et la peste en France et dans les pays Européens et Méditerranéens* (2 vols., Mouton, Paris, 1975–6).

Brockliss, Laurence and Jones, Colin, *The Medical World of Early Modern France* (Clarendon Press, Oxford, 1997).

Brooks, Francis J., 'Revising the Conquest of Mexico: Smallpox, Sources, and Populations', *Journal of Interdisciplinary History*, 24 (1993), pp. 1–29.

Bruce-Chwatt, L. J. and de Zuleta, J., *The Rise and Fall of Malaria in Europe: A Historico-Epidemiological Study* (Oxford University Press, Oxford, 1980).

Bryder, Linda, *Below the Magic Mountain: A Social History of Tuberculosis in Twentieth-Century Britain* (Clarendon Press, Oxford, 1988).

Bulst, N. and Delort, R. (eds), *Maladies et société (XIIe–XVIIIe siècles)* (CNRS, Paris, 1989).

Bynum, W. F., *Science and the Practice of Medicine in the Nineteenth Century* (Cambridge University Press, Cambridge, 1994).

Bynum, W. F. and Nutton, V. (eds), *Theories of Fever from Antiquity to the Enlightenment*, Medical History Supplement no. 1 (Wellcome Institute for the History of Medicine, London, 1981).

Bynum, W. F. and Porter, R. (eds), *William Hunter and the Eighteenth-Century Medical World* (Cambridge University Press, Cambridge, 1985).

Caplan, Arthur A., 'The Concepts of Health, Illness and Disease', in *Companion Encyclopedia of the History of Medicine*, ed. W. F. Bynum and R. Porter (Routledge, London, 1993), pp. 233–48.

Carmichael, Ann G., *Plague and the Poor in Renaissance Florence* (Cambridge University Press, Cambridge and New York, 1986).

Cipolla, Carlo M., *Public Health and the Medical Profession in the Renaissance* (Cambridge University Press, Cambridge, 1976).

Codell Carter, K., *The Rise of Causal Concepts of Disease: Case Histories* (Ashgate, Aldershot, 2003).

Coleman, William, *Yellow Fever in the North: The Methods of Early Epidemiology* (University of Wisconsin Press, Madison, 1987).

Conrad, L. I., Neve, M., Nutton, V., Porter, R. and Wear, A., *The Western Medical Tradition 800 BC to AD 1800* (Cambridge University Press, Cambridge, 1995).

Cook, David Noble, *Born to Die: Disease and the New World Conquest, 1492–1650* (Cambridge University Press, New York, 1998).

Cook, D. N. and Lovell, W. G. (eds), *The Secret Judgments of God: Native Peoples and Old World Disease in Colonial Spanish America* (University of Oklahoma Press, Norman, 1992).

Cooter, R. (ed.), *In the Name of the Child: Health and Welfare 1880–1940* (Routledge, London, 1992).

Cooter, R. and Pickstone, J. V. (eds), *Medicine in the 20th Century* (Harwood, Academic Publishers, Amsterdam, 2000).

Cooter, R., Harrison, M. and Sturdy, S., *Medicine and Modern Warfare* (Rodopi Press, Amsterdam and Atlanta, 1999).

Cooter, R., Harrison, M. and Sturdy, S. (eds), *War, Medicine and Modernity* (Sutton, Stroud, 1998).

Crosby, Alfred W., *The Columbian Exchange: Biological and Cultural Consequences of 1492* (Greenwood Press, Westport, Conn., 1972).

Crosby, Alfred W., *America's Forgotten Pandemic: The Influenza of 1918* (Cambridge University Press, New York and Cambridge, 1989).

Cunningham, Andrew and Grell, Ole P., *The Four Horsemen of the Apocalypse: Religion, War, Famine and Death in Reformation Europe* (Cambridge University Press, Cambridge, 2000).

Cunningham, A. and Williams, P. (eds), *The Laboratory Revolution in Medicine* (Cambridge University Press, Cambridge, 1992).

Curtin, P. D., *The Image of Africa: British Ideas and Action, 1780–1850* (2 vols., University of Wisconsin Press, Madison, 1964).

Curtin, P. D., *The Atlantic Slave Trade: A Census* (University of Wisconsin Press, Madison, 1969).

Curtin, Philip D., *Death by Migration: Europe's Encounter with the Tropical World in the Nineteenth Century* (Cambridge University Press, New York, 1989).

Curtin, Philip D., *Disease and Empire: The Health of European Troops in the Conquest of Africa* (Cambridge University Press, New York, 1998).

Curtin, Philip D., *Migration and Mortality in Africa and the Atlantic World, 1700–1900* (Ashgate, Aldershot, 2001).

Darmon, Pierre, *La Longue Traque de la variole: les pionniers de la médecine préventive* (Perrin, Paris, 1986).

Davidson, Roger and Hall, Lesley A. (eds), *Sex, Sin and Suffering: Venereal Disease and European Society since 1870* (Routledge, London, 2001).

Debus, Allen, *The Chemical Philosophy: Paracelsian Science and Medicine in the Sixteenth and Seventeenth Centuries* (Science History Publications, New York, 1977).

Delaporte, F., *Disease and Civilization: The Cholera in Paris, 1832*, tr. A. Goldhammer (MIT Press, Cambridge, Mass., and London, 1986).

Delaporte, F., *The History of Yellow Fever: An Essay on the Birth of Tropical Medicine* (MIT Press, Cambridge, Mass., 1991).

De Swaan, Abram, *In Care of the State: Health Care, Education and Welfare in Europe and the USA in the Modern Era* (Polity, Cambridge, 1988).

Diamond, Jared, *Guns, Germs and Steel: A Short History of Everybody for the Last 13,000 Years* (London, Vintage, 1998).

Dobson, Mary, *Contours of Death and Disease in Early Modern England* (Cambridge University Press, Cambridge, 1997).

Dols, Michael W., *The Black Death in the Middle East* (Princeton University Press, Princeton, 1977).

Dormandy, Thomas, *The White Death: A History of Tuberculosis* (Hambledon, London, 1999).

Douglas, Mary, *Purity and Danger: An Analysis of the Concepts of Pollution and Taboo* (Routledge, London, 1991 [1966]).

Duffy, John, *A History of Public Health in New York City 1625–1866* (Russell Sage Foundation, New York, 1968).

Durey, Michael, *The Return of the Plague: British Society and the Cholera, 1831–2* (Macmillan, London, 1979).

Eckart, Wolfgang U., *Medizin und Kolianimperialismus: Deutschland 1884–1945* (Ferdinand Schoeningh, Paderbon, 1997).

Eckart, W. U. and Gradmann, C. (eds), *Die Medizin und der Erste Weltkrieg* (Centaurus, Pfaffenweiler, 1996).

Eckert, E. A., *The Structure of Plagues and Pestilences in Early Modern Europe: Central Europe, 1560–1640* (Karger, Basel, 1996).

Ernst, W. and Harris, B. (eds), *Race, Science and Medicine, 1700–1960* (Routledge, London, 1999).

Evans, Richard J., *Death in Hamburg: Society and Politics in the Cholera Years 1830–1910* (Clarendon Press, Oxford, 1987).

Farmer, Paul, *Infections and Inequalities: The Modern Plagues* (University of California Press, Berkeley, 1999).

Fee, E. and Fox, D. M. (eds), *AIDS: The Burdens of History* (University of California Press, Berkeley, 1988).

Fenner, Frank, et al., *Smallpox and its Eradication* (WHO, Geneva, 1988).

Fisher, Richard B., *Edward Jenner 1749–1823* (André Deutsch, London, 1991).

Fissell, Mary, *Patients, Power, and the Poor in Eighteenth-Century Bristol* (Cambridge University Press, Cambridge, 1991).

Fleck, Ludwik, *The Genesis and Development of a Scientific Fact*, tr. F. Bradley and T. J. Trenn, ed. T. J. Trenn and R. K. Merton (University of Chicago Press, Chicago, 1979).

Foucault, Michel, 'The Politics of Health in the Eighteenth Century', in *Michel Foucault, Power/Knowledge: Selected Interviews and Other Writings 1972–1977*, ed. C. Gordon (Harvester Press, London, 1988), pp. 166–82.

Foucault, Michel, *The Birth of the Clinic*, tr. A. Sheridan (Routledge, London, 166–82 1997 [1963]).

French, R. and Wear, A. (eds), *The Medical Revolution of the Seventeenth Century* (Cambridge University Press, Cambridge, 1989).

Gallagher, Nancy E., *Egypt's Other Wars: Epidemics and the Politics of Public Health* (Syracuse University Press, Syracuse, NY, 1990).

Garrett, Laurie, *The Coming Plague: Newly Emerging Diseases in a World out of Balance* (Virago Press, London, 1994).

Geison, Gerald L., *The Private Science of Louis Pasteur* (Princeton University Press, Princeton, 1995).

Gentilcore, David, *Healers and Healing in Early Modern Italy* (Manchester University Press, Manchester, 1998).

Golinski, Jan, *Making Natural Knowledge: Constructivism and the History of Science* (Cambridge University Press, New York and Cambridge, 1998).

Gould, Tony, *A Summer Plague: Polio and its Survivors* (Yale University Press, New Haven and London, 1995).

Greenough, Paul, 'Intimidation, Coercion and Resistance in the Final Stages of the South Asian Smallpox Eradication Campaign, 1973–1975', *Social Science and Medicine*, 41 (1982), pp. 633–45.

Grmek, Mirko D., *History of AIDS: Emergence and Origin of a Modern Pandemic* (Princeton University Press, Princeton, 1990).

Guha, Sumit, 'The Importance of Social Intervention in England's Mortality Decline: The Evidence Reviewed', *Social History of Medicine*, 7 (1994), pp. 89–113.

Hamlin, Christopher, *Public Health and Social Justice in the Age of Chadwick: Britain, 1800–1854* (Cambridge University Press, Cambridge and New York, 1998).

Hannaway, C., Arden, V. A. and Parascandola, J. (eds), *AIDS and the Public Debate: Historical and Contemporary Perspectives* (IOS Press, Amsterdam, 1995).

Hardy, Anne, *The Epidemic Streets: The Rise of Preventive Medicine in London, 1850–1910* (Oxford: Oxford University Press, 1993).

Hardy, Anne, *Health and Medicine in Britain since 1860* (Palgrave, Basingstoke, 2001).

Harrison, Gordon, *Mosquitoes, Malaria and Man: A History of Hostilities since 1880* (John Murray, London, 1978).

Harrison, Mark, *Public Health in British India: Anglo-Indian Preventive Medicine 1859–1914* (Cambridge University Press, Cambridge, 1994).

Harrison, Mark, *Climates and Constitutions: Health, Race, Environment and British Imperialism in India 1600–1850* (Oxford University Press, New Delhi, 1999).

Harrison, Mark, *Medicine and Victory: British Military Medicine in the Second World War* (Oxford University Press, Oxford, forthcoming, 2004).

Haynes, Douglas M., *Imperial Medicine: Patrick Manson and the Conquest of Tropical Disease* (University of Pennsylvania Press, Philadelphia, 2001).

Hays, J. N., *The Burdens of Disease: Epidemics and Human Response in Western History* (Rutgers University Press, New Brunswick, NJ, 2000).

Herlihy, David, *The Black Death and the Transformation of the West* (Harvard University Press, Cambridge, Mass., 1997).

Hoff, Brent and Smith, Carter III, *Mapping Epidemics: A Historical Atlas of Disease* (Franklin Watts, New York, 2000).

Hooper, Edward, *The River: A Journey Back to the Source of HIV and AIDS* (Allen Lane, London, 1999).

Hopkins, A. G. (ed.), *Globalization in World History* (Pimlico, London, 2002).

Humphreys, Margaret, *Yellow Fever and the South* (Rutgers University Press, New Brunswick, NJ, 1992).

Jones, Margaret, 'The Ceylon Malaria Epidemic of 1934–35: A Case Study in Colonial Medicine', *Social History of Medicine*, 13 (2000), pp. 87–111.

Jordanova, Ludmilla, 'The Social Construction of Medical Knowledge', *Social History of Medicine*, 8 (1995), pp. 361–82.

King, Lester S., *The Medical World of the Eighteenth Century* (University of Chicago Press, Chicago, 1958).

King, Lester S., *The Road to Medical Enlightenment 1650–1695* (Macdonald, London, 1970).

Kiple, Kenneth F., *The Caribbean Slave: A Biological History* (Cambridge University Press, Cambridge, 1984).

Kiple, K. F. (ed.), *The African Exchange: Towards a Biological History of Black People* (Duke University Press, Durham, NC, 1987).

Kiple, K. F. (ed.), *The Cambridge World History of Human Disease* (Cambridge University Press, Cambridge, 1993).

Kiple, K. F. and Beck, S. V. (eds), *The Biological Consequences of European Expansion, 1450–1800* (Variorum, Aldershot, 1997).

Kraut, Alan M., *Silent Travelers: Germs, Genes, and the 'Immigrant Menace'* (Basic Books, New York, 1994).

Kunitz, Stephen J., *Disease and Social Diversity: The European Impact on the Health of Non-Europeans* (Oxford University Press, New York, 1994).

La Berge, Ann F., *Mission and Method: The Early Nineteenth-Century French Public Health Movement* (Cambridge University Press, Cambridge, 1992).

Ladurie, Emmanuel Le Roy, 'A Concept: The Unification of the Globe by Disease', in his *Mind and Method of the Historian* (Harvester, Brighton, 1981), pp. 28–83.

Landers, John, *Death and the Metropolis: Studies in the Demographic History of London 1670–1830* (Cambridge University Press, Cambridge, 1993).

Latour, Bruno, *The Pasteurization of France* (Harvard University Press, Cambridge, Mass., 1988).

Lawrence, Christopher, 'Disciplining Disease: Scurvy, the Navy, and Imperial Expansion, 1750–1825', in *Visions of Empire: Voyages, Botany, and Representations of Nature*, ed. D. P. Miller and P. H. Reill (Cambridge University Press, Cambridge, 1996), pp. 80–106.

Lawrence, Susan, *Charitable Knowledge: Hospital Pupils and Practitioners in Eighteenth-Century London* (Cambridge University Press, Cambridge, 1996).

Leavitt, J. Walzer and Numbers, R. L. (eds), *Sickness and Health in America: Readings in the History of Medicine and Public Health* (University of Wisconsin Press, Madison, 1985).

Le Fanu, James, *The Rise and Fall of Modern Medicine* (Abacus, London, 2000).

Levine, Philippa, 'Venereal Disease, Prostitution, and the Politics of Empire: The Case of British India', *Journal of the History of Sexuality*, 4 (1994), pp. 579–602.

Lindemann, Mary, *Health and Healing in Eighteenth-Century Germany* (Johns Hopkins University Press, Baltimore, 1996).

Lindemann, Mary, *Medicine and Society in Early Modern Europe* (Cambridge University Press, Cambridge, 1999).

Loudon, Irvine, *Death in Childbirth: An International Study of Maternal Care and Maternal Mortality 1800–1950* (Clarendon Press, Oxford, 1992).

Lyons, Maryinez, *The Colonial Disease: A Social History of Sleeping Sickness in Northern Zaire, 1900–1940* (Cambridge University Press, Cambridge, 1992).

Manderson, Lenore, *Sickness and the State: Health and Illness in Colonial Malaya, 1870–1940* (Cambridge University Press, Cambridge, 1996).

Markel, Howard, *Quarantine! East European Jewish Immigrants and the New York City Epidemics of 1892* (Johns Hopkins University Press, Baltimore, 1997).

Marks, L. and Worboys, M. (eds), *Migrants, Minorities and Health: Historical and Contemporary Studies* (Routledge, London, 1997).

Maulitz, Russell C., *Morbid Appearances: The Anatomy of Pathology in the Early Nineteenth Century* (Cambridge University Press, Cambridge, 1987).

McGrew, Roderick E., *Russia and the Cholera 1823–1832* (University of Wisconsin Press, Madison, 1965).

McKeown, Thomas, *The Modern Rise of Population* (Edward Arnold, London, 1976).

McNeill, J. J., 'The Ecological Basis of Warfare in the Caribbean, 1700–1804', in *Adapting to Conditions*, ed. M. Utlee (University of Alabama Press, Tuscaloosa, 1986), pp. 26–42.

McNeill, William H., *Plagues and Peoples* (Anchor Press, Doubleday, Garden City, NY, 1976).

Mendelsohn, J. Andrew, 'From Eradication to Equilibrium: How Epidemics became Complex after World War I', in *Greater than the Parts: Holism in Biomedicine 1920–1950*, ed. C. Lawrence and G. Weisz (Oxford University Press, New York, 1998), pp. 303–34.

Morris, R. J., *Cholera 1832* (Holmes and Meier, New York, 1976).

Naphy, William G., *Plagues, Poisons and Potions: Plague-Spreading Conspiracies in the Western Alps, c.1530–1640* (Manchester University Press, Manchester, 2002).

Naphy, William and Spicer, Andrew, *The Black Death: A History of Plagues 1345–1730* (Tempus, Stroud, 2000).

Ott, Katherine, *Fevered Lives: Tuberculosis in American Culture since 1870* (Harvard University Press, Cambridge, Mass., 1996).

Packard, Randall M., *White Plague, Black Labor: Tuberculosis and the Political Economy of Health and Disease in South Africa* (University of California Press, Berkeley, 1989).

Packard, Randall M., 'Malaria Dreams: Postwar Visions of Health and Development in the Third World', *Medical Anthropology*, 17 (1997), pp. 279–96.

Pelling, Margaret, *Cholera, Fever, and English Medicine 1825–1865* (Clarendon Press, Oxford, 1978).

Phillips, Howard and Killingray, David (eds), *The Spanish Influenza Pandemic of 1918–19* (Routledge, London, 2003).

Pickstone, John V., 'Ferriar's Fever to Kay's Cholera: Disease and Social Structure in Cottonopolis', *History of Science*, 22 (1984), pp. 401–19.

Pickstone, John V., *Ways of Knowing: A New History of Science, Technology and Medicine* (Manchester University Press, Manchester, 2000).

Porter, Dorothy, *Health, Civilization and the State: A History of Public Health from Ancient to Modern Times* (Routledge, London, 1999).

Porter, Dorothy (ed.), *The History of Public Health and the Modern State* (Rodopi Press, Amsterdam and Atlanta, 1994).

Porter, Roy, *The Greatest Benefit to Mankind: A Medical History of Humanity from Antiquity to the Present* (HarperCollins, London, 1997).

Powell, J. H., *Bring Out Your Dead: The Great Plague of Yellow Fever in Philadelphia in 1793* (University of Pennsylvania Press, Philadelphia, 1949).

Power, Helen J., *Tropical Medicine in the Twentieth Century: A History of the Liverpool School of Tropical Medicine, 1898–1990* (Kegan Paul International, London, 1999).

Quétel, Claude, *History of Syphilis*, tr. J. Braddock and B. Pike (Polity, Cambridge, 1990).

Ranger, T. and Slack, P. (eds), *Epidemics and Ideas: Essays on the Historical Perception of Pestilence* (Cambridge University Press, Cambridge, 1992).

Reid, Donald, *Paris Sewers and Sewermen: Realities and Representations* (Harvard University Press, Cambridge, Mass., 1991).

Riley, James C., *The Eighteenth-Century Campaign to Avoid Disease* (Macmillan, Basingstoke, 1987).

Riley, James C., *Sick, not Dead: The Health of British Workingmen during the Mortality Decline* (Johns Hopkins University Press, Baltimore, 1997).

Risse, Guenter B., *Mending Bodies, Saving Souls: A History of Hospitals* (Oxford University Press, New York, 1999).

Rosen, George, *From Medical Police to Social Medicine: Essays on the History of Health Care* (Science History Publications, New York, 1974).

Rosenberg, Charles E., *The Cholera Years: The United States in 1832, 1849, and 1856* (University of Chicago Press, Chicago, 1987).

Rosenberg, Charles E., *Explaining Epidemics and Other Studies in the History of Medicine* (Cambridge University Press, New York and Cambridge, 1992).

Rosenberg, C. E. and Golden, J. (eds), *Framing Disease: Studies in Cultural History* (Rutgers University Press, New Brunswick, NJ, 1992).

Rosner, D. (ed.), *Hives of Sickness: Public Health and Epidemics in New York City* (Rutgers University Press, New Brunswick, NJ, 1995).

Rotberg, R. I., *Health and Disease in Human History: A Journal of Interdisciplinary History Reader* (MIT Press, Cambridge, Mass., 2000).

Rothman, Sheila M., *Living in the Shadow of Death: Tuberculosis and the Social Experience of Illness in American History* (Johns Hopkins University Press, Baltimore, 1994).

Savitt, Todd L., *Medicine and Slavery: The Diseases and Health Care of Blacks in Antebellum Virginia* (University of Illinois Press, Urbana, 1978).

Schofield, R., Reher, D. and Bideau, A., *The Decline of Mortality in Europe* (Clarendon Press, Oxford, 1991).

Sheridan, Richard B., *Doctors and Slaves: A Medical and Demographic History of Slavery in the British West Indies, 1680–1834* (Cambridge University Press, New York and Cambridge, 1985).

Sirasi, Nancy, *Medieval and Early Renaissance Medicine* (University of Chicago Press, Chicago, 1990).

Slack, Paul, *The Impact of Plague in Tudor and Stuart England* (Clarendon Press, Oxford, 1985).

Smith, F. B., *The Retreat of Tuberculosis 1850–1950* (Croom Helm, London, 1986).

Sontag, Susan, *Illness as Metaphor* (Farrar, Straus and Giroux, New York, 1977).

Sontag, Susan, *AIDS and its Metaphors* (Penguin, London, 1990).

Spree, Reinhard, *Health and Social Class in Imperial Germany*, tr. S. McKinnon-Evans (Berg, Oxford, 1988).

Stepan, Nancy, *The Idea of Race in Science: Great Britain 1800–1960* (Macmillan, London, 1982).

Szreter, Simon, *Fertility, Class and Gender in Britain, 1860–1940* (Cambridge University Press, Cambridge, 1996).

Thornton, Russell, *American Indian Holocaust and Survival: A Population History since 1492* (University of Oklahoma Press, Norman, 1987).

Tomes, Nancy, *The Gospel of Germs: Men, Women, and the Microbe in American Life* (Harvard University Press, Cambridge, Mass., 1998).

Vaughan, Megan, *Curing their Ills: Colonial Power and African Illness* (Polity, Cambridge, 1991).

Wear, Andrew (ed.), *Medicine in Society: Historical Essays* (Cambridge University Press, Cambridge, 1992).

Wear, Andrew, French, Roger and Lonie, Lain (eds), *The Medical Renaissance of the Sixteenth Century* (Cambridge University Press, Cambridge, 1985).

Webster, Charles, *The Great Instauration: Science, Medicine and Reform 1626–1660* (Duckworth, London, 1975).

Webster, Charles, 'Paracelsus, Paracelsianism, and the Secularization of the Worldview', *Science in Context*, 15 (2002), pp. 9–29.

Webster, Charles (ed.), *Health, Medicine and Mortality* (Cambridge University Press, Cambridge, 1979).

Webster, C. (ed.), *Caring for Health: History and Diversity* (Open University Press, Buckingham, 2001).

Weindling, Paul, *Epidemics and Genocide in Eastern Europe, 1890–1945* (Oxford University Press, Oxford, 2000).

Weindling, Paul (ed.), *International Health Organisations and Movements 1918–1939* (Cambridge University Press, Cambridge, 1995).

Wilkinson, Lise and Hardy, Anne, *The London School of Hygiene and Public Health: A Twentieth-Century Quest for Global Public Health* (Kegan Paul, London, 1998).

Wilson, Adrian, 'On the History of Disease-Concepts: The Case of Pleurisy', *History of Science*, 38 (2000), pp. 271–319.

Wohl, Anthony S., *Endangered Lives: Public Health in Victorian Britain* (Methuen, London, 1983).

Worboys, Michael, *Spreading Germs: Disease Theories and Medical Practice in Britain, 1865–1900* (Cambridge University Press, Cambridge and New York, 2000).

Wrigley, E. A. and Schofield, R. S., *The Population History of England 1541–1871* (Edward Arnold, London, 1981).

Zinnser, Hans, *Rats, Lice, and History* (Penguin, Harmondsworth, 2000 [1935]).

Index